INSCRUTABLE MALICE

THEODICY, ESCHATOLOGY, AND THE BIBLICAL SOURCES OF *MOBY-DICK*

Jonathan A. Cook

NIU
PRESS
Dekalb, IL

© 2012 by Northern Illinois University Press
Published by the Northern Illinois University Press, DeKalb, Illinois   60115
Manufactured in the United States using acid-free paper.
All Rights Reserved
Design by Shaun Allshouse

Library of Congress Cataloging-in-Publication Data
Cook, Jonathan A. (Jonathan Alexander), 1953–
Inscrutable malice : theodicy, eschatology, and the biblical sources of
Moby-Dick / Jonathan A. Cook.
p. cm.
Includes bibliographical references and index.
ISBN 978-0-87580-464-4 (cloth : acid-free paper) —
ISBN 978-1-60909-078-4 (electronic)
1. Melville, Herman, 1819–1891. Moby Dick. 2. Theodicy in literature.
3. Eschatology in literature. I. Title.
PS2384.M62C665 2012
813'.3—dc23
2012019996

Contents

Preface

In this study I seek to examine *Moby-Dick* in the context of the author's dramatization of the problem of evil, a subject of recurrent interest in Western culture and Judeo-Christian tradition. Framing Melville's fictional exploration of this vexed question was his immersion in the Bible, especially the text of the Old Testament from which he drew prototypes for the characters of Ahab, Ishmael, and the White Whale. I argue that the book of Job serves as the basis for the novel's representation of the question of theodicy—the attempt to reconcile the justice or goodness of God with the existence of evil—while Daniel, Revelation, and other apocalyptic passages of the Old and New Testaments provide a basis for the novel's pervasive use of eschatology, the divinely ordained "last things" in the life of the individual, community, and cosmos. I demonstrate that the figure of Job was a key source for the creation of Ahab, while the book of Job's portrait of the mythical chaos monster Leviathan served as the formative model for Moby Dick. Repeated allusions to apocalyptic passages of the Bible similarly act as recurrent paradigms for both dramatic action and thematic development in Ishmael's narrative. Just as the Bible, with its composite compositional history, is ultimately inconsistent in tracing the causes of suffering and evil in human life, so Melville in *Moby-Dick* depicts a comparable range of philosophical and psychological responses to the problem of evil that are ultimately rooted in biblical tradition.

In Chapter 1, I briefly review the history of criticism of *Moby-Dick* before examining the biblical sources for the issues of theodicy and eschatology that will guide the present study. As texts with foundational authority and multiple manifestations in Western tradition, the books of Job, Daniel, and Revelation—along with other related prophetic, historical, poetic, and apocalyptic texts—provide a wealth of thematic, structural, and linguistic prototypes for Melville's whaling novel. In this chapter, I accordingly trace the complex mythological roots of the dominant biblical paradigms in the novel. Thus, we find the prototype for Ahab's pursuit of the White Whale in the Hebrew god's conquest of the marine chaos monster Leviathan, an event borrowed from earlier Mesopotamian and Canaanite myth. Moreover, the novel's eschatological structures rely on other biblical traditions depicting end-time events, especially those found in the book of Revelation, in which the demonic agents of primordial evil are overthrown and God's heavenly kingdom established on earth. I then review the Old Testament historical models for Ishmael and Ahab, which will demonstrate Melville's strategic adaptation of these two well-known outcasts from Hebrew covenantal tradition.

Chapter 2 begins with a brief overview of the antebellum American religious scene and Melville's religious upbringing as they impinge on the novel, notably the influence of the dominant evangelical culture with its pervasive ideology of reform and the role of the small sects of Quakers and Shakers. I then track Ishmael's seriocomic initiation into the whaling profession, which draws extensively on the metaphors of pilgrimage found in the writings of St. Paul and John Bunyan, the underlying theological presences in this early section of the novel. Ishmael's initiation is typified by his richly comic, mock-apocalyptic encounter with the Polynesian cannibal Queequeg, whose friendship leads to redemptive acts of conversion and covenant in the narrative. In Father Mapple's sermon on Jonah and the enigmatic encounter with the sailor Elijah, moreover, Ishmael's initiation includes a prophetic foreshadowing of some of the key moral and eschatological issues that will concern him throughout his voyage on the *Pequod*. These issues provide a backdrop to the black humor that recurs throughout Ishmael's unsettling experience of New Bedford and Nantucket, which ends with his allegorical evocation of the heroic sailor Bulkington, whose presence at the helm of the *Pequod* provides a classical model for the pursuit of moral and philosophical truth amid the sublime biblical terrors of whaling.

In Chapter 3, I examine Ahab's symbolic identity as a Job figure bringing an indictment against divine justice in his quest for Moby Dick, a modern exemplar of the biblical Leviathan evoked at the end of God's speech from the whirlwind in the book of Job. Ahab's impassioned remarks in "The Quarter-Deck" on the malignity of the White Whale are thus shown to be a synthesis of various features of the outspoken complaints of Job. The immediately ensuing chapters of the novel then trace various aspects of Ahab's aggrieved Job-like identity, and aspects of the White Whale as the book of Job's mythical chaos monster. In order to fight this alleged embodiment of divine evil, Ahab makes a Faust-like pact with the devil in the person of the Parsee Fedallah, a version of "the satan" or "adversary" of the book of Job, who appears during the *Pequod*'s first chase of a whale. As an adherent of the Zoroastrian religion, Fedallah also typifies Ahab's embrace of the pagan idolatry that characterized the reign of the biblical King Ahab. The voyage of the *Pequod* is thus launched as an unholy apocalyptic quest to destroy the ultimate source of evil in the allegedly demonic whale, a divine agent or principal within the extended theological, mythological, and literary contexts of Joban theodicy as dramatized in the novel. This narrative sequence ends with the sighting of the Spirit Spout, a demonic version of the pillar of cloud that guided the Israelites in the Egyptian desert, and the uncanny appearance of the giant squid as another proleptic anticipation of the White Whale.

In Chapter 4, I survey issues of cetology, cosmology, and epistemology in Ishmael's encyclopedic and demythologizing attempt to examine the whale both as biological species and as source for the raw materials of a major nineteenth-century American industry. This section includes Ishmael's well-known exploration of "The Whiteness of the Whale," in which he envisages Moby Dick as an apocalyptic symbol of the natural sublime, hinting at the moral ambiguity of the divine nature. Elsewhere in Ishmael's seriocomic vision (informed by the work of a broad range of writers including Dante, Rabelais, Milton, Burton, Browne, Sterne, Carlyle, Irving, and others), the whale can be seen as an embodiment of cosmological ambiguity in both the creation and the creator, while the ongoing evocations of the whale's pursuit, capture, processing, and anatomical features provide a series of moral exempla enhanced by repeated allusions to biblical wisdom literature. Throughout his detailed cetological narration and disquisition, which includes representative scenes of Ishmael on the masthead, weaving mats, helping to chase whales, stripping blubber, squeezing sperm, and steering the ship, Ishmael embraces a skeptical epistemology that is consonant with the message of the books of Job, Proverbs, and Ecclesiastes, and that further enhances the ironic critique of Saint Paul and Pauline Christianity, which began in the first narrative sequence of the novel. In this long sequence of chapters focusing on Ishmael's education into the wonders of the whale, then, we find this archetypal biblical species acting as a paradoxical embodiment of cosmological wisdom and a macrocosmic image of the natural creation.

In Chapter 5, I discuss the interplay of comedy and tragedy in several cetological episodes of *Moby-Dick* in tandem with recurrent themes and motifs relating to theodicy and eschatology. In a comic inversion of Ahab's identity as a type of the tragic Job, Ishmael is shown to be a parodic Job figure who, in his initiation into whaling, emerges as an embodiment of moral balance and comic resilience. In another comic sequence, the figure of Stubb acts as an agent of minstrel-show humor and multi-leveled satire in conjunction with the black cook, Fleece, whose well-known "sermon to the sharks" is traced to its New Testament source. I then examine Ahab's speech to the suspended whale's head in "The Sphynx" as an illustration of the captain's profound Job-like tragic insight, which coexists with an acute Oedipus-like moral blindness. Concluding this chapter is an examination of tragic and comic themes in two of the *Pequod's* nine "gams" with other whaling vessels, the *Jeroboam* and the *Virgin.* Ahab's hubris and moral blindness in the gam with the *Jeroboam,* as highlighted by the Shaker prophet Gabriel, is based on a well-known scene from the book of Daniel depicting the prophetic "writing on the wall" foretelling the fall of Belshazzar and his Babylonian kingdom. The encounter with the *Virgin,* on the other hand, is predicated on Christ's apocalyptic parable of the wise and foolish virgins, among other biblical prototypes.

In Chapter 6, I analyze the blend of hubris and heroism in the representation of Ahab in the last quarter of the novel, as well as in the depiction of ideas of mortality and immortality as conveyed by both Ahab and Ishmael in this narrative sequence. A series of dramatic scenes beginning with "The Doubloon" depicts Ahab's quest for godlike omniscience and omnipotence, which will ultimately help precipitate his fall, even as he continues to show the physical courage and moral stamina of the traditional epic hero. The supreme expression of Ahab's paradoxical blend of heroism and hubris is seen in "The Candles," which includes a remarkable synthesis of biblical and literary motifs ultimately based on Job's rhetorical attacks on the Old Testament divinity and on Gnostic traditions of an evil creator god. In addition to possessing a satanic and titanic pride, Ahab is simultaneously haunted by the deity's apparent indifference to suffering and death, as exemplified by the description of "The Dying Whale" as well as by a series of provocative metaphysical exchanges with the ship's carpenter and blacksmith, with whom he interacts in order to be fitted for a new whalebone leg. Yet as "The Whale-Watch" goes on to show, Ahab is deluded by Fedallah's prophecies about the killing of the White Whale into thinking that he is virtually immortal. A comparable concern with mortality and immortality also haunts Ishmael on his revelatory visit to the Arsacidean whale chapel—a seriocomic counterpart to Ahab's climactic encounter with the White Whale—during which Ishmael ponders the ultimate mysteries of the creation and its inextricable union of life and death. A similar concern is expressed as Ishmael witnesses the seeming impending death of Queequeg, whose carved coffin will end up serving as Ishmael's life preserver.

I begin Chapter 7 with a discussion of the mythic dimensions of Melville's basic plotline in *Moby-Dick* and Ahab's identity as an Old Testament tragic hero with typological resemblances to various figures of fallen pride. Within the novel's New Testament aspects, Saint Paul's epistle to the Romans serves as a moral touchstone for the antithetical careers of Ishmael and Ahab in the narrative. The focus of the discussion then shifts to the pathos of Ahab's rueful conversation with Starbuck in "The Symphony" immediately preceding the encounter with Moby Dick, a conversation packed with multiple biblical and literary allusions and steeped in an aura of tragic fatalism. After examining the historical prototype for the conclusion of the novel in the sinking of the whaleship *Essex* in 1820, we turn to the climax of the narrative in Ahab's three-day chase of the White Whale, whose drama and imagery closely approximate the evocation of Leviathan in the book of Job as well as passages from Psalms and Isaiah. In this confrontation, which also draws on the imagery of the war in heaven in book 6 of *Paradise Lost*, the apocalyptic themes of the novel are further elaborated and brought to their catastrophic conclusion. The final three chapters of Melville's novel thus act as the climax to Ahab's tragedy in which Aristotelian elements of recognition and reversal, terror and pity, are highlighted. Following the sinking of the *Pequod*, Ishmael as the sole survivor is the inadvertent inheritor of Ahab's Joban mantle of suffering and is symbolically reborn from the wreck of the ship to a condition of tragic knowledge and enhanced biblical wisdom.

In the Epilogue I discuss the place of *Moby-Dick* in larger theological, philosophical, and cultural traditions of theodicy and eschatology. In effect, Melville dramatized the principal justifications for natural and moral evil found in the Bible—notably in Genesis, the Hebrew prophets, Job, Ecclesiastes, the writings of Saint Paul, and Revelation—within various narrative and expository sequences of the text. By the same token, *Moby-Dick* as literary theodicy can be placed in a larger European tradition of concern with the problem of evil found in several major philosophers of the eighteenth and nineteenth centuries. The pervasive presence of the book of Job within Melville's novel is thereupon related to the Job-like circumstances of the novel's publication and its immediate aftermath, at which time Melville ironically seemed to relive the sufferings of the biblical patriarch. Finally, the novel's extensive use of apocalyptic eschatology is related to other mid- and late nineteenth-century works of American and European literature as well as to a general preoccupation with end-time events that continues into our own age in both fact and fiction.

In a letter to Sophia Hawthorne dated January 1852, Melville acknowledged the multi-level allegory that characterized *Moby-Dick* while also recognizing the astuteness of her husband, the dedicatee of the novel, in perceiving this feature in an earlier, now lost letter: "I had some vague idea while writing it, that the whole book was susceptible of an allegoric construction, & and also that *parts* of it were—but the speciality of many of the particular subordinate allegories, were first revealed to me, after reading Mr Hawthorne's letter, which, without citing any particular examples, yet intimated the part-&-parcel allegoricalness of the whole."[1] The key source for Melville's "part & parcel" use of allegory in *Moby-Dick* was, of course, the Bible, whose composite theological form and iconic 1611 translation into English as the Authorized Version helped produce the polyvalence of form and meaning in Melville's novel. Like a number of other writers before and after him, Melville creatively assimilated the Christian Bible on multiple levels, from the overarching perspective of theme, plot, characterization, and symbolism to the textual details of language, style, imagery, and trope. Included in this assimilation, too, were the pervasive rhetorical devices of paradox, irony, and ambiguity, which helped structure the complex and sometimes contradictory moral and metaphysical worlds of *Moby-Dick*—a "wicked book," the writing of which nevertheless made Melville feel "spotless as the lamb," as he famously told Hawthorne in a letter of November 1851, the month of the novel's American publication.[2]

Viewed from a wider literary perspective, Melville's use of the Christian Bible in *Moby-Dick* conforms to what Stephen Prickett has called the Romantic "appropriation" of this central text of Western culture, which came to English and American readers after a previous double act of appropriation: "Just as the Bible has appropriated the concept of a book, so, for the English-speaking world, the Authorised Version has appropriated the notion of the Bible." For many writers of the Romantic era the Bible accordingly became a primary source of "cultural renewal, aesthetic value and literary inspiration. . . . Even more significantly, the Bible had, in the process, become a metatype, the representative literary form, and the paradigm by which other works were to be understood and judged."[3] A writer highly attuned to the religious, intellectual, and artistic currents of his time, Melville shared in this embrace of the Bible as the ultimate "metatype" and model on which he could base his exploration of the nature and meaning of evil in *Moby-Dick*.

My principal goal in the present study, then, is to shed new light on the central influence of the Bible on *Moby-Dick*. As in his other works of fiction and poetry, Melville turned to this central text for an array of themes and motifs that helped shape the religious and philosophical questions infusing his imagination. I have drawn on a broad selection of recent scholarly work on the Bible, myth, and religion generally. At the same time I examine a wide variety of literary sources and influences in order to show how these combine with the biblical elements to form the densely allusive texture of

Melville's whaling novel. While presenting new evidence on the pervasive influence of the Bible on *Moby-Dick* (including a host of previously unrecognized biblical sources), I also seek in the present work to provide a comprehensive review and synthesis of the long history of criticism of the novel. It is my hope that this study will aid in the refocusing of Melville criticism toward various moral and religious issues that continue to offer significant intellectual challenges and rewards to the modern reader—issues that remain central to a full appreciation of Melville's masterpiece and of his writings generally.

For the completion of this project, I am grateful first of all to the many literary and biblical scholars whose works have shaped the parameters of my thinking on the subjects covered by this book. For various forms of assistance and intellectual fellowship I am particularly indebted to the late Walter Bezanson, Gail Coffler, Jeffrey Hotz, Eric Carl Link, Mark McCullough, Peter Norberg, Steve Olsen-Smith, Hershel Parker, and Brian Yothers; many thanks to Steve, Mark, and Brian for reading and commenting on the manuscript. I have benefited from the opportunity to present portions of this study at the May 2008 conference of the American Literature Association in a session on "Melville and His Sources," and at the May 2011 conference on "The King James Bible and Its Cultural Afterlife" at Ohio State University. My work has been aided by the staffs and facilities of the libraries of Georgetown, American, and George Mason Universities, the Library of Congress, the University of Virginia, and the Loudoun County (Virginia) Public Library system. A small portion of Chapter 2 has previously appeared as "*Moby-Dick*, Myth, and Classical Moralism: Bulkington as Hercules," *Leviathan* 5 (March 2003): 15–28; I thank Wiley-Blackwell for permission to reprint this material. Special thanks go to Amy Farranto of Northern Illinois University Press for the support she has given this project. I'm deeply grateful to the late Barbara Colgate and the Colgate family for their hospitality and generosity during my first years in the Washington, DC, area. Soraya Howard has heard much about this book over the last decade, and I'm grateful for her love, devotion, and patience during endless trips to the library. Finally, I dedicate this book to the memory of my mother, Diana Pattison Cook, who shared with me and my siblings her love of literature and the arts, together with her boundless intellectual curiosity and progressive values. *Set me as a seal upon thine heart, as a seal upon thine arm: for love is as strong as death.*

Bibliographical Note

Parenthetical citations of *Moby-Dick* are from *Moby-Dick; or The Whale*, ed. Harrison Hayford, Hershel Parker, and G. Thomas Tanselle. Evanston and Chicago: Northwestern University Press and the Newberry Library, 1988.

Parenthetical citations of the Bible are from *The Holy Bible. Authorized King James Version*. Edited by Rev. C. I. Scofield. New York: Oxford University Press, 1945.

INSCRUTABLE MALICE

CHAPTER ONE

Joban Theodicy and Apocalyptic Eschatology

A LITTLE OVER A CENTURY AGO, in a discussion of "The Sick Soul" in his *Varieties of Religious Experience* (1902), the philosopher and psychologist William James examined a human personality type that, in contrast to what he had earlier called a proponent of the "religion of healthy-mindedness," or a type that minimized the existence of evil in the world, instead tended to maximize it "based on the persuasion that the evil aspects of our life are of its very essence, and that the world's meaning most comes home to us when we lay them most to heart." Such individuals were typically subject to pathological melancholy, or what today would be termed clinical or manic depression (bipolar disorder). Surveying some of the philosophical, cultural, and psychological dimensions to this morbid-minded personality type, which included such famous victims of religious despair as Bunyan and Tolstoy, James proposed that the existential experience of evil tended to make the healthy-minded view seem "inadequate as a philosophical doctrine, because the evil facts which it refuses positively to account for are a genuine portion of reality; and they may after all be the best key to life's significance, and possibly the only openers of our eyes to the deepest levels of truth." Evoking a state of mind that he himself (and his father, for that matter) knew well, James noted the inescapable evidence that various forms of evil have pervaded both the past and present forms of life on earth—enough to confirm even an insane person's presumably delusional experience of horror.[1]

James recognized the unavoidable fact that human life was premised on predation, pain, and death: "Our civilization is founded on the shambles, and every individual existence goes out in a lonely spasm of helpless agony." The dinosaurs may seem remote from modern civilization, but various forms of horror "just as dreadful to their victims, if on a small spatial scale, fill the world about us to-day." Such reptilian predators as crocodiles and snakes remain, and "whenever they or other wild beasts clutch their living prey, the deadly horror which an agitated melancholiac feels is the literally right reaction on the situation." James concluded his discussion with the argument that some extreme forms of evil cannot be justified within systems of good; they must simply be suffered through or put out of mind. In the meantime, we should acknowledge that "systematic healthy-mindedness, failing as it does to accord sorrow, pain, and death any positive and active attention whatever, is formally less complete than systems that try at least to include these elements in their scope."[2]

Although James does not mention Melville's Ahab in his pioneering study, he might have adduced this literary figure as a prime example in his portrait of the "sick soul" whose preoccupation with evil, although produced by a morbid and melancholy temperament, is a potentially legitimate vision of the moral universe inhabited by humanity. Indeed, this morbid-minded whaling captain may arguably represent a more truthful and complete image of a predatory universe than that adduced by the healthy-minded. We might even say that James's discussion here constitutes an uncanny commentary on Melville's hero-villain, especially in such chapters as "The Quarter-Deck," "Moby-Dick," or "The Sphynx," in which Ahab justifies (or Ishmael explains) his ostensibly mad hunt for the White Whale, the imaginative equivalent of James's dinosaurs and reptiles. We should also note the fact that much of James's argument could apply to the narrator Ishmael, whose sensitivity to—if not experience of—evil is nearly equal to Ahab's but whose agile temperament is more evenly balanced than the captain's and so ultimately proves less self-destructive. James's concluding points in this section of his study concerning the incontrovertible evidence for radical evil might easily fit into one of Ishmael's philosophical disquisitions such as "The Whiteness of the Whale," "Brit," "The Try-Works," or "The Gilder." One can only speculate on the shock of recognition James might have experienced if he had read Melville's whaling epic.

James's classic study of the underlying psychology of a diverse array of religious experiences provides a window on a pervasive theme in *Moby-Dick*—the problem of evil—that stands at the center of its imaginative universe. Yet surprisingly few contemporary critics have focused on the issue. For despite widespread appreciation of its many excellencies of narration and exposition, contemporary readers often come to the novel without the conceptual vocabulary to grasp some of its most profound moral concerns. And despite the novel's canonical status in academia and its pervasive presence in modern American and even global culture, *Moby-Dick* has become increasingly distanced from the theological and mythical underpinnings of its vision.

For roughly half a century following the Melville revival in the 1920s, the religious and mythical dimensions of his writings and of his most famous novel began gradually to emerge under the critical scrutiny of such works as William Braswell, *Melville's Religious Thought* (1943); Nathalia Wright, *Melville's Use of the Bible* (1949); Lawrance Thompson, *Melville's Quarrel with God* (1952); H. Bruce Franklin, *The Wake of the Gods: Melville's Mythology* (1963); William H. Shurr, *The Mystery of Iniquity: Melville as Poet, 1857–1891* (1972); and T. Walter Herbert, Moby-Dick *and Calvinism: A World Dismantled* (1977).[3] Since then, scholarly examination of *Moby-Dick* has yielded to a growing variety of approaches, in keeping with the novel's encyclopedic scope. Yet religion and myth are often conspicuous by their absence here.

So today we have a number of articles and books that investigate *Moby-Dick*'s language, style, and narrative and allegorical techniques, its appropriation of European literary and philosophical heritages, and its incorporation of American democratic ideals and national ideologies.[4] Other studies have explored the novel's relation to varied forms of humor, popular culture, and the literary marketplace, its assimilation of epic and dramatic principles and prototypes, and its use of the visual arts and aesthetic theory.[5] Still others have examined *Moby-Dick*'s focus on the body, gender, and sexuality; its explorations of the psychology of mourning, trauma, and disaster; and its exemplification of various sciences (marine biology, oceanography, natural history), pseudo-sciences (mesmerism, phrenology, astrology), and environmentalism.[6] Finally, a number of studies have explored *Moby-Dick*'s relation to Melville's life as well as the novel's composition, recognition, and varied cultural influence.[7]

While many of these works have deepened our understanding of Melville's iconic novel, over the last few decades there has been less attention paid to the overarching religious and moral concerns that shaped Melville as a writer, such as the problem of evil, the decline of Christianity, the disappearance of God, the historicizing of the Bible. This may well be the result of the defamiliarization of the Bible and Judeo-Christian religious traditions within contemporary academia, despite the work of such influential literary critics as Northrop Frye, Frank Kermode, Robert Alter, and Harold Bloom, and despite recent advances in our understanding of the biblical text as a literary and mythological construct. There are, of course, exceptions to this loss of critical focus; indeed, the last few years have seen a limited revival of interest in *Moby-Dick* and religion. So in *Melville's Bibles*, Ilana Pardes has explored Melville's use in *Moby-Dick* of nineteenth-century exegetical traditions concerning the Old Testament figures of Job, Jonah, Ishmael, Ahab, and Rachel. In *Pen of Iron*, Robert Alter has explicated some of the Old Testament stylistic devices—poetic parallelism, narrative parataxis, homiletic discourse—that contributed to the novel's polyphonic prose. In *Sober Cannibals, Drunken Christians*, Jamie Lorentzen sheds light on some of *Moby-Dick*'s moral and religious thematics, as part of a larger study of Melville and Kierkegaard as critics of contemporary Christianity. Finally, in *All Things Shining*, Hubert Dreyfus and Sean Dorrance Kelly have explored the contrast between Ahab's enraged monotheism and Ishmael's resigned polytheism in a reading of *Moby-Dick*'s quasi-modernist religious vision.[8]

The danger of overlooking *Moby-Dick*'s overarching religious and moral concerns is nowhere more clear than in the vexed question of race and slavery in the narrative. Over the last half century, one common approach to the novel has been through the medium of antebellum political history and the mid-nineteenth-century crisis over slavery.[9] Yet critics who examine the novel from this perspective generally ignore the fact that it was set in 1840–1841, a decade earlier than it was written and a time when the slavery issue had not reached a state of crisis. And they regularly overlook the universalizing import of the novel's complex allegorical vision, which is largely moral and religious in nature. Whether postulating the White Whale as a symbol of racial ideology, or the *Pequod* as a ship of state driven by its captain's Calhoun-like fanaticism, the transformation of *Moby-Dick* into a political allegory is unavoidably reductive. Lost in such an approach is an adequate appreciation of the theological and mythical origins of Ahab's quest and the epic grandeur of his character, which was designed to be comparable to the heroes of Homer, Shakespeare, and Milton.[10]

In the present study of *Moby-Dick*, I will attempt to restore to the center of our reading experience one of the novel's primary but often neglected subjects, the problem of natural and moral evil. Such a topic necessarily begins by acknowledging the pervasive presence of the Bible in Melville's epic, for it hardly needs restating that this was the single most important literary influence on *Moby-Dick*.[11] The thesis of the present study is that biblical themes of theodicy and eschatology give distinctive shape and meaning to *Moby-Dick*. Both theodicy (the attempt to reconcile the goodness and justice of God with the existence of evil) and eschatology (the study of theological "last things") attempt to provide an answer to the problem of evil and human suffering in a universe allegedly governed by a just and righteous God. As the descendent on his father's side of several generations of Scottish Presbyterian ministers, Melville was intensely preoccupied with both these subjects, and both are deeply embedded in *Moby-Dick*.

According to the philosopher David Hume in his *Dialogues concerning Natural Religion* (restating a logical crux first set forth by the Greek philosopher Epicurus), the problem of evil had a three-part structure: "Is he [God] willing to prevent evil, but not able? Then is he impotent. Is he able, but not willing? Then is he malevolent. Is he both able and willing? Whence then is evil?" Beginning with the Fathers of the early church, Christian theologians sought to justify the existence of evil as an integral part of the divine plan—whether as punishment for original sin, a means of education and moral improvement, a necessary contrast to good in the scale of creation, a temporary defect in the universe, a metaphysical illusion, or ultimately a divine mystery. In *God's Problem*, Bart D. Ehrman has demonstrated that the Christian Bible provides an inconclusive range of answers to the problem of evil and human suffering. The "classical" view as found in the Hebrew prophets, the Deuteronomistic historian, Saint Paul, and elsewhere is based on the premise that suffering is divine punishment for human sin. On the other hand, the book of Job—the *locus classicus* of the problem of evil in the Old Testament—is generically divided between a prose folklore frame story in which suffering is represented as a test of faith and an extended poetic dialogue in which suffering is depicted as a divine mystery. In the book of Ecclesiastes, by contrast, suffering is grounded in the physical laws of the universe. Finally, in the apocalyptic books of both testaments (Daniel, Revelation), righteous suffering will be justified by an eternal afterlife, while sin will result in spiritual damnation.[12]

Having been composed and compiled over more than a thousand years of ancient history, the Christian Bible patently reflects the varied historical and theological circumstances of its redactors. In the Old Testament, an all-powerful God was responsible for both good and evil, yet the doctrine of suffering resulting from human sin had emerged by the time of the prophets and Deuteronomistic history (eighth–sixth century BCE). In a conceptual shift, late Second Temple Judaism (fourth–first century BCE) began to view evil as a cosmic force that was differentiated from Yahweh, and this view is present in the markedly dualistic world of the New Testament. Continuing the tradition of the Old Testament prophets and Deuteronomistic historian, early Christian doctrine beginning with Saint Paul held that human original sin was the ultimate source of moral evil, while natural evil stemmed from the fall of nature that accompanied the divine curse in Eden.[13]

Christian theologians, philosophers, and poets subsequently grappled with the paradox of a benign creator allowing for the existence of evil without directly authorizing it. The most influential Christian theologian on the subject of evil was Saint Augustine, who began as a Manichean dualist but after his conversion developed four basic tenets on the nature of evil. First, in keeping with the doctrines of contemporary Neoplatonism, he asserted that evil had no metaphysical existence, being the mere absence of good (*privatio boni*). Second, evil was the free moral choice of human beings in a willful act of turning away from God—an act first seen in the fall of the rebel angels and then repeated in the fall of Adam and Eve and in the ongoing sinful disposition of humankind. Third, evil must exist because it is part of the larger plenitude of the creation—a Neoplatonic concept that gave rise to the influential idea of nature as a great chain of being. Finally, evil formed part of a larger aesthetic whole in a universe that was by its nature good. As in other theological matters, Augustine's theories on the existence of evil had a determinative influence on later Christian thinkers including those of the Protestant Reformation. John Calvin emphasized the human responsibility for sin despite the predestined nature of human moral history. The classic literary embodiment of such Reformation dogma was dramatized in Milton's *Paradise Lost* (1667), which sought to "justify the ways of God to man" by depicting the Augustinian genealogy of evil from Satan's willful pride to Adam and Eve's disobedient folly.[14]

Theodicy received its classic modern philosophical formulation during the Enlightenment, notably in Leibnitz's eponymous 1705 treatise on the subject *Theodicée*, which Voltaire mocked so mercilessly in *Candide*.[15] Yet it was the contemporaneous *Historical and Critical Dictionary* of the Calvinist fideist and skeptic Pierre Bayle—the primary impetus for Leibnitz's treatise—that provided Melville with an arsenal of arguments undermining any rational reconciliation of the existence of evil with the Judeo-Christian God. Bayle's extensive discussion of heretical Gnostic sects such as the Manicheans, Marcionites, and Paulicians seemed to make an overwhelming case for either a dualistic universe (what Bayle called the "two principles") or a divine iniquity. Such a manifest absurdity seemed to demonstrate that faith and reason were fundamentally incompatible modes of cognition and evil ultimately a divine mystery: "It is no less inconceivable in Metaphysics, than it is in Ethics, that he who is goodness and holiness itself should be the author of sin."[16]

As much as Melville's thinking on the problem of evil was stimulated by Bayle, the most influential foundation for his thought on the subject was still found in the biblical text that most outspokenly attempted to confront the issue of God's apparent justification for the existence of evil: the book of Job. As Luther S. Mansfield and Howard P. Vincent have noted in their pioneering Hendricks House edition of *Moby-Dick*: "In Melville's copy of the Bible inscribed in 1850 . . . Job (with some 40 verses checked, sidelined, or underscored) was the most heavily marked book, with Ecclesiastes next. Perhaps this fact should be taken as indication that Melville was reviewing Job as he was forming his conception of *Moby Dick*."[17] With its morally embattled protagonist and its climactic representation of the sea monster Leviathan, the book of Job was indeed central to Melville's conception and composition of the novel.

In addition, one of the most salient allegorical components of *Moby-Dick* is its pervasive use of prophetic and apocalyptic eschatology (the biblical teachings concerning an individual or collective end-time), drawn from the books of Daniel and Revelation as well as a number of other passages in both testaments, including the prophets, the synoptic gospels, and the letters of Paul. The eschatological elements of *Moby-Dick*, which again raise the vexed question of divine justice in a morally ambiguous world, cast Ahab as both messianic and satanic hero-villain, whose final combat with the White Whale evokes the portentous aura of the Old Testament Day of the Lord, or Christian Judgment Day.

In his epic whaling novel, Melville dramatizes many of the key biblical components of Joban theodicy and apocalyptic eschatology and uses them as structural templates for both tragic and comic patterns of action and exposition. Readers of the novel are accordingly made aware of the author's obsessive concern with the nature and extent of evil in the universe, whether in Ahab's fixation on the White Whale or in Ishmael's more philosophical ruminations on cosmic malignity. A number of allusions to the book of Job draw attention to its thematic relevance to the novel's representation of the enigma of evil, as critics such as Mansfield and Vincent, Lawrance Thompson, C. Hugh Holman, Thornton Y. Booth, Nathalia Wright, Janis Stout, Mark Heidmann, William Young, L. Joseph Kreitzer, and Ilana Pardes have variously pointed out.[18] Still other critics—such as R. E. Watters, Joseph Thomas Ward, Grant McMillan, T. Walter Herbert, and Richard Forrer—have discussed *Moby-Dick* in the context of Melville's philosophical preoccupation with the problem of evil, or in terms of its relation to larger cultural traditions of theodicy.[19] By the same token, readers of *Moby-Dick* have often noted that Ahab's quest for the White Whale, leading to the final destruction of the *Pequod* and her crew, is noticeably "apocalyptic," and critics such as Dayton Grover Cook, Michael T. Gilmore, Lakshmi Mani, and Douglas Robinson have suggested the presence of various millennialist and apocalyptic motifs within the novel.[20] So far, however, no critic of the novel thus far has fully accounted for the pervasive and overarching influence of both Joban theodicy and apocalyptic eschatology as recurrent themes and motifs within *Moby-Dick*. Nor has their presence been fully contextualized in both testaments of the Christian Bible. Nor have they been examined in association with the tragic and comic modes that shape their significance. Yet only by combining all these critical approaches will the moral and metaphysical concerns of Melville's novel be elucidated and the intricate biblical texture of *Moby-Dick* be revealed.

In essence, *Moby-Dick* dramatizes a complex and sustained confrontation with the problem of evil, which goes to the heart of Judeo-Christian theology and tradition. The novel may be said to rest on a deep structure of biblical myth, blended with a variety of other classical and non-Western mythological traditions.[21] By demonizing Moby Dick and the whale's divine creator, Ahab embraces a morally reductive view of the cosmos that ultimately proves suicidal in its metaphysical overreaching. Ishmael, in contrast, recognizes the need for acquiring wisdom in a vision of cosmic wholeness and ultimately envisages the metaphysical coexistence of good and evil, an attitude that provides the philosophical basis for his own survival. While Ahab *re*mythologizes the White Whale into an archetypal chaos monster and an agent of divine malignity, Ishmael *de*mythologizes the whale into a part of nature and civilization, while recognizing its symbolic role in the mystery of both creator and creation. If Ahab's most characteristic traits are hubris and impiety, with the ultimate goal of self-deification, Ishmael's are skepticism and irony, leading to compassion and wry self-effacement. If Ahab enacts the familiar Old Testament role of pride and disobedience, Ishmael exemplifies the antithetical virtues of survival and witness. Finally, if *Moby-Dick* as Ahab's story subsumes the genres of tragedy and epic, in its function as Ishmael's story the novel unites the forms of comedy, anatomy, and romance.[22]

In the present study I argue that, in their attitudes toward evil, Ahab and Ishmael convey different reactions to the moral predicament of Job. Like Job, Ahab suffers a gratuitous evil that he blames on God, and just as Job is not fully tested until *physically* afflicted with a disabling skin condition (Job 2:4–8), Ahab, too, is given a comparable grievous physical injury in the loss of his leg to Moby Dick (after being branded by lightning), a cause of excruciating physical and psychic pain. Unlike Job, Ahab ultimately fails to honor—indeed, tries to usurp—the sublime power of God in nature and is ultimately destroyed by a modern Leviathan. Ishmael, on the other hand, shares with Ahab a Joban sense of dispossession and a recurrent obsession with the problem of evil, but he ultimately comes to terms with evil as a natural, not a supernatural, phenomenon. And if Ishmael, like Job, ultimately accepts the metaphysical oneness of good and evil and his modest place in the creation, Ahab demonizes both creation and creator while magnifying himself into the role of divine surrogate and messianic redeemer.[23]

By the same token, Ahab's quest for the White Whale is framed both implicitly and explicitly as an eschatological mission with both Old and New Testament precedents. In apocalyptic literature, with its eschatological framework, the world is threatened by radical evil and requires a suprahistorical force (God) to overcome it. In *Moby-Dick*, Ahab "plays God" in his attempt to vanquish the evil he imputes to Moby Dick, in imitation of God's final conquest of Leviathan (Isa. 27:1). He is ultimately destroyed in the apocalyptic drama he has created in imitation of the divine warrior's defeat of the chaos monster. In a New Testament eschatological context, Ahab's attempt to usurp the place of God invites comparison with Revelation's confederated agents of evil who are overthrown in final combat with Christ as messianic warrior. Ishmael, on the other hand, gradually distances himself from the moral absolutes of Ahab's quest, while his humanitarian values eventually associate him, however obliquely, with the millennial redemption that follows apocalyptic destruction.

The subject of theodicy, as previously noted, finds its chief biblical articulation in the book of Job, a key part of Old Testament wisdom literature that includes the books of Proverbs and Ecclesiastes. A product of Second Temple Judaism written sometime between the sixth and fourth centuries BCE, Job adapted a well-known Near Eastern folktale frame story about the faithful suffering of a devout and upright individual who is tested and rewarded by God and added an extended poetic dialogue in which human suffering is shown to be a divine mystery. The book of Job is thus a theological hybrid in which the poetic dialogues have traditionally assumed interpretive priority. Providing a historical backdrop to Job is the historical catastrophe of the destruction of Jerusalem in 586 BCE and the subsequent Babylonian captivity of the Jewish people, with its profound impact on their culture and tradition. While the existence of evil in the Old Testament is generally attributable to opposition to God's will, the book of Job explores the difficult question of evil afflicting a devout and morally pure individual, thereby addressing the universally relevant issue of how to make sense of undeserved human suffering. The cogency of its dramatization of the issue has made the book of Job a perennial touchstone of theological, philosophical, and literary speculation on the subject. Job accordingly draws on a variety of ancient wisdom traditions, creating a densely textured poetry with multiple links to biblical and extrabiblical sources. "More than any other Wisdom text from Israel," notes Leo G. Perdue, "the book of Job makes significant use of ancient Near Eastern creation mythology. And the variety of metaphors and myths of creation in Israel's cultural environment plays an important role in the articulation of the book's meaning."[24]

In a folkloric prose prologue, the book of Job opens with God's giving permission to "the satan" ("the adversary" or "accuser"), his authorized agent for detecting human fault, to test the piety of Job, whom the satan believes is devout only because he is rich in material possessions. The satan wagers that once deprived of his possessions Job will curse God to his face, but after an initial series of disasters in which his goods are taken and offspring killed, Job still demonstrates his piety. God then authorizes the satan to plague Job with a loathsome skin disease, and this has the effect of making Job curse his existence and the creation generally, but he still does not curse God. With his wealth and family destroyed, Job is visited by three friends— Eliphaz, Bildad, and Zophar (his so-called comforters)—who attribute Job's misfortunes to unacknowledged sins committed by Job or his family. In the ensuing contrapuntal debate, each friend's speech is followed by Job's answer, a pattern repeated three times (except for the final round of speeches) in an extended poetic "wisdom debate" drawing on a variety of biblical forms, primarily lamentation and disputation. The three friends' view, repeated at length, is in fact the traditional Hebrew doctrine that suffering is always attributable to human wrongdoing, in accordance with the Deuteronomic ethics governing the historical and prophetic books of the Old Testament.

Contradicting his friends' conventional wisdom, Job asserts his moral purity and laments his broken covenant with God; once a kinglike master of creation, Job is now a miserable slave. While the friends urge Job to seek reconciliation with God through prayer, Job at times adopts a forensic model of discourse in which he casts himself as a plaintiff seeking legal representation and redress from God. Following a (possibly interpolated) chapter on the difficulty of finding wisdom on earth (Job 28), Job completes his defense with a rehearsal of his virtues in abiding by all the moral laws honoring God by helping the less fortunate, followed by a summary of his present misery (chs. 29–30) and a final attestation of his innocence in a so-called Oath of Clearance (ch. 31). A final extended speech by a fourth commentator, the young Elihu (chs. 32–37), ostensibly offers a fuller exposure of Job's faults, now focused on Job's alleged pride in justifying himself to God but this, too, proves yet another example of moral obtuseness in his friends. (Some scholars believe that chapters 28 and 32–37 were late additions to the book by orthodox redactors attempting to tone down the violence of Job's attack on God; others believe the speeches ironically augment the fatuity of Job's older counselors.)

Intruding on this ideological impasse in a dramatic theophany, God now appears as a mysterious Voice from the Whirlwind to set both Job and his friends straight about the nature of the creation and divine sovereignty. Such divine whirlwinds were a regular feature of Old Testament theophanies, in keeping with Yahweh's archetypal identity as autumnal storm god and eschatological agent (2 Kings 2:1, 11; Isa. 29:6; Jer. 23:19, 25:32, 30:23; Eze. 1:4, 13:11; Amos 1:14). Speaking from the whirlwind, God formally answers Job's charges by posing a series of sarcastic rhetorical questions and comments that ostensibly put Job in his place as a creature of dust. In answer to Job's questioning of God's wisdom and justice, God thus shows Job's incompetence to govern the world, which includes the task of holding back the ever-present powers of chaos. In a series of poetic evocations of the mysteries and wonders of the natural world (chs. 38–39), God shows the wisdom that it takes to control the creation. Then, in an attempted vindication of divine justice (chs. 40–41), God reveals the ever-threatening powers of chaos—powers that only God can restrain but not eliminate—in the form of the land monster Behemoth and the sea monster Leviathan.

There now follows God's climactic evocation of Leviathan—a colossal sea creature combining features of a mythical dragon and an Egyptian crocodile that provided Melville with a full roster of literal and symbolic features for his White Whale. The rhetorical questions that begin the evocation of Leviathan in the book of Job represent God's ironic response to Job's indictment of divine justice, which imply that Job himself would rule more justly over an unruly creation. God accordingly starts with a series of sarcastic queries emphasizing human impotence before this mythic monster: "Canst thou draw out leviathan with an hook? or his tongue with a cord which thou lettest down? / Canst thou put an hook into his nose? or bore his jaw through with a thorn?" (Job 41:1–2). He goes on paradoxically to praise his "comely parts" and "proportions" before returning to the theme of Leviathan's sublime and inscrutable terror: "Who can open the doors of his face? his teeth are terrible round about. / His scales are his pride, shut up together as with a close seal. / One is so near to another, that no air can come between them" (Job 41:14–16). Leviathan in fact resembles a dragon in its incendiary breath: "Out of his mouth go burning lamps, and sparks of fire leap out. / Out of his nostrils goeth smoke, as out of a seething pot or cauldron" (Job 41:19–20). Leviathan has a heart "as firm as a stone; yea, hard as a piece of the nether millstone." Human attempts to fight the monster are futile:

> The sword of him that layeth at him cannot hold: the spear, the dart, nor the habergeon [short jacket of mail].
> He esteemeth iron as straw, and brass as rotten wood.
> The arrow cannot make him flee: slingstones are turned with him into stubble.
> Darts are counted as stubble: he laugheth at the shaking of a spear.
> Sharp stones are under him: he treadeth sharp pointed things upon the mire.
> He maketh the deep to boil like a pot: he maketh the sea like a pot of ointment.
> He maketh a path to shine after him; one would think the deep to be hoary.
> Upon earth there is not his like, who is made without fear.
> He beholdeth all high things: he is a king over all the children of pride.
> (Job 41:26–34)

Job is clearly not up to the task of subduing this deep-sea monster, which only God in his capacity as divine warrior can accomplish. In his implacable force and sublime power, moreover, Leviathan bears a symbolic likeness to God himself, a mythic conflation that Ahab will make in *Moby-Dick*. As Carol Newsom notes, "the physical description of Leviathan is uncannily evocative of the theophanic descriptions of God."[25]

Having answered Job with overwhelming evidence of divine power and having tested his piety, God rebukes Job's three comforters for their false accusations against Job, who emerges as a potential tragic hero for his prolonged anguish in the midst of inexplicable calamity. The book of Job does not end as tragedy, however, but rather as dark comedy, for God in a prose epilogue restores Job's prosperity and children to him in a fairy-tale ending that completes the frame story as a moral test, which Job has unexpectedly passed. In the end, neither his friends' doctrine of retribution nor Job's own theory of God's indifference and arbitrary power is affirmed. Instead, God's assertions of cosmic omnipotence proclaim the inscrutability of his actions and suggest the educative value of suffering. The book of Job, then, offers no obvious solution to the problem of evil but suggests that there may *be* no solution except to acknowledge that evil is part of the order of nature, for the Voice from the Whirlwind has revealed "the downright stupendousness, the wellnigh daemonic and wholly incomprehensible character of the eternal creative power."[26]

In view of the book of Job's paradoxical image of a harshly punitive but unfailingly providential God, it is perhaps not surprising that Calvin wrote 165 sermons on it and incorporated its ideas into his epoch-making *Institutes of the Christian Religion* (1536); thus the Calvinist branch of Protestant theology with its pervasive influence in Puritan America owes a significant debt to Job's unknown redactor.[27] Yet if the book of Job would seem to argue for acceptance of undeserved suffering as part of God's inscrutable plan for the creation, more modern readings of Job have highlighted the violence of Job's indictment against divine injustice and the book's challenge to traditional notions of theodicy. For according to Newsom, "Nowhere else in the Bible is such an unrestrained demolition of the traditional image of God carried out as in Job's speeches, words that once let loose have continued to resonate for millennia."[28] As the Old Testament's most searching confrontation with the problem of evil, the book of Job has influenced a number of major literary explorations of similar themes, including *King Lear, Faust,* and *The Brothers Karamazov,* not to mention the work of a host of twentieth-century writers.[29]

The only explicit reference to Job in the New Testament commends his "patience" (James 5:11), but for many modern readers Job is noteworthy for his *im*patience, while God appears like a cosmic bully, evading Job's plea for justice and providing a show of force to demonstrate that "might makes right." Contemporary evaluations of the book have noted that Job's anguished expressions of physical and mental suffering reflect a degree of pain and alienation remarkably germane to twentieth-century history. The modernity of its quasi-absurdist themes is striking. Carl Jung, for example, deconstructs the divided image of God presented in Job:

> To take the most obvious thing, what about the moral wrong Job has suffered? Is man so worthless in God's eyes that not even a *tort moral* can be inflicted on him? That contradicts the fact that man is desired by Yahweh and that it obviously matters to him whether men speak "right" of him or not. He needs Job's loyalty, and it means so much to him that he shrinks at nothing in carrying out his test. This attitude attaches an almost divine importance to man, for what else is there in the whole wide world that could mean anything to one who has everything? Yahweh's divided attitude, which on the one hand tramples on human life and happiness without regard, and on the other hand must have man for a partner, puts the latter in an impossible position. At one moment Yahweh behaves as irrationally as a cataclysm; the next moment he wants to be loved, honored, worshipped, and praised as just. He reacts

irritably to every word that has the faintest suggestion of criticism, while he himself does not care a straw for his own moral code if his actions happen to run counter to its statutes.[30]

Given the evidence found in *Moby-Dick* as well as in what we know of Melville's ambivalent attitude to the Calvinist God of his religious upbringing, we can be sure that Melville's reading of Job included some of the same unflattering critical insights into the ways of the Judeo-Christian deity. One of the advantages of Melville's pervasive use of the book of Job in the novel is the fact that the story of Job has significant thematic parallels with the Promethean, Faustian, and Gnostic myths that Melville also used in the creation of his epic narrative; and we may pause here to note their similarities. Both Aeschylus's Prometheus and the biblical Job are embodiments of exemplary physical and psychological suffering. Moreover, they both express a defiant self-righteousness toward their persecutor and are tortured by a seemingly sadistic deity. Both *Prometheus Bound* and the book of Job include a literal or symbolic "chorus" expressing conventional religious wisdom while urging the suffering hero to yield and repent, and both works end with a manifestation of the deity as storm god.[31]

So, too, in the story of Faust as formulated by Goethe, the poem begins with a prologue in heaven modeled on the prologue in Job, with Mephistopheles playing the role of "the satan" of the Old Testament. Faust is tested by the modern devil of doubt, just as Job's plight is ultimately instigated by God's "prosecuting attorney." Melville knew the Faust story from three different literary sources and blended them freely into his whaling narrative. These included the translation by Thomas Roscoe of "Doctor Faustus," based on the oldest surviving Faust chapbook and appearing in Roscoe's four-volume collection *German Novelists* (1826); Christopher Marlowe's *The Tragical History of Dr. Faustus* (1588), a dramatic adaptation of the same German source; and Goethe's two-part poetic drama *Faust* (1808, 1832). As a modern Faust, tempted through the intellect and not the senses, Melville's Ahab will aspire to supernatural control and godlike status in the hunt for his uncanny prey, taking as his demonic familiar the Parsee Fedallah with whom he has made a secret pact. Unlike the devil in the various Faust stories Melville knew, however, Fedallah is not a voluble spirit nor a wit, but a gnomic, spectral presence akin to Macbeth's witches.[32]

The pervasive Joban themes in *Moby-Dick* also mesh closely with Melville's sustained use of Gnostic motifs in the characterization of Ahab. As Millicent Bell, Thomas Vargish, William B. Dillingham, and Etsuko Taketani have all argued, a number of passages in the novel would seem to offer strong evidence of this multiform early Christian heretical belief, which viewed the physical world as the product of an evil creator god, or "demiurge," while the true god remained hidden, known only to a few adepts and carriers of the divine spark who possessed a secret wisdom or "gnosis." Melville exemplified the major tenets of Gnosticism in Ahab's self-deifying egotism and ascription of evil to both creator and creation. Yet many of the same passages in the novel that appear to provide evidence of Gnostic belief are also evocative of Job's bitter antagonism to the Old Testament deity. All we can say with certainty is that Melville performed a kind of imaginative synthesis of Greek, Hebrew, Gnostic, and Christian myth (among others) in his portrait of a heaven-defying and heretical Ahab.[33]

The subject of eschatology includes ideas about the Christian end-times in both human history and individual life. For the individual, eschatology consists of the "four last things," namely, death, judgment, heaven, and hell, while the apocalyptic eschatology that largely concerns us here consists of visionary foreshadowings of end-time events showing the vindication of the faithful and the destruction of their oppressors. Even more than the broad influence of Job discussed above, biblical apocalyptic eschatology has provided the basis for a rich variety of religious and historical movements as well as a model for an imposing number of works of Western literature. A pervasive pattern of themes, motifs, images, and symbols links *Moby-Dick* to the two apocalyptic books of the Bible—Daniel and Revelation—as well as various other related prophetic and eschatological texts.[34]

Technically speaking, the only formal apocalyptic text of the Old Testament is the book of Daniel, but eschatological ideas also inform the messages of the Hebrew prophets, notably Amos, Isaiah, Jeremiah, Ezekiel, Joel, Zephaniah, and Malachi. One repeated motif here is the Day of the Lord, or time of judgment, when God will punish the wicked and redeem the righteous "remnant." In Isaiah, from the late eighth century BCE, "the day of the Lord of hosts shall be upon every one that is proud and lofty, and upon every one that is lifted up; and he shall be brought low" (Isa. 2:12). On that day, the Lord will also "punish" Leviathan, "even leviathan the crooked serpent; and he shall slay the dragon that is in the sea" (Isa. 27:1). Isaiah's representations of the Day of the Lord will contribute to the climax of *Moby-Dick* (see chapter 7 below). In the prophet Joel's well-known description from the late sixth or early fifth century BCE, "The sun shall be turned into darkness, and the moon into blood, before the great and terrible day of the Lord come." Moreover, "whosoever shall call on the name of the Lord shall be delivered; for in mount Zion and in Jerusalem shall be deliverance, as the Lord hath said, and in the remnant whom the Lord shall call" (Joel 2:31–32). In Zephaniah, again from the late sixth or early fifth century BCE, "That day is a day of wrath, a day of trouble and distress, a day of wasteness and desolation, a day of darkness and gloominess, a day of clouds and thick darkness" (Zeph. 1:15).

In some cases, a theophany of Yahweh as divine warrior or Lord of Hosts could accompany the advent of the Day of the Lord, in keeping with Hebrew traditions of holy war.[35] Depending on historical context, the day of judgment could be invoked against other nations or against the Jewish people themselves. The disappearance of the northern kingdom of Israel following defeat by the Assyrians in 721 BCE and the Babylonian conquest of the remaining southern kingdom of Judah in 597 and again in 586 BCE were thus articulated as judgments against God's people for their worship of foreign gods or their failures of social justice (Amos 4–8, Hos. 4–10, Jer. 2–8). Old Testament prophets also condemned foreign nations for their false religions, arrogance, and wickedness (Isa. 13, Jer. 46, Ezek. 10). The natural sequel to these prophecies of doom was a period of future redemption for God's chosen people, either in the restoration of national sovereignty, or in a period of permanent peace and blessedness (Hos. 2:14–23; Joel 3:18; Isa. 2:2–4, 11:3–16, 25:6–12, 35:1–10; Jer. 31:1–37; Ezek. 16:53–63, 47:6–14). The coupling of divine destruction and restoration in the teachings of the Old Testament prophets anticipates a comparable coupling in the New Testament, in which restoration after divinely directed battle takes the form of this-worldly millennial redemption for the blessed followed by the final onset of the heavenly New Jerusalem.[36]

The historical transformation of the prophets' eschatology into the formal genre of apocalyptic literature took place in the second century BCE, well after the end of the formal prophetic tradition, when the hope for a restoration of the Davidic kingship found in Isaiah, Jeremiah, and other prophets was undermined by Israel's successive domination by Persian, Ptolmaic, Seleucid (Hellenistic), and Roman overlords. The focus on a political messiah who would restore Israel to its previous splendors yielded to a more radical program of a supernatural messiah sent by God at a time of crisis. The new tradition of apocalyptic revelation offered a vision of cosmic redemption in the face of new historical conditions, in which the hegemonic world empires of Greece and Rome appeared to threaten the very existence of the chosen people, first Jewish and then Christian. Hence the Greek term "apocalypse" denoted a literary genre based on the disclosure of divine secrets by an angelic intermediary, telling of the manner and timing of God's intervention in history. As Stephen D. O'Leary has noted, "the unique feature of apocalyptic myth is that it offers a temporal or teleological framework for understanding evil by claiming that evil must grow in power until the appointed time of the imminent end." Instead of an adversary's being sent as a deserved punishment, the genre of apocalyptic literature adduced a satanic power opposed to God in a dualistic view of the cosmos probably influenced by the Zoroastrian religion with which the Jews became familiar during two centuries of contact with their Persian overlords (539–330 BCE). The apocalyptic genre produced a mass of writings that appeared too late to be accepted into the Hebrew canon, but which now appear in the Pseudepigrapha and Apocrypha, notably 1–3 Enoch, 4 Ezra (2 Esdras), 2–3 Baruch, and the many apocalypses named for a variety of prominent Old and New Testament figures.[37]

While pretending to be set during the Babylonian captivity of the sixth century, the pseudonymous book of Daniel was written or compiled during the Maccabean revolt against Judea's Seleucid overlord Antiochus IV (dubbed Epiphanes, or "the glorious"), which began in 167 BCE. Using the figure of the devout Jew Daniel, holding onto his faith in the court of the Babylonian kings (Nebuchadnezzar, Belshazzar), the author of Daniel produced a testament of hope directed against the Jews' Hellenistic oppressor who was seeking to transform their state into a Greek satellite. The book of Daniel is divisible into two halves: the first (chs. 1–6), largely written in Aramaic, recounts legends about a legendary Hebrew exile and his companions in the court of the Babylonian king, and the second half (chs. 7–12), written in Hebrew, relates a series of Daniel's visions, glossed by an angelic intermediary. A well-known legend in the first half of the book includes the Hebrew seer's reading of the divine "writing on the wall" to the impious Belshazzar before his kingdom is invaded by Persia. (Such portentous "writing on the wall" will be a recurrent motif in *Moby-Dick*.) Beginning in chapter 7, the angel Gabriel reveals to Daniel a timetable for political redemption following defeat of a series of foreign states, symbolized by four monstrous beasts, by the divine patriarch, or Ancient of Days, and a messianic Son of Man.[38]

Two centuries after the composition of Daniel and amid an efflorescence of Jewish apocalyptic writing, the religious mission of Jesus Christ was patently eschatological in nature, his primary goal being the spiritual and ethical transformation of the Jews in preparation for the imminent kingdom of God. Christ began his career as a student of John the Baptist, a desert-dwelling millenarian ascetic who issued a call for repentance in the face of imminent divine judgment. In his subsequent teachings, Christ elaborated on the transformations of Jewish law that were needed to attain God's kingdom and the social reversals that would result from its advent. All the gospels contain numerous parables about this kingdom, and the three synoptics contain what has been called a "little apocalypse" (Matt. 24, Mark 13, Luke 21), in which Jesus predicts the tumultuous historical events and cosmological catastrophes of the last days. After this period of "great tribulation" (Matt. 24:21), the world will experience the cosmic return of the Son of Man to judgment according to a scenario drawn from Joel 2 and Daniel 7.[39]

Following Christ's crucifixion, the idea of his Second Coming, or *parousia*, became a fixture of Christian belief and guided the teachings of his chief apostles, and especially Saint Paul whose letters (both genuine and attributed) discuss eschatological themes. Yet while Christ made the practice of charity a mainstay of his messianic faith, Saint Paul posited belief in Christ's resurrection at the center of the Christian faith he helped create in his missionary activity and epistolary writings. In First Corinthians, Saint Paul envisioned the resurrection of Christ as the guarantor of spiritual afterlife for faithful Christians who will then join him at his Second Coming: "Then cometh the end, when he shall have delivered up the kingdom to God, even the father; when he shall have put down all rule and all authority and power. / For he must reign, till he hath put all enemies under his feet. / The last enemy that shall be destroyed is death" (1 Cor. 15:14–16). Paul thereupon elaborates on the "spiritual body" that Christians will inhabit following their death, when like a seed planted in the ground they will be transformed and ascend to heaven (15:35–54). The question of a spiritual afterlife derived from Pauline doctrine will be a recurrent issue throughout *Moby-Dick* (see chapter 6 below). In other letters, Paul exhorted his fellow Christians to be vigilant concerning Christ's unexpected reappearance, a sign of a general resurrection and judgment (1 Thess. 5), while he also warns about a potential satanic "man of sin" and "son of perdition" who will appear during a period of moral apostasy (or "falling away") just before Christ's return. This figure "opposeth and exalteth himself above all that is called God, or that is worshipped; so that he as God sitteth in the temple of God, shewing himself that he is God" (2 Thess. 2:4). Such a blasphemous "mystery of iniquity" was later often conflated with the mysterious figure of the "antichrist" evoked in the letters of John (1 John 2:22, 4:1–3; 2 John 7). In his usurpation of divine prerogatives, Melville's Captain Ahab will take on some of the characteristic features of the Antichrist. [40]

Like Daniel the book of Revelation, written at the end of the first century CE, was composed in another era of perceived political and existential crisis, now for the adherents of the new Christian faith in Asia Minor, who were confronted with the blasphemous imperial cult of the Roman emperor Domitian (81–96 CE) and haunted by their ruthless persecution by Nero in the mid-60s and the destruction of Jerusalem by Roman armies in 70 CE.[41] Like Daniel, Revelation was an archetypal assemblage of visionary motifs enacting revenge on the enemies of God and assuring the faithful final vindication with the advent of a messianic redeemer. Like other examples of Jewish apocalyptic, much of the symbolism and imagery of Revelation is traceable to Old Testament prophecy, notably Isaiah, Jeremiah, Ezekiel, Daniel, Joel, and Zechariah. Revelation is governed by a series of ethical dualisms organized around the conflict of the saved and the damned, beginning with a heavenly dragon that threatens the infant messiah and is defeated by the angel Michael, the guardian of the Hebrew nation. The conflict of dragon and angel from Revelation chapter 12, which provided a model for innumerable works of art and literature in Western culture, also provided a partial model for Ahab's final confrontation with the White Whale (see chapter 7 below).

In order to understand the mythical basis for Ahab's demonization of the White Whale and his elevation of its pursuit to an apocalyptic mission, we must recognize that the captain of the *Pequod* has transformed the albino whale into a mythological embodiment of evil closely related to the marine chaos monster best known by the name Leviathan, as found in several passages of the Old Testament (most prominently in the book of Job) and informing parts of the book of Revelation. These passages draw on the myths of divine combat with chaos monsters at the creation that inform the ancient cosmogonies of Babylon and Canaan and were subsequently assimilated into the Hebrew and then the Christian Bible. A brief excursus in comparative mythology will deepen our knowledge of the rich religious and mythological background to Melville's whaling epic.[42]

In the Babylonian creation epic known as the *Enuma Elish* (circa 1830–1530 BCE), the world begins with watery chaos divided between the primordial father Apsu, god of freshwater lakes, marshes, and other subterranean waters, and the primordial mother Tiamat, goddess of the salty marine waters. The creation of the other gods from these two parental figures eventually resulted in a plot by Apsu to kill them all because of their overly boisterous behavior, but instead, the leading god Ea murdered Apsu. In revenge, Tiamat organized a band of rebel gods and monsters to attack the reigning gods: "She cloaked ferocious dragons with fearsome rays, / And made them bear mantles of radiance, made them godlike, / (*chanting this imprecation*) / 'Whoever looks upon them shall collapse in utter terror!'" This formidable threat was met only by Ea's son Marduk on condition that he be rewarded the highest position in the divine assembly. The divine warrior then prepared himself for battle with a full array of weaponry:

> He fashioned a bow, designated it as his weapon,
> Feathered the arrow, set it in the string.
> He lifted up a mace and carried it in his right hand,
> Slung the bow and quiver at his side,
> Put lightning in front of him,
> His body was filled with an ever-blazing flame.
> He made a net to encircle Tiamat within it,
> Marshaled the four winds so that no part of her could escape.[43]

Marduk thereupon mounted his storm chariot against Tiamat, who took the form of a marine monster or dragon, and he killed her by driving his Evil Wind into her mouth and then shooting an arrow into her vitals. Out of the giant corpse of this sea monster, Marduk created the cosmos, using half her body to make the sky and the other half to make the watery abyss on which the earth rests. While celebrating the political ascendancy of the city of Babylon and its powerful king Hammurabi (ca. 1728–1686 BCE), this cosmogonic myth was also a reminder of the annual devastation caused by the flooding of the Tigris and Euphrates Rivers. As a result of the sixth-century BCE Hebrew captivity in Babylon when the exiles were forcibly made aware of the cosmogonic myth found in the *Enuma Elish*, the Priestly author of the account of creation in the first book of Genesis strategically transformed the conclusion to the Babylonian creation myth describing Marduk's splitting of Tiamat's body into sky and watery abyss into Yahweh's division of the waters above and below the firmament.[44]

A comparable creation story and combat myth emerged from ancient Canaanite civilization as recorded in texts from circa 1400 BCE recovered from the city of Ugarit (modern Ras Shamra) on the Syrian coast above Lebanon. The mythological literature of Canaan is divisible into three cycles of stories involving the storm and fertility god Baal ("Lord"), master of lightning and rain. The first describes Baal's fight with the Sea, or Yam (also known by the titles Prince Sea and Judge River); the second, his construction of a "house" or temple; and the third, his fight with Death, or Mot. Like the Greek pantheon (Zeus, Poseidon, and Hades), the three chief Canaanite gods were lords of storm, sea, and underworld, respectively. In an attempt to seize control over the gods, Sea (Yam) sent a message to El, the elderly supreme god (who, like the Greek Kronos, was largely detached from overseeing the affairs of the world), and to the divine assembly, demanding the surrender of Baal so that Sea could usurp his domains. Despairing of meeting this insolent challenge, the gods are rescued by Baal's bold offer to fight the Sea, with the aid of a pair of magical clubs. The description of Baal's victory exhibits the technique of linguistic parallelism—repetition with semantic accretion—that is also typical of Hebrew poetry:

> And the club danced in Baal's hands,
>> like a vulture from his fingers.
> It struck Prince sea on the skull,
>> Judge River between the eyes.
> Sea stumbled;
>> he fell to the ground;
> his joints shook;
>> his frame collapsed.
> Baal captured and drank Sea;
>> he finished off Judge River.[45]

Vanquishing both Sea and River in combat, Baal overcomes the watery principle of chaos and is rewarded, like Marduk, with kingship of the divine assembly. He celebrates with a victory banquet and eventually builds his own house-temple. In a later scene Baal sends messengers to proclaim his kingship to Mot, the god of the underworld, who invites Baal to be both his guest and the main course at his meal. In a taunting speech, Mot recognizes Baal's heroic victory over Lotan (Leviathan), the seven-headed Twisting Serpent, sending it into the underworld of the god Mot, a favorite of El:

> When you killed Lotan, the Fleeing Serpent,
>> finished off the Twisting Serpent,
>> the seven-headed monster,
> The heavens withered and drooped
>> like the folds of your robes . . .
> Now you will surely descend into the throat of El's son, Death [Mot],
>> into the watery depths of El's Darling, the Hero.[46]

The Baal story cycle ends with the confrontation between the storm god Baal and the death god Mot, a schematic opposition in keeping with the ultimate source of Canaanite myth in the annual cycles of nature. Emerging in the midst of these ancient Near Eastern religions and their creation myths, the Hebrew religion was considerably influenced by them, but unlike the myths, whose traditional function was to focus ritual celebration honoring the primordial creation of order out of chaos, the Hebrew religion embraced instead the allegedly historical event of the Exodus as the founding event of its faith. Hebrew myths of creation and chaos accordingly became not a foundational event for cultic worship but a supplemental illustration of God's continuing work of salvation. For as Bernhard Anderson notes, "Israelite prophets and poets appropriated the old chaos imagery in order to portray the continuing creative and redemptive work of God. The struggle between creation and chaos is one which goes on in the realm of history, and this historical struggle continues from the first day to the last day."[47]

The first indication of Hebrew appropriation of the Canaanite creation myth occurred in the cultic celebrations of the divine king, in which the king was honored as God's regent and an insurer of divine order according to royal covenant theology. The king here is assured of victories over his enemies that repeat the primeval victory of God over the forces of chaos, the mythical archetype that helped shape the account of the Hebrews' divinely directed victory over Pharaoh and the parting of the Red Sea during the Exodus. God's victory over the chaos monster was also invoked in some psalms by biblical redactors reflecting on their sixth-century Exile and drawing on Babylonian and Canaanite versions of the combat myth to inspire hope in the midst of captivity. Several psalms explicitly or implicitly present such key mythical and historical events in the history of God's chosen people. So in Psalm 74, "God is my King of old, working salvation in the midst of the earth. / Thou didst divide the sea by thy strength: thou brakest the heads of the dragons in the waters. / Thou brakest the heads of leviathan in pieces, and gavest him to be meat to the people inhabiting the wilderness" (Ps. 74:12–14). Psalm 89 rehearses the battle with the same chaos monster, now named Rahab (the Proud One) with implied reference to the defeat of Pharaoh at the Red Sea: "Thou rulest the raging of the sea: when the waves thereof arise, thou stillest them. / Thou hast broken Rahab in pieces, as one that is slain; thou hast scattered thine enemies with thy strong arm" (Ps. 89:9–10).

In Psalm 104, God is depicted as master of a creation that includes a peacefully subdued Leviathan: "So is this great and wide sea, wherein are things creeping innumerable, both small and great beasts. / There go the ships: there is that leviathan, whom thou hast made to play therein. / These wait all upon thee; that thou mayest give them their meat in due season" (Ps. 104:25–27). This subordinate status for Leviathan is evident in the mention of the sea monsters (or "whales," as they are called in the Authorized

Version) that were brought forth on the fifth day of creation in Genesis—an account that would seem to depend on the text of Psalm 104: "And God created great whales [more properly, "dragons" or "monsters," from the Hebrew *tannin*] and every living creature that moveth, which the waters brought forth abundantly" (Gen. 1:21). God's sovereignty over the sea as a symbol of chaos is similarly evident in several other psalms (Pss. 65:7, 77:16, 93:3–4, 107:29, 148:7).[48]

The same imagery of sea, chaos monster, serpent, and dragon informs two passages in the book of Isaiah. In the interpolated "little apocalypse" in First Isaiah (chs. 24–27), the future Day of the Lord is characterized by God's slaying of the dragon of the sea as a striking sign of his retributive might: "In that day the Lord with his sore and great and strong sword shall punish leviathan the piercing serpent, even leviathan that crooked serpent; and he shall slay the dragon that is in the sea" (Isa. 27:1). In Second Isaiah (chs. 40–55), on the other hand, the primordial chaos dragon Rahab is invoked in implied association with the parting of the Red Sea, as the psalmist encourages the deity to reassume his ancient protective powers: "awake, as in the ancient days, in the generations of old. Art thou not it [him] that hath cut Rahab, and wounded the dragon? / Art thou not it which hath dried the sea, the waters of the great deep; that hath made the depths of the sea as way for the ransomed to pass over?" (Isa. 51:9–10).

From an examination of Psalms 74 and 104 and Isaiah 27, we may conclude that the Hebrew conception of Leviathan as primordial chaos monster occupied a curiously ambiguous position in relation to the deity. On the one hand, in Psalm 74 and Isaiah 27, Leviathan is the dragon-like embodiment of watery chaos whom God has already or will soon destroy as a threat to the well-being of his people. On the other hand, in Psalm 104, Leviathan as a whalelike sea creature is an integral part of the creation and sports in the seas while awaiting nurture from God's bounteous hand; instead of being destroyed, Leviathan is tamed to be part of a cosmos ruled by the all-powerful hand of the deity.[49]

A similar ambiguity in the representation of Leviathan—both threatening chaos monster and accepted part of God's creation—can be found in the long characterization of Leviathan found in the book of Job, which draws on the Canaanite creation myth of Baal and Lotan. In the third cycle of exchanges with his friends, Job answers Bildad by reasserting God's lordship over the creation: "He divideth the sea with his power and by the understanding he smiteth through the proud [Rahab]: / By his spirit he hath garnished the heavens; his hand hath formed the crooked serpent [Leviathan]" (Job 26:12–13). Demonstrating the mystery

and majesty of the creation, God later ends his theophany as the Voice
from the Whirlwind by invoking Behemoth, the land monster (ch. 40),
and Leviathan, the sea monster (ch. 41). While the figure of Behemoth
is possibly based on a swamp-inhabiting bovine monster found in several
Near Eastern mythologies, the biblical Leviathan is manifestly borrowed
from the chaos monster of Canaanite myth, with its Near Eastern and
Mesopotamian prototypes. Resembling the Egyptian crocodile in some
of its features, especially its scaly hide, Leviathan in Job 41 is also a
composite mythical creature embodying the sea as a symbol of chaos, as
Marvin Pope, John Day, and Leo G. Perdue have demonstrated. Perhaps
the most obtrusive non-naturalistic feature of Leviathan is its dragon-like
fire-breathing capacity (Job 41:19–21). The description of Leviathan at
Job 41:9, strategically mistranslated in the Authorized Version, also bears
traces of the cowering of the gods before the marine chaos monster, as
found in both the Mesopotamian and Canaanite combat myth.[50]

The symbolic use of marine chaos monsters based on Near Eastern
creation myth is similarly evident in the two apocalyptic books of the
Bible, as the authors of Daniel and Revelation transform the primordial
combat and creation myths of Babylonian and Canaanite origin into an
eschatological event. In both Daniel and Revelation, cosmology and history
are merged and the mythical symbolism of evil directed against a political
enemy. In Daniel 7, four great beasts emerge from the sea, representative of
the four world empires—Babylonian, Median, Persian, and Macedonian—
that historically had been opposed to the Jewish people, with the "little horn"
of the last beast symbolic of the immediate Seleucid oppressor, Antiochus
IV. We may note that the third beast in this vision has four heads (Dan. 7:6),
comparable to the multiheaded Lotan that Baal kills. Just as Baal, based
on his conquest of Lotan, is given sovereignty over the council of the gods
dominated by El, the beasts of Daniel 7 have their power neutralized by
the El-like Ancient of Days and his Baal-like younger associate, the Son of
Man, whose arrival "with the clouds of heaven" recalls Baal's identity as a
storm god.[51]

The same mythical symbolism can again be found in the interrelated
beasts, dragons, and serpents of Revelation (chs. 12, 13, 17). In chapter 12, a
myth of combat against a cosmic dragon informs the image of the "great red
dragon, having seven heads and ten horns" that fights the "woman clothed
with the sun" and her messianic child. The persecution of the woman and
child here is probably based on the Greek myth of the persecution of the
goddess Leto and her child Apollo by the chaos monster Python. In this
case, the angel Michael, the guardian angel of the Israelite nation, fights

against the dragon now identified as "that old serpent, called the Devil, and Satan, which deceiveth the whole world" (Rev. 12:9). In a gesture that associates the same cosmic dragon with the primeval marine chaos monster of Near Eastern mythology, the dragon-serpent, having been expelled from heaven, now makes a last attempt to drown the woman and child: "And the serpent cast out of his mouth water as a flood after the woman, that he might causeth her to be carried away of the flood. / And the earth opened up her mouth, and swallowed up the flood which the dragon cast out of his mouth" (Rev. 12:15–16).[52]

Timothy K. Beal has noted the manner in which the dragon of Revelation 12 incorporates the traditional chaos monster of Near Eastern mythology while strategically transforming it from an integral part of the divine order into a symbol of the devil as divine adversary:

> As elsewhere in the Apocalypse, John's spectacle of the great red dragon sorts through various fragments of biblical and Greco-Roman tradition in order to piece together a new version of the monster. In the process, it attempts to *sort out* the biblical canon's deep theological ambivalence with regard to this "ancient serpent" in terms of a theologically tidier, more systematic scenario of good versus evil, God versus Devil.
>
> In other texts from the Hebrew Bible, especially in the book of Job, we have encountered visions of the world and of God in which chaos and order intertwine. In those texts, the chaos monster (Leviathan, *tannin*, etc.) emerges as a means of expressing that intertwining, engendering a sense of uncertainty and cosmic horror that is deeply theological, going to the very core of the character of God within biblical monotheism. The Apocalypse of John works against such an intertwining, peeling Leviathan the twisting serpent off the character of God and sending it to the Devil.[53]

In Revelation 13, the beast emerging from the sea has seven heads, like the primeval monster of the Canaanite creation myth, and its appearance is followed by a beast from the earth, just as the aquatic Leviathan is introduced along with the land monster Behemoth in Job. In the case of the beast from the sea, "the dragon gave him his power and his seat, and great authority," while the beast from the earth "spake as a dragon" (Rev. 13:2, 11). And in Revelation 17, the "great whore" of Babylon sits on a "scarlet-colored beast, full of names of blasphemy, having seven heads and ten horns" (Rev. 17:3), another avatar of the multiheaded chaos monster of Near Eastern creation myth.[54]

Finally, we should note that twin chaos monsters Behemoth and

Leviathan reappear in three texts of the Pseudepigrapha (4 Ezra 6:49–52; 2 Apocalypse of Baruch 29:4; and 1 Enoch 60:7–10, 24), as well as in writings from early Rabbinic Judaism. In these texts, the carcasses of Behemoth and Leviathan provide substance for a feast of the righteous at the eschatological end-time—an adaptation of the Near Eastern creation myths of a cosmos established on the carcass of the slain chaos monster, as in the story of Marduk and Tiamat.[55]

Ahab's imaginative and experiential identification of evil with the Leviathanic White Whale in *Moby-Dick* has a rich mythical and biblical background that must be acknowledged when interpreting the whale's symbolic function. In order to prime us for this identification, Melville includes strategic quotations from Genesis 1:21, Job 41:32, Psalm 104:26, and Isaiah 27:1 at the start of the "Extracts" section of *Moby-Dick*. While Melville cannot have known the Near Eastern mythological background to the Old Testament image of Leviathan (the Mesopotamian texts of the *Enuma Elish* were first discovered in the early 1850s and the Canaanite texts of the Baal myths in the late 1920s), nevertheless, as a well-informed student of the Bible, biblical commentaries, and contemporary comparative mythology, Melville was manifestly aware of the thread of symbolic continuity uniting the various chaos monsters, beasts, serpents, dragons, and devils throughout the Old and New Testament. As Robert D. Richardson has remarked, Melville "was better informed about and more deeply interested in problems of myth than any other American writer of his time."[56]

The ultimate proof of such knowledge can be found in the symbolic texture of *Moby-Dick*, for in Ahab's pursuit of the White Whale, we may read a modern version of God's fight with the marine chaos monster Leviathan wherein the divine combat is, as in the book of Revelation, transferred from a primordial to an eschatological event. And while many familiar classical and Christian myths and epic narratives dramatize the fight between a god or a hero and a terrifying monster or beast (such as Apollo and Python, Hercules and the Hydra, Perseus and the Gorgon, Theseus and the Minotaur, Saint George and the Dragon, Beowulf and Grendel), Ahab's combat, steeped in Old Testament mythology, involves an enraged attempt to usurp the divine role of holy warrior, just as the captain's appropriation of demonic powers to fight against the chaos monster further subverts the moral legitimacy of his quest. Finally, unlike the culture heroes whose dragon- or monster-slaying serves a laudable communal end, Ahab's motives for revenge are above all private and lead to the deaths of all his crew, except the surviving narrator.

In addition to the varied biblical background to the mythic status of Melville's White Whale and its human antagonist, an important range of meaning is also conveyed by the Old Testament names of *Moby-Dick*'s two main characters, Ishmael and Ahab. As Yvonne Sherwood has noted, these two figures are alienated from the mainstream of Hebrew salvationist history, being "the outcasts and the unchosen, the victims of divine deselection, who wander into *Moby-Dick* still smarting from their biblical experiences."[57] The Old Testament figure of Ishmael (whose name means "God shall hear") bears a paradoxical moral identity. As the eldest son of the patriarch Abraham and his bondswoman Hagar, Ishmael is in the line of righteous succession but he is passed over because of his illegitimacy and subsequently exiled to the wilderness with his mother, thereby repeating the fate of the original first couple without having committed their crime of disobedience. The angel of the Lord tells Hagar before Ishmael's birth not only that he will be fruitful in offspring but also that he will assume the role of rebel: "he will be a wild man; his hand will be against every man, and every man's hand against him" (Gen. 16:12). After their exile from the Abrahamic clan, Ishmael and his mother are nurtured and protected by God; indeed, Ishmael's name suits the fact that God preserves the outcasts from death in the desert because he hears the cry of both (Gen. 21:17). Following divine intervention involving the discovery of a well in the desert, "God was with the lad; and he grew, and dwelt in the wilderness, and became an archer" (Gen. 21:20). Although admitted to the Abrahamic covenant of the circumcision, Ishmael will not be included in the covenant of the Promised Land. Instead, he will found the dynasty of Ishmaelites and other peoples on the periphery of the Hebrew nation.[58]

Like the biblical Ishmael, the narrator of *Moby-Dick* early on reveals that he bears a sense of alienation and disinheritance from his cultural heritage. Just as the biblical Ishmael is an exile and a wanderer, Ishmael the sailor asserts in the first paragraph of Melville's novel that "having nothing particular to interest me on shore, I thought I would sail about a little and see the watery part of the world" (3). In his subsequent self-portrait describing his reasons for going whaling, Ishmael's "hand" is comically poised against the world when he confesses that when his "hypos" (hypochondria, or depression) gets control of his mood, "it requires a strong moral principle to prevent me from deliberately stepping into the streets and methodically knocking people's hats off" (3). By the same token, Ishmael confirms his status as rebellious "wild man" by confessing his irrepressible urge to visit exotic, uncivilized places: "as for me, I am tormented with an everlasting itch for things remote. I love to sail forbidden seas, and land on barbarous coasts" (7).

In addition, just as the biblical Ishmael was exiled as a boy because of his jealous stepmother Sarah, the young Ishmael in *Moby-Dick* (as recounted in chapter 4 of the novel) was punished by his anonymous stepmother by being sent to his room on the longest day of the year, an experience that leads to a supernatural visitation during a waking dream that is comparable to the young biblical Ishmael's protection by an angel of the Lord. And like the biblical Ishmael's youthful ordeal as an alienated wild man in the wilderness, Melville's Ishmael undergoes a spiritual testing in the comparable wilderness of the sea. As a figure of suffering and spiritual alienation, Ishmael is capable of understanding and sympathizing with Ahab's enraged quest to destroy the White Whale, but Ishmael's moral allegiance is ultimately not with Ahab's covenant of death. On the contrary, the divine blessing of the biblical Ishmael can be seen in the series of redemptive moments experienced by Melville's Ishmael, as found, for example, in his early friendship with the "savage" Queequeg in New Bedford; in his "conversion" experiences on the *Pequod*, described in "A Squeeze of the Hand" and "The Try-Works"; and in his seemingly providential survival of the wreck of the *Pequod*, comparable to the righteous remnant that survives the Day of the Lord in Old Testament prophecy.

The name of Melville's whaling captain, on the other hand, is taken from the ninth-century BCE king of Israel described in chapters 16–22 of the First Book of Kings by the antipathetic Deuteronomistic historian.[59] Married to the Tyrean (Phoenician) princess Jezebel, who introduced the cult of the Canaanite storm and fertility god Baal into Israel, Ahab allegedly "did more to provoke the Lord God of Israel to anger than all the kings of Israel that were before him" (1 Kings 16:33). The sources of such a judgment included continuing the "sins" of Jeroboam (establishing sanctuaries at Dan and Bethel dedicated to the "golden calf"), Ahab's marriage to a foreign princess, his promotion of the cult of Baal in his capital, and his making of a "sacred pole" for the cult of the goddess Asherah. As Jerome Walsh notes, "The narrator portrays for us a king whose every deed . . . stands in direct violation of the Yahwistic values on which Israel is founded."[60]

Ahab's influential ideological antagonist is the prophet Elijah the Tishbite, who is protected by God from persecution and who defeats the prophets of Baal on Mount Carmel by successfully drawing fire down from heaven (1 Kings 18:17–40). Elijah subsequently confronts Ahab over his appropriation of his subject Naboth's vineyard, after its owner has been killed by Jezebel's command—a potential symbol of the usurpation by Baal of Yahweh's sacred "vineyard" Israel. In reaction to the king's crime, Elijah predicts Ahab's end: "In the place where dogs licked the blood of Naboth shall dogs lick thy blood, even thine" (1 Kings 21:19). Although victorious against the Assyrians in early battles, Ahab's third campaign proves his downfall. After being assured of victory by his four hundred lying "house" prophets, Ahab consents to hear a prophetic opponent of his reign, Micaiah, who predicts defeat in battle. At the ensuing battle of Ramoth-gilead (circa 850 BCE), Ahab in his chariot is struck and killed by a stray arrow, as Elijah predicted, and the dogs consumed the blood in his chariot when it was later washed out in his capital of Samaria.

Like the biblical Ahab, Melville's Captain Ahab combines exemplary abilities as a political leader with an impious disregard for the moral imperatives of the monotheistic Judeo-Christian god. Just as King Ahab was a sanctified ruler of Israel who nevertheless corrupted his regime with foreign cults, Captain Ahab is a commanding figure among American whalemen, but he sets himself up as God's blasphemous antagonist and traffics in heretical religious traditions. In lieu of the Canaanite cult of Baal introduced by King Ahab's wife, Melville's Ahab has allied himself with a follower of the ancient Zoroastrian (or modern Parsee) religion in the person of Fedallah, who will assist in the hunt for Moby Dick along with his crew of four Asiatic "dusky phantoms" (216). As a visual trope for its unholy commander, the ship on which Ahab is captain is initially described as a "cannibal of a craft, tricking herself forth in the chased bones of her enemies. All round, the unpanelled, open bulwarks were garnished like one continuous jaw, with the long sharp teeth of the sperm whale, inserted there for pins, to fasten her old hempen thews and tendons to" (70). The *Pequod*'s whalebone ornamentation also evokes the distinctive "ivory house" that the biblical King Ahab made for himself as a result of his extensive foreign trade (1 Kings 22:39).

Named after an allegedly extinct Indian tribe destroyed by the Puritans in the 1630s, the *Pequod* ("destroyer") is thus typologically related to the Canaanites, who were extirpated by the Jews upon their arrival in the Promised Land; the odd-looking "wigwam" (70) that Peleg occupies while the *Pequod* is in port emphasizes this historical typology. In addition, as captain over a whaling crew drawn from around the world, Ahab has initiated a cult of diabolic revenge against God's alleged surrogate, the White Whale. Just as King Ahab unjustly seized Naboth's vineyard, Captain Ahab usurps control of the *Pequod* for his own private ends, against the will of his conscientious first mate, Starbuck. As in the story of the biblical King Ahab, too, repeated warnings of disaster fail to dissuade

Captain Ahab from his quest, and Ahab's pursuit of the White Whale, climaxed by combat and death, is repeatedly associated with moral pollution and desecration.

Melville partly modeled his whaling captain also on Job (see chapter 3 below), and by combining the biblical figures of both Ahab and Job in his protagonist, Melville would seem to be joining figures who occupy antithetical positions on a moral spectrum—King Ahab as a type of guilty apostasy and Job as the alleged type of innocent steadfast faith in the Hebrew god. But in fact both enact notorious challenges to Yahweh's system of justice, and both come close to, or actually commit, blasphemous outrages against the deity. Furthermore, a structural continuity between the book of Job and the story of King Ahab is the testing of both men by an authorized "satanic" agent of the heavenly court, a figure embodied in *Moby-Dick* in the ambiguous character of Fedallah. In Job, we recall, the satan seeks God's permission to test Job's faith by first taking away all his possessions and then, when Job fails to curse God, by afflicting him with a loathsome disease. In the First Book of Kings, the prophet Micaiah tells Ahab how God has allowed a satan-like figure to mislead King Ahab into engaging in a disastrous battle by putting a "lying spirit" into the mouth of his prophets:

> And the Lord said, Who shall persuade Ahab, that he may go up and fall at Ramoth-gilead? And one said on this manner, and another said on that manner.
>
> And there came forth a spirit and stood before the Lord, and said, I will persuade him.
>
> And the Lord said unto him, Wherewith? And he said, I will go forth and be a lying spirit in the mouth of all his prophets. And he said, Thou shalt persuade him, and prevail also: go forth, and do so.
>
> Now therefore, behold, the Lord hath put a lying spirit in the mouth of all these thy prophets, and the Lord has spoken evil concerning thee. (1 Kings 22:20–23)

As a reward for his truth-telling, Micaiah is imprisoned, while King Ahab with his characteristic willfulness fights against the Syrians at Ramoth-gildead and is defeated. While an innocent Job is physically and spiritually tested by the satan and survives his ordeal, a culpable Ahab is fatally lured into battle by a similar figure.

By bearing the name of a biblical king who outraged God more than any other Hebrew ruler, Melville's Captain Ahab carries an overdetermined moral identity involving blasphemous opposition to the deity, promotion of foreign religious practices, dangerous associations with false prophets, and a general aura of apocalyptic doom and destruction. As a literary descendent of his chief biblical prototypes, Ahab thus exemplifies the Deuteronomic principle of divine punishment for human sin; yet as a morally embattled Job figure, Ahab's character also embodies a radical critique of the traditional equation of sin and suffering. Both interpretations are seemingly valid in the polyvalent moral and metaphysical world of *Moby-Dick*.

CHAPTER TWO

Pilgrimage and Prophecy

IN THE PREVIOUS CHAPTER, we have reviewed the biblical paradigms of theodicy and eschatology that offered a potential rationale for the existence of evil and human suffering that Melville explored in *Moby-Dick*. Yet the novel also draws extensively on its immediate religious, historical, and cultural contexts. Certain key features in the religious landscape of antebellum America are thus evoked in the novel, especially in Ishmael's early experience of seeking a whaling vessel in New Bedford and Nantucket—an experience constituting a seriocomic pilgrimage through a landscape fraught with eschatological perils and prophetic warnings. As attested by the mock theatrical billing in the novel's first chapter, which placed Ishmael's voyage in the time between a *"Grand Contested Election for Presidency of the United States"* (the Harrison–Van Buren contest of November 1840) and a "BLOODY BATTLE IN AFGHANISTAN" (the Battle of Kabul in January 1842), *Moby-Dick* was largely set in the first year of Melville's own whaling voyage on the *Acushnet*, when he sailed from Fairhaven, Massachusetts, on 3 January 1841. His novel accordingly reflects, both directly and indirectly, many of the essential religious and cultural features of the era, especially the saturation of contemporary American culture by evangelical Christianity and the Bible.[1]

The first half of the nineteenth century in America saw a sustained resurgence of evangelical Christianity, in what has been called the Second Great Awakening—a protracted period of revivalism that began near the start of the century, reached a peak of cultural diffusion in the 1830s, and flowered again in the 1850s. As Alexis de Tocqueville asserted in his study of American democracy: "there is no country in the world where the Christian religion retains a greater influence over the souls of men than in

America." In a recent comprehensive survey of American theology from the mid-eighteenth to the mid-nineteenth century, Mark A. Noll has traced the synthesis of evangelical Protestantism, republican political ideology, and commonsense moral philosophy that characterized the era. Such a synthesis implied a close alliance between theological and political ideals of virtue and liberty (and their obverse, tyranny and corruption), together with a confidence in reading the mind of the creator. Christianity, in short, was deeply enmeshed in the very fabric of the nation's cultural, political, social, and moral life. Indeed, as Tocqueville noted, "It must never be forgotten that religion gave birth to Anglo-American society. In the United States, religion is therefore mingled with all the habits of the nation and all the feelings of patriotism, whence it derives a peculiar force."[2]

Extending the authority of Protestant Christianity that began with the Puritan colonization of New England, the clerical guardians of the nation and their allies promoted religion as a necessary moral counterweight to the consuming energies of democratic nation-building and the ideology of economic individualism. As a covenanted nation, America must lead the way in confronting a host of intractable social ills such as poverty, crime, delinquency, prostitution, illiteracy, disease, intemperance, and (for the Northern states) the conspicuous national sin of slavery. A new "benevolent empire" accordingly emerged, dedicated to the promulgation of Christian morality and sustained by a network of institutions and voluntary organizations dedicated to foreign and home missions, religious education, criminal justice, mental and physical health, temperance, antislavery, and a variety of other reforms, aided by the wide dissemination of scripture and other religious literature. The evangelical fervor behind this benevolent empire was geared toward the eradication of a comprehensive roster of evils through a lively appreciation of God's saving word and grace, all in a quest for moral perfection. It is perhaps only in such an environment that we can understand a mission as ambitious as Ahab's in its single-minded apocalyptic determination to destroy an embodiment of universal evil in the shape of the White Whale.[3]

A distinctive feature of the contemporary American religious scene that would strongly influence Melville's whaling novel was the widespread manifestation of millennial and apocalyptic expectations, based on the prophecies of Christ's Second Coming. Contemporary theology was divided in opinion between whether this event would be pre- or postmillennial, and contemporary national and international events were often scrutinized for tell-tale "signs of the times" (Matt. 16:3). Despite some conservative misgivings, most Americans embraced a hopeful expectation of the future, believing that the conjoined forces of material progress and divine providence made them the world's New Israel, chosen people, and redeemer nation destined to aid in the spread of Christianity and democracy around the world. Such beliefs helped set the political agenda for the era of Manifest Destiny and had an important impact on antebellum social reform movements and the development of new religious sects such as Universalism, Shakerism, Mormonism, and Adventism.[4]

The evangelical dominance of antebellum America provided a fertile ground for apocalyptic and millennial speculation, which associated the fate of the individual soul with larger patterns of Christian eschatology, as James H. Moorhead has noted:

> Apocalypticism also remained powerful because it resonated with themes at the heart of evangelical piety. Evangelical Protestantism summoned each person to move from sin to holiness, a passage requiring the acknowledgment of one's lost condition before one could enter a state of blessedness. The central dynamic was that abasement preceded exaltation in the spiritual life. These struggles surrounding conversion, along with the accompanying dreams of the heaven or hell into which death would shortly usher each person, constituted a miniature apocalypse paralleling the historical scenario of the book of Revelation. Just as the kingdom of God arrived only through overturning and judgment, so, too, believers achieved assurance of salvation only after a season of terror, during which they knew themselves to deserve hell. Indeed, the two processes were one, for the history of redemption was the sum of all individual stories of men and women fleeing the wrath to come.[5]

According to traditional Calvinist doctrine formally embodied in the Westminster Confession, the soul at death was released from the body and subject to immediate judgment in either heaven or hell. At the general resurrection at the end of history, however, the soul was reinstated in the risen "spiritual body" for the proceedings of the Last Judgment, which would determine the ultimate eschatological fate for both living and dead.

The most conspicuous movement designed to alert the nation to the imminence of the Second Coming was that promoted by William Miller in the later 1830s and early 1840s with the help of an effective Boston publicist, Joshua V. Himes.[6] A self-taught Baptist from upstate New York's "burnt-over district," Miller assembled a book-length analysis of prophetic arithmetic, premised on the visions of Daniel and Revelation, that pointed to Christ's return some time between March 1843 and 1844. Millerite Adventism was spread throughout the Northeast and beyond by means of a steadily increasing number of revivals, newspapers, camp meetings, and other "come-outer" appeals to members of the more traditional denominations that did not endorse Miller's prophetic scheme. The designated terminus of Miller's timetable was passed in March 1844, but the movement continued for another seven months based on another interpretation of a key Danielic text that hinted at the final consummation on the Jewish Day of Atonement. The Millerite movement experienced its historic "Great Disappointment" on 22 October 1844, with the nonappearance of Christ on that day. Although there is no explicit mention of the Millerite movement in *Moby-Dick*, we should note that the designated time frame of the *Pequod's* voyage in 1840–1841 coincides with the initial spread of Miller's doctrines throughout the northeast United States. Since Melville's return from nearly four years at sea occurred in mid-October 1844 in Boston, where the Millerites' Tabernacle on Howard Street was a public sensation, he can hardly have avoided knowledge of Christ's failure to reappear during the Great Disappointment of that month. Indeed, his arrival home to Lansingburgh, New York, coincided exactly with the final date set for the expected return of the messiah, as the Melville family undoubtedly knew.[7]

In addition to its grounding in the millennialist currents of antebellum America, the complex moral vision presented in *Moby-Dick* was also a function of Melville's religious upbringing, which exposed him to both liberal and conservative strains of the Protestant tradition. The son of a Unitarian father and a Dutch Reformed mother, Melville had come of age largely in the Calvinistic faith of his mother's family, with its stern predestinarian theology and its insistence on the radical divide between divine sovereignty and human depravity. The family affiliation with the Dutch church was especially important in the 1830s, when the family resided in Albany and young Herman experienced the death of his bankrupt father in 1832 and the further loss of his family's economic security during the Panic of 1837—events that led to Melville's prevailing sense of disinheritance and dispossession from the national ideology of progress and providence.[8]

Like his alter ego Ishmael, who identifies himself in chapter 10 of *Moby-Dick* as a Presbyterian (the American denomination, like the Dutch Reformed, most deeply imbued with Calvinism), Melville was indelibly marked by his early exposure to the rigors of Calvinist theology. The most direct attestation of this influence, of course, occurs in Melville's landmark 1850 review of Hawthorne's *Mosses from an Old Manse*, in which he noted that the New England author's deep understanding of evil "derives its force from its appeals to that Calvinistic sense of Innate Depravity and Original Sin, from whose visitations, in some shape or other, no deeply thinking mind is always and wholly free. For, in certain moods, no man can weigh this world, without throwing in something, somehow like Original Sin, to strike the uneven balance." Writers like Shakespeare and Hawthorne, according to Melville, demonstrated their greatness by recognizing this deep-rooted evil in their darkest works, conveying this fact in complex symbolic terms while assuming redemptive status as truth-tellers. As revealed by his *Mosses* review, Melville's mature worldview was permanently molded by the idea of a harshly punitive, unforgiving Old Testament deity, presiding over a universe tainted by moral and natural corruption. The characters of Ishmael and Ahab in *Moby-Dick* both dramatize Melville's rejection of Calvinist dogma while still adhering to its basic conception of evil as pervading both humanity and the cosmos.[9]

If the Calvinist vision of evil and the national expectation of millennial redemption both pervade *Moby-Dick*, we find ample evidence of sustained allusions to and frequent parody of evangelical texts and beliefs throughout Ishmael's initial quest for a whaling vessel, as we will find throughout this chapter. Yet the novel also reflects more particularly on a variety of specific religious trends in antebellum America. For example, two small Protestant sects—the Quakers and Shakers, both premised on different forms of "realized" eschatology—have also left an important imprint on various aspects of the novel, and we will pause here briefly to discuss their origins and beliefs.

The Quakers (or Society of Friends) dominated the religious life of the island of Nantucket until the mid-nineteenth century and inform the religious identity of the *Pequod*'s owners, Peleg and Bildad; its first mate, Starbuck; and its captain, Ahab. As a sect promoting the mystical Christology developed by George Fox in the crucible of the English Revolution, the Quakers promoted an apocalyptic spirituality or "Inner Light," while stressing notions of pacifism and unworldly asceticism. First established on Nantucket at the start of the eighteenth century, Quakerism accompanied the rise of the whaling industry there in the late eighteenth and early nineteenth centuries, although as one historian has noted, "By 1850, most Orthodox [non-Hicksite] Friends were moving closer to the dominant evangelical culture of the United States."[10] Compartmentalizing their religious principles and professional lives, Nantucket and New Bedford Quakers saw no contradiction between the indiscriminate slaughter of whales and the pacifism for which they were famous. Nor did Nantucket Quakers worry about the contrast between their quietist communal ideals and their economic interests in the business of whaling. Such contrasts are evident during Ishmael's attempt to sign on the *Pequod* when he notes in the midst of his encounter with Peleg and Bildad, the Quaker owners of the ship, that "some of these same Quakers are the most sanguinary of all sailors and whale-hunters. They are fighting Quakers; they are Quakers with a vengeance" (73). He then experiences Bildad's attempt at bargaining him out of a fair wage for signing onto the next voyage, an event that highlights the contrast between the sharp business practices of modern Christians and the otherworldly message of Christ's teachings.[11]

The Quaker background of the *Pequod*'s owners, first mate, and captain also informs the stateliness of their speech, which exhibits the archaic idiom of the King James Bible, largely seen in their use of the older forms of the second-person personal pronoun—a usage that Ishmael himself embraces in the philosophical portions of his narrative.[12] As Ishmael notes, such Quaker patterns of speech and their frequent use of biblical names help to account for the formation of a grand tragic hero like Ahab, for the captain of the *Pequod* belongs to a class of "men, who, named with Scripture names—a singularly common fashion on the island—and in childhood naturally imbibing the stately dramatic thee and thou of the Quaker idiom; still, from the audacious, daring, and boundless adventure of their subsequent lives, strangely blend with these unoutgrown peculiarities, a thousand bold dashes of character, not unworthy a Scandinavian sea king, or a poetical Pagan Roman" (73). And while the quietist principles of the Quaker faith may seem incongruous in a sacrilegious character like Ahab, the sect's reliance on the Inner Light conceivably contributed to his spiritual growth from nominal Christian to metaphysical rebel embracing elements of Gnostic, Manichean, and Zoroastrian beliefs. For Ahab is also described as a figure endowed with "greatly superior natural force, with a globular brain and a ponderous heart; who has also by the stillness and seclusion of many long night-watches in the remotest waters, and beneath constellations never seen here at the north, been led to think untraditionally and independently" (73). We should note that Ahab's embrace of unconventional religious ideas was not unprecedented among Nantucket Quaker whalers, whose experiences on long Pacific voyages sometimes changed their values and beliefs. For example, the Quaker sailor Milo Calkins, writing of an 1833 voyage on the *Independence*, claimed that his encounter with the cultures of Polynesia "opened up to my mind an entirely new and different train of ideas concerning the past, present, and future of mankind. Many of my preconceived notions imbibed from my sectarian teachings were swept away and my faith in others badly shaken."[13]

Also informing the contemporary religious background to *Moby-Dick*, but on a smaller scale, is the sect of Shakers, from whose ranks comes the "mad" prophet Gabriel of the novel's chapter 71 ("The Jeroboam"). Founded in Albany, New York, in 1774 by the immigrant Englishwoman "Mother" Ann Lee (1736–1784), the Shakers, or United Society of Believers, had by the 1840s reached their maximum expansion of about five thousand members. In Ann Lee's celibate theology, sex was the main cause of original sin. In her realized eschatology, the Second Coming and millennium had already arrived in the form of charismatic gifts of the spirit manifested during worship—hence the title of the first major statement of Shaker theology, *The Testimony of Christ's Second Appearing* (1808), and the designation of the Shaker faith as the "millennial church" in another exposition of the faith, *A Summary View of the Millennial Church, or the United Society of Believers, Commonly Called Shakers* (1823). Two of the early Shaker communities, Watervliet Village and New Lebanon, were located in the Albany area, where Melville was living with his family in the 1830s. He would almost certainly have known of the communities' well-publicized outbreaks of visions and charismatic behavior, beginning in 1837 and continuing through the mid-1840s, a phase of Shaker history called the Era of Manifestations or "Mother Ann's Work."[14]

Melville later became more familiar with the Shakers during visits in the summers of 1850 and 1851 to their communities in Hancock, Massachusetts, and New Lebanon, New York, only a few miles southwest of his new residence in Pittsfield after October 1850. On his first visit to the Shaker community in Hancock on 21 July 1850 while on vacation in the Berkshires, Melville acquired a copy of *A Summary View of the Millennial Church*. Melville marked 25 of its 384 pages, chiefly in the opening sections of the volume telling of the early history of the Shakers and their manner of worship and self-government. As Merton M. Sealts notes: "what seemingly attracted him most was the prophetic strain in the Shaker religion, with its association of exalted bodily and mental states."[15] Melville's narrator in *Moby-Dick* is similarly sensitive to the prophetic dimension of human experience in conjunction with its authoritative manifestations in the biblical prophets.

In order to get to Ishmael's narrative, we must first traverse a threshold of "Etymology" and "Extracts" about the whale, both of which convey an encyclopedic impression of the giant creature's presence throughout three thousand years of Western culture beginning with the book of Genesis, whose "great whales" (Gen. 1:21) figured at the start of the creation. Melville probably borrowed the idea for such an introductory sequence from Robert Southey's *The Doctor* (1834–1847), with hints for his drudging scholarly compilers, the consumptive "pale Usher" with his lexicons and grammars, and his doggedly research-prone "sub-sub-librarian," picked up from Sterne, Carlyle, Lamb, Irving, Poe, and Thomas Hood. Balancing the climactic appearance of the White Whale at the end of the novel, the evocation of the whale in "Etymology" and "Extracts" prepares us for the discursive nature of Ishmael's narrative art, and the wide-ranging erudition he will wield in the representation of his epic voyage. The "Late Consumptive Usher to a Grammar School" who has supplied the initial "Etymology" also serves as an emblematic figure for the death theme that haunts Ishmael's whaling saga: "He loved to dust his old grammars; it somehow mildly reminded him of his mortality" (xv). The quotations from Genesis, Job, Jonah, Psalms, and Isaiah that begin the "Extracts" similarly provide key proof texts for related biblical themes throughout the narrative. The total of some eighty prose and poetic "Extracts" subsequently reveal the whale as a universal presence in human history and an object of knowledge that, like the deity, eludes any fixed identity.[16]

From the very first paragraph of Ishmael's narrative in the first chapter ("Loomings"), the reader is immediately made aware of the religious and eschatological influences that will characterize the events of the narrative; indeed, it is not too much to say that death, judgment, heaven, and hell—the traditional "four last things"—provide the dark background to Ishmael's humorous quest for a whaling ship in the novel's early chapters. Yet if Ishmael's seemingly morbid preoccupation with death is partly a reflection of his cultural milieu, he repeatedly undercuts the evangelical piety of this culture with his ironic mockery. He does so chiefly by assuming the double role of a Pauline and a Bunyanesque picaresque pilgrim, moving through a metaphorical landscape of hellfire and damnation—a modern secular version of the travails of the New Testament apostle to the Gentiles as well as Bunyan's prototypical Christian fleeing the City of Destruction.[17]

Ishmael thus begins his narrative by describing the morbidly depressed mood, an updated equivalent to Bunyan's Slough of Despond at the start of Christian's journey, that drives him to go to sea, a realm that allegedly acts as a desired medical regime by "driving off the spleen, and regulating the circulation" (3). Posing as an upper-class valetudinarian affected by a kind of seasonal affective disorder, Ishmael asserts that going to sea as a common sailor will cure his depression but not kill his body or soul (as many of his readers might assume from the contemporary reputation of sailors). He

notes the psychological symptoms that have caused him to turn to the sea
for relief:

> Whenever I find myself growing grim about the mouth; whenever it is a
> damp, drizzly November in my soul; whenever I find myself involuntarily
> pausing before coffin warehouses, and bringing up the rear of every funeral I
> meet; and especially whenever my hypos get such an upper hand of me, that
> it requires a strong moral principle to prevent me from deliberately stepping
> into the street, and methodically knocking people's hats off—then, I account
> it high time to get to sea as soon as I can. (3)

In this characteristically allusive observation, artfully shaped by anaphora,
assonance, and alliteration, Ishmael asserts his kinship with his biblical
prototype. Ishmael represents the act of becoming a sailor as the functional
equivalent of suicide, or a "substitute for pistol and ball. With a philosophical
flourish Cato throws himself upon his sword; I quietly take to the ship"
(3). Instead of theatrically doing away with himself like the famous Roman
senator and stoic (95–46 BCE), Ishmael takes the self-effacing vocational
initiative of going to sea. Becoming a sailor is thus ambiguously represented
as both a substitute for and an inadvertent act of suicide, since it means
escaping from emotional depression on land, but then facing the high risk
of death at sea. While anticipating the absurdist, deracinated antiheroes
of twentieth-century fiction, Ishmael invokes larger questions of life and
death with self-deprecating humor, combining the philosophical acumen of
a Robert Burton or a Sir Thomas Browne with the jaunty poise of a frontier
raconteur or a New York b'hoy.[18]

Ishmael continues to justify his decision to go whaling for several
paragraphs, noting that the desire to be near water is a universal trait shared
by all human beings. Thus "of a dreamy Sabbath afternoon" one sees, lining
the wharves of Lower Manhattan, "thousands upon thousands of mortal
men fixed in ocean reveries" (4), and in the country, casual visitors, day-
dreamers, and painters will all hypnotically gravitate toward lakes, rivers,
and streams. By the same token, all inland inhabitants in the nation are
irrationally drawn toward the ocean. Influential cultures like the ancient
Greeks and Persians have even deified the sea. Using such examples,
Ishmael seeks to demonstrate that the proximity of water is vital to human
life and a source of metaphysical truth—an idea potentially confirmed by
the biblical symbolism of water generally (Gen. 2:10–14; Ps. 23:2; Isa. 11:9;
John 4:13–14, 7:37–38; Rev. 7:17, 21:6), not to mention the central role
of water in the survival of the infant Ishmael during his exile in the desert

(Gen. 21:14–19). As a primal element of the creation and a symbol of life, then, water is implicitly worshipped by humanity, whose contemplation of this hypnotic element partakes of the religious awe of the sublime.[19]

Melville's narrator ends these remarks with a key allusion to Greek myth. Thus the hypnotic allure of water is ultimately typified by "that story of Narcissus, who because he could not grasp the tormenting, mild image he saw in the fountain, plunged into it and was drowned. But that same image, we ourselves see in all rivers and oceans. It is the image of the ungraspable phantom of life, and this is the key to it all" (5). In a mythical paradigm of the problem of appearance and reality, water reflects back human identity while hinting at an inaccessible realm of truth, divinity, or immortality beyond human comprehension—a foreshadowing of the narcissistic fate of Ahab, whose inescapable rage at his disabling injury will eventually drown himself and almost all his crew.[20]

Having explained the allure of the sea to humanity in general and his own need to seek a refuge there from his "hypos," Ishmael next seeks to justify his decision to ship as a common sailor despite the fact that he comes from "an old established family in the land" by arguing that his humiliating subservience to "some old hunks of a sea-captain" is not important in the larger Christian scheme of things. "What does that indignity amount to, weighed, I mean, in the scales of the New Testament? Do you think the archangel Gabriel thinks anything the less of me, because I promptly and respectfully obey that old hunks in that particular instance? Who aint a slave?" (6). Invoking the archangel who was traditionally identified as the messenger who would blow the trumpet at the Last Judgment (Matt. 24:31; 1 Thess. 4:16), Ishmael obliquely refers here to the familiar Pauline doctrine that "he that is called in the Lord, being a servant [or slave], is the Lord's freeman: likewise also he that is called, being free, is Christ's servant" (1 Cor. 7:22). The egalitarian ethos of Christianity thus confirms the value of the human soul on its merits, not on its status as slave or master. Such teachings initiate Ishmael's self-representation as a secularized Pauline pilgrim in quest of a livelihood at sea.

Continuing his justification of his choice to go whaling, Ishmael says he always decides to go to sea as a common sailor, not a cabin passenger, because he is thereby paid for his services, and like the majority of mankind he prefers getting paid rather than himself paying—this despite the well-known belief that "money is the root of all earthly ills" (6), a maxim based on Saint Paul's (or a follower's) teaching in 1 Timothy 6. Ishmael uses this occasion to notice the universal desire for money in modern America, despite Christ's explicit assertion (Matt. 19:21–24) that "on no account can a monied man enter heaven" (6), a contradiction that highlights one of the flagrant hypocrisies of antebellum evangelical culture. In a similarly ironic vein, Ishmael concludes his counterintuitive catalogue of reasons for going to sea with the suggestion that, as a common sailor, he will breathe the "pure air of the forecastle deck" ahead of "the Commodore on the quarter-deck" who little suspects he "gets his atmosphere second hand" (6). Just as Christ dedicated his mission to inverting the social hierarchy, so that "many that are first shall be last; and the last shall be first" (Matt. 19:30; Mark 10:31; Luke 13:30), Ishmael similarly notes: "In much the same way do the commonalty lead their leaders in many other things, at the same time, that the leaders little suspect it" (6–7).

In one revealing addition to his list of reasons for going to sea on a whaling vessel, Ishmael concedes that he may have had no real choice in the matter since it was probably the responsibility of "the invisible police officer of the Fates, who has constant surveillance of me, and secretly dogs me, and influences me in some unaccountable way" (7)—an oblique way of saying that the Judeo-Christian god, the alleged source of providential care (Matt. 6:25–34, 10:29–31), was in reality an absurdist Kafkaesque secret police agent. Contributing to this mysterious exercise of divine sovereignty over Ishmael was his own "overwhelming idea of the great whale himself: Such a portentous and mysterious monster roused all my curiosity" (7). In other words, Ishmael ultimately went whaling in order to experience the mighty sea monster of Jonah and Job and the physical and metaphysical truths of the creation. For Ishmael—unlike the landlocked Sunday water gazers—will be one of those who, as the psalmist put it, "go down to the sea in ships, that do business in the great waters; / These see the works of the Lord, and his wonders in the deep" (Ps. 107:23–24).

At the end of his explanation of his decision, Ishmael remarks that "the great flood-gates of the wonder-world swung open and in the wild conceits that swayed me to my purpose, two and two there floated into my inmost soul, endless processions of the whale, and, midmost of them all, one grand hooded phantom, like a snow hill in the air" (7). Blending the "great whales" of the fifth day of creation, the animals going "two by two" into Noah's ark, and the onset of the Flood when "the fountains of the great deep [were] broken up" (Gen. 1:21, 7:9, 11), Ishmael envisages his future whaling career as a mythic journey to a primordial realm in which the snow-white "hooded phantom" of the White Whale will blend aspects of the chaos monster Leviathan and the well-known image of God the Father as the Ancient of Days in the book of Daniel, "whose garment was white as snow" (Dan. 7:9). Ishmael thus initiates the recurrent association between the White Whale and a morally ambiguous deity that will provide a major thematic leitmotif in the novel.

Just as Ishmael's initial self-portrait in "Loomings" plays on various eschatological motifs, his ensuing experiences in the port of New Bedford (a satirical Valley of the Shadow of Death of Bunyan's allegory) are characterized by a strain of black humor that makes light of the seemingly mortal threats to both body and soul confronting a green young sailor in the chief New England whaling port, which is full of alien races and unfamiliar customs. By the same token, the choice of lodging he faces ironically represents an eschatological destination—hell—that suits the Calvinism of Ishmael's Presbyterian forbears. Ishmael's attempt to find an inn for the night leads him initially to an unnamed building with the door open, but this assumed haven from the storm presents a sudden glimpse of hell and the Last Judgment. Stumbling over the "ash-box" on the porch, which momentarily makes him imagine the incendiary fate of the biblical Gomorrah, he looks through the open door: "It seemed the great Black Parliament sitting in Tophet. A hundred black faces turned round in their rows to peer; and beyond, a black Angel of Doom was beating a book in a pulpit. It was a negro church; and the preacher's text was about the blackness of darkness, and the weeping and wailing and teeth-gnashing there" (9–10). The apocalyptically minded black preacher has apparently chosen a text from the brief Epistle of Jude, an attack on heretics as doomed to hell —"to whom is reserved the blackness of darkness for ever" (l. 13)—apparently not seeing the irony of his choice of imagery for his African American congregation. Confronted with such an unexpected and threatening scene and its aura of dehumanizing minstrel-show humor, Ishmael retreats quickly, dismissing the church as an inhospitable haven: "Wretched entertainment at the sign of 'The Trap'" (10).

We should note that Ishmael's experience of the black church is a satirical recasting of Bunyan's Christian traversing the Valley of the Shadow of Death; for Christian is first warned that the Valley "is as dark as pitch" and full of "Hobgoblins, Satyrs, and Dragons of the Pit" as well as "a continual howling and yelling, as of a People under unutterable misery," containing "Clouds of confusion" and "death." And when he attempts to cross it, the Valley indeed proves to contain "the mouth of Hell" issuing "flame and smoke" and "sparks and hideous noises." But Christian—like his modern secular counterpart, Ishmael—manages ultimately to survive his symbolic ordeal and move on to the next challenge.[21]

Proceeding along his path, Ishmael soon finds an unassuming establishment bearing the sign "The Spouter Inn—Peter Coffin" and is struck by the landlord's portentous surname. Yet he thinks he can find adequate shelter from the winter weather at this inn, even though the forces of death and destruction lurk ominously in both foreground and background here too. As Ishmael notes, "the dilapidated little wooden house itself looked as if it might have been carted here from the ruins of some burnt district" (10), thereby hinting at a possible connection with the scorched cities of the plain (Gen. 19:24–25). Instead of fleeing such a locality like Lot, however, Ishmael engages in a protracted debate over whether to enter the Spouter Inn, based on three New Testament proof texts: Saint Paul's shipwreck, due to "a tempestuous wind, called Euroclydon" (Acts 27:14); the apostle's notion of the Christian body as an inviolable "temple" (2 Cor. 5); and the parable of Dives and Lazarus (Luke 16).

First noting that the Spouter Inn "stood on a sharp bleak corner, where that tempestuous wind Euroclydon kept up a worse howling than ever it did about poor Paul's tossed craft" (10), Ishmael proceeds to remark that such a wind would not be so bad if he were snug indoors, confirming the self-evident truth by facetiously citing an old "black letter" author and biblical commentator who didactically attests that it makes a large difference whether one is facing a wind like "Euroclydon" safe inside, behind a glass window, "or whether thou observest it from that sashless window, where the frost is on both sides, and of which the wight Death is the only glazier" (10). His allusion to Saint Paul's experience in Acts is eminently appropriate to Ishmael's role here as a modern-day picaresque pilgrim, yet there is a conspicuous difference between Paul, who was assured by an angel of God that no harm would come to him or his shipmates (Acts 27:23–24), and the friendless and solitary Ishmael, who must seek shelter from the potentially deadly winter wind.

Second, Ishmael makes further fun of Pauline notions of the self when he laments that the human body as a protective enclosure cannot resist the destructive forces of the elements. "Yes, these eyes are windows, and this body of mine is the house. What a pity they didn't stop up the chinks and crannies though, and thrust a little lint here and there. But it's too late to make any improvements now" (10). Here Ishmael is patently mocking Paul's assertion that the Christian believer's body is a "temple of God" (1 Cor. 3:16; 2 Cor. 6:16) and a "temple of the Holy Ghost" (1 Cor. 6:19), as well as an "earthly house" and "tabernacle" that will eventually be "dissolved" into "a building of God":

For we know that if our earthly house of this tabernacle were dissolved, we
have a building of God, an house not made with hands, eternal in the heavens.

For in this we groan, earnestly desiring to be clothed upon with our house
which is from heaven:

If so be that being clothed we shall not be found naked.

For we that are in this tabernacle do groan, being burdened: not for that we
would be unclothed, but clothed upon, that mortality might be swallowed up
of life. (2 Cor. 5:1–4; see also Rom. 8:18–25)

Paul's groaning for a new house and clothing, like the birth pangs of a
woman, is meant to convey the earnest desire to be apocalyptically reborn
into a heavenly state. Like Paul, Ishmael is indeed burdened by his mortal
body, but it is with the need to escape death by freezing not with the desire
to enter the building of God in heaven. The first few chapters of *Moby-
Dick* are in fact thematically premised on Ishmael's seriocomic quest for a
secure "earthly house" to protect his body from the elements, but as Ishmael
quickly discovers in New Bedford, Pauline notions of the self are largely
outdated for the modern would-be whaleman.

Moving on to a consideration of the parable of Dives and Lazarus (Luke
16:19–31), Ishmael likewise subverts the retributive moral of the text,
which taught the damnation of the rich Dives and the salvation of the poor
Lazarus, based on the former's refusal of charity to the latter. In real life,
a modern Lazarus can very well expire before the house of the rich Dives
without expectation of heavenly reward; ironically, he might even be willing
to "go down to the fiery pit itself in order to keep out this frost" (11). Yet if
Lazarus is dying of cold outside the rich man's door, Dives inside is freezing
from coldness of heart, living "like a Czar in an ice palace made of frozen
sighs" (11). Or at least so Ishmael claims while mimicking the language of
antebellum sentimental piety.

All of these biblically inspired meditations demonstrate Ishmael's
intense consciousness of the moral divide between America's evangelical
faith and the demoralizing realities of poverty and social class that have
driven him to the career of whaling. In the end Ishmael, like Bunyan's
Christian at the Wicket Gate, chooses to enter the Spouter Inn as a
promising inexpensive refuge from the winter storm. As we will discover,
however, he is trading the freezing winds of Euroclydon for the figurative
smoke and flames of hell, for the inn is in fact no Palace Beautiful,
Bunyan's symbol of an ideal evangelical congregation, but a seriocomic
realm of death and damnation.

The first thing that strikes Ishmael in the entryway is a "thoroughly besmoked" painting that both mystifies and beguiles him with its subject matter. "Such unaccountable masses of shades and shadows, that at first you almost thought some ambitious young artist, in the time of the New England hags, had endeavored to delineate chaos bewitched" (12). At first the painting seems to depict a seventeenth-century witches' sabbath or Faustian Walpurgisnacht. By assiduous study, however, Ishmael manages to discern that the "long, limber, portentous, black mass of something hovering in the centre of the picture over three blue, dim, perpendicular lines floating in a nameless yeast" is in fact the figure of the great Leviathan himself. The black mass of the whale is apparently "in the enormous act of impaling himself upon the three mast-heads" (13) of a foundering Cape Horn ship in a hurricane. While the subject of the painting would seem to illustrate a *lusus naturae*, or freak of nature, the association of New England hags, chaos, black mass (a likely pun), and Leviathan creates a composite association of the whale here as a modern chaos monster like that found in the book of Job.

Ishmael's imaginative list of theories of the painting's sublime subject matter—"the Black Sea in a midnight gale," "the unnatural combat of the four primal elements," "a blasted heath," "a Hyperborean winter scene," "the breaking-up of the ice-bound stream of time" (13)—suggests the same iconography of chaos latent within the cosmos of nature. In keeping with the fearful obscurity of the Burkean sublime, the smoke-begrimed painting in the entryway to the Spouter Inn, with its image of a whale in the midst of a turbulent ocean deep, acts as an emblem of the novel's cetological subject and a foreshadowing of the eventual appearance of Moby Dick and the wreck of the *Pequod*.[22]

In its more immediate context, however, Ishmael's arrival at the Spouter Inn forms a part of his ongoing encounter with a Pauline and Bunyanesque landscape of tribulation and damnation. Entering the public rooms of the inn, Ishmael discovers that the bar is located inside a symbolic hell-mouth of a whale's jaw, where the visiting whalemen can imbibe toxic alcoholic beverages from Jonah, the bartender:

> Projecting from the further angle of the room stands a dark-looking den— the bar—a rude attempt at a right whale's head. Be that how it may, there stands the vast arched bone of the whale's jaw, so wide, a coach might almost drive beneath it. Within are shabby shelves, ranged round with old decanters, bottles, flasks; and in those jaws of swift destruction, like another cursed Jonah (by which name indeed they call him), bustles a little withered old man, who, for their money, dearly sells the sailors deliriums and death. (13–14)

The language here suggests the evangelical tones of an antebellum temperance tract, for the sailors swallow the deadly drams of liquor within the mock hell-mouth of the huge whale's jaw. Appropriately enough, in Ishmael's description of the width of the whale's jaw we find an echo of Christ's well-known claim that "wide is the gate, and broad is the way, that leadeth to destruction, and many there be which go in thereat" (Matt. 7:13). The evangelical image of the wide way to hell is thus conflated with the imagery of alcohol creating a modern-day Jonah's whale hell-mouth within the men themselves. Ishmael has thus shunned lodgment at "The Trap," only to find shelter in another symbolic version of the infernal regions, where the sailors willingly seek out their own self-destruction. In its larger purposes, Ishmael's entry into the arched hell-mouth of the bar at the Spouter Inn prefigures the Jonah theme of Father Mapple's sermon, as well as the deadly terrors of the whaling industry that Ishmael will soon be joining.

The landlord of the Spouter Inn is well named for the role of a black humorist. Peter Coffin accordingly sets Ishmael up for a comic encounter with Queequeg when he tells him that the individual with whom Ishmael must share a bed is out peddling an embalmed human head that evening. The drama of Ishmael's encounter with Queequeg when the latter returns late in the evening to find his bed occupied by a stranger constitutes a wonderfully comic bedroom farce and an educational initiation for Ishmael into the world of the cultural alien and exotic, in this case a Polynesian "noble savage" whose menacing racial otherness hides a benevolent human heart.[23] As Ishmael exclaims, when Queequeg first turns around to face him, "Such a face! It was of a dark, purplish, yellow color, here and there stuck over with large, blackish looking squares" (21). His chest, arms, and back "were checkered with the same squares as his face" (22). Queequeg's outlandish appearance is suggestive of the diabolic Apollyon from *Pilgrim's Progress*: "now the Monster was hideous to behold, he was clothed with scales like a fish (and they are his pride) he had Wings like a dragon, feet like a Bear, and out of his belly came Fire and Smoak, and his mouth was the mouth of a lion." A cannibal Apollyon, Queequeg produces combustible shavings from the pocket of his grego, or short hooded coat, to burn for his ebony idol, and he makes uncouth "guttural noises" (23) while praying or singing to his god. Yet, for all his monstrous appearance and behavior, Queequeg subsequently acts on core Christian principles, beginning with the Golden Rule of moral reciprocity (Matt. 7:12), thereby demonstrating the parochialism of American attitudes toward allegedly "primitive"

peoples (which Ishmael initially shares) and the presumptuousness of the
contemporary evangelical enterprise directed at their conversion. Instead of
a menacing Apollyon, Queequeg ultimately assumes the Bunyanesque role
of Faithful to Ishmael's Christian.[24]

Geoffrey Sanborn has demonstrated that Melville modeled Queequeg
partly on the Maori chief Te Pehi Kupe who befriended an English
merchant ship's captain off the coast of New Zealand in 1824 with the
intention of procuring firearms to avenge the massacre of his children. The
Maori chief returned with the English captain to Liverpool, where they
exhibited an unusually close friendship—all as described in George Lillie
Craik's *The New Zealanders* (London, 1830).[25] Along with the historical and
anthropological insights that such an identification may evoke, however, we
must still view Queequeg as a composite Polynesian "savage" within the
larger religious and symbolic framework in which Melville has placed him,
namely, as a paradoxical pagan embodiment of traditional Christian virtues.
Upon seeing the exotic cannibal arrive in his room with his shrunken head
in tow, Ishmael is first stricken with terror and repulsion, noting that his fear
of the ghastly-looking stranger predisposed him to think the worst of his
impending bedfellow: "Ignorance is the parent of fear, and being completely
nonplussed and confounded about the stranger, I confess I was now as much
afraid of him as if it was the devil himself who had thus broken into my
room in the dead of night" (21–22).

The devil comparison operates on several symbolic levels here. Ishmael
abhorrently notes that the tattooed Queequeg's "very legs were marked, as if
a parcel of dark green frogs were running up the trunks of young palms" (22).
The reference to frogs here evokes "unclean spirits like frogs" that emerge
from the mouth of the dragon, the beast, and the false prophet, as an angel
empties the sixth vial of wrath in the book of Revelation (16:13). Queequeg's
checkered tattooing on his face and body might also suggest the telltale
"mark of the beast" (Rev. 13:15–17), while his strange mode of worshipping
his idol at first resembles a satanic rite of human sacrifice. For, as Ishmael
notes, "Remembering the embalmed head, at first I almost thought that this
black manikin was a real baby preserved in some similar manner" (22). But
the manikin turns out to be a wooden idol, and Queequeg's ensuing ritual
of putting it in the fireplace and feeding it heated ship's biscuit turns out to
be a mysterious exercise in pagan worship that expands Ishmael's cultural
horizons while comically deflating any lingering idea that Queequeg is a
devil or a devil worshipper. At the end of Queequeg's ritualized offering of
biscuit, "the little devil did not seem to fancy such dry sort of fare at all; he
never moved his lips" (23), a comic anticlimax to the seemingly portentous

pagan ritual. Queequeg's final disposal of his idol by casually putting it back in the pocket of his poncho, "as if he were a sportsman bagging a dead woodcock" (23), injects a ribald pun into the proceedings and suggests that Queequeg's small god is in fact an ineffectual Polynesian fertility idol.

In keeping with Ishmael's early role as picaresque pilgrim, there is an implicit Pauline subtext to his fascination and horror at first meeting the allegedly devil-worshipping Queequeg. In the First Letter to the Corinthians, the apostle warns against consorting with pagan idolators:

> Wherefore, my dearly beloved, flee from idolatry. . . .
>
> What say I then? that the idol is any thing, or that which is offered in sacrifice to idols is any thing?
>
> But I say, that the things which the Gentiles sacrifice, they sacrifice to devils, and not to God: and I would not that ye should have fellowship with devils.
>
> Ye cannot drink the cup of the Lord, and the cup of devils: ye cannot be partakers of the Lord's table, and of the table of devils. (1 Cor. 10:14, 19–21)

The diabolic-looking Queequeg is in fact an idolator with a vengeance. But instead of refusing to have fellowship with him, Ishmael is forced to share a bed with the cannibal and witness his devilish sacrifice—hence the delightfully drawn-out comic ordeal of Ishmael's first night at the Spouter Inn.

Although now dispossessed of any satanic associations, Queequeg nevertheless becomes an immediate physical threat to Ishmael when he jumps in bed and discovers his unexpected bedfellow, asking a frightened Ishmael, "Who-e debel you?" (23), thereby echoing Ishmael's own tendency to demonize the unknown. But after the landlord has intervened to smooth over the situation following Ishmael's cries for help, Ishmael realizes that, despite his cultural prejudices, Queequeg is "a human being just as I am: he has just as much reason to fear me, as I have to be afraid of him. Better sleep with a sober cannibal than a drunken Christian" (24). Ishmael thereupon enjoys a good night's sleep next to his strange bedfellow and in the morning discovers that Queequeg's arm is thrown over him "in the most loving and affectionate manner. You had almost thought I had been his wife" (25). The underlying irony here is that Ishmael's intimate fellowship with the idolatrous cannibal is ultimately what redeems him from the depression and alienation he finds in Christian America. Ishmael initially claimed, "No man prefers to sleep two in a bed. In fact you would a good deal rather not sleep with your own brother" (16). But he discovers in Queequeg a future sea brother whose friendship will fulfill the key biblical injunction to "love thy neighbor as thyself" (Matt. 5:43). As elsewhere in the early chapters, Melville is comically subverting the orthodoxies of contemporary evangelical culture—in this case, the sanctity of marriage in this pagan-Christian union of souls.[26]

It should be noted that the image of Queequeg's elaborately tattooed arm, which blends in with the bed's counterpane and is hugging Ishmael as he wakes up, potentially mimics the repeated Old Testament image of the protective arm of God (Exod. 15:16; Deut. 33:27; Ps. 77:15, 89:13, 98:1; Isa. 33:2, 51:5, 52:10, 53:1; Jer. 27:5). The idea of a divine prototype for Queequeg's outstretched arm (and the uncanny feeling that it conveys to Ishmael) is made explicit when Ishmael relates the comparably uncanny feeling he had when remembering a childhood experience of having his hand held by a mysterious numinous presence in a dreamlike state. Ishmael's reminiscence—the only account we get of his early life before we meet him as a self-conscious outcast in chapter 1—describes his experience as a boy after being banished to his room for misbehavior by his unnamed stepmother on the longest day of the year (21 June). After hours of misery, the young Ishmael eventually falls asleep but wakes up in the dark, now characterized as "outer darkness," the phrase used to describe the realm of the damned in the Gospel of Matthew (8:12, 22:13, 25:30):

> At last I must have fallen into a troubled nightmare of a doze; and slowly waking from it—half-steeped in dreams—I opened my eyes, and the before sunlit room was now wrapped in outer darkness. Instantly I felt a shock running through all my frame; nothing was to be seen, and nothing to be heard; but a supernatural hand seemed placed in mine. My arm hung over the counterpane, and a nameless, unimaginable, silent form or phantom, to which the hand belonged, seemed closely seated by my bedside. For what seemed ages piled on ages, I lay there, frozen with the most awful fears, not daring to drag away my hand; yet ever thinking that if I could but stir it one single inch, the horrid spell would be broken. (26)

The perception of such nightmarish terror in which the sleeper feels like he or she is awake but unable to move is now known as sleep paralysis. Just as Ishmael's nightmarish experience occurs when he is sent to bed early on the longest day of the year, sleep paralysis is often the result of a disrupted sleep schedule or circadian rhythm and can last from a few seconds to several minutes. Apparently experiencing the "hypnagogic" form of sleep paralysis that occurs after falling asleep, as opposed to the "hypnopompic" form that occurs closer to awakening, Ishmael describes his youthful experience as a frightening *mysterium tremendum*—the uncanny experience of a "nameless unimaginable form or phantom." Both hypnopompic and hypnagogic forms of sleep paralysis often consist of the feeling that someone is in the room or holding the sleeper's hand. Alternatively, the sleeper thinks that someone or something is sitting on the sleeper's chest suffocating them, an experience sometimes called the "hag" phenomenon.[27]

If the adult Ishmael is clearly recalling a youthful occurrence of sleep paralysis, the incident also has religious implications. We recall that, like Melville's Ishmael banished to his room, the biblical Ishmael with his mother was cast out into the wilderness by his stepmother, Sarah, but was saved from death by divine intervention at which point "the angel of God called to Hagar out of heaven," saying "Arise, lift up the lad, and hold him in *thine hand*; for I will make him a great nation" (Gen. 21:17–18; emphasis added). The younger Ishmael, too, has been touched by the hand of God, and his reminiscence of this event in connection with his experience of waking up next to Queequeg is an early indication of his belief in a "great democratic God" (117) who can sanction a spiritual bonding between all human beings, even those, like Queequeg, whose demonic appearance is belied by a sanctifying love absent from Ishmael's own cultural milieu. At the same time, Ishmael's memory of his childhood ghostly visitation recalls the act of prophetic calling in the Old Testament, as when Daniel exclaimed, "And behold, an hand touched me, which set me upon my knees and upon the palms of my hands" (Dan. 10:10), or as Ezekiel reported, "The hand of the Lord was upon me" (Ezek. 37:1). Job, too, experienced his divine testing as being touched by the hand of God (Job 19:21). Clearly, then, Ishmael's uncanny experience waking up next to Queequeg in part suggests both the burdensome moral responsibilities and the uncanny visionary insights of his incipient role as literary prophet.[28]

The eschatological theme of the early chapters continues as Ishmael goes out the next morning, a Sunday, to attend a service at the New Bedford Whaleman's Chapel, the modern equivalent to Christian's visit to the House of the Interpreter in *Pilgrim's Progress*. And just as the despairing Man in the Iron Cage serves as a warning to Christian in the Interpreter's House, Father Mapple delivers a sermon on the punitive captivity of Jonah in the whale. Before the arrival of the minister, Ishmael notices the series of black-bordered marble tablets forming part of the wall on either side of the chapel, commemorating the lives of whalemen lost at sea. Ishmael's view of the tablets triggers a poignant meditation on the silence and invisibility of the dead, whose metaphysical status is a profound and fearful mystery to the living:

> In what census of living creatures, the dead of mankind are included; why it is that a universal proverb says of them, that they tell no tales, though containing more secrets than the Goodwin Sands; how it is that to his name who yesterday departed for the other world, we prefix so significant and infidel a word, and yet do not thus entitle him, if he but embarks for the remotest Indies of this living earth; why the Life Insurance Companies pay death-forfeitures upon immortals; in what eternal, unstirring paralysis, and deadly, hopeless trance, yet lies antique Adam who died sixty round centuries ago; how it is that we still refuse to be comforted for those who we nevertheless maintain are dwelling in unspeakable bliss; why all the living so strive to hush all the dead; wherefore but the rumor of a knocking in a tomb will terrify a whole city. All these things are not without their meanings.
>
> But Faith, like a jackal, feeds among the tombs, and even from these dead doubts she gathers her most vital hope. (36–37)

Exhibiting the periodic style of Robert Burton and Sir Thomas Browne, Ishmael's outspoken portrayal of the mysterious fate of the dead challenges belief in the resurrection, the ultimate metaphysical foundation for the Christian religion. The implication behind Ishmael's rhetorical questions is that the dead have in fact been annihilated, not bodily resurrected to heaven. Ishmael's mention of antique Adam, lying entranced since his death roughly six thousand years ago (according to standard biblical chronology putting creation at 4004 BCE), confirms the yawning spiritual abyss that lies between the living and the dead. It also evokes the mystery of Paul's well-known assertion that, at the Last Judgment, corruption will put on incorruption: "And so it is written, The first man Adam was made a living soul [Gen. 2:7]; the last Adam [Christ] was made a quickening spirit. / Howbeit that was not first which is spiritual but that which is natural; and afterwards that which is spiritual. / The first man is of the earth, earthy: the second man is the Lord from heaven" (1 Cor. 15:45–47). Ishmael's final claim that religious faith feeds like a jackal around the tombs of the dead portrays the Christian believer as a kind of unsavory metaphysical scavenger who is willing to gather "vital hope" from "dead doubts," implying that faith in the afterlife is a kind of desperate remedy for ignorance and despair.

Ishmael's representation of the existential mystery of death is appropriate for someone who is about to put his own life in peril in the whaling profession. Yet his own answer to the despairing thoughts that arise in him from the empty tombs in the Whaleman's Chapel is a brief assertion of Platonic idealism concerning the immorality of the soul:

> Methinks we have hugely mistaken this matter of Life and Death. Methinks that what they call my shadow here on earth is my true substance. Methinks that in looking at things spiritual, we are too much like oysters observing the sun through the water, and thinking that thick water the thinnest of air. Methinks my body is but the lees of my better being. In fact take my body who will, take it I say, it is not me. And therefore three cheers for Nantucket; and come a stove boat and stove body when they will, for stave my soul, Jove himself cannot. (37)

The sentiments here are manifestly evocative of passages in Plato's *Phaedo* and *Phaedrus*, which Melville read at some point in the late 1840s. As Socrates told Simmias in the *Phaedo* while making his case for spiritual immortality, we live as "if one dwelling in the depths of the sea, should fancy his habitation to be above the waters; and when he sees the sun and stars through the waters, should fancy the sea to be the heavens." The idealist arguments of the Greek philosopher enable Ishmael to overcome his despairing glimpse of the dead whalemen's tablets, with their challenge to conventional Christian belief in the afterlife. For in Ishmael's ebullient assertion, even God (or Jove) cannot harm his immortal soul because it belongs to the world of the Platonic forms—a claim that clearly sets Ishmael apart from the Christian world of the Whaleman's Chapel.[29]

Yet there is an obvious inconsistency latent in Ishmael's dismissal of the forlorn Christian hope for the resurrection of the body, as suggested by the empty tombs of the Whaleman's Chapel, and his subsequent assertion of a Platonic belief in the immortality of the soul.[30] Is Ishmael guilty of bad faith here? Tocqueville's assertion that some form of faith in an afterlife is the only natural condition of humankind can shed light on Ishmael's unapologetic shift from a theological to a philosophical belief in immortality:

> Man alone, of all created beings, displays a natural contempt of existence, and yet a boundless desire to exist; he scorns life, but he dreads annihilation. These different feelings incessantly urge his soul to the contemplation of a future state, and religion directs his musings thither. Religion, then, is simply another form of hope, and it is no less natural to the human heart than hope itself. Men cannot abandon their religious faith without a kind of aberration of intellect and a sort of violent distortion of their true nature; they are invincibly brought back to more pious sentiments. Unbelief is an accident, and faith is the only permanent state of mankind.[31]

Ishmael's claim that his body is but the "lees of his better being" reflects the basic human instinct for faith that arises out of the hope inherent in the "boundless desire to exist," according to Tocqueville's formulation.

The service in the Whaleman's Chapel begins with a hymn that anticipates the Jonah theme of Father Mapple's sermon. Ultimately based on the first part of Psalm 18, which sets forth the psalmist's divine deliverance from danger and is quoted by Jonah himself in the belly of the whale, the hymn in the Whaleman's Chapel is adapted from the hymnbook of the Calvinistic Dutch Reformed church in which Melville was raised. In the version of the hymn sung in the Whaleman's Chapel, the Jonah-like speaker faces the deadly horrors of being swallowed by a whale, a type of eternal damnation:

> The ribs and terrors of the whale,
>   Arched over me a dismal gloom,
> While all God's sun-lit waves rolled by,
>   And left me deepening down to doom.
>
> I saw the opening maw of hell;
>   With endless pains and sorrows there;
> Which none but they that feel can tell—
>   Oh, I was plunging to despair.
>
> In black distress, I called my God,
>   When I could scarce believe him mine,
> He bowed his ear to my complaints—
>   No more the whale did me confine. (41–42)

Dramatizing the perilous physical and spiritual situation of Jonah, the hymn offers a poetic abstract of the contents of Father Mapple's sermon while demonstrating God's omnipotent power to control the whale. Like the miraculous creation of faith out of the empty tombs of the dead (beginning with Christ's own empty tomb), Jonah in the hymn finds a redemptive faith when faced with the threat of death and damnation.[32]

The stark choice between willful submission to evil and humble appeal to divine aid is the burden of Father Mapple's subsequent sermon, which casts the biblical drama of Jonah in vividly nautical terms while continuing the eschatological drama of Ishmael's experience of New Bedford.[33] Mapple's sermon is in fact a miniature masterpiece of homiletic discourse, with the biblical prophet transformed into a contemporary habitué of wharf and forecastle, a setting appropriate to Ishmael's own quest for a whaling ship to escape his crippling "hypos." The sermon illustrates the chief strategy of evangelical preaching, with its rehearsal of the sinful soul's encounter with the anxieties of death and damnation and spontaneously leading to repentance and conversion. As such it provides an essential ideological benchmark for Ahab's rebellious career, whose hardheartedness, willfulness, and heavenly defiance will shape both his exemplary stature and his tragic downfall. Mapple's sermon will thus act as a dominant moral paradigm against which Ahab will effectuate his rebellion, for unlike Jonah, the captain of the *Pequod* will emphatically *not* accept the whale as an agent of divine justice. The Hebrew prophet's divine comedy will thus be inverted in Ahab's tragic career.

The basic lesson of Mapple's Jonah sermon, the sovereignty of God and the depravity of man, is illustrative of a Calvinist dogma that still reigned supreme in many Congregational, Presbyterian, and Dutch Reformed pulpits even amid the liberalization of theology that was gradually transforming the American religious landscape in the early nineteenth century. As T. Walter Herbert has noted, Mapple's sermon echoes language and ideas found in Calvin's sermons on Jonah, demonstrating its firm grounding in Puritan theology. Father Mapple is partly modeled on "Father" Edward Taylor (1793–1871) of the nondenominational Boston Seaman's Bethel, a minimally educated ex-sailor of Methodist background whose eloquent extemporaneous sermons impressed the likes of Dickens, Harriet Martineau, Whitman, and Emerson. Emerson, for example, noted of Taylor's eloquence in his journal in March 1837: "Beautiful philanthropist! godly poet! the Shakespeare of the sailor and the poor. God has found one harp of divine melody to sing and sigh sweet music amidst caves and cellars." Melville, too, had heard Taylor preach during a visit to his wife's family in Boston in the late 1840s. Father Mapple's sermon on Jonah effectively conflates Taylor's oft-noted salty eloquence with traditional covenantal and evangelical rhetoric of New England Calvinism.[34]

One of the shortest texts of the Old Testament, the book of Jonah narrates the history of a "reluctant prophet" like Moses, Isaiah, and Jeremiah, but one who (unlike his illustrious predecessors) goes to extreme lengths to avoid God's commissioning as a prophet. Modern interpreters read Jonah as a product of Second Temple Judaism having a significant satirical component, since by the end of Jonah's ordeal the prophet has been shown up as a moral spoilsport when he resents God's forgiveness of the gentile city of Ninevah after a speedy repentance spares it from destruction.[35] Father Mapple's sermon focuses only on the first half of Jonah, which tells of the prophet's attempt to escape his commission by fleeing by ship from Joppa to the far western Mediterranean port of Tarshish. Such an evasion of divine responsibility leads to a dangerous storm, Jonah's being cast into the sea by the frightened crew, and his swallowing and regurgitation by a "great fish" traditionally viewed as a whale. Jonah's submission to Yahweh occurs in the prisonlike belly of the whale, a symbol of the traditional realm of Sheol and the underwater firmament of Hebrew cosmology. Some critics have seen Father Mapple's Jonah sermon as an incomplete version or deliberate distortion of the overall message of the book of Jonah, but this view ignores the fact that sermons were traditionally designed around a specific text, not a whole book. In the case of Mapple's sermon, the text, or exemplum, encapsulates the message of the first two chapters of Jonah: "Beloved shipmates, clinch the last verse of the first chapter of Jonah— 'And God had prepared a great fish to swallow up Jonah' [Jon. 1:17]" (42).

Following a designated text, traditional sermon structure included an "exposition" of the text's theological significance, an "application" to a real-life situation, and then a concluding "exhortation" and "peroration" to summarize the overall message. In Father Mapple's sermon, the exposition is summarized at the end of the first paragraph: "But all the things that God would have us do are hard for us to do—remember that—and hence, he oftener commands us than endeavors to persuade. And if we obey God, we must disobey ourselves; and it is in this disobeying ourselves, wherein the hardness of obeying God consists" (42–43).

The application of Mapple's discourse, the longest section of the sermon, is the vivid retelling of the prophet's career as a fugitive from God. We see Jonah appearing on the wharves of Joppa and booking a passage west, paying extra for his place. On the ship he goes down to his stateroom and falls asleep, weighed down by his guilty conscience, little knowing the divine nemesis that is following after him. For a storm at sea soon arises, and he is forced to identify himself as the cause of the storm after drawing lots with the ship's crew. Acknowledging his guilt, he asks to be thrown overboard, an act that calms the seas as Jonah sinks below the waves:

> He goes down in the whirling heart of such a masterless commotion that he scarce heeds the moment when he drops seething into the very yawning jaws awaiting him; and the whale shoots-to all his ivory teeth, like so many white bolts, upon his prison. Then Jonah prayed unto the Lord out of the fish's belly. But observe his prayer, and learn a weighty lesson. For sinful as he is,

> Jonah does not weep and wail for direct deliverance. He feels that his dreadful punishment is just. He leaves all his deliverance to God, contenting himself with this, that spite of all his pains and pangs, he will still look towards His holy temple. (46)

The big fish that has swallowed Jonah is, by implication, a sperm whale since it is the only large whale with toothed lower jaws. Here it is a modern avatar of the mythical chaos monster inhabiting the masterless commotion of the sea, whose whirling heart will eventually entrap and regurgitate Ishmael. The faint absurdity of Jonah's praying inside the fish's stomach or knowing which direction to look toward the temple in Jerusalem passes without notice in the irresistible rhetorical movement of Mapple's description, with its overwhelming depiction of human impotence in the face of God's omnipotence.

The howling of the storm outside the Whaleman's Chapel intrudes at this point, providing a vivid illustration of the stormy forces depicted in the sermon, which seem to be physically represented in the body of the preacher himself and lead him to the conclusion of his discourse with its homiletic finale. If the beginning of Mapple's sermon pertains to Ahab as tragic hero, its conclusion relates more to Ishmael as prophetic narrator of *Moby-Dick*. For after drawing a parallel between Jonah and himself "as the pilot of the living God," Mapple recounts the biblical prophet's eventual deliverance from the whale's belly after it had sounded to the bottom of the ocean for "when the whale grounded upon the ocean's utmost bones, even then, God heard the engulphed, repenting prophet when he cried" (47). We recall that Ishmael's name in Hebrew means "God hears," and the final lesson of Mapple's sermon would seem to be particularly appropriate for Melville's narrator in his role as literary prophet. When instructed to preach to the Ninevites a second time, "Jonah did the Almighty's bidding. And what was that, shipmates? To preach the Truth to the face of Falsehood! That was it!" (48).

Father Mapple's concluding peroration consists of a series of seven invocations each of "woe" and "delight" for different modes of religious behavior, the woes being directed at those "whom this world charms from Gospel duty," while "top-gallant delight is to him, who acknowledges no law or lord, but the Lord his God, and is only a patriot to heaven" (48). Mapple's admonitory woes were a staple of both Old and New Testament prophetic rhetoric (Isa. 5:20–22, 10:1, 29:15, 45:9–10; Jer. 22:13; Matt. 11:21, 23:13–16; Luke 6:24–26). The closest parallel here is the sixfold woe against Israel pronounced by the prophet Isaiah, which includes the following charges:

> Woe unto them that draw iniquity with cords of vanity, and sin as it were
> with a cart rope: . . .
> Woe unto them that call evil good, and good evil; that put darkness for
> light, and light for darkness; that put bitter for sweet, and sweet for bitter!
> Woe unto them that are wise in their own eyes, and prudent in their own
> sight! (Isa. 5:18, 20–21)

By contrast, Mapple's final woe—warning against the hypocrisy of one "who, as the great Pilot Paul has it, while preaching to others is himself a castaway!" (48), alluding to the apostle's moral caveat in 1 Corinthians 9:27—is appropriate in its reminder of the Pauline background to Ishmael's early experiences in the novel.[36]

The preacher's use of the word "delight," on the other hand, finds its verbal equivalent only in the Old Testament, notably in the Psalms (Pss. 1:2, 16:3, 37:4, 51:16, 94:19, 119:24, 77, 92, 174), with particular relevance to the images, themes, and language in Psalms 8, 23, 37, 103, and 119. In its final invocation of woes and delights, moreover, Mapple's sermon ultimately recalls the Old Testament institution of covenant, especially the conclusion to the Sinai Covenant, which included a series of blessings and curses on the two parties (Lev. 26; Deut. 28). The sermon on Jonah thus recapitulates the covenantal rhetoric that had provided a moral and political foundation for the Puritan errand in New England.[37] Mapple's concluding words amplify his message of the need for fearless prophets to deliver potentially unwelcome truths to the people of God, a message that Ishmael will take to heart in his composition of *Moby-Dick*, a secular scripture for America.[38]

In his Jonah sermon, then, Father Mapple sets forth the evangelical Christian view of the rewards of heaven and hell for those who are obedient or disobedient to God's will, conventional pieties to provide a benchmark of Christian belief and later to be offset by the unorthodox meditations of Ishmael and by Ahab's blasphemous defiance of the deity. Even where the threat of death, judgment, and hell obtrude themselves forcefully on Ishmael's attention in his visit to the Whaleman's Chapel, however, the hymn and evangelical sermon seem to have no visible effect on him. Ironically enough, his only immediate reaction to it all is to become better acquainted with the cannibal Queequeg and to worship the latter's miniature idol, a probable parody (as we will see) of Yahweh and his punitive agent against Jonah, the giant whale.

Following his visit to the Whaleman's Chapel, Ishmael returns to the Spouter Inn where he solidifies his friendship into a personal covenant with

Queequeg, whose paganism is no impediment to his behaving like an honorary Christian in his charitable behavior toward Ishmael. Indeed, Queequeg's expansive brow is so noble-looking that Ishmael humorously compares him to the noblest American of them all: "Queequeg was George Washington cannibalistically developed" (50). Such is the immediate bond of their friendship that Ishmael experiences a sentimental conversion to brotherly love from his early misanthropy, an experience that plays on Ishmael's biblical namesake, whose hand was turned against the world: "I felt a melting in me. No more my splintered heart and maddened hand were turned against the wolfish world. This soothing savage had redeemed it" (51). Just as Bunyan's pilgrim Christian feels his burden dropping off his back when, after receiving instruction at the House of the Interpreter, he unexpectedly encounters a Cross and is given assistance by three angels, so too Melville's modern pilgrim Ishmael feels a sense of disburdening following his visit to the Whaleman's Chapel when he discovers in Queequeg a spiritually redeeming companion. The pagan Queequeg's kindness to the alienated Ishmael accordingly redeems the latter's hostility toward the world by showing "no civilized hypocrisies and bland deceits" (51) but only an unspoiled simplicity of character appropriate for this prototypical noble savage.

The newfound friendship is consolidated with a shared smoke, after which Queequeg "pressed his forehead against mine, clasped me round the waist, and said that henceforth we were married; meaning, in his country's phrase, we were bosom friends; he would gladly die for me, if need should be" (51). While the pressing of the forehead and rubbing of noses was a Maori gesture of friendship, in a larger sense Queequeg is performing with Ishmael the Polynesian ritual of the "tayo," which Melville had described in detail in his second novel, *Omoo*. A socially recognized form of male bonding, the tayo constituted a nonsexual commitment to loyal friendship and shared possessions between men. In Queequeg's case, the de facto tayo ritual confirms his Christlike humanitarianism, for Queequeg will, in the end, provide in death for Ishmael's salvation, thereby fulfilling the well-known injunction of Christ: "Greater love hath no man than this, that a man lay down his life for his friends" (John 15:13). Queequeg will thus act in the coming narrative as an implicit Christ figure, whose actions and example of selfless devotion will help direct Ishmael away from his captain's egotistical quest toward a vision of fraternal community.[39]

In a spirit of reciprocity the new friends share their religions with each other. Ishmael has already given Queequeg a short lesson in the contents of the Bible, and just as Queequeg had earlier attended the service in the Whaleman's Chapel, Ishmael now agrees to worship Queequeg's black wooden idol after a mock catechism in which Ishmael comically concludes that such an act of worship represents a fulfillment of both Old and New Testament teachings. Ishmael reasons that the "magnanimous God of heaven and earth," the God of the Old Testament, could not possibly be "jealous of an insignificant bit of black wood" (52). Worshipping Queequeg's idol was actually a fulfillment of the Golden Rule of Christianity teaching that "whatsoever ye would that men should do to you, do ye even so to them" (Matt. 7:12). Ishmael thereupon rehearses the issues in a mock catechism:

> But what is worship?—to do the will of God—*that* is worship. And what is the will of God?—to do to my fellow man what I would have my fellow man to do to me—*that* is the will of God. Now, Queequeg is my fellow man. And what do I wish that this Queequeg would do to me? Why, unite with me in my particular Presbyterian form of worship. Consequently, I must then unite with him in his; ergo, I must turn idolator. (52)

Paradoxically using Christ's message of brotherly love to overturn the first and second commandments of Moses, which forbid polytheism and idolatry (Exod. 20:1–2), Ishmael decides to worship Yojo with Queequeg. By doing so, Ishmael is again flouting the well-known Pauline prohibition against participating in idolatry: "But I say, that the things which the Gentiles [pagans] sacrifice, they are sacrificing to devils, and not to God: and I would not that ye should have fellowship with devils" (1 Cor. 10:20; see also 1 Cor. 8; Gal. 5:20; Col. 3:5). As in other passages in the early chapters of *Moby-Dick*, Ishmael is subversively reformulating the writings of Paul, in this case to broaden the Christian message to include even a non-Christian cannibal. The rewriting of Christian symbolism extends also to the thirty silver dollars that Queequeg has shared with Ishmael, which mimics and conceivably redeems the thirty pieces of silver for which Judas sold Christ to the Roman authorities (Matt. 26:15). After Ishmael has helped Queequeg perform his devotions over Yojo, he notes that both he and Queequeg were "at peace with our own consciences and all the world" (52). Thus, an early redemptive moment is reached in the narrative, only to be matched by Ishmael's later experience of sperm-squeezing in chapter 94 of the novel.

It should be noted that Melville has rendered the scene of comic "idolatry" here especially significant by having Queequeg in chapter 16 casually identify the name of his small black idol as Yojo, which is almost certainly wordplay, as David H. Hirsch has indicated, on the Old Testament tetragrammaton YHWH, the ineffable name of the Hebrew God.[40] As an ironic inversion of several key features of the Old Testament deity, the black wooden Yojo looked to Ishmael like a Congolese baby, in contrast to the traditional image of Yahweh as a white-haired old man or Ancient of Days (Dan. 7:9). The idol was given ritualistic feeding with burnt biscuit, in contrast to Yahweh's required hecatombs of animal sacrifices. Finally, it was first seen by Ishmael in the fireplace of the Spouter Inn as Queequeg performed his ritual devotions, a likely parody of the scene of the burning bush in Exodus in which Moses was first told the name of the Hebrew God, "I AM THAT I AM" (Exod. 3:14)—an ambiguous assertion of divine identity that was reduced to the name YHWH throughout the Hebrew Bible. Unlike the Hebrew Yahweh, however, the idol Yojo refuses to communicate his wishes, and he is treated in a distinctly offhand manner by Queequeg, treatment that would have earned instant death for a Hebrew as in the fate of those who fatally touched the ark of the covenant (1 Sam. 6:19; 2 Sam. 6:6–7). Ishmael later notes with regard to the selection of a whaling ship for the pair: "Queequeg placed great confidence in the excellence of Yojo's judgment, and surprising forecast of things; and cherished Yojo with considerable esteem, as a rather good sort of god, who perhaps meant well enough upon the whole, but in all cases did not succeed in his benevolent designs" (68). Such a formulation burlesques the Judeo-Christian god's mixed record of success for the faithful and makes an implied satirical comment on his alleged providential care.

Following their sailboat ride to Nantucket, during which Queequeg proves himself to be a Christlike forgiver of injuries after rescuing from drowning a xenophobic bumpkin who had cast aspersions on his devilish appearance, Ishmael and Queequeg pursue their decision to ship together on a whaler from the island, a process that extends the eschatological themes informing the novel's earlier New Bedford chapters. For just as Ishmael's arrival in New Bedford on a freezing Saturday night had led to a mock glimpse of hell in the Negro church and in the bar of the Spouter Inn, so too Ishmael on Nantucket has another glimpse of perdition as he seeks accommodation at the Try Pots, whose peculiar sign catches his attention:

> Two enormous wooden pots painted black, and suspended by asses' ears, swung from the cross-trees of an old top-mast, planted in front of an old doorway. The horns of the cross-trees were sawed off on the other side, so that this old top-mast looked not a little like a gallows. Perhaps I was oversensitive to such impressions at the time, but I could not help staring at this gallows with a vague misgiving. A sort of crick was in my neck as I gazed up to the two remaining horns; yes, *two* of them, one for Queequeg, and one for

me. It's ominous, thinks I. A Coffin my Innkeeper upon landing in my first whaling port; tombstones staring at me in the whalemen's chapel; and here a gallows! and a pair of prodigious black pots too! Are these last throwing out oblique hints touching Tophet? (65–66)

As in the mock allegorical landscape of New Bedford, Ishmael is again given eschatological warning signs here, and indeed the image of death by hanging is in fact prophetic—but of Ahab's fate, not Ishmael's. Yet Ishmael's momentary fears of death and hellfire are quickly dissipated as he meets the landlady of the Try Pots, Mrs. Hosea Hussey, a comically officious matron in the lineage of Shakespeare's Dame Quickly, whose immediate preoccupation is finding out whether her two new lodgers will dine on "Clam or Cod?" (66). The Try Pots that at first seem so ominous are thus humorously deflated back to cooking pots. Even Mrs. Hussey's mention of a financially distressed whaleman who committed suicide with his harpoon at her inn (her justification for prohibiting Queequeg from carrying his harpoon into his room at night) fails to disturb the comic mood set by the landlady with her ample store of hospitable chowder.

The next day Ishmael goes out to select a whaling ship, in keeping with Yojo's alleged instructions, while Queequeg remains at the Try Pots practicing a day of "Fasting and Humiliation" (81), loosely designated by the Islamic term "Ramadan." Coming back from his expedition that day, which resulted in his selecting the *Pequod* for their whaling vessel, Ishmael discovers that Queequeg has locked the door of their room, and he soon becomes alarmed about his new friend's welfare. This seemingly ominous situation gives rise to Mrs. Hussey's renewed fears of having a suicide on her hands. But after breaking open the door, Ishmael discovers Queequeg squatting peacefully in the middle of the room, still rapt in his Ramadan. Queequeg, in fact, remains entranced for the rest of the day and evening, only ending his session the next morning when Ishmael sees him arise with his first glimpse of the sun. While professing an openness to all religions, Ishmael nevertheless lectures Queequeg about the unhealthiness of his religious asceticism, ending his harangue with a bold statement of the physiological origins of the state of hell: "In one word, Queequeg, said I, rather digressively; hell is an idea first born on an undigested apple-dumpling; and since then perpetuated through the heredity dyspepsias nurtured by Ramadans" (85). Ishmael's comic reduction of hell to a condition of indigestion, the alleged cause of nightmares according to contemporary medicine, is in keeping with his other comic subversions of evangelical orthodoxy and its Pauline eschatology; indeed, the apple dumpling provides a mischievous reminder of the mythological source of the Fall.

The subversion of orthodoxy here is enhanced if we factor in a probable reference to *Pilgrim's Progress* in this episode, for Queequeg's assumed suicide has a potential model in the visit of Christian and Hopeful to Doubting Castle of Giant Despair, who counsels the two pilgrims to commit suicide. "Here then they lay, from *Wednesday* morning till *Saturday* night, without one bit of bread, or drop of drink, or any light, or any to ask how they did." The Giant Despair subsequently told them that "since they were never like to come out of the place, their only way would be, forthwith to make an end of themselves, either with Knife, Halter or Poison." Ishmael's fear of hanging when seeing the sign of the Try Pots Inn and Queequeg's feared suicide with his harpoon while a guest there thus obliquely parody the events that unfold at Bunyan's Doubting Castle. Yet unlike the pilgrims of Bunyan's allegory who manage to escape from Doubting Castle after Christian discovers the Key of Promise (assurance of salvation) around his neck, Ishmael opposes Queequeg's religious self-mortification with good-natured common sense, not Christian dogma.[41]

If the novel's early chapters reveal Ishmael's repeated encounter with the four last things of Christian eschatology, the formal debut of its larger apocalyptic symbolism occurs when he and Queequeg join the crew of the *Pequod*, whose voyage will soon become an epic quest for the White Whale as an embodiment of cosmic evil. After Ishmael has negotiated their joining the crew of the ship (see chapter 3 below), Queequeg's signing the papers to enlist as a harpooner provides Bildad with the occasion to give him a Millerite-type pamphlet warning of the approaching end-times ("The Latter Day Coming; or No Time to Lose") and hyperbolically to assert Queequeg's need to repent: "Spurn the idol Bel and the hideous dragon; turn from the wrath to come; mind thine eye, I say; oh! goodness gracious! steer clear of the fiery pit!" (89). While the first part of Bildad's warning draws on two obscure tales from the Apocrypha (elaborating on Daniel 3 and 6), the latter part constitutes standard New Testament and evangelical formulas of apocalyptic admonition. Despite the solemn warning, however, the speech is the occasion for another of Bildad and Peleg's comic altercations over Bildad's inappropriate use of biblical teachings in the practical business of whaling. This has been seen earlier in the novel in Bildad's misuse of the Sermon on the Mount to cheat Ishmael out of his fair share of the *Pequod's* "lays," an action satirically confirmed by the underlying meaning of Peleg's biblical name, "to divide" (Gen. 10:25).

Having signed on to the *Pequod*, Ishmael and Queequeg are immediately confronted by the mysterious one-armed, pockmarked sailor prophet Elijah, who asks them whether they are fully informed about Ahab's past. The figure of Elijah here is, of course, an implicit reminder of the history of the biblical King Ahab and the prophet who denounced his idolatry for sanctioning the religion of Baal following his dynastic marriage to Queen Jezebel of Tyre. The first indication of the prophet Elijah's opposition to King Ahab was his declaration of a three-year drought over Israel, during which time the prophet dwelt by the dried-up brook Cherith: "And it came to pass after a while, that the brook dried up, because there had been no rain in the land" (1 Kings 17:7). The initial portrait of the shabbily attired Elijah in chapter 19 of *Moby-Dick* evokes this episode, for the sailor's face is scarred by a "confluent small pox," which "left it like the complicated ribbed bed of a torrent, when the rushing waters have been dried up" (91). Elijah's emphatic act of pointing at the *Pequod*—by "drawing back his whole arm, and then rapidly shoving it straight out from him, with the fixed bayonet of his pointed finger darted full at the object" (91)—also hints at the finger of God that is evident in the prophetic careers of Moses and Daniel (see Exod. 8:19, 31:18; Deut. 9:10; Dan. 5:5). In a series of remarks reminiscent of the biblical Elijah's opposition to King Ahab's idolatrous regime, the wharf-side Elijah of chapter 19 repeatedly hints at Captain Ahab's moral recusancy, insinuating that Ishmael and Queequeg have given away their souls by signing aboard the *Pequod*. Elijah accordingly calls Ahab by the name of Old Thunder (obliquely recalling the biblical Ahab's association with the storm god Baal) and hints at several incidents that have marked Ahab's character, mentioning a three-day period suspended between life and death off Cape Horn; a "deadly scrimmage" with an unnamed Spaniard in a church in Santa, Peru; the act of spitting into a "silver calabash," probably a communion cup in the same church; and the loss of his leg on his most recent voyage, the fulfillment of an unidentified prophecy. All of Elijah's examples—mock crucifixion, sacrilegious violence, deliberate blasphemy—hint at violently antichristian acts on Ahab's part, but in keeping with the equivocal nature of his prophecy Ishmael dismisses the warning message of the ragged old sailor. Even so, the eerie encounter leaves Ishmael with "all kinds of vague wonderments, and half-apprehensions" (93) about the captain under whom he will be sailing.

Ishmael is rightly concerned about the warning from this nautical prophet, not only because of the ominous suggestions arising from the name of Elijah in connection with the blasphemous King Ahab but also in terms of the apocalyptic associations implicit in Elijah's name. For in the final words of the book of the prophet Malachi, the last book in the Old Testament, God announces that the reappearance of the prophet Elijah would be the sign of impending apocalyptic destruction, the Day of the Lord:

> For, behold, the day cometh, that shall burn as an oven; and all the proud, yea, all that do wickedly, shall be stubble: and the day that cometh shall burn them up, saith the Lord of hosts, that it shall leave them neither root nor branch.
>
> But unto you that fear my name shall the Sun of righteousness arise with healing in his wings . . .
>
> Behold, I will send you Elijah the prophet before the coming of the great and dreadful day of the Lord. (Mal. 4:1–2, 5)

In the New Testament, the role of Elijah is associated with both John the Baptist and Christ as messianic agents of apocalyptic transformation (Matt. 11:10–16, 16:13–23, 17:10–13). In *Moby-Dick*, the appearance of the sailor Elijah in chapter 19 imaginatively fulfills the biblical prophecy of messianic expectation and divine vengeance following the appearance of a prophet bearing the same distinctive name.

If Elijah's mysterious appearance in chapter 19 provides an early indication of the relevance of Captain Ahab's biblical prototype for an understanding of his character, the prophet's second appearance in chapter 21, when Ishmael and Queequeg are about to board the *Pequod* at dawn the next day, adds a final apocalyptic note to the portentous atmosphere that the sailor prophet has created at the start of the *Pequod*'s voyage. Indeed, we may say that his implied function in this later chapter is to create a symbolic link between Old Testament prophecy and New Testament apocalyptic. Unexpectedly presenting himself before Ishmael and Queequeg, Elijah now asks whether they are still planning to go onboard Ahab's ship and, upon hearing the affirmative, asks them if they have noticed the strange-looking crewmen going aboard before them: "Did ye see anything looking like men going towards that ship [the *Pequod*] a while ago?" (99). The mysterious men, we discover later, are Fedallah and his crew of four Malay sailors who will man Ahab's whaleboat—demonic familiars, in the symbolic frame of the novel, who will ultimately lead Ahab to his doom. Failing to obtain a response to his leading questions, Elijah decides that Ishmael is too dim to understand the nature of the voyage on which he is soon to embark, even as Elijah's final words of dismissal imply that he will not see Ishmael and Queequeg before the Last Judgment: "Oh! I was going to warn ye against—but never mind, never mind—it's all one, all in the family too;—sharp frost this morning, ain't it? Good bye to ye. Shan't see ye again very soon, I guess, unless it's before the Grand Jury" (99). Elijah's "cracked words" dismiss Ishmael and Queequeg to their fate while hinting that the evil he foresees for Ahab and his crew is an ineluctable part of the human condition: "it's all one, all in the family too" (99). Dismissing the ragged prophet's words as humbug, Ishmael, together with Queequeg, boards the *Pequod*, which then departs on Christmas Day, launched on the secret messianic mission of its "mad" captain.

The final departure of the *Pequod* from port on Christmas Day is evoked in chapter 22 ("Merry Christmas"), at which time Peleg and Bildad pilot the ship into the North Atlantic and give their final instructions for the voyage. As in Ishmael's first encounter with the owners in port, their actions again convey an ironic dichotomy between pious and profane aspects of their shared religious culture, with Peleg swearing at the men like a devil and giving Ishmael his first kick, and Bildad singing hymns and urging godly behavior in the crew. Such a dichotomy is offset by two other symbolic indications of the holiday on which the ship is sailing, with Ishmael conveying a sense of cosmic hope in keeping with the Christmas spirit: "Spite of this frigid winter night in the boisterous Atlantic, spite of my wet feet and wetter jacket, there was yet, it then seemed to me, many a pleasant haven in store; and meads and glades so eternally vernal, that the grass shot up by the spring, untrodden, unwilted, remains at midsummer" (104). Despite Ishmael's hopeful sense of a "haven" (or heaven) in store, however, the *Pequod*'s captain, like the Judeo-Christian god, is nowhere to be seen. In a potential pun on the nonappearance of the infant messiah that day, and the larger ineffectuality of Christianity in the sailors' world, Bildad's sister Charity "had placed a small choice copy of Watts [the Protestant hymnal] in each seaman's berth" (103), even though the sailors still sing a profane song about "the girls in Booble Alley [Liverpool], with hearty good will" (103). In the meantime, the ship itself presents a savage appearance in the gathering night, as the "long rows of teeth on the bulwarks glistened in the moonlight" (104), and following the final departure of the two pilot-owners, it "blindly plunged like fate into the lone Atlantic" (105). The tone is ominous here, but a more telling prophetic hint of the *Pequod*'s coming voyage is to be found in the next chapter, in the portrait of the heroic sailor Bulkington.

Shortly after the *Pequod* is launched on her apocalyptic voyage, Ishmael discovers the figure of Bulkington at its helm, a sailor who, just returned to

Nantucket from a four-year voyage on the *Grampus*, was already shipping out again. Bulkington's life and death are celebrated in chapter 23 ("The Lee Shore") in a brief "six-inch chapter" that substitutes for the six-foot "stoneless grave" Bulkington received in his "ocean-perishing." It is thematically appropriate that an evocation of death and immortality completes the initial narrative sequence of Melville's novel with its recurrent eschatological concerns. Bulkington's stoneless grave is thus a textual equivalent to the empty tombs in the Whaleman's Chapel and the "stoneless" sepulcher of Christ (Mark 16); but Ishmael's shipmate here is envisaged as having earned heroic fame, like a Homeric hero, through his moral courage not his religious faith. Like the two chapters involving the figure of Elijah just discussed, "The Lee Shore" is another foreshadowing of disaster for the *Pequod*, yet the mood of the chapter is not so much foreboding as heroically assertive. The symbolic frame of reference here again changes from biblical to classical, as it did earlier in "The Chapel." For the figure of Bulkington is a modern embodiment of the classical hero Hercules (or Herakles), whose great physical strength was supplemented by a history of moral fortitude, as represented in the well-known allegorical "Choice of Hercules" between Vice and Virtue.[42]

Like Hercules, Bulkington is an icon of both physical and moral strength. Initially mentioned in "The Spouter Inn" as part of the *Grampus* crew returning after a four-year whaling voyage, Bulkington was there described by Ishmael as "full six feet in height, with noble shoulders, and a chest like a coffer-dam. I have seldom seen such brawn in a man. His face was deeply brown and burnt, making his white teeth dazzling by contrast; while in the deep shadows of his eyes floated some reminiscences that did not seem to give him much joy" (16). A melancholy soul like Ishmael and Ahab, Bulkington is celebrated in "The Lee Shore" as having the moral courage to go from one protracted and dangerous whaling voyage to another within a matter of days. Ishmael posits an analogy between Bulkington's leaving port so quickly and the ship that avoids the lee (windward) shore for fear of shipwreck. Although we know very little about Bulkington's life at this point, Ishmael uses his mere physical presence at the helm of the *Pequod* to celebrate the intellectual quest for truth amid the inhibiting influences of dogma and convention, the chief impediments to truth in the evangelical America from which Ishmael is escaping by going whaling:

> Know ye now Bulkington? Glimpses do ye seem to see of that mortally intolerable truth; that all deep, earnest thinking is but the intrepid effort of the soul to keep the open independence of her sea; while the wildest winds of

heaven and earth conspire to cast her on the treacherous, slavish shore?

But as in landlessness alone resides the highest truth, shoreless, indefinite as God—so, better is it to perish in that howling infinite, than be ingloriously dashed upon the lee, even if that were safety! For worm-like, then, oh! who would craven crawl to land! Terrors of the terrible! is all this agony so vain? Take heart, take heart, O Bulkington! Bear thee grimly, demigod! Up from the spray of thy ocean-perishing—straight up, leaps thy apotheosis! (107)

This Faustian, Romantic credo of fearless mental independence, contrasting the ocean's sublimely destructive power with the false security of the inhabited land, recalls the impetuous Taji of Melville's earlier *Mardi* while echoing another literary example of the conflict between intellectual freedom and social convention in Emerson's essay on "Intellect" from the *Essays: First Series* (1841), which urges the strenuous pursuit of "truth" over the comforts of "repose." Bulkington is thus portrayed as an archetypal Romantic quester whose nonconformity to contemporary theological dogma earns Ishmael's proleptic epitaph, the only such memorial to a member of the crew in the novel. At the same time, Ishmael's evocation of the appeal of "landlessness" as a terrifying, "howling infinite"—exemplifying the "highest truth, shoreless, indefinite as God"—shows the supreme appeal of the masculine oceanic sublime as an aesthetic and philosophical realm over the more tame appeal of the nurturing maternal land, an adaptation of traditional Burkean aesthetics of the sublime and beautiful. Bulkington is thus an exemplary hero whose anticipated "ocean-perishing" gives the reader a preview of further events to come.[43]

Ishmael accordingly creates a matrix of both classical and Christian symbolism in his salute to Bulkington's life and death. The analogy of the ship here suggests one of several poetic metaphors for the soul in the Platonic dialogues, while the whole passage states a thematic message that is antithetical to the Jonah lesson of Father Mapple's sermon. If Jonah found redemption in godly submission during his misguided sea voyage, Bulkington finds it in philosophical independence, even at the price of death and disaster. And if Father Mapple's sermon would seem most applicable to the career of Ahab, the example of Bulkington, encouraging heroic mental independence, seems most applicable to Ishmael as secular prophet. The classical context of the passage is evident also in the Neoplatonic image of the truth as "shoreless, indefinite as God" and in the imagery of Bulkington as a demigod whose apotheosis leaps straight up from the spray of his "ocean-perishing." The phenomenon of apotheosis was alien to Judeo-Christian tradition but was instead applicable in classical mythology to those semidivine beings, like Hercules, who were given immortality with the gods because of their divine ancestry or special achievements. The contrast between the image of Bulkington undergoing heroic apotheosis in his ocean-perishing and the empty tombs in the Whaleman's Chapel again reveals the ongoing debate between Christian and classical notions of the afterlife that thread their way through the early chapters of *Moby-Dick*.

We may conclude, then, that chapter 23 ("The Lee Shore") is yet another prophetic text anticipating the moral tenor of the upcoming voyage of the *Pequod* and the question of the afterlife. Yet instead of the eschatological issues of death, judgment, heaven, and hell that we encountered during Ishmael's stays in New Bedford and Nantucket, we find here a classical celebration of heroic life and death, with an emphasis on nondogmatic philosophical thinking alien to the Judeo-Christian tradition. Also conspicuous in Ishmael's commemoration of Bulkington is the loneliness of the latter's quest, showing that the search for truth requires a painfully ascetic dedication and heroic stamina. We will now discover another kind of ascetic hero in Captain Ahab, whose larger identity is firmly rooted in the theological world of the Old Testament.

CHAPTER THREE

Chaos Monster and Unholy Warrior

IF THE APOCALYPTIC and eschatological themes of *Moby-Dick* are repeatedly invoked in the early chapters of the novel as Ishmael goes in search of a whaling vessel (as we have seen above), the Joban theme follows a more gradual pattern of development, being hinted at the start of the novel but made fully manifest only when Ahab makes his first appearance in chapter 28. Thus, while speculating at the start of the novel on his reasons for deciding to sign onto a whaling ship, Ishmael noted "the overwhelming idea of the great whale himself. Such a portentous and mysterious monster roused all my curiosity" (7). Although the description here may recall the sperm whale's enormous bulk and obscure natural history, a significant part of Ishmael's fascination with the "great whale" is doubtless the creature's archetypal representation as Leviathan in the Old Testament. The figures of Leviathan and Yahweh are symbolically linked both in the book of Job and in the mind of Melville's whaling captain, whose deranged self-appointed mission is to extirpate the primordial source of evil in the albino whale that has injured him—an atavistic reversion to the magical thinking of myth, shaped by the contours of Judeo-Christian tradition. In this chapter, then, we will explore the early Joban and apocalyptic roles of Moby Dick and Ahab as modern exemplars, respectively, of the archetypal biblical chaos monster, and the divine warrior of biblical myth blended with the rebellious Job of the poetic dialogues.

After its elliptical initial introduction, the Joban theme of *Moby-Dick* makes its formal debut in chapter 16 ("The Ship") when Ishmael investigates the possibility of signing himself and Queequeg on as crewmen of the

Pequod. The two Quaker owners whom Ishmael encounters here are the comically matched pair of Peleg and Bildad, the latter bearing the name of one of Job's comforters and (in keeping with this identity) exhibiting a dour religious orthodoxy, as contrasted with his business partner's more worldly personality. Called on to give counsel to his friend Job, the biblical Bildad—like his associates Eliphaz and Zophar—asserts the conventional wisdom that Job must be guilty of wrongdoing since God only punishes the wicked. The Bildad of the *Pequod* is a similarly pious hypocrite who would like to sign Ishmael on as a crewman at the low rate of the 777th "lay," or fraction of profit, justifying his action by punningly appealing to Christ's Sermon on the Mount in which it is stated that one should "lay" up treasures in heaven, not on earth. Bildad's biblical identity is blended in this way with a durable comic stage type, the Yankee peddler, while it also hints at a type of American businessman who incongruously attempts to justify sharp commercial practices with Christian ethics.

Noting Bildad's seemingly effortless reconciliation of the Quaker principle of nonviolence with his lifelong killing of whales for profit, Ishmael comments on such compartmentalization of beliefs and actions: "How now in the contemplative evening of his days, the pious Bildad reconciled these things in the reminiscence, I do not know; but it did not seem to concern him much, and very probably he had long since come to the sage and sensible conclusion that a man's religion is one thing, and this practical world quite another. This world pays dividends" (74). The all-important motive of money thus usurps all moral principle in Bildad's religious practice. Like his Old Testament namesake, Melville's Bildad is thus guilty of a flagrant hypocrisy as even his partner Peleg recognizes when he comically challenges his co-owner's unfair offer of wages to Ishmael: "'Why, blast your eyes, Bildad,' cried Peleg, 'thou dost not want to swindle this young man! he must have more than that'" (77). But in defending himself, Bildad is more than ready to rebuke his volatile, profane partner in the harsh moralistic manner of Job's inflexible friend: "as thou art still an impenitent man, Captain Peleg, I greatly fear lest thy conscience be but a leaky one; and will in the end sink thee foundering down to the fiery pit, Captain Peleg."[1]

Yet despite the initial introduction of Bildad as a satirical exemplar of religious hypocrisy, the tragic Joban theme of *Moby-Dick* formally emerges near the end of chapter 16 when Ahab is first described in Peleg's reply to Ishmael's request to see the captain of the *Pequod*. Peleg comments on the ambiguity of the secluded captain's physical condition by noting that he's "sort of sick, and yet he don't look so. In fact he ain't sick; but no, he isn't well either" (78). The shipowner assures Ishmael that he has nothing to fear from Ahab, who is then described in paradoxical Joban terms as a morally divided soul, distinguished for both his reticence and his eloquence: "He's a grand, ungodly, god-like man, Captain Ahab; doesn't speak much; but, when he does speak, then you may well listen" (79). After noting that Ahab is a man with broad experience at sea, Peleg exonerates Ahab of any negative associations of his biblical name:

> "I know Captain Ahab well; I've sailed with him as mate years ago; I know what he is—a good man—not a pious, good man, like Bildad, but a swearing good man—something like me—only there's a good deal more of him. Aye, ay, I know that he was never very jolly; and I know that on the passage home, he was a little out of his mind for a spell; but it was the sharp shooting pains in his bleeding stump that brought that about, as any one might see. I know, too, that ever since he lost his leg last voyage by that accursed whale, he's been a kind of moody—desperate moody, and savage sometimes; but that will all pass off." (79)

In this, the reader's first introduction to Ahab, the resemblances to Job are suggested in the notion that Ahab is a good man who has been suffering from a terrible physical affliction, like the one that "the satan" has imposed on Job. Ahab, of course, has not lost his worldly goods like the biblical patriarch. But the loss of his leg does represent a climactic physical injury to complement an earlier trauma (as we will eventually learn) in being struck by lightning—the equivalent of Job's initial loss of his children and property, after which the second messenger informs Job that the "fire of God is fallen from heaven, and hath burned up the sheep, and the servants, and consumed them" (Job 1:16). Since Job's faith remains firm amid these devastating losses, the satan tells God after this first series of disasters to "put forth thy hand now, and touch his bone and his flesh, and he will curse thee to thy face" (Job 2:5). As a second test of his faith, God then gives Job a disfiguring case of "sore boils from the sole of his foot unto his crown" (Job 2:7). In like manner, Ahab becomes an outspoken rebel against God when he loses his leg in an encounter with Moby Dick during his previous voyage, a loss of the "bone" and "flesh" that the satan told God to "touch" (harm) in God's further test of Job.

Ahab had then suffered an agonizing wound to his groin from his artificial whalebone leg just before the sailing of the *Pequod* from Nantucket (as we learn in chapter 106), an implied emasculation and further violation of flesh and bone that eventuates in Ahab's desire to "dismember" his "dismemberer" (168). Like Job, Ahab might well complain that God "breaketh me with a tempest, and multiplieth my wounds without cause" (Job 9:17). Ahab's excruciating physical and psychological pain, stemming from his lost leg and pierced groin, duplicates the physical and psychological pain that pervades the book of Job following his inexplicable loss of family, property, and physical health, all in rapid succession. Both Ahab's and Job's attributing the cause of their suffering to a malign or inscrutable god is in keeping with the findings of modern psychological research, in which human beings, in the absence of other probable causes, instinctively associate excessive, anomalous suffering with a divine agent.[2]

Captain Ahab's Joban traits continue to be evident throughout our early introduction to his character. Immediately following Job's physical affliction by the satan, his wife tells him to "curse God, and die," to which Job replies, "Thou speakest as one of the foolish women speaketh" (Job 2:9–10). Nevertheless, Job's first extensive verbal reaction to his afflictions is to curse the day of his birth, along with all the rest of creation (Job 3). In an apparent variation of this motif, our first introduction to Ahab involves the notion that Ahab is possibly cursed by both his biblical name and his distinctive birthmark or scar. As Ishmael learns from Captain Peleg when he signs onto the *Pequod*, Ahab received his damning biblical name as "a foolish ignorant whim of his crazy, widowed mother, who died when he was only a twelvemonth old" (79). Ishmael's first sight of Ahab after several days at sea reveals a man who shows "no sign of common bodily illness about him, nor of the recovery of any," but he is nevertheless scarred with "a slender rod-like mark, lividly whitish" (123), starting on his head and continuing down his body. The rodlike mark suggests Ahab's branding by lightning, just as the "fire of God" had consumed Job's sheep and servants at the beginning of his divinely sanctioned ordeal (Job 1:16).

Ahab is literally a marked man, whose prominent, overdetermined scar— comparable to Satan's scarring by thunder in *Paradise Lost* (I.600–604), God's mark on the brow of Cain (Gen. 4:15), the mark of the beast in Revelation 13, and the prophet Zoroaster's full-body scar by lightning as recorded in Bayle's *Dictionary*—is explained as a possible birthmark or the product of some violent incident at sea: "Whether that mark was born with him, or whether it was the scar left by some desperate wound, no one could certainly say." However, "once Tashtego's senior, an old Gay-Head Indian among the crew, superstitiously asserted that not till he was full forty years old did Ahab become that way branded, and then it came upon him, not in the fury of any mortal fray, but in an elemental strife at sea" (123–24). The Manxman in the crew, on the other hand, having "preternatural powers of discernment" has claimed "that if ever Captain Ahab should be tranquilly laid out—which might hardly come to pass, so he muttered—then, whoever should do that last office for the dead, would find a birthmark on him from crown to sole" (124). Ahab's presumed birthmark here recalls Job's disfiguring physical affliction by the satan "from the sole of his foot unto his crown" (Job 2:7). Ahab's body is clearly branded with a mark from God, whether from birth (in a manner recalling the satan's blighting of Job's body) or as a result of Ahab's earlier fire worship (as he implies in chapter 119). At the same time, Ahab's body-length scar identifies him as having a divided soul, in keeping with his identity as an embodiment of nineteenth-century Faustian man.

Ahab's trio of physical injuries, the branding of his body, the loss of his leg to Moby Dick, and the agonizing wound to his groin caused by his artificial whalebone leg, all make him a Job-like victim of a physical affliction that has resulted in violent metaphysical rebellion. Ishmael's description of Ahab's first appearance on the deck of the *Pequod* as the ship sails south is suitable for a man who has undergone a Job-like (or Christlike) physical and psychological punishment. Showing "an infinity of firmest fortitude" in his bearing, "moody stricken Ahab" stood before his fellow officers "with a crucifixion in his face; in all the nameless regal overbearing dignity of some mighty woe" (124). Job and his three friends are silent for a week following his divine affliction: "none spake a word unto him: for they saw that his grief was very great" (Job 2:13). Similarly, Ahab has been sequestered in his cabin during the first days of the *Pequod's* voyage before he finally emerged to Ishmael's view: "Not a word he spoke; nor did his officers say aught to him; though by all their minutest gestures and expressions, they plainly showed the uneasy, if not painful, consciousness of being under a troubled master-eye" (124).

By the time of his first appearance in chapter 28, Ahab is firmly established as a Joban tragic hero whose suffering rivals that of the biblical patriarch, yet it is only in the sequence of five dramatic tableaux beginning with chapter 36 ("The Quarter-Deck") that we witness Ahab's emergence as a fully formed tragic figure. From its classical beginnings, tragedy has depicted the existential encounter of a hero with an irrational and opportunistic evil as in Ahab's tormented response to his injury by the White Whale. Since the publication of F. O. Matthiessen's *American Renaissance* (1941), Ahab's identity as a tragic hero in a distinctly Shakespearean mold has been examined in a number of studies. So we find, for example, traces of Hamlet in Ahab's drawn-out revenge scheme, melancholic temperament, and metaphysical questionings; traces of Lear in Ahab's enraged challenge to divine justice, felt weight of years, mental instability, and protective relationship with his deranged "fool," Pip; and traces of Macbeth in Ahab's tyrannical control of his crew, steadily increasing usurpation of power, and overconfident reliance on supernatural signs and agents.[3]

Other aspects to Melville's whaling narrative point to the model of Greek tragedy, notably *Prometheus Bound* and *Oedipus the King*, as well as to the Aristotelian specifications for the genre. We accordingly witness the terror and pity of Ahab's physical and psychological suffering, his self-destructive flaws of pride, rage, and blasphemy, and his fatal entrapment by events, which include final scenes of recognition and reversal. As a semi-dramatic narrative fiction bridging the realms of classical and modern tragedy, *Moby-Dick* may thus be categorized under the rubric of revenge tragedy, a perennially popular form because of its combination of visceral appeal and moral complexity as attested by its long trajectory from Aeschylus's *Oresteia* through *Hamlet* and beyond.[4]

In the formulation of Ahab's tragic persona, we should also note the influence of various strains of English and European Romanticism, notably the convention of the morally divided hero-villain conspicuous in the protagonists of Goethe and his German peers, the English Gothic novel, and Byron's oriental romances and closet dramas. Such figures as Goethe's Faust and Beckford's Vathek, Godwin's Falkland and Mary Shelley's Frankenstein, Percy Shelley's Prometheus, and Byron's Conrad, Manfred, and Cain, and other moral rebels and metaphysical overreachers—many influenced by the Romantic revaluation of Milton's Satan, a figure who also gives distinctive shape to Ahab's character—carry their revolt to self-destructive ends. Together they demonstrate the social and theological limits of a world hostile to such moral rebellion or impious aspiration.[5]

Granted the importance of Ahab's classical, Renaissance, and Romantic lineages, we may still argue that his tragic predicament is ultimately grounded in the world of the book of Job, which provided the dominant source for Ahab's and the White Whale's symbolically interlinked identities.[6] *Moby-Dick*'s Joban theme thus emerges fully-fledged when we first hear Ahab reveal the true mission of the *Pequod* in chapter 36, in a scene replete with Job-like attacks on the deity and evocations of the hated White Whale in terms of the biblical Leviathan. As a result of his long watches at sea, during which time he has apparently shed all notions of Christian orthodoxy, Ahab has come to the conclusion that the seeming malignity of the universe can only be explained by postulating a malign creator god. The focus of his anger, we soon learn, is the albino sperm whale that sheared off his leg in the Pacific during his previous whaling cruise. As Ahab tells Starbuck, following his announcement to the crew of the forthcoming hunt for Moby Dick:

> "Hark ye yet again,—the little lower layer. All visible objects, man, are but as pasteboard masks. But in each event—in the living act, the undoubted deed— there, some unknown but still reasoning thing puts forth the mouldings of its features from behind the unreasoning mask. If man will strike, strike through the mask! How can the prisoner reach outside except by thrusting through the wall? To me, the white whale is that wall, shoved near to me. Sometimes I think there's naught beyond. But 'tis enough. He tasks me; he heaps me; I see in him outrageous strength, with an inscrutable malice sinewing it. That inscrutable thing is chiefly what I hate; and be the white whale agent, or be the white whale principal, I will wreak that hate upon him. Talk not to me of blasphemy, man; I'd strike the sun if it insulted me. For could the sun do that, then could I do the other; since there is ever a sort of fair play herein, jealousy presiding over all creations. But not my master man, is even that fair play. Who's over me? Truth hath no confines." (164)

Ahab's famous explanation to Starbuck of the reason for his pursuit of Moby Dick might be interpreted as variously influenced by Platonic, Gnostic, or Romantic-Transcendental tradition. In keeping with the latter, the speech echoes Diogenes Teufeldröckh's remarks on the emblematic nature of reality in book 1, chapter 11, of Carlyle's *Sartor Resartus*.[7] But in the speech's radical confrontation with the seemingly malign mysteries of the cosmos, Ahab is clearly assuming a Job-like stance, for in his first cycle of speeches, Job is an enraged questioner of God's seemingly amoral, inscrutable, and sadistic power:

> If he [man] will contend with him [God], he [God] cannot answer him [man] one of a thousand. . . .
>
> Lo, he goeth by me, and I see him not: he passeth on also, but I perceive him not.
>
> Behold, he taketh away who can hinder him? who will say unto him, What doest thou? . . .
>
> He will not suffer me to take my breath, but filleth me with bitterness.
>
> If I speak of strength, lo, he is strong: and if of judgment, who shall set me a time to plead? . . .
>
> This is one thing, therefore I said it, He destroyeth the perfect and the wicked.
>
> If the scourge slay suddenly, he will laugh at the trial of the innocent.

The earth is given into the hand of the wicked: he covereth the faces of the judges thereof; if not, where, and who is he? . . .

For he is not a man, as I am, that I should answer him, and we should come together in judgment.

Neither is there any daysman [mediator] betwixt us, that might lay his hand upon us both.

Let him take his rod away from me, and let not his fear terrify me: . . .

I will say unto God, Do not condemn me; shew me wherefore thou contendest with me.

Is it good unto thee that thou shouldest oppress, that thou shouldest despise the work of thine hands, and shine upon the counsel of the wicked?

Hast thou eyes of flesh? or seest thou as man seeth? (Job 9:3, 11–12, 18–19, 22–24, 32–34, 10:2–4)

Ahab's initial explanation of the White Whale's metaphysical meaning substantially duplicates the complaints of Job about his relationship to the deity. In both Job and Ahab we find extended complaints about God (or the White Whale) as bafflingly invisible, brutally omnipotent, and legally unaccountable. Leo G. Perdue notes that Job's first cycle of speeches (chapters 3–10) attacks God for his inversion of several key traditional roles—divine warrior, just judge, cosmic artist, and nurturing parent—with regard to the creation:

> In the first cycle, Job deconstructs the root metaphors of the two traditions of creation: cosmos and humanity. Battle, word, artistry and fertility are turned upside down. Not only is God the Divine Warrior who has attacked creation, but also the wicked and corrupt judge who laughs at the destructive force of his own evil decisions. As artist God has created not a human object of beauty and delight, but rather one for sadistic torture. As divine parent, God conceives, forms, and nurtures Job in the womb, not out of love, but out of the desire to bring suffering and pain.[8]

Such an inversion of roles is also evident in Ahab's attitude toward the White Whale. Ahab's description of his desire for revenge against Moby Dick posits the latter as engaged in all-out war against him. His chief grievance is that "outrageous strength" should be allied with "inscrutable malice." The whale's quasi-divine omnipotence is destructively allied with evil instead of good, a subversion of the central tenet of theodicy as well as of the notion that human beings are divinely made creatures. Just as Job complains that he has been condemned without a trial or hearing, Ahab resorts to legal language to lodge his protest against injustice. Ahab is thus a moral and metaphysical prisoner, and the White Whale is the claustrophobic wall in this prison. Calling the whale the agent or principal of an "undoubted deed," Ahab asks for fair play. He claims the equality of "all creations" before the tribunal of truth, holding that human beings are on an equal plane with the "sun" in this regard. Ahab imagines the deity as hiding behind the "pasteboard masks" of his creation; Job complains that God "covereth the faces of the judges." So, too, Job puts himself on an equal plane with his creator when voicing his unmerited suffering. Ahab makes a claim to being an American democratic hero by insisting that he is capable of obtaining cosmic justice through the force of his individual will. As Tocqueville noted, "to seek the reason of things for oneself, and in oneself alone; to tend to results without being bound by means, and to strike through the form to the substance—such are the principal characteristics of what I shall call the philosophical method of the Americans."[9]

Still another conceptual link uniting Job and Ahab is their perception of human enslavement.[10] Just as Job believes that God has wantonly subjected him to the misery of slavery, Ahab expresses a feeling of enslavement when he notes that the idea of Moby Dick "tasks" him and "heaps" him. The feeling of being overloaded with work—tasked and heaped—is the complaint of a slave. So, too, the White Whale for Ahab is paradoxically both an oppressive presence *and* a symbol of divine absence: "Sometimes I think there's naught beyond" (164). The same paradox is evident in Job, for as James Crenshaw observes, "Job both complains because God is too near and also grieves over the fact that the deity has withdrawn into the heavens."[11]

In a study of Job as a psychiatric case history of trauma and recovery, Jack Kahn notes that after the inexplicable loss of his family, possessions, and health, Job exhibits the characteristic symptoms of both depression and paranoia.[12] A like experience of suffering has resulted in Ahab's deep melancholy and paranoid delusions of persecution by the White Whale as an instrument of the deity. Just before the famous quarterdeck speech quoted above, Ahab's first mate, Starbuck, had attempted to challenge the factual basis of Ahab's apparent delusion, relegating Moby Dick to the realm of living creatures that strike by instinct against their attackers: "'Vengeance on a dumb brute!' cried Starbuck, 'that simply smote thee from blindest instinct! Madness! To be enraged with a dumb thing, Captain Ahab, seems blasphemous'" (163–64). To the conventionally pious Starbuck, Ahab's picture of a universe characterized by divine malice is deeply offensive. Starbuck's horrified reaction to Ahab's blasphemies duplicates Job's friends' equally horrified reaction to Job's attacks on divine justice. But Starbuck, unlike Job's friends, is not secure in his own orthodoxy; indeed, he is already showing signs of vulnerability to his captain's overwhelming rhetoric and force of personality.

Significantly, Ahab attempts to win his first mate's loyalty using several classic rhetorical fallacies. First, Ahab claims that since all the other crew members are committed to his private mission of revenge, Starbuck can not hang back, thereby drawing on "bandwagon" or "in-crowd" appeal. Second, Ahab's characterization of the crew as unreflecting, savage animals ("The Pagan leopards—the unrecking, unworshipping things, that live; and seek, and give no reason for the torrid life they feel!") also reminds Starbuck that his brand of Christian piety is an exception onboard the *Pequod*—in effect, a veiled threat. Third, Ahab claims that hunting Moby Dick will be just like hunting any other sperm whale, thus creating a false analogy. Last, Ahab asserts that Starbuck's skills as a harpooner ("the best lance out of all Nantucket" [164]) will help the hunt for the White Whale—an appeal to flattery.[13]

Yet, in a final telling aside Ahab reveals that his recruitment of Starbuck to join his mission is an act of spiritual coercion: "Something shot from my dilated nostrils, he has inhaled it in his lungs. Starbuck now is mine; cannot oppose me now, without rebellion" (164). Imagining himself like God creating Adam—"And the Lord God formed man of the dust of the ground, and breathed into his nostrils the breath of life; and man became a living soul" (Gen. 2:7)—or a Homeric god inspiring a warrior with martial fortitude, Ahab begins to reveal the tyrannical power he will wield over his crew, and over Starbuck in particular. It is an ironic conclusion to his preceding complaints about divine oppression and injustice. Ahab's condition of enslavement in relation to the deity is thus inversely mirrored in his despotic enslavement of his crew, as his allegedly noble ends are used to justify his ignoble means.

Immediately following Ahab's Job-like challenges to the deity in chapter 36, the four succeeding chapters, ranging from chapter 37 ("Sunset") to chapter 40 ("Midnight, Forecastle"), are taken up with dramatic vignettes describing the repercussions of Ahab's announcement of the *Pequod*'s hitherto unacknowledged mission to kill Moby Dick. So we first find Ahab soliloquizing on the spiritual costs to his planned vengeance, then the devout Starbuck expressing fear of the consequences of Ahab's "blasphemous" quest, then humorous Stubb expressing a comic fatalism about the future, and finally the crew celebrating the hunt with orgiastic revels leading to violence that is interrupted only by the opportunistic arrival of a squall. Each dramatic vignette embodies an illustration of the different reactions to the newly announced mission of the *Pequod* to destroy a monstrous form of evil.[14]

Ahab's soliloquy in chapter 37 begins in a mood of pathos with the captain's meditation, as the sun sinks below the horizon, on the ambiguous symbol of power he feels on his brow: "The diver sun—slow dived from noon,—goes down; my soul mounts up! she wearies with her endless hill. Is, then, the crown too heavy that I wear? this Iron Crown of Lombardy?" (167). With a self-conscious weariness of his soul suggestive of Richard II's well-known meditation on the vicissitudes of kingship in Shakespeare's history play (*Richard II*, III.ii.144–77), Ahab depicts himself wearing a crown symbolizing both despotic political power and Christlike martyrdom. The famous Iron Crown of Lombardy, which allegedly contained a nail from the True Cross, was traditionally used for coronations of Holy Roman emperors and had crowned both Napoleon in 1803 and Franz Joseph in 1848.[15] The implication here is that, following his Job-like challenges to divine justice in "The Quarter-Deck," Ahab has in fact usurped divine power, but the messianic jeweled crown he now wears may also be one of thorns (Matt. 27:29). Ahab accordingly confesses that "the jagged edge galls me so, my brain seems to beat against the solid metal" (167).

Continuing his meditation in "Sunset," Ahab regrets his tragic alienation from the light (or the "good") as a result of his embrace of vengeance. In accents reminiscent of Milton's Satan and Goethe's Faust, Ahab meditates on the "fallenness" of his perceptual powers that has resulted from his intellectual obsession with the sources of evil: "This lovely light, it lights not me; all loveliness is anguish to me, since I can ne'er enjoy. Gifted with the high perception, I lack the low, enjoying power; damned, most subtly and most malignantly! damned in the midst of Paradise!" (167). Ahab's complaint here evokes the portrait of Milton's Satan outside Eden, who reflects on the desolate condition of separation from the original divine sources of his being: "the more I see / Pleasures about me, so much more I feel / Torment within me, as from the hateful siege / Of contraries" (*Paradise Lost*, IX.119–22). Ahab's speech similarly recalls Faust's initial despairing meditation at his desk at night: "I'm not afraid of Hell and the Devil, / But all my joy has left me too" (*Faust*, ll. 369–70).[16]

Yet Ahab's meditation in chapter 37 leads to a reassertion of will to complete his quest. It is here that his direct challenges to the gods again reveal the captain's Job-like protests of injustice, now combined with the prophetic powers of the suffering Greek Titan Prometheus in his defiance of Zeus:

> The prophecy was that I should be dismembered; and—Aye! I lost this leg.
> I now prophesy that I will dismember my dismemberer. Now, then, be the
> prophet and the fulfiller one. That's more than ye, ye great gods, ever were.

I laugh and hoot at ye, ye cricket-players, ye pugilists, ye deaf Burkes and blinded Bendigoes! I will not say as schoolboys do to bullies,—Take some one of your own size; don't pommel *me*! No, ye've knocked me down, and I am up again; but *ye* have run and hidden. Come forth from behind your cotton bags! I have no long gun to reach ye. (168)

While Ahab's allusions to the gods as contemporary prizefighters bespeak his kinship with Prometheus, his sense of unjust punishment and desperate wish to see his opponent continue to imply his Job-like identity. As Philippe Nemo notes, "Job plants himself in God's way and 'looks for' God, like the pugilist who 'looks for' his adversary by the exit-doors in order to settle some old score."[17] Like Ahab, Job obsessively details his physical abuse by God: "I was at ease, but he hath broken me asunder: he hath also taken me by my neck, and shaken me to pieces, and set me up for his mark. / His archers compass me round about, he cleaveth my reins [kidneys] asunder, and doth not spare; he poureth out my gall upon the ground" (16:12–13). And like Ahab, Job complains of the invisibility of the deity, no matter where he searches:

> Oh that I knew where I might find him! that I might come even to his seat!
> I would order my case before him, and fill my mouth with arguments....
> Behold, I go forward, but he is not there; and backward, but I cannot perceive him;
> On the left hand, where he doth work, I cannot behold him: he hideth himself on the right hand, that I cannot see him. (Job 23:3–4, 8–9)

As in his earlier speech in "The Quarter-Deck," Ahab's divine adversary in "Sunset" is still invisible. Ahab is still seeking (literally) "fair play" in his quest for revenge, but it is now the gods who oppose him, not just Moby Dick. His tone has assumed a boisterous humor as he mocks these gods as bullying pugilists who have hidden themselves after striking blows against him. Ahab's challenges here exhibit a paradoxical combination of democratic empowerment and autocratic hubris—a combination that in the next chapter ("Dusk") fills Starbuck with despair as he meditates on Ahab's tyrannical assumption of control over the crew: "Who's over him, he cries;—aye, he would be a democrat to all above; look, how he lords it over all below! Oh! I plainly see my miserable office,—to obey, rebelling; and worse yet, to hate with touch of pity!" (169). Unlike Job's friends, who are confident in their moral rectitude when confronted with the blasphemous Job, Starbuck feels overwhelmed by Ahab's rhetorical and charismatic power. He ends his meditation here with a desperate plea for heaven to support his moral cause against the captain: "Stand by me, hold me, bind me, O ye blessed influences!" (170).

Yet at the end of the sequence of dramatic tableaux in "Midnight, Forecastle," we find an implied refutation of Starbuck's hope for divine protection in the penultimate comments of the old Manx sailor on the readiness with which some of the *Pequod's* crew are willing to fight and possibly kill each other during their orgiastic Walpurgisnacht-like revels. As the oracular Manxman remarks of the ring in which Daggoo and a Spanish sailor are ready to face off, "Ready formed. There! the ringed horizon. In that ring Cain struck Abel. Sweet work, right work! No? Why, then, God, mad'st thou the ring?" (178). The final question highlights the narrative's ongoing representation of the question of theodicy, placing homicide within the larger context of creation theology, asking why a good God would sanction the evil of intrahuman violence and warfare here symbolized by the "ring," a term applicable to both the boxing arena and the world encircled by the horizon.

It is important to note that, while the initial depiction of Ahab's obsession with Moby Dick has an essential biblical dimension, Ahab's fixation on the whale's seemingly deliberate malice is also grounded realistically in the well-attested perils of the contemporary whaling industry. The industry was rife with stories of deadly encounters with aggressive bull sperm whales that fought back against their captors. Unlike other species of whales, sperm whales were dangerous at both ends of their enormous bodies, inflicting damage with their powerful flukes as well as their massive heads and toothed lower jaws. In an 1832 account recorded by Captain John O. Morse of the *Hector* of New Bedford, for example, an angry sperm whale destroyed two boats and then chased a third, which came to its crewmates' rescue, for half a mile. According to a newspaper report of the incident, the whale "seemed to possess the spirit of a demon, and looked as savage as a hungry hyena." While sailing off Chile in 1847, the *Acushnet*—the whaling vessel in which Melville had originally shipped in early 1841—encountered an aggressive sperm whale, which fought against the three whaleboats that harpooned it. After shattering one boat, the whale swam off with another in tow, while the third cut its line in order to come to the aid of the men from the first vessel. The whale eventually turned on and destroyed the third boat, using its flukes to break it to pieces. As one historian of whaling has affirmed: "Plenty of evidence may be found in the old whaling records to substantiate the reputed malevolence of Moby Dick."[18]

We may better understand Ahab's desire for vengeance against Moby Dick, then, if we know something about the deadly nature of the pursuit of sperm whales in which the American whaling industry specialized. The climax to the initial representation of Ahab's desire for vengeance against Moby Dick in retaliation for his dismembering occurs in chapter 41 ("Moby Dick"), in which we are given an extended account of the lethal career of the White Whale. And it is here that the legendary whale is revealingly transformed from a naturalistic to a quasi-mythical identity. After describing the "wild, mystical, sympathetical feeling" (179) that followed his sworn oath to hunt Moby Dick, Ishmael notes that the prolonged voyages and irregular communications in the sperm whale fishery had not allowed for a fully coherent account of Moby Dick's ferocity to become common knowledge, so that whalemen still lowered to hunt him. "But at length, such calamities did ensue in these assaults—not restricted to sprained wrists and ankles, broken limbs, or devouring amputations—but fatal to the last degree of fatality; those repeated disastrous repulses, all accumulating and piling their terrors upon Moby Dick; those things had gone far to shake the fortitude of many brave hunters, to whom the story of the White Whale had eventually come" (180). Such experiences had given birth to wild rumors about the whale, for both the "ignorance and superstitiousness hereditary to all sailors" and their exposure to "whatever is appallingly astonishing in the sea" (180) both predispose the whaleman to such ideas: "No wonder, then, that ever gathering volume from the mere transit over the widest watery spaces, the outblown rumors of the White Whale did in the end incorporate with themselves all manner of morbid hints, and half-formed foetal suggestions of supernatural agencies, which eventually invested Moby Dick with new terrors unborrowed from anything that visibly appears" (181). The two chief ideas that are born from this marriage of nautical superstition and fatal experience are, as Ishmael notes, the belief that Moby Dick is both ubiquitous and immortal; in other words, the White Whale has been magnified to a godlike status in many whalemen's estimation.

Several critics have commented on Melville's use of the mythic imagination in his depiction of the White Whale in chapter 41. Janez Stanonik, for example, has suggested that the symbolic significance of Moby Dick ultimately stems from a variety of nautical legends of a white whale dating from the first half of the nineteenth century, while H. Bruce Franklin has highlighted the manner in which Moby Dick is informed with a mythic identity by drawing on contemporary schools and theories of myth.[19] The characterization of the whale in chapter 41 of *Moby-Dick* is clearly meant to trace the process whereby folktale, legend, and popular superstition combine to create the outlines of a modern mythic belief. Yet Ishmael's bestowal of a mythical status on Moby Dick here is largely dependent on two key literary prototypes: the nineteenth-century "Mocha Dick" of nautical legend and the ancient biblical Leviathan, which together help create an image of the whale as modern avatar of the archetypal chaos monster.[20]

It has long been known that Melville found an initial literary prototype for the White Whale in the account of "Mocha Dick: or the White Whale of the Pacific: A Leaf From a Manuscript Journal" by J. N. Reynolds, published in the May 1839 *Knickerbocker Magazine*.[21] In this exciting nautical adventure tale, the frame narrator, while cruising off the Chilean coastline, listens to the story of the killing of the legendary albino whale Mocha Dick, named after a small Chilean coastal island. The narrator of the story is the first mate of a Nantucket whaler on which the frame narrator is a visitor during a gam. While the indirect method of narration serves to enhance the whale's portentous identity, the depiction of Mocha Dick here hints at the legendary status given by the sailors to Moby Dick, with the difference that the whale in Reynolds's story eventually proves mortal. Reynolds (as frame narrator) writes initially of the uncanny ferocity of Mocha Dick, and he notes that the whale's celebrity continued to increase until Pacific whalemen were in the habit of concluding their meetings at sea with questions of news about Mocha Dick (as Ahab repeatedly does concerning Moby Dick). Taking over the narration of the story, the first mate of the whaler tells of his ship's first encounter with the uncanny-looking whale: "As he drew near, with his long curved back looming occasionally above the surface of the billows, we perceived that it was *white as the surf around him*; and the men stared aghast at each other, as they uttered, in a suppressed tone, the terrible name of MOCHA DICK!" (556). Refusing to be intimidated by the legendary whale, the mate in Reynolds's story urges his harpooner to strike the whale, but the youthful whaleman is unnerved by the sight of its ferocity and barely grazes its back with his harpoon:

> The young harpooner, though ordinarily as fearless as a lion, had imbibed a sort of superstitious dread of Mocha Dick, from the exaggerated stories of that prodigy, which he had heard from his comrades. He regarded him, as he had heard him described in many a tough yarn during the middle watch, rather as some ferocious fiend of the deep, than a regular-built, legitimate whale! Judge then of his trepidation, on beholding a creature, answering the wildest dreams of his fancy, and sufficiently formidable, without any superadded terrors, bearing down upon him with thrashing flukes and distended jaws! (556)

After two ineffectual harpoons are thrown, the whale escapes: "The giant animal swept on for a few rods, and then, as if in contempt of our fruitless and childish attempt to injure him, flapped a storm of spray in our faces with his broad tail, and dashed far down into the depths of the ocean, leaving our little skiff among the waters where he sank, to spin and duck in the whirlpool" (556). After a remarkably dramatic buildup, however, the seemingly unassailable whale is unexpectedly killed, thanks to the heroic stamina of the mate. The final message of the story is thus not the uncanny power and ferocity of the whale but the intrepid courage of the American whaleman as the narrative shifts emphasis from nautical sensationalism to spread-eagle patriotism.

Like the historical records of nineteenth-century American whaling, Reynolds's story of the fabled albino sperm whale Mocha Dick demonstrates that the legendary aura and imputed malevolence of Melville's Moby Dick had ample precedent in the sperm whale fishery. Yet when we compare Melville's whale with its literary prototype in "Mocha Dick," it is immediately apparent that Moby Dick has been given a more complex mythic identity, and this complexity stems largely from Melville's association of the White Whale with the Leviathan of the Old Testament. Thus, Ahab's whale is not only a deadly bull sperm whale but also the embodiment of a primordial chaos monster present since the creation, as implied in Job chapter 41. Based on the importance of Job both in the characterization of Ahab and in the depiction of his monstrous opponent, we may even go so far as to say that Melville's naming of his whale *Moby* Dick, based on Reynolds's original *Mocha* Dick, is probably attributable to the centrality of the book of Job in Melville's narrative.[22]

In chapter 41 of *Moby-Dick* we become familiar with the aura of legend that surrounds the White Whale because of the frequently fatal experiences of those who encountered it and to the power of sailor superstition to magnify its lethal power. To this is added the still sketchy facts of the natural history of the sperm whale, which confirm the remarkable distances that it swims and the still unfathomed mysteries of its deep-sea existence. All of this leads up to Ishmael's extended representation of both the imaginary impression and the actual appearance of the White Whale, together with the ascription of an intelligent and almost supernatural malignity to its career: "Forced into familiarity then, with such prodigies as these; and knowing that after repeated, intrepid assaults, the White Whale had escaped alive; it cannot be much matter of surprise that some whalemen should go still further in their superstitions; declaring Moby Dick not only ubiquitous, but immortal (for immortality is but ubiquity in time)" (183). The combination of the whale's uncommon bulk, peculiar snow-white wrinkled forehead, and "high, pyramidical white hump" terrify the whale's pursuers, as well as the "unexampled intelligent malignity which according to specific accounts, he had over and over again evinced in his assaults" (183).

> Already several fatalities had attended his chase. But though similar disasters, however little bruited ashore, were by no means unusual in the fishery; yet, in most instances, such seemed the White Whale's infernal aforethought of ferocity, that every dismembering or death that he caused, was not wholly regarded as having been inflicted by an unintelligent agent.
>
> Judge, then, to what pitches of inflamed, distracted fury the minds of his more desperate hunters were impelled, when amid the chips of chewed boats, and the sinking limbs of torn comrades, they swam out of the white curds of the whale's direful wrath into the serene, exasperating sunlight, that smiled on, as if at a birth or a bridal. (183–84)

On close examination, it is evident that the implicit mythical basis for the characterization of the White Whale in chapter 41 of *Moby-Dick* is God's portrayal of the indomitable Leviathan of chapter 41 in Job, and it is probably no coincidence that both mythical whales are found in the same chapter of their respective texts.[23] In Job 41, the predominant feature of Leviathan is its immunity to assault from any human foe, as the divine Voice from the Whirlwind indicates when it discounts the force of any weapons that may be used against the sea monster (Job 41:26–29). Ishmael's image of Moby Dick as invulnerable to attack by the tools of the whaling trade suggests the basic message of this passage from Job, just as the images of the White Whale's destructive wake—"white curds of the whale's direful wrath"—are reminiscent of the shiny, hoary path the Leviathan leaves behind: "He maketh a path to shine after him; one would think the deep to be hoary" (Job 41:32). And just as Moby Dick seems a creature of "unexampled, intelligent malignity," the image of Leviathan in Job seems to embody God's contemptuous attitude toward humanity as evinced by his sarcastic tauntings to Job, as well as Leviathan's exhibition of humanlike perception and volition—he "esteemeth," "laugheth," "maketh," "beholdeth" (Job 41:27, 29, 31, 34), which allegedly all demonstrate (as in Moby Dick) an "infernal aforethought of ferocity."

If the Leviathan of chapter 41 of Job is an implicit model for the image of the White Whale in chapter 41 of *Moby-Dick*, the narrative reveals the obsession with revenge that motivates Ahab against Moby Dick after the whale has bitten off Ahab's leg:

> The White Whale swam before him as the monomaniac incarnation of all those malicious agencies which some deep men feel eating in them, till they are left living on with half a heart and half a lung. That intangible malignity which has been from the beginning; to whose dominion even the modern Christians ascribe one-half of the worlds; which the ancient Ophites of the east reverenced in their statue devil;—Ahab did not fall down and worship it like them; but deliriously transferring its idea to the abhorred white whale, he pitted himself, all mutilated, against it. All that most maddens and torments; all that stirs up the lees of things; all truth with malice in it; all that cracks the sinews and cakes the brain; all the subtle demonisms of life and thought; all evil, to crazy Ahab, were visibly personified, and made practically assailable in Moby Dick. He piled upon the whale's white hump the sum of all the general rage and hate felt by his whole race from Adam down; and then, as if his chest had been a mortar, he burst his hot heart's shell upon it. (184)

The well-known description of Ahab's demonization of Moby Dick here is made more comprehensible when we realize that the mad captain's monomania against the whale is a morbid combination of narcissistic rage, messianic violence, and atavistic mythologizing in which a modern Leviathan is given the creature's original biblical significance as a primeval marine chaos monster. Joseph Adamson has astutely demonstrated the degree to which Ahab suffers from the shameful mortification of his disabling injury by the whale and the narcissistic injury to the ego that ensues.[24] Such a physical and psychic injury leads to a mythological reaction formation. In Ahab's imagination, evil has become a metaphysical principle associated with the "intangible malignity" allegedly present at the creation, acknowledged by modern Christians (in the person of the devil), and worshipped in the ancient world by the Gnostic sect of Ophites (as discussed in Irenaeus's *Against Heresies* and Origen's *Against Celsus*), who revered the serpent of Eden for communicating knowledge of good and evil to Adam and Eve, thus enlightening them about the evil Demiurge who allegedly created the world. Already an opponent of Christianity before the loss of his leg (as we have learned from the prophet Elijah), Ahab underwent a deliriously painful ordeal in the weeks following the injury, during which he became insanely fixated on the idea that the White Whale was a monstrous embodiment of cosmic evil.

The archetypal nature of Moby Dick's identity is evident in the description of Ahab's mythologizing of the whale into a symbol of evil that has existed from the beginnings of the human race; indeed, it is coextensive with the universe, either as part of the divine nature or as a separate but equal entity. As the incarnation of all "intangible malignity" and "all the subtle demonisms of life and thought" (184), Moby Dick is manifestly a modern embodiment of the chaos monster (or demon) of ancient Near Eastern myth—a creature embodying the symbolic form of all the destructive forces in the cosmos to the pre-Christian cultures of this region, as Joseph Fontenrose notes:

> The chaos demon (or demons) represented not only primeval disorder, but all dreadful forces that remain in the world and periodically threaten the god-won order: hurricane, flood, fire, volcanic eruption, earthquake, eclipse, disease, famine, war, crime, winter, darkness, death. They imagined either that the demon himself came back to life and renewed combat, or that his progeny continued the war against the cosmos, ever striving for disorder and a return to primeval inactivity. His death amounted to no more than banishment from the ordered world: he was cast into the outer darkness beneath the earth or beyond it, that is, he was thrown back into the primeval chaos from which he came, where he and his minions lived on, ever ready to invade the god-established order and undo the whole work of creation. For the cosmos has been won from the chaos that still surrounds it, as a cultivated plot from the encompassing wilderness.[25]

In the book of Job and elsewhere, the sea-inhabiting Leviathan subdued by God was a primordial creature of insuperable destructive power and the ultimate justification for divine control of the universe. In the Old Testament chaos monster tradition, human sinfulness can awaken the temporarily vanquished forces of evil and disorder subdued by God at the creation. Ahab's blasphemous acts on land and sea before his fateful meeting with Moby Dick are, in this mythic paradigm, potential grounds for the appearance of the White Whale as divine nemesis.

Ishmael's ensuing description of the etiology of Ahab's mental condition provides key documentation of the combination of physical and metaphysical causes of Ahab's "monomania," the recently coined term to describe a form of madness in which delusions on certain subjects do not disturb rational function in other areas of mental life. Ahab's monomania did not take "its instant rise at the precise time of his bodily dismemberment" (184); it was only during his long voyage back to Nantucket that "his torn body and gashed soul bled into one another; and so interfusing, made him mad" (185).

In reaction to the excruciating pain of his injury, the captain for a time raved in madness, but as his body healed, Ahab, "in his hidden self, raved on. Human madness is oftentimes a cunning and most feline thing. When you think it fled, it may have but become transfigured into some still subtler form. Ahab's full lunacy subsided not, but deepeningly contracted" (185). His final mental condition is a paradox revealingly expressed in a rhetorical figure of chiasmus for, "in his narrow-flowing monomania, not one jot of Ahab's broad madness had been left behind; so in that broad madness, not one jot of his great natural intellect had perished" (185).[26]

Ahab's monomania aligns the captain with a distinctively modern form of mental illness that was thought to be particularly characteristic of the unsettled conditions of democratic America, as Joan Burbick has shown.[27] Burbick thus demonstrates how the whaling captain's monomania is grounded in the national discourse of mental and physical health, in which mental labor was valorized within the developing ideology of middle-class life. Such cerebral exertions, together with their attendant risks of obsession, paranoia, insomnia, and exhaustion, were associated with the destiny of the nation. According to contemporary medical thought, monomania led to "moral insanity"—the loss of a sense of good and evil, alienation from family and friends, and a morbid preference for solitude—for which the career of Melville's whaling captain provides an abundance of evidence. The only cure for such a condition was thought to be emotional and psychological reintegration with loved ones, an option repeatedly shunned by Ahab throughout the latter chapters of the novel in several scenes with Starbuck and Pip.

While Ahab's monomania has a firm cultural grounding in the antebellum discourse of mental health, in his obsession with a single source for all his bodily and spiritual woes, Ahab nevertheless shows his archetypal Job-like identity for throughout the book of Job the protagonist is similarly obsessed with the single assumed source of his suffering. As John T. Wilcox notes, "one of the striking features of this book is the way in which Job fastens *exclusively* on God as the source of the world's evils, as if he saw little efficacy in the natural and human forces which—on the surface—caused those evils."[28] Yet implicit in the description of Ahab's obsession with revenge against Moby Dick as a personification of archetypal evil (chapter 41) is not only the mythological symbolism of Job but also the basic tenets of Gnosticism. Ishmael's reference to Ahab's attempt to embody the general "rage and hate felt by the whole race from Adam down" (184) implies an allusion to humanity's mythic progenitor as a Gnostic symbol of primeval man, who was surrounded by the evil creation of the Demiurge and must seek to overcome his entrapped spiritual condition through the attainment of knowledge of his divine origins, indicated by an interior spark of light. This Gnostic theme is elaborated in the description of Ahab's "larger, darker, deeper part" (185), which lies hidden inside him, just as (to make an archaeological analogy) the modern Hotel de Cluny in Paris is built over an older subterranean Roman Hall of Thermes, a historical site that Melville had visited in December 1849:

> This is much; yet Ahab's larger, darker, deeper part remains unhinted. But vain to popularize profundities, and all truth is profound. Winding far down from within the very heart of this spiked Hotel de Cluny where we here stand—however grand and wonderful, now quit it;—and take your way, ye nobler, sadder souls, to those vast Roman halls of Thermes; where far beneath the fantastic towers of man's upper earth, his root of grandeur, his whole awful essence sits in bearded state; an antique buried beneath antiquities, and throned on torsos! So with a broken throne, the great gods mock that captive king; so like a Caryatid, he patient sits, upholding on his frozen brow the piled entablatures of ages. Wind ye down there, ye prouder, sadder souls! Question that proud, sad king! A family likeness! aye, he did beget ye, ye young exiled royalties; and from your grim sire only will the old State-secret come. (185–86)

Harrison Hayford has explored the potential mix of mythical (Adam, Enceladus, Prometheus, Atlas), literary (Milton's Satan, Keats's Hyperion, Byron's rebellious heroes), and biographical sources for Ishmael's pregnant image of the "captive king," noting that similar motifs of physical and psychological incarceration are found throughout Melville's later fiction.[29] William B. Dillingham, on the other hand, has argued that the comparison of Ahab's identity with the underground "captive king" is a version of the mythical Adam buried within the Gnostic adept, in keeping with the Gnostic belief in human entrapment within the physical universe.[30] The identification of this "captive king" with a mythical Adam figure (and thus Ahab) is in fact confirmed near the end of the novel, in "The Symphony," when Ahab tells Starbuck, "I feel deadly faint, bowed, and humped, as though I were Adam, staggering beneath the piled centuries since Paradise" (544).

The captive king is indeed a figure of the "Old Adam," but since the Gnostic theme in *Moby-Dick* frequently overlaps with questions of theodicy dramatized in the book of Job, the image of the captive king may be seen as a conflation of Gnostic and Joban paradigms. In the book of Job chapter

15, Eliphaz accuses him of assuming the role of an Adamic "primal man" who was possessed of a wisdom that came from divine sources: "Art thou the first man that was born? or wast thou made before the hills? / Hast thou heard the secret of God? And dost thou restrain wisdom to thyself? / What knowest thou, that we know not? what understandest thou, which is not in us?" (Job 15:7–9).The first man referred to here is a primeval Adam figure, deputized by God to live in Paradise and guard the tree of life—the basis for the Near Eastern myth that formed the foundation of the story of the Garden of Eden.[31] In the myth, this "first" or primal man rebels against God by attempting to assume the divine status of the creator by obtaining the knowledge or wisdom that is the exclusive preserve of God, as in fact occurred when Adam and Eve ate the fruit of the tree of knowledge. The first couple's eating of the fruit, of course, leads to the punishment of exile, toil, pain, and death. Related myths of disastrous overreaching for a godlike status relevant to Ahab's case can also be found in the biblical attack on the divine presumptions of the King of Babylon as a light-bringing god of the dawn (Lucifer) in Isaiah 14, and in the critique of the overreaching ambitions of the prince of Tyre in Ezekiel 28, in which the primal man attempts to occupy the throne of God and is hurled from the sacred mountain El into the pit of hell.

This archetypal Old Testament myth of human overreaching is implicitly invoked in the description of the captive king in chapter 41 of *Moby-Dick*, an archaeological embodiment of Ahab's subconscious mind reminiscent of Jung's psychic model of the collective unconscious. Just as Ahab has recently announced his attempt to usurp the role of divine warrior in his desire to kill Moby Dick, a modern incarnation of the primordial chaos monster, the "proud, sad king" sits buried underground, a monitory figure mocked by the gods for his attempt to usurp their privileges of supreme knowledge and immortality. The Adam figure here is undoubtedly called a "king" because in the myth of Eden, Adam was initially God's vice regent on earth and a de facto king of creation. In his fallen condition this antique Adam is, genealogically speaking, humanity's regal "root of grandeur" sitting on a broken, postlapsarian throne. In a final rhetorical gesture, Ishmael tells humanity's "prouder, sadder souls" to question this buried statue of their progenitor concerning their genealogy; they are in fact "exiled royalties" because of the Fall, and only from this silent stony Adam can they attain the "State-secret" of the creation.[32]

Given the pervasive presence of the book of Job in chapter 41 of *Moby-Dick* and indeed throughout the novel, it is only fitting that the chapter ends with an explicit reference to this biblical text in Ishmael's summary description of the voyage of the *Pequod*, led by an autocratic captain who has mysteriously inspired his crew with his own private, infatuated obsession with revenge against a "Job's whale": "Here, then, was this grey-headed, ungodly old man, chasing with curses a Job's whale around the world, at the head of a crew, too, chiefly made up of mongrel renegades, and castaways, and cannibals" (186). While this description depicts Ahab as though he is engaged in an act of futility and pathos, the nature of Ahab's ultimate hold on his crew is more sinister:

> Such a crew, so officered, seemed specially picked and packed by some infernal fatality to help him to his monomaniac revenge. How it was that they so aboundingly responded to the old man's ire—by what evil magic their souls were possessed, that at times his hate seemed almost theirs; the White Whale as much their insufferable foe as his; how all this came to be—what the White Whale was to them, or how to their unconscious understandings, also, in some dim, unsuspected way, he might have seemed the gliding great demon of the seas of life,—all this to explain, would be to dive deeper than Ishmael can go. (187)

Ishmael confesses himself unable to fathom the psychological depths of the crew's cooperation with Ahab's mission, but we can assume that it is largely based on the charismatic nature of Ahab's authority, the naturally superstitious minds of the crew, and the archetypal nature of the creature they are pursuing. Ahab's galvanizing of the crew for revenge is, in modern parlance, a form of male bonding that results in a mission-driven cult led by a fanatical and autocratic cult leader.

It is readily apparent, then, that Ahab's quarrel with Moby Dick—as depicted in chapters 28, 36, 37, and 41 of Melville's novel—borrows extensively from the argument in the book of Job in which a morally innocent Job challenges God to justify the reasons for his suffering. So, too, the initial depiction of the legendary White Whale patently evokes the mythic Leviathan of Job. We have seen that Ahab's speeches offer many similar rhetorical strategies to those found in Job, as well as Job-like indictments of God's seeming responsibility for worldly evil. Yet these same chapters of the novel are also laced with hints about the potentially apocalyptic nature of the *Pequod*'s voyage. With Ahab's personal appearance in chapter 28 we get an extensive representation of the images and motifs that will govern this biblical paradigm. While the sailing of the *Pequod* on

Christmas Day prepares us for a view of Ahab as messianic redeemer, the symbolic identity that emerges from chapters 28, 36, and 41 is of a man who simultaneously embodies both great suffering and sin, evoking the examples of Job, Milton's Satan, and the apocalyptic image of the devil and Antichrist from the New Testament.[33]

If Melville's Ahab is initially described as looking "like a man cut away from the stake" (a description hinting at the fate of a victim of the Spanish Inquisition), the first distinctive physical characteristic that Ishmael notices is the remarkable scar that extends from the top of his head "down one side of his tawny scorched face and neck, till it disappeared in his clothing" (123). Ahab's scar evokes Milton's initial portrait of Satan:

> but his face
> Deep scars of Thunder had intrencht, and care
> Sat on his faded cheek, but under Browes
> Of dauntless courage, and considerate Pride
> Waiting Revenge:
> 　　　　　　(*Paradise Lost*, I.600–604)

Ahab's blasted features and Satan-like overweening pride are suitable for his apocalyptic role as divine adversary and Antichrist. We have already noted the resemblance of Ahab's scar to the mark of Cain as well as to the physical affliction of Job. A third possible association here is to the "mark of the beast," which characterizes those dedicated to the service of the devil, serpent, false prophet, and Antichrist, as described in Revelation 13:16. Ahab's satanic associations and his role as end-time counterpart to Christ are both apparent in his initial characterization, which blends stubborn pride and superhuman suffering in the manner of Milton's Satan: "There was an infinity of firmest fortitude, a determinate, unsurrenderable wilfullness, in the fixed and fearless, forward dedication of that glance." However, Ahab's appearance also conveys tragic pathos in the look of "crucifixion in his face; and in all the nameless regal overbearing dignity of some mighty woe" (124).

Ahab's formal announcement in "The Quarter Deck" that the real goal of the voyage of the *Pequod* will be the killing of Moby Dick gives additional details to Ahab's antichristian identity. In this chapter Ahab reveals it was Moby Dick that sheared off his leg, and he arouses the excitement of the crew to hunt the whale, offering the gold doubloon as a reward to the seaman who first sights it. In response to Starbuck's dismayed reaction to his newly announced quest for the whale, Ahab elaborates on the metaphysical significance of the White Whale as an agent or principal of divine malice, in the process representing himself with all the pride of Milton's Satan, as when he claims that he would "strike the sun" if it insulted him. We have already looked at this speech in the context of Ahab's Joban identity; we must now look at it from the perspective of its explicitly antichristian message, for Ahab's defiant pride also evokes, among other things, that "man of sin" and "son of perdition; Who opposeth and exalteth himself above all that is called God, or that is worshipped" (2 Thess. 2:3–4). The word "sun" in Ahab's speech also implicitly draws on the traditional Christian pun of sun/son, based on the conflation of Christ with the "Sun of righteousness" mentioned in Malachi 4:2. In his announcement of vengeance against Moby Dick, Ahab deliberately subverts the Christian doctrine of nonviolence as set forth in the Sermon on the Mount: "resist not evil; but whosoever shall smite thee on thy right check, turn to him the other also" (Matt. 5:39). Ahab, on the contrary, will tolerate no "sun" of righteousness to dictate a passive acceptance of evil but will instead embrace the well-known *lex talionis* of the Mosaic Law (Exod. 21:24–25).

In keeping with his antichristian identity, Ahab seeks to obtain the fanatical devotion of his crew now by having them perform a mock Black Mass, beginning with a shared drink of grog and continuing with a sacrilegious ceremony of crossed lances and harpoons held by his three mates and three harpooners. The elaborately antichristian nature of the ceremony is confirmed by Ahab's inverted allusions to traditional Christian ritual. Ahab thus begins by passing grog around to all his crew, which fills them with demonic energy: "Round with it, round! Short draughts—long swallows, men; 'tis hot as Satan's hoof. So, so; it goes round excellently. It spiralizes in ye; forks out at the serpent-snapping eye" (165). Ahab instructs his three mates to cross their lances so that he can charge them with his electrical energy by grasping the lances at their intersection, a galvanizing exercise that mocks the vivifying nature of the mass while it plays on the new thaumaturgical "science" of animal magnetism or mesmerism.[34]

After this ritual, Ahab insists that his three "Christian" mates pay homage to his three pagan harpooners: "And now, ye mates, I do appoint ye three cupbearers to my three pagan kinsmen there—you three most honorable gentleman and noblemen, my valiant harpooners. Disdain the task? What, when the great Pope washes the feet of beggars, using his tiara for ewer? Oh, my sweet cardinals! your own condescension, *that* shall bend ye to it" (166). Implicit in Ahab's sacrilegious analogy here is the long Protestant tradition of identifying the pope as a potential Antichrist. Requiring that Christian serve pagan in his mock communion, Ahab finishes the ritual by having his three mates offer the three harpooners drinks from the sockets of the up-ended harpoon irons. As satanic priest, Ahab desecrates the traditional meaning of the communion by calling the harpoon sockets "murderous chalices" and then commands the crew to swear a formal oath of vengeance against the White Whale: "Death to Moby Dick!" (166). Ahab's actions, dominating his crew and demonizing Moby Dick, set in place a process that will lead to the captain's moral corruption and spiritual damnation despite the heroic nature of his philosophical quest. For Ahab's assumption of absolute control over his crew represents his commitment of the unpardonable sin of violating others' spiritual autonomy—a theme often associated with the fiction of Melville's friend Hawthorne in such characters as Roger Chillingworth and Ethan Brand.[35]

If Ahab's quasi-religious ritual of binding his crew to his mission of revenge evokes the prophet Isaiah's "covenant with death, and with hell" (Isa. 28:15), Ahab's act also has close ties to the Faust legend. Indeed, in the later uncanny appearance of Fedallah on the *Pequod* we find the Mephistophelean figure with whom Ahab has entered into his Faustian pact. In a subsequent sequence of chapters, we witness Ahab's demonic "possession" by Fedallah, who emerges as an apocalyptic figure incorporating elements of the prosecutorial satan of the book of Job, the traditional demonic Satan of the New Testament, and the empowering and enabling Mephistopheles of the Faust dramas of Marlowe and Goethe.[36]

In chapter 44 ("The Chart"), Ahab is seen poring over a set of nautical charts in order to calculate the probable location of Moby Dick at certain times of the year—a calculation based on the fact that sperm whales have predictable times and locations for feeding throughout the oceans of the world. The result of such calculations is that Ahab will seek the White Whale during the Season-on-the-Line, that is, along the equator in the mid-Pacific at the beginning of the year. The *Pequod* thus has a year to hunt for whales until the ship reaches the Pacific after cruising south in the Atlantic, rounding the Cape of Good Hope, passing through the Indian Ocean, and then finally entering the Pacific at a time when Moby Dick may be found in its known feeding grounds. Ahab's intense scrutiny of his charts in chapter 44 leads to the onset of a kind of demonic possession, as his ongoing obsession with the whale creates a transformation in both his work habits and his personality. The image of Ahab's obsession with revenge here first shows him as a tormented demonic antitype of the crucified Christ: "Ah, God! what trances of torments does that man endure who is consumed with one unachieved revengeful desire. He sleeps with clenched hands; and wakes with his own bloody nails in his palms" (201).[37] The ensuing description of Ahab's state of mind provides a key insight into the etiology of Ahab's tortured and demon-haunted madness, together with his tortured Joban predicament:

> Often, when forced from his hammock by exhausting and intolerably vivid dreams of the night, which, resuming his own intense thoughts through the day, carried them on amid a clashing of phrensies, and whirled them round and round in his blazing brain, till the very throbbing of his life-spot became insufferable anguish; and when, as was sometimes the case, these spiritual throes in him heaved his being up from its base, and a chasm seemed opening in him, from which forked flames and lightnings shot up, and accursed fiends beckoned him to leap down among them; when this hell in himself yawned beneath him, a wild cry would be heard through the ship; and with glaring eyes Ahab would burst from his state room, as though escaping from a bed that was on fire. (201–2)

Ahab's nighttime anguish duplicates that of the tormented Job, whose condition is not relieved by sleep, as the latter reveals in his first answer to Eliphaz:

> As a servant earnestly desireth the shadow, and as an hireling looketh for the reward of his work:
> So am I made to possess months of vanity, and wearisome nights are appointed to me.
> When I lie down, I say, When shall I arise, and the night be gone? and I am full of tossings to and fro unto the dawning of the day. . . .
> Am I a sea, or a whale, that thou settest a watch over me?
> When I say, My bed shall comfort me, my couch shall ease my complaint;
> Then thou scarest me with dreams and terrifiest me through visions:
> So that my soul chooseth strangling, and death rather than life.
> (Job 7:2–4, 12–15)

In an ironic transformation of Job's complaint at 7:12, which plays on the notion of God as the vigilant guardian over the chaos monster (here appearing as "sea" and "whale"), Ahab is himself keeping close watch over the whale, which represents the same type of mythical creature to him. And like Job, Ahab finds no relief in sleep but is tormented by terrifying dreams and visions, effectively reducing him to the misery of a slave.

Unlike Job, however, the visions that Ahab sees are specifically demonic in nature, as hell seems to open up from his subconscious mind in a manner more suggestive of the Faust legend than the story of Job. The description of Ahab's complex oceanographic calculations and mental perturbations in his cabin (a nautical version of the alchemist's study, as described in chapter 44) represents a dramatic counterpart to the scene of Faust's formal bond with the devil found in both Marlowe's and Goethe's versions of the story. Ahab's mental transformation is depicted as an amalgam of faculty psychology, Christian demonology, and classical mythology, all rooted in the self-willed damnation of the German overreacher and suggestive of both Aeschylus's bound Titan and Mary Shelley's gothic monster and its creator. Ahab is thus seen fleeing in horror from his hammock at night, when his "living principle or soul" sought escape from the "scorching contiguity" of the "characterizing mind":

> But as the mind does not exist unless leagued with the soul, therefore it must have been that, in Ahab's case, yielding up all his thoughts and fancies to his one supreme purpose; that purpose, by its own sheer inveteracy of will, forced itself against gods and devils into a kind of self-assumed, independent being of its own. Nay, could grimly live and burn, while the common vitality to which it was conjoined, fled horror-stricken from the unbidden and unfathered birth. Therefore, the tormented spirit that glared out of bodily eyes, when what seemed Ahab rushed from his room, was for the time but a vacated thing, a formless somnambulistic being, a ray of living light, to be sure, but without an object to color, and therefore a blankness in itself. God help thee, old man, thy thoughts have created a creature in thee; and he whose intense thinking thus makes him a Prometheus; a vulture feeds upon that heart for ever; that vulture the very creature he creates. (202)

The elaborate battle described here is between Ahab's revenge-obsessed mind and his life principle or soul, which in sleep flees in horror from the faculty that has usurped its proper function and declared itself independent. Ahab's traumatic conflict suggests the mental condition of not only Job but also Aeschylus's Prometheus, Marlowe's Faustus, Milton's Satan, and Goethe's Faust. At the end of Aeschylus's play in Elizabeth Barrett Browning's translation, for example, Zeus's acquiescent messenger Hermes gives a preview of Prometheus's agonizing torture, claiming that it would be his own fault for violating divine authority:

and Zeus's winged hound,
The strong carnivorous eagle, shall wheel down
To meet thee,—self-called to a daily feast,—
And set his fierce beak in thee, and tear off
The long rags of thy flesh, and batten deep
Upon thy dusky liver! Do not look
For any end, moreover, to this curse,
Or ere some god appear, to bear thy pangs
On his own head vicarious, and descend
With unreluctant step the darks of hell,
And the deep glooms enringing Tartarus!—[38]

Unlike the callous Hermes, Ishmael laments Ahab's "sheer inveteracy of will" in his obsessive pursuit of the White Whale, thus resembling the chorus of Aeschylus's play more than the divine messenger.

Ahab's intense study of his nautical charts and resulting split in his personality similarly recalls Marlowe's Doctor Faustus, who signs his bond with Mephistopheles despite an initial physiological reaction against doing so (his blood refuses to flow to provide a medium for writing). Thus, in answer to Faustus's question about the location of hell, Marlowe's Mephistopheles informs his new victim that "Hell hath no limits, nor is circumscribed / In one self place, for where we are is hell, / And where hell is must we ever be" (Scene 5, ll. 123–25). In Milton's epic as well, Satan confessed that wherever he went he carried a hell within himself: "Which way I fly is Hell; myself am Hell" (*Paradise Lost*, IV.75). Finally, the description of Ahab's condition also exemplifies Faust's famous lament in Goethe's play: "Alas, I house two souls in me / And each from each wants separation" (ll. 1112–13).[39]

As an illustration of what antebellum psychology called monomania, Ahab appears to be the victim here of a psychotic breakdown, depicted in the older language of mental illness as spirit possession. The final comparison with the fate of Prometheus emphasizes that Ahab's aggravated melancholy and his quest for forbidden secrets create a pathologically self-destructive *psychomachia* in accordance with the Renaissance image of the Greek Titan suffering a self-inflicted mental punishment, as found in the writings of Francis Bacon and Robert Burton.[40] In like manner, the monster created by Dr. Frankenstein in Mary Shelley's novel turned against his creator; and the description of the "unbidden and unfathered birth" of the monstrous transformation of Ahab would seem to suggest the comparable doppelgänger-like creature found in *Frankenstein*. What is being described in Ahab's case in "The Chart" is nothing less than the birth of an independent demonic agent within his mind, soon to take the tangible form of the ghostly Fedallah, who occupies a borderland between hallucination and reality as a kind of exterior soul of Ahab.[41]

Following the symbolic birth of a demonic agent within Ahab, we find the captain beginning the hunt for other sperm whales besides Moby Dick in order to occupy the time before the arrival at the Season-on-the-Line and to demonstrate to the officers and crew that the quest for the White Whale will not undermine the *Pequod's* commercial mission, as Ishmael sets forth in a chapter entitled "Surmises." It is during the first whale hunt that we discover the existence of the Parsee Fedallah and his mysterious crew of Malay sailors who will man Ahab's whaleboat. As Ahab's demonic familiar, and in exchange for his soul, Fedallah gives Ahab access to forbidden power and knowledge, according to the model of Mephistopheles and Faust. As a version of the satan of the book of Job, Goethe's Mephistopheles is given license to test Faust, whom God believes to be essentially good. The newly identified source for Melville's notes on an imagined Faustian pact with the devil—inscribed in the back of his copy of the seventh volume of Shakespeare's plays—confirms that the original Faust story, with its reformulation by Marlowe and Goethe, was, in addition to his biblical models, a key source for the conception of Ahab, particularly in relation to Fedallah.[42]

Like Mephistopheles, Fedallah is allied to the powers of blackness, yet he is not simply a two-dimensional devil but rather a portmanteau figure— prophet, psychopomp, devil, fire-worshipper, and envoy of fate—who acts as Ahab's nihilistic shadow and nemesis, ultimately perishing in anticipation of Ahab's own death. Such a composite identity would explain the relevance of Fedallah's Arabic name, "servant" or "sacrifice" of God. Possessed of an Islamic name because of Arabian conquest of Persia in the seventh and eighth centuries, Fedallah is a Parsee, the name given to adherents of the Zoroastrian religion who fled Persia for the northwest coast of India in the tenth century. As a biblically inspired presence, Fedallah assumes the symbolic role of the divinely sanctioned "lying spirit," who misleads the Israelite King Ahab to fight against the Syrians at Ramoth-gilead; he is also affiliated symbolically with the satanic adversary in both Job and Revelation. A metaphysical double agent, Fedallah thus fills the ambiguous role of "prosecuting attorney" of the deity (as in Job) and God's ostensible apocalyptic adversary (as in Revelation).[43]

Fedallah and his exotic crew are first described in chapter 48 ("The First Lowering"), when they emerge from their seclusion in the hold of the *Pequod* to hunt the first whale of the ship's voyage:

> The figure that now stood by its bows was tall and swart, with one white tooth evilly protruding from its steel-like lips. A rumpled Chinese jacket of black cotton funereally invested him, with wide black trowsers of the same dark stuff. But strangely crowning this ebonness was a glistening white plaited turban, the living hair braided and coiled round and round upon his head. Less swart in aspect, the companions of this figure were of that vivid, tiger-yellow complexion peculiar to some of the aboriginal natives of the Manillas;—a race notorious for a certain diabolism of subtilty, and by some honest white mariners supposed to be the paid spies and secret confidential agents on the water of the devil, their lord, whose counting room they suppose to be elsewhere. (217)

Fedallah exhibits a countenance and dress combining black and white, a likely comment on his ambiguous moral identity, while the plaited turban of white hair and the single fang-like tooth, "evilly protruding from its steel-like lips," contribute a serpentine, diabolic aspect to the image. The portrait of Fedallah and his crew is obviously intended to evoke a gothic frisson in the reader, based on their association with the "aboriginal" East that would later haunt Joseph Conrad's imagination. An embodiment of non-Western, Asiatic identity, Fedallah thus bears an Arabic name, practices a Persian religion, comes from the Indian subcontinent, wears a Chinese jacket, and is accompanied by a Malay crew. Yet a key factor in Fedallah's moral identity is his ancestral Zoroastrian faith, the oldest revealed religion in the world.[44]

A dualistic religion founded by the Indo-Iranian prophet Zoroaster (or more properly, Zarathustra) more than a thousand years before Christ, Zoroastrianism is based on the idea of a combat between the forces of goodness and light, embodied in the god Ormuzd, and the forces of evil and darkness, embodied in the god Ahriman.[45] At the end of time, the forces of good, embodied in a world savior, will triumph and evil be permanently destroyed at the Last Day. Adherents worship fire as the primary symbol of the godhead, just as Fedallah worships the fire of the corposants in chapter 119 ("The Candles"). The presence of a Parsee with an Islamic name as Ahab's closest adviser confirms the captain's rejection of the Christian religion, in keeping with the history of his biblical prototype King Ahab, who was punished by Yahweh for admitting the worship of the Canaanite god Baal into Israel. Fedallah's Zoroastrian fire worship thus ambiguously blends with his diabolical identity, while the predominantly black color of his dress and appearance implies the ascendency of the forces of darkness in his character. As a modern Zoroastrian, Fedallah is an adherent to a dualistic religion that has been linked to the development of the genre of apocalyptic writing that flourished in late Second Temple Judaism and early Christianity. The Parsee's association with this tradition was anticipated early in the novel when the sailor prophet Elijah warned Ishmael and Queequeg about the phantom shapes boarding the *Pequod* and claimed he would not see the two new crew members until the Last Judgment.

Potential confirmation of Fedallah's apocalyptic and demonic identity takes place during the first lowering for whales, when all the *Pequod*'s whaleboats are in eager pursuit and each officer exhibits different verbal means of inspiring the crew to row harder. In contrast to the inventive and colorful humor employed by Flask and Stubb with their crews, Ahab's verbal incitement of his savage-looking crew involves pronouncing words that are literally unspeakable: "But what it was that inscrutable Ahab said to that tiger-yellow crew of his—these were words best omitted here; for you live under the blessed light of the evangelical land. Only the infidel sharks in the audacious seas may give ear to such words, when, with tornado brow, and eyes of red murder, and foam-glued lips, Ahab leaped after his prey" (223). One can only guess what blasphemous, incantatory words Ahab might have spoken to his crew, but the language of New Testament apocalyptic gives us a sense of what he is probably saying. Ahab may be imitating the demonic "beast of the sea" of the book of Revelation while inciting his crew: "And there was given unto him a mouth speaking great things and blasphemies; ... / And he opened his mouth in blasphemy against God, to blaspheme his name, and his tabernacle, and them that dwell in heaven" (Rev. 13:5–6). Ahab's "tiger-yellow" crew hears blasphemies appropriate only for the "infidel sharks," just as the mythical beast of the sea of Revelation is initially associated with the predatory leopard, lion, and dragon (Rev. 13:2). This first lowering for whales provides Ahab with a rehearsal of the means he will be using to hunt Moby Dick, even though this particular hunt is ultimately interrupted by a squall that leaves Ishmael's whaleboat soaked and stranded overnight.

After our initial introduction to Fedallah during "The First Lowering," two chapters later in "Ahab's Boat and Crew, Fedallah," a description of Ahab's manning and equipping of his whaleboat, we are informed that such creatures as Fedallah and his associates are not unknown among the crew of whaling vessels, for "now and then such unaccountable odds and ends of strange nations come up from the unknown nooks and ash-holes of the earth to man these floating outlaws of whalers" (230)—indeed, "Beelzebub himself might climb up the side and step down into the cabin to chat with the captain, and it would not create any unsubduable excitement in the forecastle" (231). The history of Ahab's association with Fedallah and the nature of the relationship remains a mystery, although Fedallah's appearance hints at a mythic identity consonant with his exotic Asiatic origins, where the antiquity of the civilization seems to go back to humankind's primordial beginnings:

> He was such a creature as civilized, domestic people in the temperate zone only see in their dreams, and that but dimly; but the like of whom now and then glide among the unchanging Asiatic communities, especially the Oriental isles to the east of the continent—those insulated, immemorial, unalterable countries, which even in these modern days still preserve much of the ghostly aboriginalness of earth's primal generations, when the memory of the first man was a distinct recollection, and all men his descendants, unknowing whence he came, eyed each other as real phantoms, and asked of the sun and moon why they were created and to what end; when though, according to Genesis, the angels indeed consorted with the daughters of men, the devils also, add the uncanonical Rabbins [Rabbis], indulged in mundane amours. (231)

Fedallah thus appears to come from a mythical time that Ishmael describes as when some of earth's early inhabitants were the offspring of fallen angels. The concluding reference above is to the antediluvian world of Genesis, when "the sons of God saw the daughters of men" and "took them wives of all which they chose," creating a race of heroes and legendary warriors, "the mighty men which were of old" (Gen. 6:2, 4). The uncanonical version of the same story—as told in the intertestamental Jewish apocalyptic literature associated with the biblical patriarch Enoch (1 Enoch 6–36, known as *The Book of the Watchers*)—describes the condemnation by God of the "watcher" angels, who were appointed to guard the universe. Led by Semyaza (or Semihazah) and his lieutenant Azaz'el, a group of two hundred lustful watcher angels violated the divine order by mating with earthly women, begetting a race of giants (*nephilim* or "fallen ones"), who subsequently begat a race of devouring devils. These fallen angels introduced the arts of magic, weaponry, violence, and injustice to the human world. A cosmic combat ultimately ensued between good and evil angels, followed by a divine prediction that the latter would be defeated and condemned to hell in seventy generations.[46]

Ishmael's elaborate introduction to Fedallah's character thus seeks to create a mythic backdrop blending cosmogony and demonology, in which it is implied that his ancestry may even go back to the legendary precursors of the Christian devil. In this manner, Fedallah's combined role in both the Joban and apocalyptic dimensions of the novel gains additional imaginative depth. With his imputed ancestry as a descendent of fallen angels, Fedallah is implicitly linked to the varied near-Eastern combat myths that underlie the larger mythic structure of Melville's novel.

Although it is not explicitly mentioned in chapter 36, Ahab's successful dominance of his crew to pursue his goal of private revenge was contingent on his sailing the *Pequod* toward the Cape of Good Hope. Instead of following the traditional American whaling route of rounding Cape Horn to enter the Pacific, with the usual stops along the South American coast for supplies and possible shore leave for the crew (the route taken by Melville on the *Acushnet* in 1841), Ahab will head east to the Pacific for the Season-on-the-Line, with no stops along the way at traditional foreign whaling ports. In this way, too, Ahab will protect himself from possible legal consequences of his act of unauthorized usurpation in pursuit of the Leviathan-like White Whale.

It is dramatically appropriate that with the first appearance of the ghostly Fedallah thus comes the first ghostly anticipation of Moby Dick as the *Pequod* travels down the coast of Africa. For soon after the emergence of Fedallah and his Malay crew and the ultimately frustrating chase for whales described in chapter 48, there appears in chapter 51 the nocturnal and mysterious Spirit Spout that seems to lure the *Pequod* onward around the Cape of Good Hope and then toward the Indian and Pacific Oceans. The first sighting occurs on a moonlit night, "when all the waves rolled by like scrolls of silver; and, by their soft, suffusing seethings, made what seemed a silvery silence, not a solitude: on such a silent night a silvery jet was seen far in advance of the white bubbles of the bow. Lit up by the moon, it looked celestial; seemed some plumed and glittering god uprising from the sea" (232). In the initial description here, the plenitude of sibilants in Ishmael's language vividly evokes the nocturnal scene on the cruising ship, but these sounds could also suggest the hissing of a serpent. In view of his role as Ahab's prophetic guide in the hunt for Moby Dick, it is appropriate that Fedallah is the first to see the mysterious spout and announces its presence with his "unearthly voice": "Had the trump of judgment blown, they [the crew] could not have quivered more; yet still they felt no terror; rather pleasure" (233).

In its ghostly appearance, the Spirit Spout mimics the pillar of cloud by day and pillar of fire by night that led the Israelites through the wilderness (Exod. 13:21–22; Neh. 9:19), but according to Ishmael, the spout also looked "as if it were treacherously beckoning us on and on, in order that the monster might turn round upon us, and rend us at last in the remotest and most savage seas" (233). In its relation to the mysterious spout, the *Pequod* thus more closely resembles the armies of Pharaoh that drowned in the Red Sea (Exod. 14) than the chosen people following God's lead. But in his representation of the Spirit Spout, Melville is also joining a biblical image to a literary and mythological prototype—the Greek Titan Adamastor who opposes the voyage of Vasco da Gama around the Cape of Good Hope, as described in Canto 5 of Camoëns's epic *Lusiads*. This threatening mythological spirit, a personification of the "Cape of Storms," first appears to Gama's crew as a huge dark cloud but then materializes into a grotesque-looking giant who warns them of future disasters and narrates his own story of eternal punishment for seeking to ravish the beautiful sea goddess Tethys (Thetis). The repeated appearance of the Spirit Spout in Melville's narrative over the next few weeks as the *Pequod* rounds the same cape will accordingly inspire the sailors with increasing dread of disaster, while the conclusion will eventually confirm the analogy with the fate of both Pharaoh and the Africa-rounding Portuguese mariners.[47]

In addition to these biblical and mythological echoes, the formal advent of Fedallah as Ahab's lieutenant in chapter 50 and the appearance of the Spirit Spout in chapter 51 also signal the influence of Coleridge's *Rime of the Ancient Mariner*, for after the shooting of the albatross the Mariner's ship is haunted by the bird's offended polar spirit just as the *Pequod* is led on by the mysterious Spirit Spout directly following Ahab's unleashing of his savage crew. The *Pequod's* rounding of the Cape of Good Hope, sailing from Atlantic to Indian Oceans, is comparable to the mariner's haunted journey from South Atlantic to Pacific waters. And just as the mariner's ship in part 2 appears during a calm "As idle as a painted ship / Upon a painted ocean" (ll. 117–18), in chapter 51 of *Moby-Dick*, "the silent ship, as if manned by painted sailors in wax, day after day tore on through all the swift madness and gladness of the demoniac waves" (235).[48]

It is revealing that immediately after the sighting of the Spirit Spout, the *Pequod* has an eerie encounter with a whaler named the *Albatross*, which Ishmael describes as a skeletal-looking ship: "As if the waves had been fullers, this craft was bleached like the skeleton of a stranded walrus" (236). With its tell-tale literary name, the bleached and deathly appearance of the *Albatross* is evocative of the phantom ship in Coleridge's *Rime of the Ancient*

Mariner, which appears after the mariner has offended the polar spirit by killing the harmless albatross:

Alas! (thought I, and my heart beat loud)
How fast she nears and nears!
Are those *her* sails that glance in the Sun,
Like restless gossamers?

Are those *her* ribs through which the Sun
Did peer, as though a grate?
And is that Woman all her crew?
Is that a DEATH? and are there two?
Is DEATH that woman's mate?

       * * *

The naked hulk alongside came,
And the twain were casting dice;
"The game is done! I've won! I've won!"
Quoth she, and whistles thrice.
        (ll. 181–89, 195–98)

Like the sinister phantoms on Coleridge's "spectre bark," the three "long-bearded look-outs" on the *Albatross* are figures suspended between life and death: "Standing in iron hoops nailed to the mast, they swayed and swung over a fathomless sea." Even when the two ships cross paths, "those forlorn-looking fishermen, mildly eyeing us as they passed, said not one word to our own look-outs, while the quarter-deck hail was being heard from below" (236). Just as the mariner's killing of the albatross initiates his unholy ordeal, the silent encounter with the bleached-looking *Albatross* is a prophetic sign of Ahab's self-willed isolation and provocation of the divine powers of nemesis.

It is significant that the *Albatross* passes the *Pequod* without any verbal communication. The captain drops his speaking trumpet into the sea when trying to respond to Ahab's query about Moby Dick—a portentous reminder of the ineffable nature of the White Whale. A rising wind also keeps the two captains from meeting for the traditional gam, but since the other whaler is also from Nantucket, Ahab shouts to it: "Ahoy there! This is the Pequod, bound round the world! Tell them to address all future letters to the Pacific ocean! and this time three years, if I am not home, tell them to address them to—" (237). Ahab breaks off his words because he sees that the fish swimming alongside the *Pequod* now desert to the other ship passing in its wake. Ahab's portentous failure of speech has an implied conclusion in the word "hell," and the apocalyptic subtext of the setting here makes it natural that hell should come after this visionary "death ship." The obvious message of the encounter with the *Albatross* is that the hunt for Moby Dick will likely be a doomed enterprise. But in a recurrent motif from the book of Daniel governing Ahab's willful resistance to supernatural signs and omens, like the Babylonian Belshazzar he is unable to read this nautical writing on the wall. Although the desertion of the shoals of fish to the other whaler inspires Ahab with a "deep helpless sadness," he promptly regains his determination and commands the steersman to continue their course "around the world!" (237).

In a final coda, the chapter ends with Ishmael commenting on the paradoxical excitement and futility of sailing around the world, as the *Pequod* is set to do: "But in pursuit of those far mysteries we dream of, or in tormented chase of that demon phantom that, some time or other, swims before all human hearts; while chasing such over this round globe, they either lead us on in barren mazes or midway leave us whelmed" (237). Here Ishmael is implicitly universalizing Ahab's quest as an instinctive human search for divine truth, the elusive nature of which recalls the Israelites' forty years of wandering in the wilderness and Pharaoh's army drowned in the Red Sea. The implied biblical analogy here forms a symbolic complement to the earlier appearance of the alluring but ultimately sinister Spirit Spout modeled on the divine pillar of cloud of Exodus.

In the ensuing depiction of the giant squid in chapter 59, we find still another anticipation of the White Whale in the formless white mass of animate matter after Ahab has temporarily given chase to the white apparition, thinking it might be Moby Dick. The largest-known species of invertebrate, sometimes reaching lengths of over fifty feet, the giant squid or *architeuthis* (the legendary sea monster known as the "kraken") forms an important part of the sperm whale's diet and remains one of the ocean's most mysterious inhabitants, rarely seen at the surface and largely known even today only through dead specimens. As Ishmael describes it, the squid is a grotesque life form suggestive of a ghostly hydra-headed monster: "A vast pulpy mass, furlongs in length and breadth, of a glancing cream-color, lay floating on the water, innumerable long arms radiating from its center, and curling and twisting like a nest of anacondas, as if blindly to clutch at any hapless object within reach. No perceptible face or front did it have; no conceivable token of either sensation or instinct; but undulated there on the billows, an unearthly, formless, chance-like apparition of life" (276).[49]

The mass of the giant squid is comparable to the appearance of the strange water snakes in part 4 of Coleridge's *Rime*:

> Beyond the shadow of the ship,
> I watched the water-snakes:
> They moved in tracks of shining white,
> And when they reared, the elfish light
> Fell off in hoary flakes.
>
> (ll. 272–76)

Yet in contrast to the mariner's subsequent blessing of the snakes as part of God's creation, we find instead in *Moby-Dick* a lingering sense of dread at the sight of the monstrous snakelike creature. At the sight of this rarely seen species of squid Starbuck voices his superstitious fears: "Almost rather had I seen Moby Dick and fought him, than to have seen thee, white ghost!" (276). Like the earlier Spirit Spout, the giant squid is another portentous anticipation of the White Whale, luring the *Pequod* forward to its climactic encounter with a modern form of Job's Leviathan in the Pacific.

CHAPTER FOUR

Cetology, Cosmology, Epistemology

IN THE PREVIOUS CHAPTER, we have explored the influence of Joban theodicy and apocalyptic eschatology on the characterizations of Ahab and the White Whale. As an anguished victim of divine malevolence like Job, Ahab has mythologized Moby Dick into a modern version of the archetypal Leviathan—becoming, in the process, an exemplar of both eloquent protest, like Job, and blasphemous impiety, like the demonic figures of biblical apocalyptic. In the present chapter, our focus shifts to the significance of the White Whale (and of whales, generally) to Ishmael, whose quest for knowledge of Leviathan raises interrelated questions of cetology, cosmology, and epistemology. If such questions frequently overlap, it is because his systematic examination of the whale leads Ishmael into speculations on the subject of cosmology (the study of the origin and structure of the universe, including questions of space, time, causality, and freedom), largely because of the whale's status as a primordial sea creature associated with both creation and creator in the Old Testament. At the same time, Ishmael's ongoing attempts to unriddle the mysteries of the whale often lead him to a sustained engagement with epistemology, that branch of philosophy dealing with the method and grounds of knowledge. While drawing on the Lockean empiricism that traditionally undergirded contemporary American science and culture as well as the era's Romantic idealism, Ishmael frequently ends his investigations of the whale with doubt and suspended judgment—a position of Pyrrhonian skepticism reinforced by Melville's recent readings in Pierre Bayle's *Historical and Critical Dictionary* and his family inheritance of Calvinism, with its emphasis on the fallen state of human cognition. This chapter, then, will examine the interrelated issues of cetology, cosmology, and epistemology in a survey of the extended middle of Ishmael's narrative, which Howard P. Vincent in his study of Melville's whaling sources long ago dubbed the cetological center of Melville's novel.[1]

We have seen that the divine portrait of Leviathan in Job provided Ishmael with a persuasive image of the whale as mythological monster whose identity and power would never be comprehended by humankind— an image reflected in Ishmael's frequent expressions of wonder over sperm whale anatomy. Part of Ishmael's mission in the novel's cetological chapters is to attain both practical and philosophical wisdom from his whaling experience. It is no coincidence, then, that significant allusions to biblical wisdom literature occur in Ishmael's frequent homiletic discourses in this section. Biblical wisdom (Hebrew *hokmah*) includes the book of Proverbs, which offers prudential advice about the allegedly unvarying moral laws of the universe (especially the notion that right behavior creates worldly success), as well as the books of Ecclesiastes and Job (the so-called higher wisdom), which subvert the idea that the universe is governed by equitable or benign laws. Authorship of both Proverbs and Ecclesiastes was traditionally ascribed to Solomon, in accordance with the Hebrew king's legendary capacity for wisdom, despite the antithetical moral message of each book. A text in which Melville found deep "unspeakable" meanings, Ecclesiastes taught that good and evil were arbitrary events in human life, for the world was governed by impersonal natural forces, oblivious to human welfare. Without the benefit of personal immortality or divine providence, individuals should thus enjoy this life's simple pleasures in sympathy with the rest of the creation, for all life was ultimately vanity—an idea that Ishmael endorses emphatically in chapter 96. At the same time, throughout his cetological discussions Ishmael continues the ironic inversions of Pauline teachings that characterized the early chapters, again revealing the flaws in orthodox Christian doctrine.[2]

An important component of Ishmael's secularized wisdom in the cetological chapters is his demythologizing and partial humanizing of the whale. Thus, as Robert Zoellner notes, "Ishmael's redemption depends on his breaking free of Ahab's version of Leviathan as deific correlate. Leviathan must be demythologized before he can be re-mythologized. The physiological facts of the whale serve this process of de-mythification. Much of the mystery and terror of Ishmael's 'murderous monster' dissipates as he—and we—learn that Leviathan has a brain like our brain, lungs like our lungs, and an eye like our eye." As J. A. Ward also points out, the novel's cetological chapters designedly provide a firm grounding in the world of whaling in order to offset the larger metaphysical themes of the narrative.[3] Ishmael's cetological lore is accordingly indebted to the extensive literature of whaling that Melville assimilated while composing the novel.[4] Yet Ishmael's study of cetology—which encompasses an encyclopedic review of the whale from the perspectives of biology, natural history, medicine, law, art, economics, history, philosophy, and psychology (among others)— ultimately reveals the relativity and limitation of human knowledge. In effect, "Ishmael functions as the artist of the sublime as he attempts to represent the unrepresentable."[5]

By the same token, Ishmael's review of cetology reflects the contemporary Romantic critique of science, together with a reliance on older metaphorical languages of myth and mysticism. Randall Bohrer has identified the pervasive presence in *Moby-Dick* of a microcosm-macrocosm system of correspondence in which objects in nature embody and reflect larger cosmological entities: "The one and the many are unified both in the sense that the same images are reciprocally shared by the multitude of mirroring parts and in the sense that a mirror is a single thing that nevertheless has the capacity to contain the images of a multitude of things in a single image." In effect, the novel is a "cosmic Leviathan, a microcosm that reflects or incorporates within its structure the multiplicity of the macrocosmic body of the world."[6] Such a concept provides a useful gloss on many passages in *Moby-Dick*, and it is particularly relevant to the chapters on cetology, for the whale as anatomized by Ishmael acts as both a microcosmic and a macrocosmic image of God, nature, and humanity.

Finally, in keeping with Melville's remarkably assimilative mind, the epistemology of Ishmael's discussion of whales and whaling subsumes a broad range of literary prototypes. Ishmael's playful gigantism when discussing whales, for example, hints at the outsized world of Rabelais, while his encyclopedic "anatomy" of the whale's body follows in the erudite tradition of Robert Burton. Ishmael's debunking of popular and scientific misinformation on whales is indebted to Sir Thomas Browne's well-known explosion of *Vulgar Errors*, and his evocation of the ineffable sublimities of the whale often relies on the sublime cosmological visions of Dante and Milton. By the same token, Ishmael's skeptical mind-set and improvisational narrative technique are decisively shaped by *Tristam Shandy* and *Sartor Resartus*—for if the recurrent digressive play of mind found in Sterne's novel, a comic dramatization of the Lockean association of ideas, provided an important paradigm for Ishmael's unsettled epistemological explorations, then Carlyle's fictionalized biography of the Diogenes Teufelsdröckh, which seamlessly joined narration and philosophical commentary, contributed to Ishmael's (and Ahab's) narrative and discursive concerns with deciphering the symbolic meanings of the universe. Last of all, the contemporary essayistic writings of De Quincey, Lamb, and Irving similarly contributed to Ishmael's play of sensibility and humor. We will now see how these varied literary, philosophical, and biblical influences play out in the novel's cetology chapters.[7]

In his ongoing explorations of cetology, Ishmael constantly hovers between a representation of the whale as empirical reality and ineffable symbol, alternating, as Samuel Otter has noted, "between accepting, Job-like, divine embargoes against the pursuit of knowledge and continuing to search for corporeal answers."[8] In the final chapters of Job, we recall, Yahweh demonstrates Job's ignorance and impotence with regard to the complex workings of the cosmos, and although he performs an encyclopedic examination of the whale as species, Ishmael often reaches the same conclusion. Unlike Ahab, however, who has magnified the White Whale into an embodiment of divine malice, beginning in chapter 32 ("Cetology"), Ishmael seeks to demythologize Leviathan by creating a revised taxonomy and natural history of the whale while recognizing that his concerted efforts, in the spirit of Sterne's narrator, are merely "the draught of a systemization of cetology" (136). Ishmael sets himself to the task of classification with mock heroic ambition, asserting his ability to know the whale despite divine interdiction. At first he mimics the role of divine architect and creator as represented by the psalmist: "Of old hast thou laid the foundation of earth: and the heavens are the work of thy hands" (Ps. 102:25). But then Ishmael claims the right to classify the whale according to his own broad experience, using an implied Shandian birth metaphor:

> To grope down into the bottom of the sea after them [whales]; to have one's hands among the unspeakable foundations, ribs, and very pelvis of the world; this is a fearful thing. What am I that I should essay to hook the nose of this leviathan! The awful tauntings of Job might well appal me! "Will he (the leviathan) make a covenant with thee? Behold the hope of him is vain!" But I have swam through libraries and sailed through oceans; I have had to do with whales with these visible hands; I am in earnest; and I will try. (136)

Daniel Hoffman usefully reminds us that "Ishmael's basis for his enterprise is a very Emersonian assertion of the superiority of first-hand experience over book-learning." Yet Ishmael's self-reliant cetology here is also a symptom of his democratic faith, for as Tocqueville noted, "Equality begets in man the desire of judging everything for himself; it gives him in all things a taste for the tangible and the real, a contempt for tradition and for forms." Such a democratic tendency would help explain Ishmael's subsequent deference to two Nantucket whalemen (Simeon Macey and Charley Coffin) in his assertion that the whale was not a mammal, as in the scientific Linnaean classification of the whale, but a fish: "how shall we define the whale, by his obvious externals, so as conspicuously to label him for all time to come? To be short, then, a whale is *a spouting fish with a horizontal tail*" (137). The biological identity of whales was still a disputed issue in the early nineteenth century, as most prominently displayed in a high-profile 1818 New York lawsuit, *Maurice v. Judd*, between the state "fish" oil inspector (James Maurice) and a New York merchant and purveyor of whale oil (Samuel Judd) over whether whales were fish or mammals. "Fish" oil, used by the tanning industry, was subject to a new tax that merchants were unwilling to pay; the jury conservatively decided in favor of whales as fish. Thus Ishmael's opting to call the whale a fish does not deny its mammalian features but defers to the traditional belief, as did the New York jury, that the biblical orders of creation, whether sea, land, or air, ultimately determined each species' ultimate identity.[9]

Ishmael's ensuing mock heroic system of cetology attempts to substitute empirical fact for a varied assemblage of conflicting data. Announcing his ambitious project, Ishmael states: "It is some systematized exhibition of the whale in his broad genera, that I would now put before you. Yet it is no easy task. The classification of the constituents of chaos, nothing less is here assayed" (134). Ishmael ostensibly refers to the disarray in cetacean classification, but the invocation of chaos with regard to the whale also implicitly evokes the primordial identity of Leviathan in biblical myth. The creation of order out of chaos is now the assigned task of literary artists such as Ishmael rather than the mandate of a divine creator; Ishmael is thus an American Adam, naming the great whales of the creation. In keeping with his scholarly predilections, Ishmael classifies whales, with the assistance of a small library of cetological authorities (beginning with an article on "Whales" in the *Penny Cyclopaedia*), into three different-sized "books" (folio, octavo, duodecimo) or genera, each with a variety of "chapters" (species) according to the animal's size and characteristics. While performing a task akin to Sir Thomas Browne's quasi-scientific review of "vulgar errors" (from which Ishmael in fact borrowed his information on the Narwhale), Ishmael's use of textual metaphors in "Cetology" ultimately suggests the traditional theological idea of nature as a cosmic book written by the divine author, a concept Melville would have found articulated in both Sir Thomas Browne's *Religio Medici* and Carlyle's *Sartor Resartus*.[10]

Explaining his own system of classification after reviewing the confusion arising from others, Ishmael punningly notes that "nothing remains but to take hold of the whales bodily, in their entire liberal volume, and boldly sort them that way. And this is the Bibliographical system here adopted" (140). With Shandian wit, Ishmael claims that he will sort the "liberal volume" of the various species of whales into his own system, a heroically ambitious task worthy of Sterne's Uncle Toby. Ishmael now reviews the characteristics of six folio, five octavo, and three duodecimo whales of special note, followed by a list of other whale names of as yet uncertain classification. The discussion focuses on the significance of the whale's name (or in some cases, names), as well as its distinctive appearance and habits. Throughout his descriptions, Ishmael creates a series of lively vignettes describing a diverse group of species with distinctive shapes and personalities, from the magisterial sperm whale to the scampish-looking mealy-mouthed porpoise. One species even bears Ishmael's own whimsical designation of Huzza Porpoise because it "swims in hilarious shoals, which upon the broad sea keep tossing themselves to heaven like caps in a Fourth-of-July crowd" (143). The ultimate effect of Ishmael's portrait gallery is to celebrate the plenitude and vitality of the creation in the various forms of cetacean species, modern descendents of "that leviathan, whom thou [God] hast made to play" in the oceans (Ps. 104:26).

In the end, Ishmael admits that his brief survey of cetacean species is necessarily incomplete as a summary of natural history. Indeed, he concludes his chapter on cetology by arguing that his account must remain "unfinished, even as the great Cathedral of Cologne was left, with the crane still standing upon the top of the uncompleted tower. For small erections may be finished by their first architects; grand ones, true ones, ever leave the copestone to posterity. God keep me from ever completing anything. This whole book is but a draught—nay, but the draught of a draught" (145). With Rabelaisian or Shandian wordplay and a Romantic ethos of incompletion, Ishmael announces that his study of the whale will be an ongoing process, not an immutable product. This demonstrates that, unlike Ahab's fixed image of Moby Dick, Ishmael's own skeptical quest for knowledge of the whale will never be fully complete, nor will the creation presumably yield all its secrets.[11]

While Ishmael's excursus on cetology in chapter 32 establishes some of his imaginative credentials for an ongoing examination of the whale as a species, in chapter 35 ("The Mast-Head") Ishmael raises issues of cosmology and epistemology in a discussion of the important role of the panoramic "mast-head" in the business of whaling—and in the quest for truth generally. In effect, he points out the dangers of Platonic idealism and the modern pantheism of the Transcendentalists (traceable to Spinoza and Goethe) at the end of a humorous overview of the function of the masthead watcher in the sighting of whales. Ishmael begins by contrasting the different facilities for aerial observation in whalers in the northern and southern hemispheres. Thus, in the southern whale fishery in which Ishmael is engaged, the masthead watcher is completely exposed to the elements with only a watch-coat for protection, a condition that allows Ishmael covertly to mock Saint Paul's claim for the ideal Christian's desire to be in heaven. Ishmael accordingly notes that:

> properly speaking the thickest of watch-coats is no more of a house than the unclad body; for as the soul is glued inside its fleshly tabernacle, and cannot freely move about in it, nor even move out of it, without running great risk of perishing (like an ignorant pilgrim crossing the snowy Alps in winter); so a watch-coat is not so much of a house as it is a mere envelope, or additional skin encasing you. You cannot put a shelf or chest of drawers in your body, and no more can you make a convenient closet of your watch-coat. (156–57)

As in Ishmael's earlier critique of Pauline cosmology and eschatology when seeking shelter in New Bedford, he again subverts the apostle's confident assertion: "For we know that if our earthly house of this tabernacle were dissolved, we have a building of God, an house not made with hands, eternal in the heavens. / For in this we groan, earnestly desiring to be clothed upon with our house which is from heaven" (2 Cor. 5:1–2). Ironically, Ishmael's masthead watcher is figuratively situated in the heavens, but he still faces a mortal peril to his body, without the consolations of Christianity and with a very un-Pauline terror of death. For Ishmael, the human body is obviously not a secure "temple of the Holy ghost" (1 Cor. 6:19) but an easily perishable entity that only an "ignorant pilgrim" (another cut at Saint Paul) would not properly clothe.

In the northern whale fishery, by contrast, the masthead watcher has the benefit of a more protected crow's nest, the alleged invention of one Captain Sleet. The latter is, of course, a Shandian pseudonym for the pioneering arctic whaling captain William Scoresby, Sr., whose son's account of the father's accomplishments in opening up the arctic whaling fishery is wryly burlesqued here. But the eventual point of Ishmael's humorous comparison of southern and northern whale fishery mastheads is to demonstrate the hidden dangers of the former, which despite "the widely contrasting serenity of those seductive seas" (158) still poses a mortal peril to the philosophically inclined young whaleman. For if, as we have seen, a Christian metaphysics of the soul is dangerously inadequate to Ishmael's experience of whaling, the alternative of Platonic idealism is equally risky. Ishmael assumes an admonitory Carlylean tone in discussing the dangers to whalers of educated young Platonists who inadvertently let the hypnotic atmospheric effects of masthead duty put them into a potentially fatal mystical trance; when "lulled into such an opium-like listlessness of vacant, unconscious reverie is this absent-minded youth by the blending cadence of waves with thoughts, that at last he loses his identity" (159):

> In this enchanted mood, thy spirit ebbs away to whence it came; becomes diffused through time and space; like Wickliff's sprinkled Pantheistic ashes, forming at last a part of every shore the round globe over.
>
> There is no life in thee, now, except that rocking life imparted by a gentle rolling ship; by her, borrowed from the sea; by the sea, from the inscrutable tides of God. But while this sleep, this dream is on ye, move your foot or hand an inch; slip your hold at all; and your identity comes back in horror. Over Descartian vortices you hover. And perhaps, at mid-day, in the fairest weather, with one half-throttled shriek you drop through that transparent air into the summer sea, no more to rise for ever. Heed it well, ye Pantheists! (159)

In a June 1851 letter to Hawthorne, Melville criticized those who endorsed Goethe's advice to "Live in the All" by positing the shortcomings of such an injunction to those suffering intense physical pain such as a raging toothache.[12] In "The Mast-Head," Ishmael is performing a similar critique to those of his contemporaries who would "live in the all" without taking account of the natural limits of such an act of solipsism, for the rocking of the mast induces a naïve and infantilized self-hypnosis in which any movement may cause a fatal plunge. The risk of such a benignly idealized cosmology is the sudden reminder of the precarious position in which the masthead observer is located. As elsewhere in the novel, the beauty of appearances hides a potentially deadly reality—in this case, the underlying "Descartian vortices" in which all matter was believed to move in Cartesian physics, the precursor to the modern Newtonian physics of gravity. It is appropriate that Ishmael cites Descartes, the creator of modern scientific rationalism separating mind from matter, as a potential threat to the idealism of the "young Platonist" on the masthead whose budding career as a student of the Emersonian Oversoul or Coleridgean Pantheism may be cut short by the sudden intrusion of an unforgiving reality symbolized by the vortex, an allegedly universal mechanical motion devoid of any transcendent purpose.[13]

Readers may recognize that the myth of Narcissus, which Ishmael cited in the novel's first chapter, is also a relevant prototype for his warning about the masthead here, but the chapter's emphatic moral also has an overlooked biblical source in the book of Proverbs, in a discussion of the dangers of intoxication. To those who "tarry long at the wine," the Solomonic author warns, "thou shalt be as he that lieth down in the midst of the sea, or as he that lieth upon the top of a mast. / They have stricken me, shalt thou say, and I was not sick; they have beaten me, and I felt it not: when shall I awake?" (Prov. 23:30, 34–35). The same warning against sleeping on the masthead is cited in part 1 of Bunyan's *Pilgrim's Progress* when Christian encounters three men asleep with leg irons (Simple, Sloth, and Presumption), and cries, "You are like them that sleep on top of a Mast, for the dead Sea is under you, a Gulf that hath no bottom: Awake therefore, and come away."[14] The warning that terminates Ishmael's chapter on the masthead, then, demonstrates the seductions of any philosophical idealism that ignores the reality of evil; and the Hebrew wisdom tradition here, supplemented by an episode in Bunyan's allegory, reinforces Ishmael's message about the dangerous intoxications inherent in modern idealism's Pantheistic and Transcendentalist variants. As Tocqueville similarly asserted in his study of American democracy: "Among the different systems by whose aid philosophy endeavors to explain the universe I believe pantheism to be one of those most fitted to seduce the human mind in democratic times."[15] Ishmael will later acknowledge that he is a student of Transcendentalist epistemology in "The Fountain," but he is not an advocate of the school's naïve Neoplatonic ontology of evil that denies its very existence.

While Ahab formally announces his view of the White Whale as an agent or principal of apocalyptic evil in chapter 36 ("The Quarter-Deck"), Ishmael correspondingly sets forth his own philosophical evaluation of the significance of Moby Dick in chapter 42 ("The Whiteness of the Whale"). And if the depiction of Moby Dick in chapter 41 casts the White Whale as a modern version of Job's Leviathan, the ambiguous whiteness of Moby Dick in the next chapter implicitly reconfigures God's depiction to Job of the chaos monster. Lacking Ahab's motive of revenge caused by his physical suffering, Ishmael finds grounds for an instinctive intellectual antipathy to the whale because its whiteness signifies "a colorless, all-color of atheism from which we shrink" (195). Ahab demonizes the White Whale as a monstrous, quasi-mythical embodiment of evil; Ishmael sees its unusual coloring as typifying the underlying unity of good and evil in a nihilistic cosmos devoid of any divine principle. Surveying a broad range of evidence from the realms of natural history, geography, astronomy, physics, history, myth, and religion, Ishmael builds a case for interpreting the very structure of the universe as conveying a terrifying message of death-in-life. Yet at the heart of Ishmael's meditation on whiteness is an apocalyptic vision mediated by the terrors of the sublime, ultimately producing a sustained expression of fear complementing the insensate rage governing Ahab's pursuit of Moby Dick.[16]

Rather than making the White Whale, alone, the focus of his epistemological obsessions, as Ahab does, Ishmael enlists the whole cosmos in his meditation on whiteness and uses amplification and antithesis as the key rhetorical components. As Richard S. Moore argues, "the chapter presents in sequence associationism, sensationism, and intuitive idealism, the three epistemological theories available in Melville's day. As Ishmael takes up each theory, he tests its capacity to explain the power of whiteness."[17] The presence of the apocalyptic sublime here is made known at the end of the very first paragraph of Ishmael's disquisition, in its associationist phase. After commenting on the multiple positive associations of whiteness—including beauty, royalty, nobility, majesty, divinity—in a number of concessive subordinate clauses, Ishmael comes to the association of whiteness and Christianity. He then terminates his incantatory one-sentence paragraph with an allusion to the last book of the Bible:

> though in the Vision of St. John, white robes are given to the redeemed, and the four-and-twenty elders stand clothed there in white before the great white throne; and the Holy One that sitteth there white like wool; yet for all these accumulated associations, with whatever is sweet, and honorable, and sublime, there yet lurks an elusive something in the innermost idea of this hue, which strikes more panic to the soul than the redness which affrights in blood. (189)

Ishmael alludes here to Saint John's initial throne vision in Revelation 4, one of several examples of the association of whiteness and divinity in this biblical book. While conceding that such sacred associations of whiteness are "sweet, and honorable, and sublime," Ishmael proceeds to convert them into a rationale for cosmic apocalyptic terror. In the process, he moves from the classical Longinian sense of the sublime as a rhetorical elevation (as found in the Hebrew Bible) to the more contemporary Burkean sense of the sublime as a psychological inducement to terror, through qualities that included obscurity, power, privation, vastness, and infinity—attributes that suggest the origins of the Enlightenment idea of the sublime in the terrifying vastness of the Copernican universe, with its naturalization of the traditional qualities of divinity. At the start of part 2 of his influential treatise, which outlined the core of his theory of the natural sublime, Burke provided a summary of the onset of sublime passion in a manner that anticipates Ishmael's increasingly fear-driven meditation on the metaphysical meanings of the whiteness of Ahab's hated whale:

> The passion caused by the great and sublime in *nature*, when those causes operate most powerfully, is Astonishment; and astonishment is that state of the soul, in which all its motions are suspended, with some degree of horror. In this case the mind is so entirely filled with its object, that it cannot entertain any other, nor by consequence reason on that object which employs it. Hence arises the great power of the sublime, that far from being produced by them, it anticipates our reasonings, and hurries us on by an irresistible force.[18]

Ishmael's state of mind in chapter 42 duplicates Burke's evocation of the natural sublime. Melville's narrator can thus be described as having the motions of his soul suspended in horror (as Burke put it), and his mind completely filled with its object, to the extent that his explanations of the terror inspired by the whale's white color inspire an inconclusive set of reasonings which culminate, through an irresistible force, in nihilistic despair. In the end, the combination of apocalyptic vision and sublime aesthetics in this chapter associates the terror of death and spiritual annihilation with a rewriting of traditional Christian apocalyptic.

Following his initial paragraph, much of Ishmael's meditations associate whiteness with death. When Ishmael contemplates a series of white animals such as the polar bear, the shark, the albatross, and the White Steed of the Prairies, he associates terror and death with their existence in natural worlds inimical to humanity. At the same time he finds whiteness associated with terror and death in the human world:

> Nor, in some things, does the common, hereditary experience of all mankind fail to bear witness to the supernaturalism of this hue. It cannot well be doubted, that the one visible quality in the aspect of the dead which most appals the gazer, is the marble pallor lingering there; as if indeed that pallor were as much the badge of consternation in the other world, as of mortal trepidation here. And from that pallor of the dead we borrow the expressive hue of the shroud in which we wrap them. Nor even in our superstitions

do we fail to throw the same snowy mantle round our phantoms; all ghosts rising in a milk-white fog—Yea, while these terrors seize us, let us add, that even the king of terrors, when personified by the evangelist, rides on his pallid horse. (192)

Ishmael sees the pallor of the dead as hinting at their consternation regarding the afterlife—presumably the horror of facing eternal damnation, or more likely, spiritual annihilation. Ishmael terminates the first stage of his frightful meditation on whiteness with allusions to both Job and Revelation. Bildad thus presents a chilling portrait of the guilty man's fear of mortality in the book of Job: "His confidence shall be rooted out of his tabernacle, and it shall bring him to the king of terrors" (Job 18:14). And in Saint John's initial throne vision, when the Lamb of God opens the fourth of seven seals, John beholds "a pale horse: and his name that sat on him was Death, and Hell followed with him" (Rev. 6:8). Associating Job's king of terrors with the well-known personification of death found in Revelation, Ishmael creates an obsessive image of the apocalyptic sublime as a chilling conflation of whiteness and death.

While the first half of Ishmael's disquisition on whiteness as a source for apocalyptic terror is completed by the allusion to Revelation, the second half constitutes an inquiry into this terror's likely causes, using sensationist and intuitionist models. Ishmael's rhetorical method in this sequence is aimed to present whiteness as a terminally ambiguous and problematic phenomenon. Although associated with majestic or sacred objects, whiteness originates or intensifies the fearsome appearance of objects of terror. Ishmael obsessively reiterates various descriptions of whiteness in nature and history while conceding that "without imagination no man can follow another into these halls" (192). He cites two examples of the terror inspired by whiteness in the experience of sailors: first, in the "superstitious dread" (193) inspired by shoal waters around coastlines and, second, in the appearance of "the scenery of the Antarctic seas; where at times, by some infernal trick of legerdemain in the powers of frost and air, he, shivering and half shipwrecked, instead of rainbows speaking hope and solace to his misery, views what seems a boundless church-yard grinning upon him with its lean ice monuments and splintered crosses" (194). The rainbow, the Old Testament's sign of God's covenant not to destroy the human race (Gen. 9:9–17), is here replaced by a frozen churchyard demonically mimicking its human counterpart. Drawing on information about the Antarctic regions newly available in Charles Wilkes's *Narrative of the U.S. Exploring Expedition* (1845), Ishmael raises insuperable doubts about the benignity of the creation, associating whiteness here with shipwreck and death in forbidding polar seas. His increasingly horrified meditation on whiteness in nature is enhanced by the chilling effect of his allusions to the polar regions, which might be considered a subversion of God's depiction of a providential creation in the book of Job: "Hast thou entered into the treasures of the snow? or hast thou seen the treasures of the hail, . . . / Out of whose womb came the ice? and hoary frost of heaven, who hath gendered it? / The waters are hid as with a stone, and the face of the deep is frozen" (Job 38:22, 29–30).

Ishmael cites the example of a young colt in Vermont affrighted by the smell of the buffalo robe shaken in front of him despite being unexposed to this dangerous creature, which demonstrates that "the instinct of the knowledge of the demonism in the world" (194) is universal in the animal creation. His own instinctive fears, aroused by various natural manifestations of whiteness, assume a similar primordial function: "the muffled rollings of a milky sea; the bleak rustlings of the festooned frosts of mountains; the desolate shiftings of the windrowed snows of the prairies; all these, to Ishmael are as the shaking of that buffalo robe to the frightened colt!" (194). Ishmael augments this subversion of divine providence by noting, "Though in many of its aspects this visible world seems formed in love, the invisible spheres were formed in fright" (195). Ishmael's language here implicitly undermines Saint Paul's assertion of God's providential ubiquity: "For the invisible things of him from the creation of the world are clearly seen, being understood by the things that are made, even his eternal power and Godhead" (Rom. 1:20).

In view of Ishmael's implicit reliance on the aesthetics of the apocalyptic sublime, his technique of biblical allusion and inversion is appropriate in this chapter, given the basis of the Burkean sublime in the realms of infinity, power, and obscurity—all of them traditional characteristics of the deity. In a supreme expression of these characteristics, Ishmael's final paragraph implicitly locates the terror of whiteness in the very physical structure of the universe. He asks whether "by its indefiniteness it [whiteness] shadows forth the heartless voids and immensities of the universe, and thus stabs us from behind with the thought of annihilation, when beholding the white depths of the milky way?" (195). At the start of Genesis, God created light, saw that it was good, and divided light from darkness (Gen. 1:4). By contrast, Ishmael's terror of spiritual annihilation stems from the assumption that the "white depths of the milky way" preclude the traditional ideas of a benevolent creator God. But an even more appalling idea for Ishmael lies in the very composition of light itself, the ultimate source of all appearance of color in the universe, which Newton's *Opticks* and Locke's *Essay on Human*

Understanding had famously reduced to a secondary quality of matter. Ishmael's horrified conclusion here is that even the most delicate beauties are, according to the new science of optics, inherently deceitful:

> And when we consider that other theory of the natural philosophers, that all other early hues—every stately or lovely emblazoning—the sweet tinges of sunset skies and woods; yea, and the gilded velvets of butterflies, and the butterfly cheeks of young girls; all these are but subtle deceits, not actually inherent in substances, but only laid on from without; so that all deified Nature absolutely paints like the harlot, whose allurements cover nothing but the charnel-house within. (195)

The spectacle of "deified Nature," the visible manifestation of divinity, being condemned as a deadly harlot conspicuously negates the popular natural theology of the day, which looked from the wondrous design of the creation to the wonderful creator. For the beauty of nature here merely disguises the horrors of death and annihilation. Ishmael completes his somber meditation by noting that "the mystical cosmetic which produces every one of her [nature's] hues, the great principle of light, for ever remains white or colorless in itself." Thus "the palsied universe lies before us a leper; and like willful travelers in Lapland, who refuse to wear colored and coloring glasses upon their eyes, so the wretched infidel gazes himself blind at the monumental white shroud that wraps all the prospect around him. And of all these things the Albino whale was a symbol" (195). In mid-nineteenth-century England and America, the fear of atheism was grounded in the terrifying implications of the idea of a godless materialist universe; Christianity provided the protective veil against such a vision. In his meditation on whiteness, Ishmael dissolves this veil by inverting the traditional religious connotations of white. In the Old Testament, the deity himself wears a garment that is "white as snow" (Dan. 7:9). In the New Testament, Jesus as sun of righteousness and son of God was the "true Light" (John 1:9), while in the apocalyptic New Jerusalem, "the city had no need of the sun, neither of the moon, to shine in it: for the Lamb is the light thereof" (Rev. 21:23). Ishmael's evocation of the traveler in Lapland who succumbs to snow blindness creates a vivid metaphor for the individual who unwisely fixates on the literally appalling significance of light in the cosmos.

In addition to its apocalyptic symbolism, "The Whiteness of the Whale" voices an implicit critique of Enlightenment science and philosophy, drawing on arguments Melville found in reading Bayle's article on Pyrrho, as Millicent Bell has noted.[19] The Newtonian discovery of the composition of light turns, in Ishmael's meditations on whiteness, into a nightmare vision of a universe stripped of living color, with a corollary conviction that the deity is a deceiver like the God famously hypothesized in Descartes's *Meditations*—a God who intentionally misleads humanity through a false representation of reality. Bayle's article on the Greek skeptic Pyrrho, the progenitor of classical and modern skepticism, could have provided Melville with the philosophical rationale for Ishmael's depiction of a creation that paints itself deceptively into a spectrum of colors, thereby implying a systematic deceit in the creator:

> But now the new Philosophy speaks more positively: heat, smell, colours, etc. are not in the objects of our senses; they are only some modifications of my soul; ... for if the objects of our senses appear coloured, hot, cold, smelling, tho' they are not so, why should they not appear extended and figured, at rest and in motion, though they had no such thing. ... Ever since the beginning of the world all men, except, perhaps one in two hundred millions, do firmly believe that bodies are coloured, and yet it is a mistake. I ask, whether God deceives men with respect to those colours? If he deceives them in that respect, what hinders but he may deceive them with respect to extension.[20]

The argument presented in Bayle's essay on Pyrrho provides potential support for Ishmael's vision of the deceptive nature of all physical objects, since their appearance is not found in themselves but in the qualities of light. If Ishmael in "The Whiteness of the Whale" affirms that light itself paradoxically can be "the very Veil of the Christian Deity" as well as "the very intensifying agent in things the most appalling to mankind" (195), he also hints here that the divine creator of good might also be the creator of evil—if there is indeed a god ruling the world. And if Ahab, based on his personal injury, has definitively cast God in chapter 41 as an agent of universal malignity, Ishmael in chapter 42 provisionally agrees with this idea, based on his encyclopedic survey of the cosmos. "Wonder ye then at the fiery hunt?" (195).

The beginning of Ishmael's actual experiences with the whale hunt in chapter 47 ("The Mat-Maker") provides another important representation of his cosmology. Ishmael's extensive acquaintance with the whale originates with the fact that Ahab realizes he cannot make the quest for Moby Dick the exclusive goal of the *Pequod*'s cruise. So the normal pursuit and capture of whales must proceed, while Ahab secretly directs the voyage to its ultimate confrontation with the White Whale in the Pacific Ocean. Immediately following the description of Ahab's secret strategy in chapter 46, we begin the description of the first chase for whales. This is prefaced by Ishmael's meditation, in chapter 47, on the varying roles played by necessity, free will, and chance in determining the unfolding of human destiny—an alternative to Ahab's fatalistic and deterministic cosmology, as recently illustrated in "The Chart." Ishmael's own cosmological meditation emerges out of his occupation with Queequeg of weaving a mat to affix to the side of their whaleboat, with Ishmael plying the weaver's shuttle and Queequeg wielding the "sword" with which to drive the marline or woof into the lengthwise fixed yarns of the warp. In a philosophical reverie comparable to his earlier experience on the masthead in chapter 35, and with a change of metaphor from chapter 1 when the Fates were theatrical stage managers, Ishmael notes, "it seemed as if this were the Loom of Time, and I myself were a shuttle mechanically weaving and weaving away at the Fates":

> There lay the fixed threads of the warp. Subject to but one single, ever returning, unchanging vibration, and that vibration merely enough to admit of the crosswise interblending of other threads with its own. This warp seemed necessity; and here, thought I, with my own hand I ply my own shuttle and weave my own destiny into these unalterable threads. Meantime, Queequeg's impulsive, indifferent sword, sometimes hitting the woof slantingly, or crookedly, or strongly, or weakly, as the case might be; and by this difference in the concluding blow producing a corresponding contrast in the final aspect of the completed fabric; this savage's sword, thought I, which thus finally shapes and fashions both warp and woof; this easy, indifferent sword must be chance—aye, chance, free will, and necessity—no wise incompatible—all interweavingly working together. The straight warp of necessity, not to be swerved from its ultimate course—its every alternating vibration, indeed, only tending to that; free will still free to ply her shuttle between given threads; and chance, though restrained in its play within the right lines of necessity, and sideways in its motions modified by free will, though thus prescribed to by both, chance by turns rules either, and has the last featuring blow at events. (214–15)

With its anticipation in the title of chapter 1 ("Loomings") and its later thematic elaborations in chapter 93 ("The Castaway") and chapter 102 ("A Bower in the Arsacides"), Ishmael's symbolic tableau here evokes several literary and mythical prototypes, namely, the three Fates of Greek mythology who weave, measure, and cut the thread of human life; the debates among

Milton's fallen angels "Of Providence, Foreknowledge, Will, and Fate, / Fixt
Fate, Free will, Foreknowledge absolute" (II.559–60); the song of the earth
spirit at the beginning of Goethe's *Faust*: "I work at the hurtling loom, I
make / Of time God's living cloak" (ll. 508–9); and Carlyle's use of clothes
and weaving metaphors throughout *Sartor Resartus*, which he adapted from
Goethe and German Romantic philosophy.[21]

The reconciliation of fate and free will has been a perennial concern in
the history of philosophy, and it is no accident that it arises in Ishmael's
cosmological meditations—with the key addition of the element of chance.
Ishmael's vision of the interplay of necessity, free will, and chance is an
important component of his skeptical epistemology, in contradistinction to
Ahab's belief in a fixed fate that creates an apocalyptic order to history. Like
the Satan of Milton's epic, whose journey into the realm of chaos reveals
that the "high Arbiter / Chance governs all" (*Paradise Lost*, II.909–10),
Ishmael, anticipating Thomas Hardy, insists on contingency as the final
arbiter of human destiny, denying the Christian ideal of a providential order.
At the same time, Ishmael's message in "The Mat-Maker" conforms to one
significant aspect of biblical wisdom in Ecclesiastes, which claimed that
events in human life were arbitrary because "time and chance happeneth to
them all" (Eccles. 9:11). While such a cosmological vision governs Ishmael's
thought throughout the novel, at the end we see this vision confirmed in
action in his escape—by chance—from the sinking of the *Pequod* after a
complex series of chance events allow him to float free of the wreck on
Queequeg's coffin–life preserver.[22]

Following Ishmael's anticlimactic experience of hunting his first whale,
beginning in chapter 47, and his seriocomic resignation to the dangers
of whaling, we find an interlinked series of chapters that emphasize both
the destructive nature of the world's oceans and the ubiquitous dangers of
the whaling industry. These chapters add to Ishmael's literary cosmology
since they posit the ocean as a primordial realm of death and destruction.
Presenting an almost Darwinian view of nature, chapter 58 ("Brit") begins
with a description of the vast fields of brit, the small planktonic crustacea
on which baleen whales feed, and then moves on to a meditation on the
supremely destructive power of the sea and its predatory inhabitants.
Ishmael points out that the sea is the scene of repeated "mortal disasters"
so that "however baby man may brag of his science and skill, and however
much, in a flattering future, that science and skill may augment; yet for
ever and for ever, to the crack of doom, the sea will insult and murder him,
and pulverize the stateliest, stiffest frigate he can make; nevertheless, by
continual repetition of these very impressions, man has lost that sense of

the full awfulness of the sea which aboriginally belongs to it" (273). In order to restore that sense of awfulness, Ishmael conducts a brief natural history of marine destruction, starting with the story of Noah's Flood—a history that includes the element's seemingly unnatural and ruthless killing of "its own offspring." In a Homeric simile, Ishmael notes that even whales are victims of the sea's cruel power: "Like a savage tigress that tossing in the jungle overlays her own cubs, so the sea dashes even the mightiest whales against the rocks, and leaves them there side by side with the split wrecks of ships. No mercy, no power but its own controls it" (274). Ishmael's somber vision here strategically subverts the hymn to creation found in Psalm 104, in which ships and whales live under divine nurture and protection:

> O Lord, how manifold are thy works! in wisdom has thou made them all: the earth is full of thy riches.
>
> So is this great and wide sea, wherein are things creeping innumerable, both small and great beasts.
>
> There go the ships: there is that leviathan, whom thou hast made to play therein.
>
> These wait all upon thee; that thou mayest give them their meat in due season. (Ps. 104:24–27)

Ishmael's dark meditation reaches its climax with an assertion of the "universal cannibalism of the sea; all whose creatures prey upon each other, carrying on eternal war since the world began" (274). The ghastly Hobbesian vision of life here confirms the tradition of the sea as a realm of chaos, as symbolized in the Bible by the Leviathan of Job and the beasts from the sea of Daniel and Revelation. Yet the realm of chaos that Ishmael depicts is not absolute; for he ends the chapter, in habitual homiletic fashion, claiming that a macrocosmic contrast between "this green, gentle, and most docile earth" and the sea can be found within the microcosm of each individual as a consolatory memory: "For as this appalling ocean surrounds the verdant land, so in the soul of man there lies one insular Tahiti, full of peace and joy, but encompassed by all the horrors of the half known life. God keep thee! Push not off from that isle, thou canst never return!" (274). In accents that suggest the Neoplatonic and pantheistic frame of Wordsworth's famous "Immortality Ode," Ishmael thus re-creates the Judeo-Christian myth of the Fall as a primitivist fable in which the soul of man mirrors both cosmos and chaos, proposing that all human beings carry within themselves a lost paradise analogous to their prenatal existence. At the same time, Robert Alter notes, two distinct biblical echoes are set up by the passage—in the traditional divine blessing "God keep thee!" (Num. 6:24; Prov. 4:6; Phil. 4:7) and in the final admonition, which obliquely evokes the prudential wisdom of Proverbs on the deadly appeal of a seductress: "For her house inclineth unto death, and her paths unto the dead. / None that go unto her return again, neither take they hold of the paths of life" (Prov. 2:18–19).[23]

In "Brit," then, Ishmael continues to present a dualist cosmology in which the sea is a symbol of evil, outweighing good in both the physical and moral universe. In the subsequent chapter on "The Line," detailing the intricate and potentially lethal manner in which the hempen whale line is strung throughout the whaleboat, the fact that human beings live in the midst of danger and death does not mean they can't enjoy life on its own terms. "The Line" begins as a discussion of the fine Manilla rope that the modern American whaleman uses to secure the harpooned whale, anticipating the depiction of the first actual whale killing of the voyage (by Stubb) in the next chapter. While detailing the careful coiling and stowage of this line in tubs in the whaleboats, Ishmael mentions that "the least tangle or kink in the coiling would, in running out, infallibly take somebody's arm, leg, or entire body off" (279), inadvertently foreshadowing Ahab's manner of death at the end of the novel. And, as Ishmael notes, the threat from the line to the men in the whaleboat extends throughout the whole craft because "the whale-line folds the whole boat in its complicated coils, twisting and writhing around it in almost every direction. All the oarsmen are involved in its perilous contortions; so that to the timid eye of the landsman, they seem as Indian jugglers, with the deadliest snakes sportively festooning their limbs" (280). While the images of snakes and Indian jugglers here suggest a circus sideshow performance, the potentially fatal whale line implicitly assumes a classical, Laocoön-like symbolism as it ineluctably surrounds the whalemen during the chase; yet the image here is ultimately biblical in origin, based on the wisdom of Ecclesiastes.

For the ultimate message of "The Line" is the fact that the perpetual presence of such a deadly arrangement of moving ropes does not keep whalemen from enjoying high spirits during the chase. Indeed, it enhances the jollity of the crew: "Gayer sallies, more merry mirth, better jokes, and brighter repartees, you never heard over your mahogany, than you will hear over the half-inch white cedar of the whale-boat, when thus hung in hangman's nooses" (280). The moral of the chapter in effect comprises a modern variation on the traditional wisdom motifs of carpe diem and memento mori, as the whalemen's comic exhilaration is offset by the invisible threat of the halter to the convicted criminal: "All men live enveloped in whale-lines. All are born with halters round their necks; but it is only when caught in the swift, sudden turn of death, that mortals realize the silent, subtle, ever-present perils of life" (281). In Ishmael's fatalistic tableau, the proximity of sudden death both frames and intensifies the human need for festivity.

In the end, Ishmael's theme in "The Line" is inspired by the fatalistic vision of Ecclesiastes, which memorably teaches the lesson of "seize the day," or carpe diem: "Then I commended mirth, because a man hath no better thing under the sun, than to eat, and to drink, and to be merry" (Eccles. 8:15). Yet Ecclesiastes is also the source for Ishmael's reminder, or memento mori, of the danger of unforeseen death that faces all men: "For man also knoweth not his time: as the fishes that are taken in an evil net, and as the birds that are caught in the snare; so are the sons of men snared in an evil time, when it falleth suddenly upon them" (Eccles. 9:12). The sudden death caused by a tangled whale line is thus comparable to the fatal entrapment of birds and fish by hunters, putting human beings on the same level as the rest of the creation. "The Line" adds to Ishmael's earlier philosophical paradigm of fate, free will, and chance by presenting the ropes used in whaling as emblems of the invisible web of fate that surrounds all individuals and at some random moment will extinguish their lives, like the hunter's snare evoked in Ecclesiastes.

The final use of the rope as cosmological metaphor, which began with "The Mat-Maker," occurs in chapter 72 ("The Monkey-Rope"), an explanation of the process whereby one whaleman (Ishmael) secures another (Queequeg) with a monkey-rope while the latter places a hook into the half-submerged whale's blubber and thus facilitates the stripping of the whale by the ship's tackle as the huge body revolves in the water, shedding its outer layer of fat. The peculiarly vulnerable position of both Ishmael on the ship's side and Queequeg positioned below him on the slippery whale's back amid a rout of hungry sharks leads to Ishmael's meditation on the combination of legal, economic, moral, philosophical, and spiritual lessons found in such an interdependent relationship:

> So strongly and metaphysically did I conceive of my situation then, that while earnestly watching his motions, I seemed distinctly to perceive that my own individuality was now merged in a joint stock company of two: that my free will had received a mortal wound; and that another's mistakes or misfortunes might plunge innocent me into unmerited disaster and death. Therefore, I saw that here was a sort of interregnum in Providence; for its even-handed equity never could have sanctioned so gross an injustice. And yet still further pondering—while I jerked him now and then from between

the whale and the ship, which would threaten to jam him—still further pondering, I say, I saw that this situation of mine was the precise situation of every mortal that breathes; only, in most cases, he, one way or other, has this Siamese connexion with a plurality of other mortals. If your banker breaks, you snap; if your apothecary by mistake sends you poison in your pills, you die. True, you may say that, by exceeding caution, you may possibly escape these and the multitudinous other evil chances of life. But handle Queequeg's monkey-rope heedfully as I would, sometimes he jerked it so, that I came very near sliding overboard. (320)

In substance, Ishmael's description of the function of the monkey-rope comments on the workings of the modern market economy, in which individuals formed contractual relationships with others, all ultimately guided by the invisible hand of the market. Such a legally shared relationship violated the traditional laws of morality and religion in which individuals alone were responsible for their actions. There could in fact be no "particular" providence when another's mistakes, such as those made by one's banker or apothecary, could involve one in financial ruin or accidental death.

It should be noted, however, that Ishmael's "metaphysical" estimate of his situation at the monkey-rope also has a significant biblical component. On a superficial level, Ishmael's view of his obligatory tie to Queequeg may be seen as physically enacting one of the maxims of Ecclesiastes on the benefits of cooperative labor: "Two are better than one; because they have a good reward for their labour. / For if they fall, the one will lift up his fellow; but woe to him that is alone when he falleth; for he hath not another to help him up" (Eccles. 4:9–10). Yet the ironic tenor of Ishmael's philosophical meditation on the monkey-rope shows that it is ultimately a critique of the injustice arising from such interdependence. As such, it is a subversive reformulation of Saint Paul's well-known allegory on the Christian believers who make up the corporate body of Christ. As the apostle asserted, each bodily "member" such as a foot, ear, or eye cannot consider itself apart from the larger body of Christians: "For as the body is one, and hath many members, and all the members of that one body, being many, are one body: so also is Christ" (1 Cor. 12:12). God has created this arrangement in order that "there should be no schism in the body; but that the members should have the same care one for another. / And whether one member suffer, all the members suffer with it; or one member be honored, all the members rejoice with it" (1 Cor. 12:25–26). Saint Paul is asserting that all Christians were obliged by their faith to function as one social unit, caring for and rejoicing with each other. Ishmael, on the other hand, notes that human beings are legally tied to each other for good and for ill; yet there is no providential scheme involved in such an arrangement. And while borrowing the frame of Saint Paul's religious view, Ishmael strips it of its consolatory Christian message to assert the potential dangers implied in such an interdependent relationship as he has with Queequeg.

Continuing his description of the figure of Queequeg on the whale's back surrounded by sharks, which are being kept at bay by the razor-sharp whale spades wielded by Tashtego and Daggoo, Ishmael now presents an iconic interpretation of the harpooner's perilous plight, which is slightly different from Ishmael's previous description of his own perilous situation: "Well, well, my dear comrade and twin-brother, thought I, as I drew in and then slacked off the rope to every swell of the sea—what matters it, after all? Are you not the precious image of each and all of us men in this whaling world? That unsounded ocean you gasp in, is Life; those sharks, your foes; those spades, your friends; and what between sharks and spades you are in a sad pickle and peril, poor lad" (321). As in "The Mat-Maker," we are again presented with a trio of allegorical entities governing the individual's life, with an added critique of Saint Paul's allegory of the body in that Queequeg emphatically does not belong to the "body" of Christian believers; for Ishmael imagines the vulnerable harpooner as praying to Yojo for protection and then giving up "his life into the hands of his gods" (321). Queequeg's permanent condition of peril implicitly evokes the many "perils" that Saint Paul faced in his ministry, as when he was "in perils of waters," "in perils by the heathen," "in perils of the wilderness," and "in perils in the sea" (2 Cor. 11:26). A final comic critique of Pauline doctrine, and of Christian morality generally, occurs at the end of this chapter when Stubb insists that the steward give the exhausted Queequeg alcohol-laden grog for his pains, not the tepid "ginger and water" originally given to the ship's crew by the temperance-minded Aunt Charity whose "gift" is accordingly "freely given to the waves" (322). We recall the importance of "gifts" and "charity" in Paul's epistles, especially the "free gift" of grace offered by Christ (Rom. 5:15). St. Paul is again the implicit butt of Ishmael's comic criticisms as he subversively revises some New Testament ethics and metaphysics to his own purposes.

Throughout his discussions of cetology Ishmael might implicitly be responding to God's taunting questions to Job, but he nevertheless has a detailed personal knowledge of the whale's actual appearance, unlike many of his land-bound contemporaries. Ishmael's inclination toward debunking the scientific world's overly schematic images of the whale informs a trio of chapters on the visual representation of cetacean subjects. In the three so-called pictorial chapters of the novel (chapters 55–57), Ishmael provides an encyclopedic survey of the whale's representational possibilities ultimately inspired by book 5 of Sir Thomas Browne's *Pseudodoxia Epidemica* (*Vulgar Errors*), entitled "Of Many Things Questionable as They are Commonly Described in Pictures."[24]

In chapter 55 ("Of the Monstrous Pictures of Whales"), Ishmael begins by identifying misleading portraits of the whale, "those curious imaginary portraits of him which even down to the present day confidently challenge the faith of the landsman" (260). Surveying a host of imagery (including ancient religious art, older collections of voyages, Baroque painting, and modern scientific treatises), Ishmael points out the salient shortcomings in all such previous representations. Stuart M. Frank has provided an invaluable gallery of visual sources for Ishmael's allusions here and in the next two chapters, demonstrating the extraordinary range in representations of various cetacean species, including the dragon-like sea monsters that passed for whales throughout the sixteenth, seventeenth, and even eighteenth centuries.[25] In referring to the allegedly oldest image of the whale in India, for example ("the incarnation of Vishnu in the form of leviathan, learnedly known at the Matse Avatar"), Ishmael notes that the creature's lower body "looks more like the tapering tail of an anaconda, than the broad palms of the true whale's majestic flukes" (261). Moving forward in time to examples of whales as sea monsters in Renaissance and Baroque art and illustration, Ishmael examines Guido's *Perseus and Andromeda* and Hogarth's *Perseus Descending* as well as the old bookbinders' or publishers' insignia of whales (or dolphins) and anchors. In the Hogarth print, the "huge corpulence" of the monster ludicrously "undulates on the surface, scarcely drawing one inch of water" and has a "distended tusked mouth into which the billows are rolling"; while in "the vignettes and other embellishments of some ancient books you will at times meet very curious touches at the whale, where all manner of spouts, jets d'eau, and hot springs and cold, Saratoga and Baden-Baden, come bubbling up from his unexhausted brain" (261). Clearly, Ishmael's representation of various "monstrous" images of whales here comically deflates the intimidating bulk of Leviathan, transferring it from the realm of the sublime to the ridiculous.

In the first half of chapter 55, Ishmael is involved in the act of demythologizing the Joban Leviathan by discounting the mythic overlay that continued to influence depictions of the whale in modern Europe. In the second half of the chapter, on the other hand, he explores the distortions in the representations of the whale in "those pictures of Leviathan purporting to be sober, scientific delineations, by those who know" (261–62). Here Ishmael examines the illustrations of such allegedly informed mariners and naturalists as Captain James Colnett, Oliver Goldsmith, Count de Lacépède, William Scoresby, Jr., Frederick Cuvier, and Anselm Desmarest. Yet, in each case, Ishmael finds significant inaccuracies. The basic problem is that "the living Leviathan has never yet fairly floated himself for his portrait" because of its size and the element in which it lives. Ishmael effectively remythologizes the whale by concluding that "the great Leviathan is that one creature in the world which must remain unpainted to the last" (264). Claiming that going whaling is the only way to know the whale for real, he paradoxically adds that doing so puts one at risk of "being eternally stove and sunk by him. Wherefore, it seems to me you had best not be too fastidious in your curiosity touching this Leviathan" (264). Ishmael's final message about the difficulty of fully imagining the whale is in keeping with God's depiction of Leviathan as chaos monster in Job: "Behold, the hope of him is in vain" (Job 41:9). It is also suggestive of the general Old Testament ban on seeing the deity directly, as in God's interdiction to Moses of seeing him face to face (Exod. 33:20), or representing him in art, as found in the prohibition on "graven images" in the second commandment of the Decalogue (Exod. 20:4).

Despite Ishmael's apparent dismissal of all attempts to represent the whale accurately, in the following chapter ("Of the Less Erroneous Pictures of Whales, and the True Pictures of Whaling Scenes") he commends the cetacean images found in the whaling narratives of Thomas Beale and J. Ross Browne, and in two engraved acquatints by the contemporary French artist Garneray (misnamed Garnery by Melville) depicting the tumultuous hunt for sperm and right whales. Each of these two scenes is carefully evoked and the painter praised for his knowledge of the realistic details of whaling. In the description of these images, the living Leviathan becomes part of a genre scene exhibiting principles of picturesque contrast, as in the depiction of the right whale hunt in which "the thick-lipped leviathan is rushing through the deep, leaving tons of tumultuous white curds in his wake, and causing the slight boat to rock in the swells like a skiff caught nigh the paddle-wheels of an ocean steamer. Thus, the foreground is all raging commotion; but behind, in admirable artistic contrast, is the glassy level of a sea becalmed, the drooping unstarched sails of the powerless ship, and the inert mass of a dead whale" (266).

Ishmael does not rest satisfied, however, in these closer approximations to the living image of the modern Leviathan. In chapter 57 ("Of Whales in Paint; in Teeth; in Wood; in Sheet-Iron; in Stone; In Mountains; In Stars") he completes his survey of the image of the whale, starting in the microcosmic realm of folk art and expanding outward to the macrocosmic forms of the earth and sky. In the process, Ishmael compiles a full Whitmanesque catalogue of cetacean objects and images. Here the issue is not so much a question of the scientific accuracy of human representations of the whale as it is the sheer ubiquity of its image or outline in the visible world. We now find the whale depicted by Ishmael as a pantheistic presence infusing the cosmos, recalling the Neoplatonic and alchemical tradition of "divine signatures" as well as the Romantic theory of the world as divine text or hieroglyphic.

On the level of folk art, the whale has become a species of totemic animal as the object of artistic ingenuity among sailors, who show their skill by fashioning items both decorative (scrimshaw) and useful (pie crimps, corset busks) out of sperm whale teeth and bone. In addition, the whale appears on commercial signs, door knockers, and weathervanes, reminding the inhabitants of the civilized world of the source of their lamplight. Completing this catalogue of folk art based on the whale's form is its appearance in the very shape of the earth and pattern of stars. Thus Ishmael notes the images of the "petrified forms of the Leviathan" evident in the "bony, ribby regions of the earth, where at the base of high broken cliffs masses of rock lie strewn in fantastic groupings upon the plain" (270). Alternatively, "in mountainous countries where the traveler is continually girdled about by amphitheatrical heights; here and there from some lucky point of view you will catch passing glimpses of the profiles of whales defined along the undulatory ridges" (270–71). In both cases, Ishmael is asserting that in sublime rocky or mountainous landscapes, the spirit and even the profile of the whale are pantheistically present, embedded in the very forms of the earth itself. In a final elaboration of the same conceit, he notes that glimpses of Leviathan can even be found in the constellations of the Northern and Southern Hemispheres, so that one can "trace out great whales in the starry heavens, and boats in pursuit of them" (271). Thus the universe is imprinted with the image of the whale as a primordial cosmic monster and quasi-divine being that humankind hunts through eternity.

With a concluding flourish, Ishmael imagines himself mounting the constellation Cetus, or the Whale, with "a frigate's anchors for my bridle-bitts and fasces of harpoons for spurs," in order to "leap the topmost skies, to see whether the fabled heavens with all their countless tents really lie encamped beyond my mortal sight!" (271). Ishmael's conceit here casts him as a kind of celestial Arion on the back of a dolphin trying to ascertain the epistemological truth of a heavenly realm. While drawing on a passage in Plato's *Phaedo* describing the appeal of the idealized realm of forms (as Merton M. Sealts has noted), Ishmael also borrows from the language of Second Isaiah, in which God "sitteth upon the circle of the earth" and "stretchest out the heavens as a curtain, and spreadeth them out as a tent to dwell in" (Isa. 40:22).[26] The whale is thus again implied to be co-eternal with the creation, and Ishmael's poetic conceit of a cognitive search for heaven on the whale's back provides a suggestive dramatic contrast to the example of the heaven-defying Ahab on a lethal quest for Moby Dick.

While Ishmael's trio of chapters reviewing whale imagery continues the analytical study of cetology begun in the earlier chapter by that name, after Stubb's killing of the first sperm whale in chapter 61, we eventually move to a more experiential cetology in a series of "anatomical" chapters examining the body of the whale as it is stripped of its blubber and decapitated for its celebrated spermaceti oil. As in the earlier chapters, various echoes of the biblical image of Leviathan thread their way through Ishmael's writing. Some time ago, Lawrance Thompson argued that each of these chapters was "a sarcastic answer to the taunting insistence of Job's God that Leviathan is inscrutable and untouchable." Ilana Pardes has provided a more balanced appraisal, however, when she asserts that "Leviathan in *Moby-Dick* is at once an imaginary demonic-divine phantom . . . and a concrete marine mammal, caught, dissected, and sold as a commodity in one of America's largest industries. With unique Romantic irony and humor . . . Melville situates Joban sublimity between the metaphysical and the physical." A key concept in Ishmael's discussion of the physical characteristics of whale anatomy is accordingly the paradoxical idea of binary opposition or bipolar unity, a philosophical concern of Romantic writers ultimately related to the theodicy question found throughout the novel.[27]

The first step in the processing of the dead sperm whale involves stripping its blubber from its body, which is performed by attaching a giant hook to a segment of blubber and then rotating the body until all the blubber is removed in a continuous thick band. A subtext to Ishmael's detailed description of this process is God's initial words to Job concerning the chaos monster: "Canst thou draw out leviathan with an hook? . . . / Canst thou put an hook through his nose? or bore his jaw through with a thorn?" (Job 41:1–2). The crew of the *Pequod* render this divine interdiction null and void when the ponderous "great blubber hook" is lowered into position and the whale is peeled like a piece of fruit: "Now as the blubber envelopes the whale precisely as the rind does an orange, so is it stripped off from the body precisely as an orange is sometimes stripped by spiralizing it" (304). Yet even if the sperm whale can, with suitable effort, be divested of its blubber with a hook, Ishmael in chapter 68 ("The Blanket") still marvels over the mysterious texture and patterning of its gelatinous "skin," an "infinitely thin, isinglass substance" (306) that covers the body of the whale. For the whale's skin is "all over obliquely crossed and re-crossed with numberless straight marks in thick array," some of which strike Ishmael as "hieroglyphical; that is, if you call those mysterious cyphers on the walls of pyramids hieroglyphics" (306). Leviathan's outer integument may be hooked and stripped by the modern whaleman, but the designs on his body are still a mystery to Ishmael, thereby confirming God's words to Job on Leviathan's appearance: "Who can discover the face of his garment?" (Job 41:13).

Ishmael's discussion of the whale's skin in "The Blanket" also comments on the remarkable coat of blubber that encases the body of the sperm whale, the source of the "blanket pieces" that are stripped from the dead whale for later processing into oil. "It is by reason of this cosy blanketing of his body, that the whale is enabled to keep himself comfortable in all weathers, in all seas, times, and tides" (307). If the strangely transparent and hieroglyphically marked skin of the whale is an insoluble mystery to Ishmael, the whale's thick blanket of blubber is more easily understood as the means by which a warm-blooded whale can survive equally well in both polar and tropical seas. In fact, the whale's coat of blubber inspires Ishmael with a concluding didactic message that anticipates the many seriocomic homilies he will later deliver on the whale's anatomy: "Oh, man! admire and model thyself after the whale! Do, thou, too, remain warm among ice. Do thou, too, live in this world without being of it. Be cool at the equator; keep thy blood fluid at the Pole. Like the great dome of St. Peter's and like the great whale, retain, O man! in all seasons a temperature of thine own" (307).

Ishmael's injunction to maintain spiritual equilibrium, anticipating his climactic spiritual awakening in chapter 96 ("The Try-Works"), initially suggests the Stoic doctrines of *apatheia* (emotional detachment) and *autarkia* (self-control), but the ultimate source of Ishmael's homily here is actually Saint Paul's well-known injunction to his fellow Christians to remain untainted by the world: "be not conformed to this world: but be ye transformed by the renewing of your mind, that ye may prove what is that good, and acceptable, and perfect, will of God" (Rom. 12:2). In Ishmael's secularized adaptation of Pauline doctrine, the apostle's encouragement of conformity to God is transformed into conformity to the godlike whale, while the biblical source of Ishmael's wisdom is hidden behind an analogy with Saint Peter's dome. The analogy is completed in Ishmael's final comment in the chapter, which subsumes a Rabelaisian pun on "erections" and "peter" in a mock-solemn expression of wonder at the uniquely spacious and sublime creations of man and nature: "But how easy and how hopeless to teach these fine things! Of erections, how few are domed like St. Peter's! of creatures, how few vast as the whale!" (307). In his praise of the vast bulk and sublime equilibrium of the whale, then, Ishmael is (to vary the familiar phrase) covertly robbing Saint Peter's to pay mock rhetorical tribute to Saint Paul.

Following Ishmael's descriptions of stripping the whale in "Cutting In" and "The Blanket," he continues his exploration of cetacean anatomy in a comparison of the sperm whale's and right whale's heads in chapters 74–75. Stubb and Flask have earlier killed a right whale in accordance with Fedallah's instructions to hang both whales' head on either side of the ship to ensure it against capsizing. Ishmael's ensuing discussion of the whales' heads, which continues for several chapters, provides a sequence of insights into the polyvalent significance of this part of the whale's anatomy in the two species that "present the two extremes of all the known varieties of the whale" (329). In Bert Bender's analysis of the allegory of the whale's head, he identifies an overarching conflict of head and heart illustrated therein. Yet the binary oppositions found in these chapters—between good and evil, life and death, body and spirit, male and female, sublime and beautiful, among others—extend into an encyclopedic range of subjects that act as an extended macrocosmic object lesson for the microcosm of man.[28]

Ishmael's first comment on the whale's head is to note the diminutive size of the eyes and ears in both sperm and right whales. Remarking on the position of the whale's eyes on either side of its massive head, Ishmael speculates on the seemingly godlike stereoscopic visual capabilities that result from this anatomical feature. He asks, "is his brain so much more comprehensive, combining, and subtle than man's, that he can at the same moment of time attentively examine two distinct prospects, one on one side of him, and the other in an exactly opposite direction?" (331). Any advantage that may accrue to the whale from such a feature, however, is potentially undermined when the whale is attacked by man, in which case a "helpless perplexity of volition" may result from "their divided and diametrically opposite powers of vision" (331).[29] Ishmael's depiction of the contrast between the whale's unique perceptual omniscience and its seeming impotence to save its own life anticipates the paradoxical, frequently androgynous nature of the whale's anatomy in general—as seen, for example, in the ensuing contrast between the sperm whale's "beautiful and chaste-looking mouth" and its "portentous lower jaw" (332). Despite the whale's visual disadvantage when faced with human predators, however, its small eyes and ears serve it well in its vast oceanic habitat. Indeed, they provide human beings with an ironic object lesson in the pragmatic advantages of intellectual refinement and discrimination over amplification and redundancy, in a humorous critique of Lockean sensationalism: "But if his eyes were broad as the lens of Herschel's great telescope; and his ears capacious as the porches of cathedrals; would that make him any longer of sight, or sharper of hearing? Not at all.—Why then do you try to 'enlarge' your mind? Subtilize it" (331).

The most striking physical difference between the heads of the sperm and right whales, of course, is the design of their mouths, for the sperm whale has a slender tooth-lined lower jaw adapted to seizing its underwater prey (the giant squid), while the right whale has a massive structure of baleen designed to filter seawater for its tiny floating food (krill). The sperm whale's mouth allegedly suggests "a speculative indifference as to death" in accordance with the philosophy of Plato, especially as found in the *Phaedo*, while the right whale's mouth exhibits "an enormous practical resolution in facing death" (335) suitable for a stoic such as Marcus Aurelius. If, according to Montaigne, to philosophize is to learn to die, the sperm and right whales are bona fide philosophers who can provide human beings with lessons in accepting mortality, just as their organs of sight and hearing might provide models for the Lockean acquisition of knowledge. Ishmael playfully anthropomorphizes the whales' heads while drawing on the Renaissance tradition of erudite humor assimilated by Melville from Rabelais and Robert Burton.

Lest we imagine that the sperm whale's head is merely the subject of learned sport on Ishmael's part, the representation in chapter 76 ("The Battering Ram") of the immense power contained in it should correct our impression, as Ishmael again remythologizes the sperm whale into an inexorable divine surrogate. The "front of the Sperm Whale's head," Ishmael notes, "is a dead, blind wall, without a single organ or tender prominence of any sort whatsoever," being in fact a tough wadded mass from which the "severest pointed harpoon, the sharpest lance darted by the strongest human arm, impotently rebounds" (336–37). The sperm whale is thus capable of extraordinary destructive power when it rams an object with the "dead, impregnable, uninjurable wall" (337) of its head. We may compare Ishmael's remarks here to God's evocation of Leviathan's insuperable power: "His heart is as firm as a stone; yea as hard as a piece of the nether millstone," moreover, "the arrow cannot make him flee" while "Darts are counted as stubble" (Job 41:24, 28, 29). The sublime destructive force of the sperm whale's head prepares us for the conclusion of the novel, while again suggesting a probable analogy between the whale head and the godhead: "For unless you own the whale, you are but a provincial and sentimentalist in Truth. But clear Truth is a thing for salamander giants only to encounter; how small the chances for provincials then? What befell the weakling youth lifting the dread goddess's veil at Sais?" (338). The whale's power—like the sublime realm of divinity, here typified by the shrine of Isis, represented in Schiller's poem "The Veiled Statue at Sais"—is unimaginable to humans who, following Ishmael's oxymoron, must be fireproof like the salamander in medieval legend and godlike in size like a giant in order to survive the terrifying revelation of ultimate truth, an experience that will drive the cabin boy Pip mad, as we will soon witness.

A similar emphasis on sacred mystery and danger is evident in the pair of chapters describing the baling of the precious oil found in the sperm whale's head. In chapter 77 ("The Great Heidelburg Tun") and chapter 78 ("Cisterns and Buckets"), Ishmael describes the intoxicating secrets of the whale's huge "case," the repository for "the highly-prized spermaceti, in its absolutely pure, limpid, and odoriferous state" (340). The "ticklish business" of baling the whale's case is thereupon evoked, as the Gay Head Indian Tashtego carefully probes the suspended head for an opening to the case in which a bucket guided by a pole can be inserted to draw forth the precious spermaceti. The presence of aromatic "sperm" in the whale's gigantic head, together with the insertion of Tashtego's "pole" into the head to draw it forth, suggests a Rabelaisian sexual allegory here of the sperm whale's head as a bisexual embodiment of both fertility and reproduction, testes and womb. The Gay Head Indian "mounts" the head to bale the case; while in the end "Tashtego has to ram his long pole harder and harder, and deeper and deeper into the Tun, until some twenty feet of the pole have gone down" (342).

The analogy to sexual intercourse is patent here, and in a weird parody of orgasm, Tashtego accidentally falls headfirst into the whale's case. The ensuing seriocomic drama describes how the huge whale's head accidentally breaks loose from the tackle holding it in place and starts to sink into the ocean, with Tashtego struggling inside. Without an instant's hesitation, Queequeg jumps into the water to effect a rescue, and the manner of Tashtego's subsequent delivery from the whale's head continues the sexual, reproductive allegory. Queequeg used his sword "to scuttle a large hole" near the bottom of the head and then "had thrust his long arm far inwards and upwards, and so hauled out our poor Tashtego by the head" after turning him around to make sure "he came forth in the good old way"

(343), that is, head first. "And thus, through the courage and great skill in obstetrics of Queequeg, the deliverance, or rather, delivery of Tashtego, was successfully accomplished, in the teeth, too, of the most untoward and apparently hopeless impediments" (344). Ishmael finishes his representation of Tashtego's comic birthing from the womb of the whale's head with a vision of what would have happened if the Indian had "perished in that head," for he would have been "smothered in the very whitest and daintiest of fragrant spermaceti; coffined, hearsed, and tombed in the secret inner chamber and sanctum sanctorum of the whale" (344). The bisexual womb-tomb of the sperm whale's case might have provided a perverse kind of embalmed immortality, but Tashtego is instead reborn in a parody of Jonah-like deliverance. The incident ultimately demonstrates that, in nature, death and life are paradoxically intertwined, contrary to the teachings of Pauline Christianity, while Queequeg again demonstrates his mock Christlike identity by resurrecting his shipmate from death, allowing Tashtego to be born again from the womb-tomb of the whale's head.[30]

Ishmael's next pair of cetological chapters—chapter 79 ("The Prairie") and chapter 80 ("The Nut")—examine the features of the sperm whale's "full front" and recessed brain, respectively, in order to interpret the whale's "character" in the context of the contemporary pseudosciences of physiognomy and phrenology, both of which ultimately fail to provide insights into the whale's head.[31] "If the Sperm Whale be physiognomically a Sphinx, to the phrenologist his brain seems that geometrical circle which it is impossible to square" (348). Such a message implicitly confirms God's query to Job concerning Leviathan: "Who can open the doors of his face?" (Job 41:14). Ishmael's main point in "The Prairie" is to note the absence of expressive features on the sperm whale's head, finding there instead a faceless blank expanse that would dumbfound students of both physiognomy and phrenology, both of which relied on exterior features to read innate character traits. Lacking anything resembling a nose (a Shandian multivalent organ), the sperm whale has a vast blank brow that is "sublime" in aspect. Comparing the sperm whale's brow to the expansive foreheads of remarkable intellects such as Shakespeare or Melancthon, Ishmael remarks:

> But in the great Sperm Whale, this high and mighty god-like dignity inherent in the brow is so immensely amplified, that gazing on it, in that full front view, you feel the Deity and the dread powers more forcibly than in beholding any other object in living nature. For you see no one point precisely; not one

distinct feature is revealed; no nose, eyes, ears, or mouth; no face; he has none, proper; nothing but that one broad firmament of a forehead, pleated with riddles, dumbly lowering with the doom of boats, and ships, and men. (346)

The sperm whale's brow is thus an apt symbol of the Judeo-Christian deity's brutal power and radically impersonal identity, devoid of human feature. In a reversal of his earlier humanization of the whale, Ishmael now seems to be implying that Ahab's mythologized view of the whale as an inscrutable, ruthlessly destructive, divine agent may be legitimate.

Continuing his explorations of the sperm whale's head, Ishmael locates the whale's brain in chapter 80 ("The Nut") as "at least twenty feet from his apparent forehead in life" (348). It is evident that "phrenologically the head of this Leviathan, in the creature's living intact state, is an entire delusion" (349). The contours of the whale's head do not express the differing qualities of its brain, as claimed in the science of phrenology with its map of cranial bumps. However, Ishmael suggests that a better way to gauge the "prodigious bulk and power" (349) of the sperm whale is by examining the huge disks of its vertebrae, which indicate the massive size of the spinal chord extending down its spine. Indeed, if the sperm whale's brain fails to yield any phrenological features, the distinctive hump of its spine might better indicate the whale's true character according to Ishmael's whimsical conclusion: "From its relative situation then, I should call this high hump the organ of firmness or indominableness in the Sperm Whale" (350). In his comic conclusion, Ishmael playfully celebrates the supreme physical power of Leviathan as described by the deity: "In his neck remaineth strength . . . / The flakes of his flesh are joined together: they are firm in themselves; they cannot be moved. / His heart is as firm as a stone; yea, as hard as a piece of the nether millstone" (Job 41:22–24).

The last chapter to discuss a feature of the sperm whale's head proper is chapter 85 ("The Fountain"), a disquisition on the spout that forms a symbolic complement to the next chapter on the whale's powerful tail (chapter 86); the two chapters juxtapose the whale's ethereal respiratory "fountain" with its massive locomotive "back parts" in a dichotomy of spirit and body. In "The Fountain," after a discussion of the whale's remarkable lung capacity, which allows it to remain underwater for extended periods of time using one breath, Ishmael examines the disputed composition of the whale's vaporous exhalations of its spout. As in an earlier admonition about gaining an idea of the "living contour" (264) of the whale, Ishmael again warns against being "over curious touching the precise nature of the whale spout" (373). According to some whalemen, the whale's spout is deemed "poisonous" (373)—a sailor superstition appropriate to the biblical image of the whale as the dragon-like chaos monster of Job: "Out of his nostrils goeth smoke, as out of a seething pot or cauldron. / His breath kindleth coals, and flame goeth out of his mouth" (Job 41:20–21). But according to Ishmael's demythologizing hypothesis, this mysterious fountain is in fact "nothing but mist" (373).

Whimsically associating the whale with other "ponderous profound" beings such as Plato, Pyrrho, the Devil, Jupiter (or God), and Dante, whose heads allegedly emit "a certain semi-visible steam, while in the act of thinking deep thoughts" (374), Ishmael facetiously identifies himself with this group when he describes his head as steaming while writing a treatise on eternity and drinking tea on a hot August day. Ishmael ends his discussion with the image of the whale's fountain as resembling the rainbow that God used as the sign of covenant with Noah not to destroy the human race again (Gen. 9:8–17): "And how nobly it raises our conceit of the mighty, misty monster, to behold him solemnly sailing through a calm tropical sea; his vast, mild head overhung by a canopy of vapor, engendered by his incommunicable contemplations, and that vapor—as you will sometimes see it—glorified by a rainbow, as if Heaven itself had put its seal upon his thought" (374). In this allusive description, the sperm whale is seen as a surrogate divinity like the creator in the Psalms—"He causeth the vapours to ascend from the ends of the earth" (Ps. 135:7)—while displaying the sign of the rainbow as in the story of Noah. Moreover, the whale forms a part of a benevolent creation, as in Psalm 104, while the seal on the whale's thoughts recalls the seal of the living God put on the foreheads of the servants of God in Revelation (Rev. 7:2–3). Ishmael's final comment is to associate the vapor of the whale's spout with his own unsettled religious identity as neither believer nor infidel: "through all the thick mists of the dim doubts in my mind, divine intuitions now and then shoot, enkindling my fog with a heavenly ray" (374). The interpretation of the whale's fountain typifies Ishmael's characteristic blend of Pyrrhonian skepticism and Romantic idealism, which together allow him to maintain his psychological balance when confronting the cosmos.

If the whale's "fountain" in chapter 85 evoked a creature with an almost godlike self-sufficiency of breathing, whose vaporous exhalation could be interpreted as a sign of divine covenant (rainbow) or curse (poison), the description of the tail in chapter 86 depicts an equally ambiguous organ, for this massive locomotive organ has characteristics that are both male and female, angelic and demonic. In "The Tail," Ishmael accordingly evokes the extraordinary power embodied in the whale's horizontal tail flukes. Just as God described Leviathan's "comely proportions" (Job 41:12), Ishmael begins by noting the striking beauty evident in the shape of the whale's flukes: "In no living thing are the lines of beauty more exquisitely defined than in the crescentic borders of these flukes" (375). The eighteenth-century English artist Hogarth was famous for theorizing a curvilinear "line of beauty"; here Ishmael applies the phrase to the design of the huge horizontal fins that create the whale's forward mobility, in addition to several other functions. One of the latter is "peaking," when the whale prepares to make a prolonged dive by extending its tail and half its body vertically before plunging below the surface. As Ishmael notes of this impressive movement, "Out of the bottomless profundities the gigantic tail seems spasmodically snatching at the highest heavens. So in dreams, have I seen majestic Satan thrusting forth his tormented colossal claw from the flame Baltic of Hell" (378). If the first image of the tail "snatching at the highest heaven" is reminiscent of the dragon of Revelation, whose "tail drew the third part of the stars of heaven, and did cast them to the earth" (Rev. 12:4), the second image of Satan's colossal claw, with its visionary sublimity, is evocative of the freezing, upside-down confinement of Satan at the bottom of Dante's *Inferno.*

Ishmael subsequently remarks that, depending on the viewer's mood, the whale's tail in the act of peaking can evoke either the devils of Dante or the archangels of Isaiah: "But in gazing at such scenes, it is all in all what mood you are in; if in the Dantean, the devils will occur to you; if in that of Isaiah, the archangels [see Isa. 6:1–8]" (378). Viewed from either perspective, the colossal tail is an organ of sublime power and terror, and it is thus appropriate that Ishmael ends his description of the tail by confessing that he is unable to interpret its "mystic gestures." Indeed, his inability to explicate the sublime gestures of the whale's flukes extends back to his inability to fathom the whale's featureless face as well: "Dissect him how I may, then, I but go skin deep; I know him not, and never will. But if I know not even the tail of this whale, how understand his head? much more, how comprehend his face, when face he has none? Thou shalt see my back parts, my tail, he seems to say, but my face shall not be seen" (379). Referring to the whale's "back parts," Ishmael is quoting Yahweh's words to Moses asserting his divine inscrutability (Exod. 33:21–23). But the final message of "The Tail" (as of "The Prairie") also confirms the basic message of Job, in which God's rhetorical questions concerning Leviathan's physical attributes cause Job to renounce his attempt to understand "things too wonderful for me, which I knew not" (Job 42:3).

Following Ishmael's excursus on the whale's fountain and tail, the narrative regains some of its previous momentum for an evocation of the remarkable social life of the sperm whale in chapter 87 ("The Armada"), in conjunction with the *Pequod's* arrival at the straits of Sunda, gateway to the Pacific Ocean. The sudden advent of Malay pirates at this point creates an ironic inversion of the theme of Ahab's quest for vengeance, with the pursuer now temporarily assuming the role of the pursued in a locale famous for its piracy. Yet the main interest of the chapter lies in the sudden windfall of sperm whales for capture, together with a revelation of the social and reproductive secrets of sperm whales unveiled to Ishmael's wondering eyes. The immense aggregation of sperm whales is first seen by Ishmael "forming a great semicircle, embracing one half of the level horizon," while "a continuous chain of whale-jets were up-playing and sparkling in the noon-day air" (382). As Marius Bewley has noted, the description of the concentric rings of sperm whales into which Ishmael and his fellows glide borrows imagery and symbolism from Canto XXVIII of *Paradise*, in which Dante reaches the Ninth Heaven and sees the luminous circles of angelic hierarchies circling around a divine point of light.[32]

It is in this chapter, then, that Ishmael (like Pip in chapter 93) discovers some of the mysteries of the oceanic abyss in a privileged vision of natural creation, followed by the intrusion of violent human destruction. While frantically engaged in killing and "drugging" as many whales as possible, Ishmael and his fellow whalemen are drawn into the "innermost heart of the shoal" (386) of a huge semicircular flotilla of whales:

> Yes, we were now in that enchanted calm which they say lurks at the heart of every commotion. And still in the distracted distance we beheld the tumults of the outer concentric circles, and saw successive pods of whales, eight or ten in each, swiftly going round and round, like multiplied spans of horses in a ring; and so closely shoulder to shoulder, that a Titanic circus-rider might easily have overarched the middle ones, and so have gone round on their backs. (387)

The rings of whales here duplicate Dante's wheeling rings of fire, the innermost of which is swiftest "because of burning love that urges it" (*Paradise*, XXVIII, 45). Appropriately enough, Ishmael is magically able to see an underwater nursery of young sperm whales: "suspended in those watery vaults, floated the forms of nursing mothers of the whales, and those that by their enormous girth seemed shortly to become mothers" (387). Moreover, "Some of the subtlest secrets of the seas seemed divulged to us in this enchanted pond. We saw young Leviathan amours in the deep" (388). If Tashtego in "Cisterns and Buckets" enacted an allegory of sexual intercourse and rebirth in connection with the (male) sperm whale's head, here we see the same processes in all their actual physical wonder as the newborn whales are nursed with milk and protected by their mothers, even as the crewmen of the *Pequod* are hunting in their midst. The innermost circle of sperm whales in this scene, as in Dante's beatific vision, is thus united by love. If Moby Dick is, for Ahab, a modern chaos monster inspiring hate, the whale as a social species here is a creature of order and affection mimicking the circular workings of the cosmos.[33]

As a result of viewing the scenes of nursing whales and their humanlike reproductive habits, Ishmael finds a spiritual lesson in the microcosmic-macrocosmic analogy between the protective herd formation of the whales and his own sense of inner joy, a lesson that ostensibly inverts the earlier message of "Brit" about the inevitability of all human beings' losing their inner psychological paradise:

> And thus, though surrounded by circle upon circle of consternation and affrights, did these inscrutable creatures at the centre freely and fearlessly indulge in all peaceful concernments; yea, serenely revelled in dalliance and delight. But even so, amid the tornadoed Atlantic of my being, do I myself still for ever centrally disport in mute calm; and while ponderous planets of unwaning woe revolve around me, deep down and deep inland there I still bathe me in eternal mildness of joy. (388–89)

Ishmael's sense of spiritual security—a combination of prenatal well-being, prelapsarian innocence, and baptismal purification—suggests an inviolable paradise at the heart of the human psyche, in the manner of the psalmist who has assurance of divine security: "He maketh me to lie down in green pastures: he leadeth me beside the still waters. . . . / Yea, though I walk through the valley of the shadow of death, I will fear no evil" (Ps. 23:2, 4). Unlike Ahab, who is numb to any positive pleasures or enjoyments in his life because of his obsession with his own physical and psychic injuries, Ishmael enjoys a playful sense of imaginative pleasure while feeling protected from the pervasive threats of the outside world. Yet the vision of cetacean social harmony he witnesses in "The Grand Armada" is soon destroyed by the actions of the *Pequod*'s crew, as he describes the panic that affects the school of whales when one of their number, wounded with a cutting spade, is "tossing the keen spade about him, wounding and murdering his own comrades" (389).

While Ishmael's momentary vision of Leviathanic creation and destruction leads to the revelation of ineffable paradisiacal secrets of the deep, the experience of Pip in chapter 93 ("The Castaway") offers another mystical experience of underwater cosmology. Yet here the description of the cabin boy's descent into madness from being abandoned at sea is depicted as an unmediated insight into the divine. Pip in effect becomes a holy fool—a modern counterpart to the wise fool of Shakespeare's *King Lear*—endowed with the otherworldly "wisdom" that is a prime biblical virtue, especially as expounded by Saint Paul in 1 Corinthians. The young Negro boy becomes an embodiment of biblical wisdom based on his discovery of humanity's existential loneliness in the universe. Pip had first leaped out of the boat when the harpooned whale hit the planks beneath him, and the cabin boy then accidentally got caught with the whale line around his neck (a foreshadowing of Ahab's ultimate fate), so the line had to be cut to save his life. The second time that Pip leaps nervously from the boat during the chase, Stubb leaves him behind, thinking that one of the other two whaleboats will pick him up; but Pip remains several hours alone in the middle of the ocean until the *Pequod* accidentally finds him, in a foreshadowing of Ishmael's later fate.[34]

As Ishmael notes: "The intense concentration of self in the middle of such a heartless immensity, my God! who can tell it?" (414). Pip's abandonment echoes Ishmael's own fear of the cosmic void in the chapter on "The Whiteness of the Whale," even as his solitary fate provides an ironic contrast with the symbiotic social groupings of the sperm whale in "The Armada." The cabin boy's wits are turned by the terror of his experience as a castaway, yet Pip allegedly gains a series of unique cosmological insights while immersed in mid-ocean:

> The sea had jeeringly kept his finite body up, but drowned the infinite of his soul. Not drowned entirely, though. Rather carried down alive to wondrous depths, where strange shapes of the unwarped primal world glided to and fro before his passive eyes; and the miser-merman, Wisdom, revealed his hoarded heaps; and among the joyous, heartless, ever-juvenile eternities, Pip saw the multitudinous, God-omnipresent, coral insects, that out of the firmament of waters heaved the colossal orbs. He saw God's foot upon the treadle of the loom, and spoke it; and therefore his shipmates called him mad. So man's insanity is heaven's sense; and wandering from all mortal reason, man comes at last to that celestial thought, which, to reason, is absurd and frantic; and weal or woe, feels then uncompromised, indifferent as his God. (414)

As Ishmael implies in his final comment here, Pip's experience represents an oblique confirmation of Saint Paul's well-known claim that "If any man among you seemeth to be wise in this world, let him become a fool, that he may be wise. / For the wisdom of this world is foolishness with God" (1

Cor. 3:18–19). Pip accordingly becomes a holy fool, whose derangement is associated with divine insight and autonomy. On the other hand, the title of the chapter in which Pip is abandoned, "The Castaway," may remind us of Paul's use of this word, expressing his fear of spiritual abandonment if he fails in his moral mission (1 Cor. 9:27). Pip's very name, another word for "seed," is in fact a Pauline metaphor for the soul embedded within the body, as in the apostle's discussion of the basis for spiritual resurrection: "But God giveth it [the soul] a body as it hath pleased him, and to every seed his own body" (1 Cor. 15:38). Pip is just such a Pauline "seed" whose spiritual conversion comes at the expense of his sanity.

The nature of Pip's newly acquired "wisdom" is also deeply rooted in the Old Testament link between wisdom and creation. Ishmael's evocation of Pip's visionary experience as he loses his sanity involves a mythic journey to the bottom of the sea where what he sees constitutes a pattern of motifs based on Jonah, Genesis, Psalms, Proverbs, and Job.[35] On one level, Pip's traumatic abandonment at sea makes him a juvenile Jonah figure, whose "conversion" experience (seeing the underwater secrets of the creation in lieu of being swallowed by a great fish) transforms him into a prophet for the rest of the *Pequod*'s voyage. Pip's visions of the bottom of the sea also re-create the scene of the second day of creation when "God said, Let there be a firmament in the midst of the waters, and let it divide the waters" (Gen. 1:6). In accordance with the divine mandate Pip sees the "multitudinous God-omnipresent, coral insects, that out of the firmament of waters heaved the colossal orbs," making the creation of coral atolls ("colossal orbs") in the Pacific into a symbol of creation generally. In the same vein, the psalmist writes that those who "go down to the sea in ships, that do business in great waters; / These see the works of the Lord and his wonders in the deep" (Ps. 107:23–24). Pip's vision of "God's foot on the treadle of the loom," however, envisages the continuing process of creation in a weaving metaphor that is less biblical than Romantic being based on the song of the Earth Spirit in the prologue to Goethe's *Faust*, which provided a key metaphor for the process of creation in Carlyle's *Sartor Resartus*.

Pip's vision of the "unwarped primal world" also includes the personification of "the miser-merman, Wisdom," seen atop his "hoarded heaps." In the book of Proverbs, "woman wisdom" is depicted as being co-eternal with the creation, including sky and sea. As she recounts: "When he [God] prepared the heavens, I was there: when he set a compass upon the face of the depth: / When he established the clouds above: when he strengthened the fountains of the deep: / When he gave to the sea his decree, that the waters should not pass his commandment" (Prov. 8:27–29). The "miser-merman, Wisdom," in Pip's undersea vision conflates the primeval female figure of wisdom in Proverbs, a companion to the divine architect of the creation, with a mythological male guardian of deep-sea treasures. In the famous "hymn to wisdom" in Job 28, moreover, wisdom is first depicted as hidden from human knowledge: "But where shall wisdom be found? and where is the place of understanding? . . . / The deep saith, It is not in me: and the sea saith, It is not in me" (Job 28:12, 14). But the end of the biblical chapter resolves the mystery of wisdom's riddle-like hidden whereabouts in the simple formula: "Behold, the fear of the Lord, that is wisdom; and to depart from evil is understanding" (Job 28:28). After his oceanic immersion, Pip has indeed found this godly wisdom, for one of his chief roles will henceforth be as mouthpiece for cryptic warnings against the hunt for Moby Dick. Assuming the role of licensed fool to Ahab, Pip, like the fool to Shakespeare's Lear, acts as a potentially healing agent and good angel to the sick soul of Ahab, countering the demonic influence of the captain's bad angel, Fedallah. The final narrative of Ahab's tragedy subsumes a kind of implicit psychomachia between these two prophetically inspired moral agents.

Many critics have noted that Ishmael symbolically washes himself clean of Ahab's blasphemous quest in chapter 94 ("A Squeeze of the Hand"), in which Ishmael engages, along with his crewmates, in the task of squeezing out the congealed spermaceti globules from the whale's "case." Coming just after the account of Pip's abandonment in the middle of the ocean, this chapter offers a counter vision of human solidarity around a "Constantine's bath." So, too, it will provide a proleptic counter example to Ahab's infernal baptism of his harpoon in chapter 113 ("The Forge"). Ishmael's evocation of the scene of squeezing spermaceti from the whale's "case" at first suggests a rich metaphorical experience of baptism and the remission of sins, but the passage leads inexorably to the articulation of a holy brotherhood in which social evil has theoretically been eradicated. The symbolism of the passage is appropriate in view of the original significance of Christian baptism, which involved the exorcising of demonic spirits from the newly immersed subject:

> As I sat there at my ease, cross-legged on the deck; after the bitter exertion at the windlass; under a blue tranquil sky; the ship under indolent sail, and gliding so serenely along; as I bathed my hands among those soft, gentle globules of infiltrated tissues, woven almost within the hour; as they richly broke to my fingers, and discharged all their opulence, like fully ripe grapes

their wine; as I snuffed up that uncontaminated aroma,—literally and truly, like the smell of spring violets; I declare to you, that for the time I lived as in a musky meadow; I forgot all about our horrible oath; in that inexpressible sperm, I washed my hands and my heart of it; I almost began to credit the old Paracelsan superstition that sperm is of rare virtue in allaying the heat of anger: while bathing in that bath, I felt divinely free of all ill-will, or petulance, or malice, of any sort whatsoever.

Squeeze! squeeze! squeeze! all the morning long; I squeezed that sperm till I myself almost melted into it; I squeezed that sperm till a strange sort of insanity came over me; and I found myself unwittingly squeezing my co-laborers' hands in it, mistaking their hands for the gentle globules. Such an abounding, affectionate, friendly, loving feeling did this avocation beget; that at last I was continually squeezing their hands, and looking up into their eyes sentimentally; as much as to say,—Oh! my dear fellow beings, why should we longer cherish any social acerbities, or know the slightest ill-humour or envy! Come; let us squeeze hands all round; nay, let us all squeeze ourselves into each other; let us squeeze ourselves universally into the very milk and sperm of kindness. (415–16)

To many modern readers, Ishmael's act of squeezing sperm suggests a tongue-in-cheek hymn to masturbation, and Melville is doubtlessly mocking here the contemporary medical belief associating self-abuse with insanity.[36] But to limit Ishmael's remarks to a sexual joke or homoerotic rhapsody would be otiose. Nineteenth-century American whaling literature reveals that Ishmael was not alone in remarking on the paradoxically sensual and sacramental qualities of processing spermaceti oil, for another whaleman later noted the same experience in similarly erotic and biblical language: "it was luxurious to wade deep in the try-pots filled with this odorous unguent . . . No king of earth, even Solomon in all his glory, could command such a bath. I almost fell in love with the touch of my own legs, as I stroked the precious ointment from the skin."[37]

Ishmael's description of sperm-squeezing is in fact a secularized act of Christian conversion replete with biblical language and imagery. Ishmael's "strange sort of insanity" from sperm-squeezing, as in the recent madness of Pip, thus suggests the unworldly foolishness of the state of being described by Saint Paul as becoming a "fool of Christ" (1 Cor. 4:10). But the essential New Testament proof text underlying Ishmael's earnest desire for an end to all "social acerbities" and the promotion of "kindness" is to be found in the First Epistle of Peter, in a classic description of the "born again" experience:

> Seeing ye have purified your souls in obeying the truth through the Spirit unto unfeigned love of the brethren, see that ye love one another with a pure heart fervently:
>
> Being born again, not of corruptible seed, but of incorruptible, by the word of God, which liveth and abideth for ever. . . .
>
> Wherefore laying aside all malice, and all guile, and hypocrisies, and envies, and all evil speakings,
>
> As newborn babes, desire the sincere milk of the word, that ye may grow thereby: (1 Peter 1:22–23, 2:1–2)

Unlike the baptism of the spirit or rebirth through the "milk of the word" described in Peter, which will allegedly eliminate a variety of moral evils, Ishmael subversively conveys the same message of social harmony and spiritual rebirth through a secularized ritual baptism and laying on of hands while immersed in the natural "seed" (sperm) of the whale. Ishmael's injunction for individuals to squeeze themselves into "the very milk and sperm of kindness" humorously conflates Peter's well-known words with those of Shakespeare's Lady Macbeth, who famously described her husband as too full of the "milk of human kindness" (*Macbeth*, I.v.17).

We recall that, as a result of his enforced exile from the covenant, the biblical Ishmael's "hand is against all men's," just as the narrator Ishmael appears at the start of *Moby-Dick*, when his "maddened hand" is "turned against the wolfish world" (51). But in chapter 94, Ishmael is now literally and figuratively purifying his hands of their potential violence toward others, as he emotionally distances himself from Ahab's vengeful quest for the White Whale. Ishmael's claim to feel "divinely free of all ill will, or petulance, or malice" while bathing his hands in the spermaceti is also implicitly millennial, for the passage's description of a complete cleansing of human malice can only take place in the traditional era when Satan has been chained for a thousand years and the Christian martyrs resurrected to a kingdom of perfect peace (Rev. 20). Ishmael's concluding injunction that the human community should all join hands and "squeeze" themselves into each other is thus a sign of his growing recognition of the sacred bonds of humanity and a message of egalitarian social concord—the secular equivalent to millennial peace.[38]

Ishmael expresses the desire that he could squeeze whale sperm forever, but since this is clearly impossible he concludes with the ultimate lesson that he has learned from the activity: man must "lower, or at least shift, his conceit of attainable felicity; not placing it anywhere in the intellect or the fancy; but in the wife, the heart, the bed, the table, the saddle, the fire-side, the country; now that I have perceived all this, I am ready to squeeze case eternally. In thoughts of the visions of the night, I saw long rows of angels in paradise, each with his hand in a jar of spermaceti" (416). In contrast to the millennial implications of sperm-squeezing, Ishmael now offers a pastoral ideal of domestic affection as a means to personal fulfillment. The message is one that the "preacher" of Ecclesiastes had also advocated: "Live joyfully with the wife whom thou lovest all the days of the life of thy vanity, which he hath given thee under the sun, . . . for that is thy portion in this life, and in thy labour which thou takest under the sun" (Eccles. 9:9). In general, Ishmael's shift in felicity represents a conversion from the values of the head (as articulated, for example, in "The Lee Shore") to those of the heart. It is a move away from the intellectual allurements of Platonic or Romantic idealism to a wise enjoyment of life's pleasures, as Ecclesiastes teaches.[39]

Yet Ishmael is still fixated on his sperm-squeezing experience when he ascribes the activity to the angels in heaven (as the end of the passage quoted above indicates), for he now makes subversive use of a phrase employed by Job's first comforter, Eliphaz, to describe the onset of a mystic vision of God: "In thoughts from the visions of the night, when deep sleep falleth on men, / Fear came upon me, and trembling, which made all my bones to shake" (Job 4:13–14). Eliphaz is describing the uncanny state in which he learnt from God that all creatures were morally flawed, since even "his angels he charges with folly" (Job 4:18). In Ishmael's comic transvaluation of the passage from Job, the angels are now agents of joyful illumination based on the sensual delight of sperm-squeezing. Ishmael climaxes his millennial dream with a heavenly sanction for sperm-squeezing, enlisting the angels in a playful Rabelaisian fantasy of cosmic harmony that comically subverts the text of Job.[40]

If "A Squeeze of the Hand" constitutes a statement of Ishmael's millennial dreams of human fraternity in a baptismal renunciation of his verbal oath to Ahab to aid the hunt for Moby Dick, the scene evoked two chapters later, in "The Try-Works," represents a symbolic exorcism in his act of foreswearing allegiance to Ahab's self-destructive view of the White Whale. In its description of his moral awakening from illusion to reality, the chapter accordingly constitutes Ishmael's ultimate statement of a personal theodicy and cosmology, which recognizes the psychological distortions that have led to Ahab's fixation on evil and his attendant demonization of the deity.

The chapter begins as a detailed description of how the whale blubber is "tried out" in the great boiling vats of the try-works, but the arrival of midnight soon transforms the messy process into a scene of hellish suggestiveness:

> Standing on this [the hatch] were the Tartarean shapes of the pagan harpooneers, always the whale-ship's stokers. With huge pronged poles they pitched hissing masses of blubber into the scalding pots, or stirred up the fires beneath, till the snaky flames darted, curling, out of the doors to catch them by the feet. The smoke rolled away in sullen heaps. To every pitch of the ship there was a pitch of the boiling oil, which seemed all eagerness to leap into their faces. (423)

In Ishmael's impressionable state of mind, the infernal spectacle becomes a visual trope for Ahab's obsessed soul:

> Their tawny features, now all begrimed with smoke and sweat, their matted beards, and the contrasting barbaric brilliancy of their teeth, all these were strangely revealed in the capricious emblazonings of the works. As they narrated to each other their unholy adventures, their tales of terror told in words of mirth; as their uncivilized laughter forked upwards out of them, like the flames from the furnace; as to and fro, in their front, the harpooners wildly gesticulated with their huge pronged forks and dippers; as the wind howled on, and the sea leaped, and the ship groaned and dived, and yet steadfastly shot her red hell further and further into the blackness of the sea and the night, and scornfully champed the white bone in her mouth, and viciously spat round her on all sides; then the rushing Pequod, freighted with savages, and laden with fire, and burning a corpse, and plunging into that blackness of darkness, seemed the material counterpart of her monomaniac commander's soul. (423)

The infernal atmospherics of the scene have completely transformed the three pagan harpooners and crew into demonic characters out of the world of Dante's *Inferno*, while the ship itself has become a diabolic nocturnal steed from the world of German Romantic balladry (recalling the folk etymology of the word "night*mare*"). Mesmerized by this unholy vision of seemingly diabolic activity, Ishmael falls into a trance-like state that causes him to turn around at the tiller, a near fatal error that is corrected just in time when he wakes up and realizes what has happened. The near disaster here anticipates the very real destruction of the *Pequod* that will be caused by Ahab's inexorable determination to follow his own demonic vision of the White Whale. Ishmael's change of heart or "conversion" (*metanoia*) to a new view of truth following his hallucinatory near-death experience also follows a well-documented pattern in the psychology of religion in which a close encounter with death gives one an enhanced understanding of the value of life.

Howard P. Vincent has noted that the nighttime description of the try-works in chapter 96 builds on similar descriptions in the nonfiction whaling narratives of Frederick Debell Bennett and J. Ross Browne, noting that the latter compared the burning try-works on his whaling ship to Dante's images of hell.[41] Giving more tangible form to Browne's passing reference, Melville imbues the scene in "The Try-Works" with a sublime terror partly adapted from the *Inferno*, for the scene evokes the representation of the Fifth Bolgia in Canto XXI of the *Inferno* where "barrators" (sellers of professional positions in church or state) are immersed in boiling pitch as a tribe of minor devils or Malebranche ("evil claws") stick them with prongs. In this scene in "Hell" (as it was called in the Cary translation that Melville read), the devils are at one point compared to cooks with "flesh-hooks" as they deal with a troublesome inmate:

> They grappled him with more than hundred hooks,
> And shouted: "Cover'd thou must sport thee here;
> So, if thou canst, in secret mayst thou filch."
> E'en thus the cook bestirs him, with his grooms,
> To thrust the flesh into the caldron down
> With flesh-hooks, that it float not on the top.[42]

Like the malicious and mischievous devils described here and in the following canto, the pagan harpooners move about "with their huge pronged forks and harpoons" while the begrimed crew are full of mirthful anecdotes as "their uncivilized laughter forked upwards out of them." Like Dante the Pilgrim, Ishmael is silently appalled by their spectacle, which eventually causes him to turn around unknowingly at the tiller just as Dante eventually realizes when exiting with Virgil from the bottom of Hell in Canto XXXIV that he has been upside down while descending the circles of the infernal regions. And like Dante exiting from Hell into Purgatory and glimpsing the light of the sun (*Purgatory* II, 1–12), Ishmael evokes the image of the sun as a truer image of the creation than his demonic vision.

Ishmael's lesson from his "unnatural hallucination of the night" in chapter 96 is to warn against the morally corrupting influence of the "ghastly light" of an "artificial fire"—a misleading ephemeral appearance that substitutes for a more complete reality:

Look not too long in the face of the fire, O man! Never dream with thy hand on the helm! Turn not thy back to the compass; accept the first hint of the hitching tiller; believe not the artificial fire, when its redness makes all things look ghastly. To-morrow, in the natural sun, the skies will be bright; those who glared like devils in the forking flames, the morn will show in far other, at least gentler, relief; the glorious, golden, glad sun, the only true lamp—all others but liars! (424)

In their redemptive symbolism, Ishmael's allusions to the "natural sun" and the "glorious, golden, glad sun" both invite potential puns on the Son (Christ), confirming the secularized nature of Ishmael's vision. For Ishmael's "exorcism" from his vision of evil is ensured by the beneficent power of the radiant sun—not the divine son who exorcised demons in the New Testament. In addition, Ishmael is asserting the basic psychological truth that the perception of evil is magnified in the dark by the imagination, whereas natural sunlight restores one's moral perspective to a healthy balance. The example of Spenser's Red Cross Knight with his near disastrous subjection to the illusions of Archimago in the *Faerie Queene*, book 1, thus provides a prototype for Ishmael's experiences in chapter 96. In his conversion experience from fiery darkness to salutary sunlight, Ishmael may also be echoing Milton's famous invocation to the light at the start of book 3 of *Paradise Lost*: "Taught by the heav'nly Muse to venture down / The dark descent, and up to reascend, / Though hard and rare: thee I revisit safe, / And feel thy Sovran vital Lamp" (III.19–22).

In addition, the perverse psychological effects of an imaginative obsession with evil is one that Melville's literary friend and Berkshire neighbor Nathaniel Hawthorne excelled in depicting, and the similarity of Ishmael's experience in "The Try-Works" to the experiences of Hawthorne's Ethan Brand, Goodman Brown, and Giovanni Guasconti is no accident. Like these misguided heroes, Ishmael's imputation of a satanic sinfulness to his shipmates leads to a demonization of the cosmos and an inversion of his moral compass. The whole experience gives rise to a perception of the real versus the imaginary extent of evil in the cosmos, together with the need for an informed understanding of evil for attaining psychological maturity. The message of "The Try-Works" thus supplements the message found in chapter 35 ("The Mast-Head"), in which Ishmael warns against dreamy youths keeping watch in the ship's masthead, who put themselves in mortal danger by slipping into reveries that transform the cosmos into a beneficent symbol of the soul. In "The Try-Works," Ishmael accepts the fact that the sun can never disguise the earth's desert places, whether on land or sea, an observation that leads to his most explicit statement of a naturalistic theodicy to be found in the novel, based on the tenets of Old Testament wisdom literature:

> Nevertheless, the sun hides not Virginia's Dismal Swamp, nor Rome's accursed Campagna, nor wide Sahara, nor all the millions of miles of deserts and of griefs beneath the moon. The sun hides not the ocean, which is the dark side of this earth, and which is two thirds of this earth. So, therefore, that mortal man who hath more of joy than sorrow in him, that mortal man cannot be true—not true, or undeveloped. With books the same. The truest of all men was the Man of Sorrows, and the truest of all books is Solomon's, and Ecclesiastes is the fine hammered steel of woe. "All is vanity." ALL. This willful world hath not got hold of unchristian Solomon's wisdom yet. But he who dodges hospitals and jails, and walks fast crossing grave-yards, and would rather talk of operas than hell; calls Cowper, Young, Pascal, Rousseau, poor devils all of sick men; and throughout a care-free lifetime swears by Rabelais as passing wise, and therefore jolly:—not that man is fitted to sit down on tomb-stones, and break the green damp mould with unfathomably wondrous Solomon. (424)

Following his ascription of absolute evil to the midnight scene just described, modified by the assertion that daylight restores the world to a more reassuring perspective, Ishmael now makes the final point that, even in sunlight, a majority of the surface of the earth is inimical to human life, a sign that evil outweighs good in the very physical foundations of the world. In Christian myth, nature participated in the Fall of humankind. But the source of natural evil here is more attributable to classical Greek physics (the Aristotelian idea that the realm beneath the moon is subject to decay) than to divine fiat. After suggesting the relative preponderance of natural evils in the macrocosm, Ishmael examines the knowledge of moral evil in the microcosm of man, adducing two key figures of biblical wisdom who accepted evil as a given in human life. The "truest of all men" is Christ, the so-called man of sorrows (Isa. 53:3), because of his recognition of universal human sinfulness, while the "truest of all books" is the collection of wisdom writings traditionally ascribed to Solomon, especially the book of Ecclesiastes ("the fine-hammered steel of woe"), which repeatedly asserts that human life is ultimately characterized by futility, or "vanity," and suffering is an integral part of the composition of the universe. In keeping with Ishmael's claims here, Ecclesiastes taught that "Sorrow is better than laughter: for by the sadness of the countenance the heart is made better. /

The heart of the wise is in the house of mourning; but the heart of fools is in the house of mirth" (Eccl. 7:3–4).

In these meditations on the inherent evils in the cosmos, Ishmael is essentially restating one traditional answer to the question of theodicy, namely, that suffering serves to educate individuals and bring them to psychological maturity through the realization that evil is an ineluctable part of the natural and moral order. Ishmael's subsequent recommendation of the works of Cowper, Young, Pascal, and Rousseau over those of Rabelais, while hardly fair to the latter author, reaffirms the point that a comprehensive image of human life must include the darker realities of human existence. The argument here takes us back to William James's contrast between the superficial "healthy minded" and the more discerning "morbid minded" temperament in their respective perceptions of evil (see chapter 1). From a biographical perspective, the passage also criticizes Melville's New York friend Evert Duyckinck, at the center of a circle of writers who made a cult of Rabelaisian jollity; whereas Melville's new Berkshire friend Hawthorne was clearly a man who could sit on tombstones and exchange Solomonic wisdom.[43]

Drawing on both Proverbs and Ecclesiastes, Ishmael's concluding remarks in this chapter make the vital distinction between a wisdom that incorporates a recognition of evil and so leads to educative "woe" (Ishmael) and an overwhelming "woe" that leads to "madness" (Ahab): "But even Solomon, he says, 'the man that wandereth out of the way of understanding shall remain' (*i.e.* even while living) 'in the congregation of the dead' [Prov. 21:16]. Give not thyself up, then, to fire, lest it invert thee, deaden thee; as for a time it did me. There is a wisdom that is woe; but there is a woe that is madness" (424–25). Ishmael's final distinction here was enunciated by the "preacher" in Ecclesiastes: "And I gave my heart to know wisdom, and to know madness and folly: I perceived that this also is vexation of spirit. / For in much wisdom is much grief: and he that increaseth knowledge increaseth sorrow" (Eccles. 1:17–18). Confirming Solomon's warning in Proverbs against the spirit-killing insanity that can afflict the morally deranged man (with implicit reference to Ahab), Ishmael seeks the attainment of psychological balance between "the wisdom that is woe" and the "woe that is madness," a quasi-Aristotelean golden mean of self-control or temperance (*sophrosyne*) leading to psychological maturity. The balance between opposing extremes is ultimately typified by the "Catskill eagle" that "can alike dive down into the blackest gorges, and soar out of them again and become invisible in the sunny spaces. And even if he forever flies within the gorge, that gorge is in the mountains; so that even in his lowest swoop the mountain eagle is still higher than other birds upon the plain, even though they soar" (425). The Catskill eagle typifies a mind or soul that can acknowledge the powers of light and darkness, good and evil, with equal ability, a distinction only possible in a morally balanced, heroically elevated character. While suggesting the epic poetic vision of a Dante or a Milton, which can encompass the realms of heaven and hell, Ishmael's eagle more directly reflects the combination of sunlight and shadow that allegedly resided in Hawthorne's literary imagination according to a key point in Melville's review of Hawthorne's *Mosses from an Old Manse*.[44]

As his most explicit statement of the preponderance of evil in the world, Ishmael's experience in "The Try-Works" invites comparison to the Joban theodicy that informs the characterization of Ahab. If the satan in God's heavenly court is the ultimate instigator of the disasters that befall Job, Ishmael is also afflicted with a satanic fantasy of the *Pequod* as a realm of hell, as well as the material embodiment of Ahab's soul. Unlike Ahab's bodily dismemberment however, which epitomizes for Ahab the willful injustice of the deity, Ishmael's experience is only a hallucinatory fantasy of hell, and unlike Ahab, who persists in his demonization of the White Whale until the *Pequod* is destroyed, Ishmael wakes up from his diabolical dream in time to save the ship from capsizing. After this experience of near disaster, Ishmael still acknowledges that evil is more pervasive than good in the world just as the sea covers a larger portion of the earth's surface than the land and even the land is characterized by deadly swamps and deserts. Ishmael is thus able to resist the totalizing Joban vision of evil that infects Ahab, because he is able to acknowledge the "glorious, gold, glad sun" as "the only true lamp—all others but liars" (424). The existence of the sun as a beneficent source of light, life, and knowledge supersedes Ishmael's earlier nihilistic vision of white light within a moribund universe, and Ishmael's awareness of this sets him apart from Ahab's obsession with an artificial fire providing more heat than light.

The wisdom of Ecclesiastes continues to be of relevance until the end of the novel's prolonged cetological sequence in chapter 98 ("Stowing Down and Cleaning Up"), a description of the final stages of disposing of the whale and cleaning up the ship. The refined oil is poured into large casks, which are then stored in the hold, and the decks, rigging, and equipment are thoroughly cleansed of whale oil and soot. Despite the immaculate condition of the ship, the hunt for whales inevitably continues, which will lead to another laborious round of exhausting tasks for the crew and another chaotic mess on deck. Ishmael's sermonic conclusion summarizes the underlying moral of this unending routine of repetitive labor:

Oh! my friends, but this is man-killing! Yet this is life. For hardly have we
mortals by long toilings extracted from this world's vast bulk its small but
valuable sperm; and then, with weary patience, cleansed ourselves from its
defilements, and learned to live here in clean tabernacles of the soul; hardly is
this done, when—*There she blows!*—the ghost is spouted up, and away we sail
to fight some other world, and go through young life's old routine again! (429)

Ishmael's reference here to the need to live in "clean tabernacles of the soul"
without "defilement" inevitably recalls the Pauline language and metaphors
that Ishmael mimics periodically throughout the novel; for the soul as a
"tabernacle" derives from Paul's now familiar assertion that "we know that
if our earthly house of this tabernacle were dissolved, we have a building of
God, an house not made with human hands, eternal in the heavens" (2 Cor.
5:1). Paul also warns: "If any man defile the temple of God, him shall God
destroy; for the temple of God is holy, which temple ye are" (1 Cor. 3:17).
Such language takes us back to Paul's sanctimonious metaphysics of the body,
which Ishmael again subverts by demonstrating its impractical idealism.

Yet, as Zachary Hutchins notes, the dominant proof text for Ishmael's
remarks in chapter 98, as it often is elsewhere in the chapters on cetology, is
the wisdom of Ecclesiastes, namely, its message that "all is vanity" (Eccles.
1:2). The repetitive tasks of whale hunting thus provide another example
of the repetitive events of the cosmos: "The thing that hath been, it is that
which shall be; and that which is done is that which shall be done: and
there is no new thing under the sun" (Eccles. 1:9). At the end of his detailed
evocation of cetological labor and lore, then, Ishmael, anticipating Camus,
acknowledges the endless routines of human labor as a metaphor for all of
human life in its seeming monotony, absurdity, and futility.[45]

CHAPTER FIVE

Comic and Tragic Variations

WHILE QUESTIONS OF CETOLOGY, cosmology, and epistemology, as we have seen, inform a number of chapters within the cetological center of Ishmael's narrative, the modes of comedy and tragedy, similarly imbued with biblical import, also help structure a number of scenes from the same extended middle portion of the narrative. Although comedy and tragedy as dramatic forms have their origins in ancient Greek religious ritual, many of their operative principles can also be found in a number of the world's major religions and scriptures, including the Christian Bible, where the moral dramas enacted in Job and Revelation are especially noteworthy for incorporating elements of both comedy and tragedy. The righteous individuals in these narratives accordingly experience intense suffering as in tragedy, but they also find redemption in theophanic endings that reward the faithful and result in a newly formed society characteristic of comedy. The eighteenth-century biblical commentators Robert Lowth and J. G. Herder compared the book of Job to Greek tragedy, and the comparison was continued by the philosopher Horace M. Kallen in the early twentieth century in his recasting of Job as Euripidean tragedy and then confirmed again at midcentury in the poet Archibald MacLeish's modern dramatic adaptation *J.B.* The book of Job has also been interpreted as comedy, notably by J. William Whedbee, who has argued that because it allegedly exhibits comedy's U-shaped plot, conventional character types (boasters and fools), literary devices (caricature, irony, parody, satire), and life-affirming vision, Job properly belongs to the mode of the comic. The same mixed form characterizes the book of Revelation, which Milton in *The Reason of Church Government* (1662) called a tragedy, but which has since been used by numerous writers as a template for both comedy and satire. As a grand liturgical drama of human suffering with a monstrous cast of supernatural villains but a supremely happy ending, the book of Revelation, like Job, can accordingly be read as a generic hybrid of tragedy and comedy, as Stephen D. O'Leary has argued. For if much of the narrative depicts the tragic suffering of the faithful, the heavenly combat of the armies of Christ and Antichrist eventually leads to the final catastrophic defeat of the devil's party and the comic rebirth and holy marriage of the faithful with Christ in a New Jerusalem.[1]

If biblical scholars have interpreted Job and Revelation as possessing both tragic and comic components, literary artists had long anticipated such findings in plays, poems, and narratives that drew on the potential tragic or comic dimensions of both these biblical texts. Shakespeare, for example, divided the tragic suffering of Job between the characters of Lear and Gloucester in *King Lear*. Goethe drew on the folkloric frame story of Job to conceptualize the epic drama of *Faust*, with its tragicomic depiction of the hero's relentless moral development. Milton relied heavily on the book of Revelation for the mythological combat depicted in *Paradise Lost* and the tragic fall of the hero in *Samson Agonistes*. Some of Hawthorne's short fiction from *Mosses from an Old Manse* blended apocalyptic symbolism from Revelation with a variety of satirical themes and motifs. All these literary works, with their accompanying tragic or comic perspectives, left significant traces within Melville's whaling novel.[2]

A number of critics have examined the presence of both tragic and comic forms in *Moby-Dick*, usually on a separate basis. In fact, Melville structured the novel as an antiphonal blend of comedy and tragedy strategically centered around the key biblical paradigms of Joban theodicy and apocalyptic eschatology. The narrative presents comic variations on these biblical paradigms in a number of chapters involving Ishmael and then the second mate Stubb, as we will see at length in the discussion below. By the same token, the basic components of Ahab's tragedy lie in the captain's Job-like and Lear-like moral blindness and insight, laid out, for example, in "The Sphynx" (for more on Ahab's role as tragic hero see chapters 6 and 7 below). Finally, the nine encounters with other whalers that periodically occur within the narrative, and two in particular (the encounters with the *Jeroboam* and the *Virgin*), similarly illustrate opposing modes of tragedy and comedy within the larger biblical structures of the narrative.

An early example of Ishmael's ongoing comic inversion of Job can be found in his response in chapter 24 ("The Advocate") to the general low opinion of whaling, which includes the belief that "*The whale has no famous author, and whaling no famous chronicler.*" To this an indignant Ishmael replies: "Who wrote the first account of our Leviathan? Who but mighty Job!" (111). By making Job the author of the biblical book that bears his name, Ishmael is taking obvious liberties with the biblical text. Indeed, the hyperbolic adjective "mighty" is conceivably better applied to the chaos monster evoked therein than to the physically and psychologically maimed patriarch. But the semantic slippage is symptomatic of Ishmael's general tendency to transform the book of Job into mock-heroic burlesque for many of the cetological chapters of the narrative.

Mark Heidmann notes that if Ahab interprets his sufferings as the personal attack of a hostile deity, Ishmael interprets his adversities in a more impersonal, dispassionate, and universal light; yet both attitudes have their source in different aspects of the book of Job.[3] We have seen how the protracted presentation of Ahab's obsession with the White Whale is an adaptation of Job's experience of divine justice, while the whale itself is a modern version of the biblical chaos monster Leviathan. It is both ironic and appropriate, then, that when we witness Ishmael's initial experience of whaling while in pursuit of the first sperm whales encountered by the *Pequod*, Ishmael's characterization of the experience casts him as a kind of parodic anti-Job. Ishmael originally justified his going to sea as a common sailor by arguing that adversity was a universal experience, for "however the old sea-captains may order me about—however they may thump and punch me about, I have the satisfaction of knowing that it is all right; that everybody else is one way or other served in much the same way—either in a physical or metaphysical point of view, that is" (6). Ishmael, then, is primed to accept physical abuse as the crewman of a whaler, and his experience on the *Pequod* only confirms this uncomplaining and very un-Job-like resilience of spirit.

A key chapter for revealing the anti-Job aspect to Ishmael's identity is chapter 49 ("The Hyena"), named after the carrion-feeding scavenger of Africa or Asia with an unnerving "laugh." In this chapter, a newly initiated Ishmael spends the night adrift in a swamped whaleboat after a squall has interrupted the chase for a sperm whale—his uncomfortable initiation into the dangers of the chase. Nightfall keeps the whaleboat from returning to the *Pequod* and threatens its sodden occupants with being lost at sea. Reflecting on the unpredictable perils of whaling, in which violent death is a constant danger, Ishmael comments on the kind of punch-drunk attitude, a "genial, desperado philosophy," that overcomes someone like himself under such conditions of extreme tribulation: "He bolts down all events, all creeds, and beliefs, and persuasions, all hard things visible and invisible, never mind how knobby; as an ostrich of potent digestion gobbles down bullets and gun flints. And as for small difficulties and worryings, prospects of sudden disaster, peril of life and limb; all these, and death itself seem to him only sly, good-natured hits, and jolly punches in the side bestowed by the unseen and unaccountable old joker" (226). Ishmael's mention of "sudden disaster" and "peril of life and limb" here implicitly evokes the example of Job, while the "unseen and unaccountable old joker" suggests the amoral god of Job, who tests the latter on a wager with the satan. Nothing could distance Ishmael further from Ahab than his humorous acceptance of death and disaster at the hands of an amorally playful divine pugilist. We recall that in chapter 37 Ahab mimicked Job when he had told the "gods" while looking out his cabin window: "I will not say as schoolboys do to bullies,—Take someone of your own size; don't pommel me! No, ye've knocked me down, and I am up again; but *ye* have run and hidden" (168). The injustice of such treatment doesn't seem to faze Ishmael since he accepts it as part of the whaling enterprise.[4]

Following his uncomfortable initiation into the perils of his new profession, Ishmael interviews three successive crewmates—Queequeg, Flask, and Stubb—about the risks he has run in becoming part of a whaling crew. All of them confirm that incidents such as he has just experienced, involving overnight foundering after a strenuous day of rowing, are not uncommon on a whaling voyage. After realizing that such dangers are ubiquitous in whaling, even though he's a crewman in the boat of Starbuck, the most careful and conscientious of the *Pequod*'s three officers, Ishmael comically decides it is time to go below and make a will. Having done so, Ishmael confesses to feeling a sense of relief: "a stone was rolled away from my heart. Besides, the days I should now live would be as good as the days that Lazarus lived after his resurrection" (227–28). He feels he has been spiritually resurrected like Christ or Lazarus and that for the rest of the voyage he will be living a posthumous existence. Having become his own ghost and familiar spirit, he is no longer fearful of death: "I survived myself; my death and burial were locked up in my chest. I looked round me tranquilly and contentedly, like a quiet ghost with a clean conscience sitting inside the bars of a snug family vault" (228). The pun on the word "chest" here contributes to the metaphysical comedy, implying that Ishmael has made his peace with death both legalistically and emotionally. His belated recognition of the dangers of whaling has created a cheerful stoical attitude, which makes him immune to the Job-like indictment of divine violence and injustice that motivates Ahab.

As previously noted, Ishmael's careful scrutiny of the whale's anatomy and the industrial processing of its body on board the *Pequod* may be said to refute

God's taunting representation of the chaos monster Leviathan's inscrutable appearance and immunity to capture. Indeed, Ishmael's prolonged review of the sperm whale seems deliberately keyed to God's depiction of Leviathan. If Ishmael at times assumes the identity of a parodic anti-Job, a number of his descriptions of the sperm whale in the novel's cetological center transform the animal into a kind of demythologized anti-Leviathan. One of the most salient comic acts of subversion of Leviathan occurs in chapter 95 ("The Cassock"), where Ishmael describes the use to which the outer casing of the whale's penis is dedicated in protecting the "mincer" of whale blubber during the final process of preparing the blubber for "trying-out." The appropriation of the sperm whale's phallus here is a latent parody of Yahweh's boast to Job about Leviathan's prowess: "I will not conceal his parts, nor his power, nor his comely proportions" (Job 41:12). If God will not conceal Leviathan's powerful "parts," then neither will Ishmael. In chapter 37, Ahab prophesized grandly that he would "dismember my dismemberer" (168). In chapter 95, the sailors of the *Pequod* parodically perform this feat on a captured sperm whale.[5]

Ishmael hints at the phallic identity of this "unaccountable cone" when describing it as "longer than a Kentuckian is tall, nigh a foot in diameter at the base, and jet-black as Yojo, the ebony idol of Queequeg. And an idol, indeed, it is; or, rather, in old times, its likeness was. Such an idol as that found in the secret groves of Queen Maachah in Judea" (419). Ishmael is comparing the whale's member here to the idol of Asherah (the elderly Canaanite god El's consort), worshipped by the Judean King Asa's mother, Maachah—an alleged fertility symbol in the form of a wood or stone pillar that was destroyed according to the Judean king's fight on behalf of ritual purity: "And [Asa] took away the sodomites out of the land, and removed all the idols that his fathers had made. / And also Maachah his mother, even her he removed from being queen, because she had made an idol in a grove; and Asa destroyed her idol, and burnt it by the brook Kidron" (1 Kings 15:12–13). Ishmael's implication that the Judean queen's idol was a phallic symbol is not found in the Authorized Version of the Bible but is ultimately based on Saint Jerome's Latin Vulgate Bible, which mistakenly associated the Canaanite idol with the Roman fertility god Priapus.[6] In other respects, the appropriation of the whale's phallus on the *Pequod* is in keeping with the biblical story of King Ahab, who sanctioned his Tyrian wife Jezebel's dedication to Baal, a fertility god whose worship involved rituals that were an abomination to the devotees of Yahweh.

Yet it is not so much the whale's penis that is being used by the whalemen of the *Pequod* but, rather, its elastic outer casing, or what one might call its foreskin. Circumcision was the principal sign of God's covenant with the Hebrew nation, beginning with Abraham (Gen. 17:9–14); indeed, the foreskin was a "token" of the covenant between Yahweh and Abraham and a sign of the latter's faith. In *Moby-Dick*, the whale's cassock-like foreskin is given a mock-sacramental meaning on the body of the mincer, acting as a symbolic token of Ishmael's subversive humor—directed at both Leviathan, as Yahweh's tamed chaos monster, and the Christian priesthood, as purveyors of divine ritual. The subsequent paragraphs of "The Cassock" accordingly describe how one of the sailors cuts off the whale's "grandissimus," peels off its outer skin, stretches and dries it on the rigging, and then uses it for a protective garment for mincing the "horse-pieces," or blocks of whale blubber. "The mincer now stands before you invested in the full canonicals of his calling. Immemorial to all his order, this investiture alone will adequately protect him, while employed in the peculiar functions of his office" (420). The chapter ends with a Rabelaisian joke in the description of the mincer, dressed in his black cassock, comparable to a minister or priest at the pulpit, both being intent on "bible leaves"—in the mincer's case, making the slices as thin as the "leaves" of a Bible: "Arrayed in decent black; occupying a conspicuous pulpit; intent on bible leaves; what a candidate for an archbishoprick, what a lad for a Pope were this mincer!" (420). The sexual humor here constitutes a pungent satire on the pretensions of both Protestant and Catholic ecclesiastical hierarchies (especially their highest officials), and the Carlylean notion that clothes make the man—in this case, the man of God. "The Cassock" may thus be read as a satirical inversion of the chapter on "Church Clothes" in book 3 of Carlyle's *Sartor Resartus*, with Ishmael obscenely burlesquing Christian ritual in the carnivalesque spirit of the medieval Feast of Fools.[7]

Other comic variations on biblical themes in *Moby-Dick* can be found in the discursive interludes of chapters 82 and 83. The first of these chapters humorously mythologizes the status of the American whaleman in a spoof of the new science of comparative religion, while the second demythologizes the legend of Jonah in a comparable satire on the new Higher Criticism of the Bible.[8] In "The Honor and Glory of Whaling," Ishmael appropriates the mixed figures of Perseus, Saint George, Hercules, and Vishnoo as heroic prototypes for the modern whaleman, satirically transforming the varied chaos monsters they confronted into ocean-going Leviathans, again drawing on book 5 of Sir Thomas Browne's *Vulgar Errors* for some of his comic debunking.[9] In contrast to Ahab's hubristic self-aggrandizement into the god-defying figures of Job, Prometheus, Satan, or Faust, Ishmael humorously elevates the lowly vocation of whaleman, himself included, into an improbable gallery of legendary Western and Eastern gods and heroes while conflating the sperm whale with a host of legendary sea monsters and dragons.

Improbable as it may seem, Ishmael's elucidations here have some scholarly merit. His rationale for glossing Saint George's dragon as a whale, for example, is based on the fact that "in many old chronicles whales and dragons are strangely jumbled together, and often stand for each other. 'Thou art as a lion of the waters, and as a dragon of the sea,' saith Ezekiel; hereby, plainly meaning a whale; in truth, some versions of the Bible use that word itself" (362). The Old Testament does in fact variously use the Hebrew nouns *tannin* (Gen. 1:21), *Leviathan* (Ps. 73:13–14, 104:26; Job 41; Isa. 27:1), and *Rahab* (Ps. 87:4; Isa. 51:9; Ezek. 29:3, 32:2) to refer to a non-naturalistic marine monster or sea dragon. In Ishmael's quotation from Ezekiel, the Egyptian pharaoh is being addressed as Rahab. The Authorized Version reads: "Thou art like a young lion to the nations, and thou art as a whale in the seas: and thou camest forth with thy rivers [the Nile], and troublest the waters with thy feet, and fouledst their rivers" (Ezek. 32:2). Ishmael has inadvertently substituted "dragon" for the Authorized Version's "whale," but both are legitimate translations of the Hebrew Rahab, an embodiment of the sea as primeval chaos monster that God will capture with a net, as the prophet announces. The passage from Ezekiel denouncing a self-aggrandizing Pharaoh is in fact one in a number of portraits of biblical overreachers who are potential prototypes for Ahab.[10]

Ishmael speculates that the frequent depiction of Saint George's dragon with a "griffin-like shape" reflects the traditional ignorance of the whale's exact form. This allows Ishmael to claim Saint George as a fellow harpooner, and the modern American whaleman as belonging by right to the Order of Saint George, better known as the Order of the Garter—the highest order of English knighthood, founded in 1349 and expanded in 1831 under King William IV to include the royal family and foreign sovereigns. Ishmael's unlikely elevation of the American whaleman to the highest chivalric honor in England belongs in the tradition of frontier humor like the contemporary Crockett almanacs. As in that tradition, a strategy of outrageous exaggeration serves the democratic purpose of elevating the common man to heroic proportions. Ishmael's comic aggrandizement of the American whaleman climaxes in the latter's alleged kinship with the Hindu Vishnu, who was transformed into a whale in his first incarnation in order to retrieve the Vedas from the bottom of the sea, thus literally becoming a whaleman. The comic apotheosis of the American whaleman is complete in his transformation into an avatar of divine wisdom.[11]

Ishmael's democratic elevation of the American whaleman to chivalric honor in "The Honor and Glory of Whaling" presents an implicit burlesque of Ahab's apocalyptic drama of divine warrior and chaos monster. In the next chapter, "Jonah Historically Regarded," we find a humorous review of the historicity of the story of Jonah as an exercise in hermeneutical literalism within Ishmael's ongoing subversion of biblical myth. The exercise was partly inspired by Pierre Bayle's ironic article on "Jonas" in his famous *Dictionary* and by John Kitto's more orthodox entry on the prophet—written by the Scottish Presbyterian John Eadie—in Kitto's well-known reference work, the *Cyclopaedia of Biblical Literature* (1845).[12]

To begin the discussion, Ishmael refers to the authority of a Sag Harbor whaleman, a determined skeptic (like Pierre Bayle) who has expressed doubt about the possibility of Jonah's being swallowed by a whale since the image of the whale found in his old illustrated Bible gives the creature two spouts, implying that it is a right whale, and such baleen-mouthed whales could not swallow any object as large as a man. The whaleman's objections here may remind us of Tocqueville's observation that democracy gives a man "the desire of judging everything for himself; it gives him in all things a taste for the tangible and the real, a contempt for tradition and for forms."[13] In answer to this whaleman's most reasonable caveat, Ishmael cites Bishop Jebb's improbable claim, borrowed from Eadie, that Jonah might have only been held in the whale's mouth, thus beginning an ironic pose of pretending to side with the orthodox Christian defenders of the Jonah legend against the commonsensical American whaleman.

The Sag Harbor whaleman's second objection to the Jonah legend involves the likely action of the whale's gastric juices on the biblical prophet over three days—an objection met by various absurd theories such as the idea that the "whale" was really a ship or an inflatable life preserver. The whaleman's third and final objection is to Jonah's alleged journey from the Mediterranean coast to the city of Ninevah on the Tigris River in three days. In a mock peroration, Ishmael ironically attacks the old whaleman's entirely reasonable questioning of biblical authority as only showing "his foolish, impious pride, and abominable, devilish rebellion against the reverend clergy" (365) and then cites a Portuguese Catholic priest for whom "this very idea of Jonah's going to Ninevah via the Cape of Good Hope was advanced as a signal magnification of the general miracle" (366). It goes without saying that this anonymous Portuguese priest is hardly a disinterested party, since patriotic pride in the achievements of

Vasco da Gama in circumnavigating Africa for the first time favors such an itinerary for Jonah.

By remarking that even non-Christians such as "the highly enlightened Turks devoutly believe in the historical story of Jonah" (366), Ishmael evokes the traditional enemy of the Christian faith to score a dubious point for the orthodox believer. Allegedly clinching the argument that Jonah's providential experiences must have really happened, Ishmael has by now completely undermined any further belief in the biblical legend and miracle of Jonah. In its comic representation of the ultimate conflict between clergy and layman, faith and reason, religion and science, Ishmael's ironic reductio ad absurdum of the Jonah legend provides a satirical coda to Father Mapple's orthodox treatment of the Jonah theme, while again casting Ishmael in the role of a parodic anti-Job figure for whom Leviathan has been tamed by the powers of skepticism and human reason.

An important addition to Ahab's and Ishmael's Joban and anti-Joban models of experience in relation to the issue of theodicy can be found in several medial chapters of *Moby-Dick* which offer a seriocomic reappraisal of this same subject, now focused on the character of Stubb. In these chapters, Stubb engages in actions and conversations that lead to several dark satirical critiques of the beneficence of the creator God in the face of a fiercely carnivorous animal creation. The first of these conversations follows Stubb's killing of a sperm whale in chapter 63 and his subsequent order in chapter 64 to Fleece, the pious old black cook, for a steak cut from the newly killed whale. As a figure who implicitly subverts the threat of God's chaos monster Leviathan, Stubb is at the center of an extended "black" comedy that begins with his request for a rare whale steak and continues through Fleece's ensuing "sermon" to the sharks and Stubb's subsequent catechism of the cook's beliefs, all of which constitute a sustained satirical attack on Christian morality and metaphysics. A largely unnoticed subtext to this dramatic sequence is the fact that Stubb's eating of a whale steak and its aftermath constitutes a parody of the legendary feast of the righteous on the body of Leviathan at the apocalyptic end-time.[14]

The notion of the feasting of the righteous on the body of Leviathan (and in some cases on Behemoth as well) has a long history in ancient Hebrew culture and early Rabbinic Judaism. In chapter 41 of the book of Job, Leviathan was claimed by God as being beyond the range of human conquest or consumption: "Shall the companions make a banquet of him? shall they part him among the merchants?" (Job 41:6). Yet a conspicuous countertradition in the Bible and Pseudepigrapha asserts that just such a feast is the ultimate reward of the righteous. In Psalm 74, for example, Leviathan's corpse provides nourishment for the chosen people in the wilderness following their miraculous crossing of the Red Sea because of God's control over this chaotic element: "Thou brakest the heads of leviathan in pieces, and gavest him to be meat to the people inhabiting the wilderness" (Ps. 74:14). In this tradition, the divine combat with the primordial chaos monsters of sea and land, Leviathan and Behemoth, would ultimately result in end-time feasting by the righteous on their gigantic carcasses. In 4 Ezra, for example (which Melville read and annotated in one of his Bibles under its older name 2 Esdras), cosmogony and eschatology are combined in the description of God's providential care: "to Leviathan thou didst give the seventh part of the watery world; and thou has kept them [Behemoth and Leviathan] to be eaten by whom thou wilt, and when thou wilt" (4 Ezra 6:52). Similarly, in 2 Apocalypse of Baruch, God tells the Jewish prophet: "And Behemoth will reveal itself from its place, and Leviathan come from the sea, the two great monsters which I created on the fifth day of creation and which I shall have kept until that time. And they will be nourishment for all who are left" (2 Apoc. Bar. 29:4). In 1 Enoch, the early patriarch Enoch reports: "And the angel of peace who was with me said to me, 'These two monsters [Leviathan and Behemoth] are prepared for the great day of the Lord (when) they shall turn into food'" (1 Enoch 60:24). Finally, in a dozen texts of early Rabbinic Judaism, Leviathan and Behemoth are again variously depicted as final nourishment for the end-time remnant.[15]

Viewed in the context of this tradition, the scene of Stubb's consumption of raw whale steak—while surrounded by a host of sharks feeding on the carcass of the whale—gains ironic dimensions. For, unlike the righteous of the end-time, it is the irreligious and Epicurean Stubb who enjoys the steak, while the ghastly and ruthlessly predatory sharks feed hungrily on the carcass. Both human and marine carnivores represent challenges to the providential care of the creator that is suggested by the end-time feast of the righteous. Ishmael draws out the grotesque implications of the scene of Stubb's supper, as the murderous feeding of the sharks acts as a dramatic backdrop to the equally savage nature of man, best seen in the institutions of war and slavery, the latter illustrated by the horrors of the infamous Middle Passage. The result is a mordant Swiftian satire on the cannibalistic norms of human and animal nature, packed in one appalling periodic sentence, followed by a shocking conclusion about the evil at the heart of nature:

Though amid all the smoking horror and diabolism of a sea-fight, sharks will be seen longingly gazing up to the ship's decks, like hungry dogs round a table where red meat is being carved, ready to bolt down every killed man that is tossed to them; and though, while the valiant butchers over the deck-table are thus cannibally carving each other's live meat with carving-knives all gilded and tasseled, the sharks, also, with their jewel-hilted mouths, are quarrelsomely carving away under the table at the dead meat; and though, were you to turn the whole affair upside down, it would still be pretty much the same thing, that is to say, a shocking sharkish business enough for all parties; and though sharks also are the invariable outriders of all slave ships crossing the Atlantic, systematically trotting alongside, to be handy in case a parcel is to be carried anywhere, or a dead slave to be decently buried; and though one or two other like instances might be set down, touching the set terms, places, and occasions, when sharks do most socially congregate, and most hilariously feast; yet is there no conceivable time or occasion when you will find them in such countless numbers, and in gayer or more jovial spirits, than around a dead sperm whale, moored by night to a whale-ship at sea. If you have never seen that sight, then suspend your decision about the propriety of devil-worship, and the expediency of conciliating the devil. (293)

The midnight setting and the sharks' eager consumption of human as well as whale flesh add to the somber diabolism of the scene, while the comparison of sharks to hungry dogs in the service of their master, man, only makes the overall satirical point sharper.

In addition to the grotesque comedy of Stubb's supper with its Old Testament-related subtexts, we also find an implied satirical critique of the New Testament ethic of nonviolence when Stubb gets the ship's elderly cook, Fleece, to preach a mock sermon to the sharks to get them to desist from their savage feeding. Fleece's nickname suggests the innocence of the lamb, and his devout demeanor makes him a suitable candidate to deliver a spontaneous Christian homily, but his attempt to sermonize the sharks is a manifestly absurd endeavor, despite the legitimate Christian language and doctrine contained in his message. The only real hope of transforming the predatory nature of the shark into something more harmless, of course, is the arrival of the Old Testament messianic age or the Christian millennium. Fleece's sermon to the sharks is a satire on the remoteness of the apocalyptic elimination of evil, despite the fervent evangelical faith of antebellum America, and on the general inadequacy of nonviolent Christian ethics in the world of nature.[16]

The first phase of Stubb and the cook's conversation involves Fleece's mock sermon to the sharks to moderate their savagery, in accordance with Stubb's satirical request: "Cook, go and talk to 'em; tell 'em they are welcome to help themselves civilly, and in moderation, but they must keep quiet" (294). Fleece is at first inclined to swear at the sharks to "stop dat dam noise dar" (294), but Stubb convinces him that a more gentlemanly approach might be more productive. Thus the sharks become a particularly recalcitrant congregation in whose ill-disposed nature Fleece is himself implicated. The black comedy of the scene soon comes into focus in the verbal interplay between the connoisseur of whale flesh Stubb and the ancient black cook, a figure of comic obtuseness whose conversation with Stubb recalls the comic exchanges of Tambo and Bones in contemporary minstrel shows. Fleece's ensuing brief sermon forms a symbolic counterpart to Father Mapple's sermon on Jonah earlier in the narrative with Mapple's text and message conveying an Old Testament doctrine of fearful submission to God as opposed to Fleece's New Testament message of loving cooperation with one's fellow man—even as both sermons preach a shared Judeo-Christian ethic of self-denial. Fleece begins by addressing the sharks as "Belubed fellow-critters" and then raises the issue of their "woraciousness":

> "Well, den, Belubed fellow-critters:" —
>
> "Right!" exclaimed Stubb, approvingly, "coax 'em to it; try that," and Fleece continued.
>
> "Dough you is all sharks, and by natur wery woracious, yet I zay to you, fellow-critters, dat dat woraciousness—'top dat dam slappin' ob de tail! How you tink to hear, 'spose you keep up such a dam slappin' and bitin' dare?"
>
> "Cook," cried Stubb, collaring him, "I wont have that swearing. Talk to 'em gentlemanly."
>
> Once more the sermon proceeded.
>
> "Your woraciousness, fellow-critters, I don't blame ye so much for; dat is natur, and can't be helped; but to gobern dat wicket natur, dat is de pint. You is sharks, sartin; but if you gobern de shark in you, why den you be angel; for all angel is not'ing more dan de shark well goberned. Now, look here, bred'ren, just try wonst to be cibil, a helping yourselbs from dat whale. Don't be tearin' de blubber out your neighbor's mout, I say. Is not one shark good right as toder to dat whale? And, by Gor, none on you has de right to dat whale; dat whale belong to some one else. I know some o' you has berry brig mout, brigger dan oders; but den de brig mouts sometimes has de small bellies; so dat de bigness ob de mout is not to swallow wid, but to bite off de blubber for de small fry ob sharks, dat can't get into de scrouge to help demselves."
>
> "Well done, old Fleece!" cried Stubb, "that's Christianity; go on." (295)

David S. Reynolds has identified a likely source for Fleece's homiletic discourse in the urban humor of William H. Levison, the author of a series of burlesque sermons by an imaginary Negro preacher, Julius Caesar Hannibal, published in the *New York Picayune* in the late 1840s and collected into two volumes entitled *Julius Caesar Hannibal* and *Black Diamonds*. "Melville's contemporary readers would have found a familiar amusement in the fact that Fleece uses sharks as his text, because Levison's Hannibal had preached funny sermons about many strange animals: the crocodile, the lobster, the monkey, the elephant, the hog, and the whale. Nor would they have been surprised by Fleece's ultimately cynical message—the horrifying voraciousness of the sharks, symbolizing the universal cannibalism of humankind and nature—for Hannibal frequently emphasized human savagery."[17]

Yet if Fleece's sermon would seem to have a topical source in the popular humor of the day, the distinctive language and content of his address would also seem to hint at an actual biblical source. Indeed, given the fact that Father Mapple's sermon was based on a text from the Old Testament, a New Testament source for Fleece's sermon to the sharks would seem to be a logical complement. While the basic message of his sermon might suggest passages in several Pauline epistles, the main source for Fleece's remarks is in fact the First Epistle of Peter, a letter of encouragement and exhortation addressed to the new gentile Christian converts in the provinces of Asia. In the second chapter of his letter, the author emphasizes the need for spiritual rebirth, self-denial, and submission to authority for the new believer:

> Dearly beloved, I beseech you as strangers and pilgrims, abstain from fleshly lusts, which war against the soul;
>
> Having your conversation honest among the Gentiles: that, whereas they speak against you as evil-doers, they may by your good works, which they shall behold, glorify God in the day of visitation.
>
> Submit yourselves to every ordinance of man for the Lord's sake: whether it be to the king, as supreme;
>
> Or unto governors, as unto them that are sent by him for the punishment of evildoers, and for the praise of them that do well.
>
> For so is the will of God, that with well doing ye may put to silence the ignorance of foolish men:
>
> As free, and not using your liberty for a cloke [cloak] of maliciousness, but as the servants of God. (1 Peter 2:11–16)

Several key words and ideas here correlate to Fleece's sermon. First, when addressing his predatory animal audience, Fleece parodies the "dearly beloved" of 1 Peter 2:11, a phrase (along with the simpler "beloved") found in several New Testament epistles. In addition, just as Fleece reprimands the voracious appetite of the sharks, so Peter enjoins the faithful to "abstain from fleshly lusts." And just as Fleece tells the sharks to "gobern dat wicked natur," so Peter tells believers to submit to all "governors" as representatives of the civil power of the state sent "for the punishment of evil-doers."

In addition to the second chapter of 1 Peter, the content of Fleece's sermon also seems partially based on admonitions made two chapters later, in which the writer tells his flock that the time is past when as gentiles they could indulge their appetites without limit:

> when we walked in lasciviousness, lusts, excess of wine, revellings, banquetings, and abominable idolatries.
>
> Wherein they [the new converts' former companions] think it strange that ye run not with them to the same excess of riot, speaking ill of you....
>
> And above all things have fervent charity among yourselves: for charity shall cover the multitude of sins.
>
> Use hospitality one to another without grudging.
>
> As every man hath received the gift, even so minister the same one to another, as good stewards of the manifold grace of God. (1 Peter 4:3–4, 8–10)

Just as the New Testament author tells his fellow Christians to stop engaging in "banquetings and abominable idolatries," Fleece addresses the sharks in their similar pursuit of "banqueting" on raw whale meat. And just as the author argues that "charity shall cover a multitude of sins," Fleece is urging the sharks to be "cibil" and exercise charity toward each other by sharing their food.

No matter if Fleece's comic sermon to the sharks, like any other contemporary Christian sermon, has a biblical text at its core, it falls on deaf ears. The congregation of sharks continue their devouring of the carcass, and Stubb tells him to pronounce a final benediction on the creatures. Instead, Fleece issues a parting curse, which inverts everything he has just said in his sermon: "Cussed fellow-critters! Kick up de damndest row as ever you can; fill you dam' bellies 'till dey bust—and den die" (295). The honesty and inherent logic of the curse are perhaps more convincing than all the previous idealism of the gospel-based injunction for self-control. In this scene of subversive humor we find the irreligious Stubb manipulating the old black cook, whose name ostensibly conveys the Christian ideal of lamblike innocence, into an absurd demonstration of the limitations of

Christian ethics in a savage carnivorous world typified by hungry sharks.

The comic subversion is not over yet, however. For in a mock catechism Stubb attacks Fleece for his alleged ignorance of how to cook a whale steak and criticizes Fleece's religious beliefs. Inquiring into the place of his birth, Stubb mockingly tells the cook he must "be born over again" (296) to the knowledge of cooking whale meat—an appropriate biblical phrase, given its provenance in the same epistle of Peter that Fleece used as the text of his sermon. When Fleece insists that the meat he cooked tastes good, Stubb attacks him for his lack of conscience in asserting such a dreadful lie, reminding Fleece of possible retribution in the afterlife: "Where do you expect to go to, cook?" Hearing that Fleece expects to ascend to heaven, Stubb remains in a stubbornly this-worldly mind-set: "But don't you know the higher you climb, the colder it gets? Main-top, eh?" (297). To Stubb, getting into heaven must be done by the ticklish business of climbing the rigging, not "crawling through the lubber's hole." However, "none of us are in heaven yet" (297)—and Stubb, with his resolutely materialist vision, is not likely to get there any time soon. A convinced Epicurean, Stubb returns to the subject of how to cook a whale steak, which he insists must be barely cooked at all: "Hold the steak in one hand, and show a live coal to it with the other; that done, dish it, d'ye hear?" (297). He then tells Fleece to pickle the tips of the whale's fins and flukes—and to prepare him a breakfast of "Whale-balls." Fleece's final verdict on Stubb's culinary preference for raw meat and unlikely body parts brings us back to the original subject of sharks, with a new ironic twist: "I'm bressed if he ain't more of shark dan Massa Shark hisself" (297).[18]

Fleece's self-defensive ironic association of Stubb with the sharks is part of the minstrel show format of chapter 64 providing an amusing dramatic framework to the more serious ethical implications of the scene, which are based on the abhorrent sight of predatory nature and which extend into the next two chapters. The irreverent comedy of "Stubb's Supper," behind which lies the Epicurean temper of the second mate, is thus immediately followed by Ishmael's brief disquisition on "The Whale as a Dish" in chapter 65, which investigates the history of the whale as an item of human consumption.[19] In contrast to Fleece's disapproval of Stubb's culinary tastes, Ishmael's investigation here represents a vindication of Stubb's taste for whale meat, for Ishmael undercuts the baseless prejudice of "landsmen" against whalemen consuming any part of the newly killed whale "by its own light." Ishmael's homiletic rejoinder is that human beings regularly kill and consume the meat of freshly killed cattle, a point that leads him into an attack on cruelty to animals by the allegedly "civilized and enlightened gourmand" (300) in a satirical passage that reverses the values of civilized and savage in their use of food:

> Go to the meat-market of a Saturday night and see the crowds of live bipeds staring up at the long rows of dead quadrupeds. Does not that sight take a tooth out of the cannibal's jaw? Cannibals? who is not a cannibal? I tell you it will be more tolerable for the Fejee that salted down a lean missionary in his cellar against a coming famine; it will be more tolerable for that provident Fejee, I say, in the day of judgment, than for thee, civilized and enlightened gourmand, who nailest geese to the ground and feastest on their bloated livers in thy paté-de-foie-gras.
>
> But Stubb, he eats the whale by its own light, does he? and that is adding insult to injury, is it? Look at your knife-handle, there, my civilized and enlightened gourmand dining off that roast beef, what is that handle made of?—what but the bones of the brother of the very ox you are eating? And what do you pick your teeth with, after devouring that fat goose? With a feather of the same fowl. (300)

The whole passage constitutes a modern update to Montaigne's well-known essay on cannibalism, with its relativistic notions on the moral judgment of non-Western cultures by European standards, and Swift's ironic apology for cannibalism in "A Modest Proposal." The argument here is framed in biblical terms, for Ishmael's assertion that the cannibal who "salted down a lean missionary in his cellar against a coming famine" will fare better in the day of judgment than the consumer of paté de foie gras echoes Christ's claim: "Verily I say unto you, It shall be more tolerable for the land of Sodom and Gomorrah in the day of judgment, than for that city [the city that refuses to receive the twelve disciples]" (Matt. 10:15, also 11:22, 24, 12:36). The moral challenge here is that needless cruelty to animals in order to indulge overdeveloped tastes in cuisine will ultimately be judged more harshly even than the Fejee cannibal (the implied equivalent to the inhabitants of the Cities of the Plain) who eats a missionary for purely nutritional purposes. Ishmael's subsequent condemnation of the "civilized and enlightened gourmand" who might attack Stubb for eating the whale "by its own light" also has an underlying biblical proof text in the Sermon on the Mount: "Judge not, that ye be not judged. For with what judgment ye judge, ye shall be judged: and with what measure ye mete, it shall be measured to you again" (Matt. 7:1–2). The final message here is that civilized and savage peoples are not so far removed in their moral norms and habits as the comfortable denizens of the civilized world would like to believe.

Ishmael's vindication of Stubb's taste for whale meat, then, performs the paradoxical task of using Christ's teachings to defend an act of carnivorous consumption that is, in itself, implicitly a satirical critique of a New Testament ethic of nonviolence. The final word in this ironic sequence focusing on Stubb's challenge to divine beneficence and Christian ethics comes in chapter 66 ("The Shark Massacre"), in which the sharks that were consuming the whale carcass are killed with whaling spades, so that the huge body isn't totally consumed overnight. The sharks' ferocity is evident when they attack each other after receiving a wound from the whaling spade, and even bend around to eat their own obtruding entrails in an instinctive act of self-cannibalism. The ultimate instance of their astonishing malignancy occurs when a dead shark hoisted on deck nearly bites off Queequeg's hand when he tries to shut its jaw, proving that a "sort of generic or Pantheistic vitality seemed to lurk in their very joints and bones, after what might be called individual life had departed" (302). Queequeg's reaction to his wound is a spontaneous indictment of the god, whether pagan or Christian, who created the shark: "'Queequeg no care what god made him shark,' said the savage, agonizingly lifting his hand up and down; 'wedder Feejee god or Nantucket god; but de god wat made shark must be one dam Ingin'" (300). Queequeg's spontaneous, racist indictment of God as the savage author of evil is an epigrammatic statement summarizing Ahab's whole case against the deity who was, in his view, responsible for the loss of his leg.

Stubb's consumption of the whale steak, with its counterpart in the feasting sharks, offers a grotesque comedy of cannibalistic appetites in both humankind and nature, and the black cook's enjoining the sharks to "gobern dat wicked nature" adds a satiric critique of Christian ethics. Rather than governing their evil natures or helping the less fortunate, as the cook commands, the sharks are so voracious they will even consume their own entrails. These chapters illustrating the pervasive consumption of flesh in the animal kingdom show Stubb acting as both object and agent of satirical comedy in relation to the act of eating the raw flesh of the sperm whale, a modern embodiment of the archetypal Leviathan.[20]

The final grotesque illustration of the savagery of nature's universal cannibalism occurs in chapter 69 ("The Funeral"), as the sperm whale carcass drifts through the ocean, consumed by hungry sharks and birds. Instead of illustrating the apocalyptic feasting of the righteous on the body of Leviathan, the "funeral" of the sperm whale reveals the horrible indignity of nature's great creation attacked by predators whose sable appearance may simulate human mourning attire but whose real interest is in the food available. In his best vein of black humor, Ishmael notes: "There's a most doleful and most mocking funeral! The sea-vultures all in pious mourning, the air-sharks all punctiliously in black or speckled. In life but few of them would have helped the whale, I ween, if peradventure he had needed it; but upon the banquet of his funeral they most piously do pounce. Oh, horrible vulturism of the earth! from which not even the mightiest whale is free" (308). The image here (as in the chapter "Brit") is of the sea as a realm of relentless war between species up and down the food chain in which we again find a subversion of the benign biblical image of the creation as found, for example, in Psalm 104. As if this savage vision is not unsettling enough, Ishmael notes the absurd fact that the whale's carcass is sometimes mistaken by ships for shoal water, thereby creating an imaginary hazard on future maps—a striking example of the survival of outdated precedents, traditions, and "old beliefs never bottomed on the earth, and now not even hovering in the air! There's orthodoxy!" (309). The whale's carcass is a prime example of both nature's grotesque savagery and the unlimited power of human credulity, with its willingness to accept obsolete dogmas and superstitions— including the dogmas of Christian tradition premised on a beneficent creator, despite all evidence to the contrary.

Perhaps the most explicit statement of the Joban theme of God's ultimate responsibility for allowing evil in the world occurs in a comic dialogue between Stubb and Flask, in chapter 73, during which Stubb narrates an updated nautical version of the folktale opening of the book of Job describing the wager between God and the satan for Job's soul.[21] The chapter, entitled "Stubb and Flask Kill a Right Whale; and Then Have a Talk over Him," describes the killing of a right whale so that its head may be hoisted upon the side of the *Pequod* opposite a sperm whale's head according to Fedallah's occult belief that the ship would thereby be magically protected against capsizing. In the process of preparing the whale for towing back to the *Pequod*, Stubb and Flask discuss the Parsee's mysterious presence on the ship. Stubb insists facetiously that he's the devil in disguise. After some whimsical joking about how Fedallah manages to hide his tail, Stubb also asserts that Ahab made a Faustian bargain with the Parsee, and the latter promised Ahab the White Whale in exchange for Ahab's soul. Stubb begins the conversation with an intentionally naïve question:

"What's the old man have so much to do with him for?"

"Striking up a swap or a bargain, I suppose."

"Bargain?—About what?"

"Why, do you see, the old man is hard bent after that White Whale, and the devil there is trying to come round him, and get him to swap away his silver watch, or his soul, or something of that sort, and then he'll surrender Moby Dick."

"I don't know, Flask, but the devil is a curious chap, and a wicked one, I tell ye. Why, they say as how he went sauntering into the old flag-ship once, switching his tail about devilish easy and gentlemanlike, and inquiring if the old governor was at home. Well, he was at home, and asked the devil what he wanted. The devil, switching his hoofs, up and says, 'I want John.' 'What for?' says the old governor. 'What business is that of yours,' says the devil, getting mad,—'I want to use him.' 'Take him,' says the governor—and by the Lord, Flask, if the devil didn't give John the Asiatic cholera before he got through with him, I'll eat this whale in one mouthful. But look sharp—aint you all ready there? Well, then, pull ahead, and let's get the whale alongside."

"I think I remember some such story as you were telling," said Flask, when at last the two boats were slowly advancing with their burden towards the ship, "but I can't remember where."

"Three Spaniards? Adventures of those three bloody-minded soldadoes? Did ye read it there, Flask? I guess ye did?"

"No: never saw such a book; heard of it, though. But now, tell me, Stubb, do you suppose that that devil you was speaking of just now, was the same you say is now on board the Pequod?"

"Am I the same man that helped kill this whale? Doesn't the devil live for ever; who ever heard that the devil was dead? Did you ever see any parson a wearing mourning for the devil? And if the devil has a latch-key to get into the admiral's cabin, don't you suppose he can crawl into a port-hole? Tell me that, Mr. Flask?" (325–26)

In Stubb's pungent reformulation of the beginning of the book of Job (with echoes of both Marlowe's and Goethe's Faust stories), the "devil" is the authorized "adversary" figure; the old flagship is the heavenly court; the old governor is the God of the Old Testament; John is Job (or Johan Faust); and the devil's infliction of the Asiatic cholera on John (alluding to the notorious cholera pandemic of 1831–1833) is comparable to the attack of skin disease (traditionally boils) inflicted on Job by the satan. God gives permission to the satan to test Job's religious commitment by depriving him of his fortune, family, and physical health, while in Stubb's parodic rendition, a "sauntering" devil is given unquestioned authority to inflict harm on John. The subversive message is that God—the old governor—gives permission for the devil's destructive actions. Although based on the Job story, in which the satan is an authorized agent of the heavenly court, in Stubb's retelling he acts more like the traditional Christian devil, especially in his modern embodiment (following Goethe) as the suave but heartless Mephistopheles.

Stubb's exchange with Flask here is reminiscent of the whimsical conversation in *Doctor Faustus* of Faust's assistant, Wagner, with the clown Robin, itself a parodic commentary on John Faustus's recent dealings with Mephistopheles in scene 4 of Marlowe's play. That Flask has only a vague recollection of Stubb's story demonstrates his unsurprising lack of familiarity with the contents of the Bible. Indeed, Stubb tweaks him for his ignorance, suggesting that the story came from a popular novel of the era, George Walker's *The Three Spaniards* (1800). Whatever his own source of knowledge of the Job and Faust stories in his conversation with Flask, Stubb demonstrates his understanding of the Job-like or Faust-like situation Ahab has taken on for himself in the hunt for Moby Dick while the sescond mate jauntily laughs off the mysterious figure of Fedallah.

The full theological implications of Stubb's parable are made more explicit further along in Stubb and Flask's conversation when Flask questions Stubb's bravado about what the latter might do to rid the *Pequod* of the patently diabolical Fedallah:

> "But see here, Stubb, I thought you a little boasted just now, that you meant to give Fedallah a sea-toss, if you got a good chance. Now, if he's so old as all those hoops of yours come to, and if he is going to live for ever, what good will it do to pitch him overboard—tell me that?"
>
> "Give him a good ducking, anyhow."
>
> "But he'd crawl back."
>
> "Duck him again; and keep ducking him."
>
> "Suppose he should take it into his head to duck you, though—yes, and drown you—what then?"
>
> "I should like to see him try it; I'd give him such a pair of black eyes that he wouldn't dare to show his face in the admiral's cabin again for a long while, let alone down in the orlop there, where he lives, and hereabouts on the upper decks where he sneaks so much. Damn the devil, Flask; do you suppose I'm afraid of the devil? Who's afraid of him, except the old governor who daresn't catch him and put him in double-darbies, as he deserves, but lets him go about kidnapping people; aye, and signed a bond with him, that all the people the devil kidnapped, he'd roast for him? There's a governor!" (326–27)

The implied basis for Stubb's remarks is again the book of Job in which God has authorized the satan's actions, except that Stubb now indicts the old governor for allowing the devil to kidnap people with impunity. Indeed, according to Stubb, God has signed a bond with the devil so that the latter would roast all his kidnap victims—as a service to God. (In the Faust story, it is Faust himself who signs a bond with the devil.) Since there is no mention of hell in connection with the satan's actions in the book of Job (the Old Testament Sheol was only a weak anticipation of the Christian hell), Stubb is again conflating the Old Testament figure of "the adversary" with the more familiar Christian concept of the devil (Satan), whose deeds are performed in opposition to, not in cooperation with, the deity. In Stubb's view, God is apparently afraid of the devil, even as he subcontracts his dirty work of damnation to his subordinate. The implied indictment of divine justice here is on a par with Ahab's early fulminations against Moby Dick; Stubb is just presenting a comic folkloric version of the same idea. Stubb ends his conversation with Flask with the claim that he's going to keep an eye out for Fedallah in case he tries to kidnap Ahab, and if the Parsee shows any sign of trouble, he'll pull his tail off with the capstan (an image of castration), thereby causing Beelzebub to lose face (or vital force) and thus desist from causing trouble. Stubb's comic parable inadvertently confirms the centrality of Job to Ahab's symbolic identity even as it serves as a simplified cartoon version of Ahab's grand quest for Moby Dick.

In addition to the assimilation of biblical paradigms of theodicy and eschatology to the comic portions of *Moby-Dick*, the same key texts are also blended with the novel's use of the tragic Shakespearean mode in the overarching story of Ahab's vengeance. While Shakespearean parallels can be found throughout *Moby-Dick*, we will here examine Melville's conjoined appropriation of Job and *King Lear* in two chapters of the novel. Harold Fisch and Steven Marx have examined the Joban dimensions to Shakespeare's *Lear*, which split the experience of Job between the old king and Gloucester, both of whom suffer seemingly gratuitous family disinheritance and disaster; the former undergoes exposure to the forces of chaos in a storm, the latter is redeemed from Job-like despair in a mock suicide and recovery on the cliffs of Dover.[22] The contiguous chapters 70 ("The Sphynx") and 71 ("The Jeroboam's Story") develop Ahab's stature as a Job-like or Lear-like tragic hero paradoxically capable of both probing moral insight and self-destructive blindness.

In chapter 70, Ahab is seen alone on deck during an intense noontime calm, addressing the huge severed head of Stubb's recently killed sperm

whale, hanging at the side of the *Pequod* and half-immersed in the ocean.
Envisaging the head as a modern version of the ancient Egyptian sphinx but
also assuming the role of Oedipus confronting the Theban monster (which
posed the famous riddle to Oedipus, the reverse of Ahab's questioning of
the sphinx-like whale's head), Ahab addresses the giant whale's head as a
guardian of cosmic and apocalyptic secrets, based on the fact that the sperm
whale was the deepest diver of all whales.[23] (The thirty-foot height of the
Egyptian sphinx's human head is comparable to a full-grown male sperm
whale's head.) Ahab implicitly assumes that, having been made on the fifth
day of creation when animal life was first produced, the "great whales" (Gen.
1:21) would know the master plan of the divine architect. Like Oedipus
seeking to answer the divine riddle of human existence in a seemingly
amoral universe, Ahab asks the whale head, as a surrogate godhead, to reveal
its knowledge of the deeps in which millions of human beings have suffered
and died:

> "Speak, thou vast and venerable head," muttered Ahab, "which, though
> ungarnished with a beard, yet here and there lookest hoary with mosses; speak,
> mighty head, and tell us the secret thing that is in thee. Of all divers, thou
> hast dived the deepest. The head upon which the upper sun now gleams, has
> moved amid this world's foundations. Where unrecorded names and navies
> rust, and untold hopes and anchors rot; where in her murderous hold this
> frigate earth is ballasted with bones of millions of the drowned; there, in that
> awful water-land, there was thy most familiar home. Thou hast been where
> bell or diver never went; hast slept by many a sailor's side, where sleepless
> mothers would give their lives to lay them down. Thou saw'st the locked
> lovers when leaping from their flaming ship; heart to heart they sank beneath
> the exulting wave; true to each other, when heaven seemed false to them.
> Thou saw'st the murdered mate when tossed by pirates from the midnight
> deck; for hours he fell into the deeper midnight of the insatiate maw; and
> his murderers still sailed on unharmed—while swift lightnings shivered the
> neighboring ship that would have borne a righteous husband to outstretched,
> longing arms. O head! thou has seen enough to split the planets and make an
> infidel of Abraham, and not one syllable is thine!" (311–12)

Ahab's soliloquy here is a tour de force of anguished inquiry into the
enigma of the unfathomable suffering of the innocent and the grotesque
impunity of the guilty in a world without any sign of divine providence—a
message that echoes the anguished complaints of Job: "He [God] destroyeth
the perfect with the wicked. / If the scourge slay suddenly, he will laugh at

the trial of the innocent. / The earth is given into the hand of the wicked: he covereth the faces of the judges thereof; if not, where, and who is he?" (Job 9:22–24). Like Ahab, Job demands an explanation for injustice: "Is it good unto thee that thou shouldest oppress, that thou shouldest despise the work of thine hands, and shine upon the counsel of the wicked? / Hast thou eyes of flesh? or seest thou as man seeth?" (Job 10:3–4). Ahab, like Job, perceives both the monstrous injustice of the human condition and the silence of the God who allegedly oversees it. In this respect, too, Ahab—especially in his final assertion that the whale has "seen enough to split the planets"—evokes the enraged Lear on the heath, calling down destruction on a monstrously immoral world ("Blow, winds, and crack your cheeks! rage, blow! / You cataracts and hurricanes, spout / Till you have drench'd our steeples"), or reacting to the news of the murder of his beloved youngest daughter: "Had I your tongues and eyes, I'd use them so / That heaven's vault should crack" (*King Lear*, III.ii.1–3, V.iii.259–60). Lear's desire for cosmic destruction here parallels Job's curse on the creation for giving him birth (Job 3), following the disasters that have afflicted him.

Ahab's soliloquy depicts him in perhaps his most noble light, as a champion of the human race in the midst of its immemorial and inexplicable suffering—in effect, an inquirer into the traditional mysteries of theodicy now focused on the primeval realm of the sea as a symbol of chaos. Like his cabin boy, Pip, in "The Castaway," Ahab imagines the sublime scene in the depths of the ocean, but instead of finding the life-affirming wisdom of the creation as Pip does, he finds only apocalyptic death and destruction. It is one of the paradoxes in his character that his tragic insights here are followed immediately by a representation of his intractable moral blindness in the next chapter, which recounts the *Pequod*'s encounter with the whaler *Jeroboam*. In the lead-up to his encounter with the crew of this whaler, Ahab is interrupted from his meditations on the whale's head by the announcement of a sail on the horizon. He is immediately cheered by this sign of a rising wind, as he wishes for the presence of Saint Paul to bring him the strong eastern wind (Euroclydon) that buffeted Paul's ship on the way to Rome (Acts 27:14). Feeling his mood improve with the breeze, Ahab ends his address to the whale's head with an assertion of the ineffable link between cosmos and consciousness: "O Nature, and O soul of man! how far beyond all utterance are your linked analogies! not the smallest atom stirs or lives in matter, but has its cunning duplicate in mind" (312).

This recognition of the interpenetration of matter and mind evokes the current Romantic theory of correspondence and the relation of macrocosm to microcosm, as notably articulated by Schelling, Wordsworth, and

Emerson. Yet in his ensuing experience with the *Jeroboam*, Ahab abruptly loses his philosophical acumen, and his obsessive revenge scheme reasserts itself. Like another Oedipus, Ahab moves from the insights of his encounter with the sphinx-like whale's head to the blindness of his encounter with the Tiresias-like prophet Gabriel of the *Jeroboam*, whose crew, like the inhabitants of Thebes, are laboring under the scourge of a malignant plague.

The nine encounters or gams between the *Pequod* and other whaling vessels throughout *Moby-Dick* create an antiphonal blend of comic and tragic motifs incorporated within the novel's larger biblical themes. These nine encounters can be divided into contiguous or thematically related pairs and triads. The *Pequod*'s brief salutation of the first ship encountered, the deathly silent *Albatross*, is thus followed by the prolonged gam with the crew of the *Town-Ho*, with its involved saga of mutiny and providential intervention by Moby Dick. The encounter with the French captain and crew of the sensually obsessed *Rosebud* (*Bouton de Rose*), whose captain is the butt of Stubb's practical joke, is followed by the gam with the humorous, commonsensical English captain and doctor of the *Samuel Enderby*, the ship being named after a notable English merchant house in keeping with the fact that England was the leading commercial nation in the world. The meeting with the desperate oil-deprived Germans of the *Virgin* (*Jungfrau*) is followed some time later by the brief salutation of the oil-rich American *Bachelor*, its crew merrily celebrating a full cargo. The gam with the grieving captain of the *Rachel* is soon followed by the funerary scene observed on the decks of the *Delight*, both vessels having recently lost crew members to the depredations of Moby Dick. In terms of structural triads, the encounters with the *Rosebud*, the *Samuel Enderby*, and the *Virgin* are all based on the humorous representation of foreign stereotypes while the encounters with the domestic *Albatross*, *Rachel*, and *Delight* all convey ominous messages of mortality.

Varying from brief evocations (the *Albatross*, *Bachelor*, *Rachel*, and *Delight*) to extended dramatic episodes (the *Town-Ho*, *Jeroboam*, *Jungfrau*, *Rose Bud*, and *Samuel Enderby*), these inset chapters serve a variety of thematic and structural functions in the narrative. For as Walter E. Bezanson notes, "The ships the *Pequod* passes may be taken as a group of metaphysical parables, a series of biblical analogues, a masque of situations confronting man, a pageant of the humors within men, a parade of the nations, and . . . concrete and symbolic ways of thinking about the White Whale." Moreover, in the absence of stops at traditional whaling ports, as Edward Stone points out, the gams with the other ships act as comparable occasions of social exchange even as they maintain the *Pequod's* isolation amid an atmosphere of cumulative foreboding.[24]

In addition, James Dean Young has shown that the *Pequod's* encounters with other whalers highlight the general problem of human communication while also indicating antithetical attitudes of belief or disbelief in the existence of the White Whale, several of the ships acting as unheeded omens of disaster for the captain of the *Pequod*.[25] For example, the first ship encountered, the *Albatross*, is unable to respond to Ahab's query about the White Whale because its captain drops his speaking trumpet. The long gam with the *Town-Ho* involves the story of the mutinous standoff between the sailor Steelkilt and the abusive mate Radney, ending in the latter's retributive and seemingly providential death caused by Moby Dick, a conclusion that never reaches Ahab's ears because of the crew's reluctance to risk sharing its unwelcome message. During the *Pequod's* encounter with the *Jeroboam*, a similar failure of communication is evident in the prophet Gabriel's unheeded warnings of apocalyptic doom. In the *Pequod's* subsequent encounter with the *Virgin* (*Jungfrau*), the German captain knows nothing about Moby Dick. The French captain of the *Rosebud* can't communicate with Stubb in English and thereby sets himself up for Stubb's elaborate joke on his obtuseness. In the gam with the *Samuel Enderby*, Ahab refuses to be warned by the English captain Boomer, who has also lost a limb to Moby Dick, while the jovially self-satisfied *Bachelor*, her deck and hold full with sperm oil and her crew preoccupied with revelry, has nothing to tell Ahab about the White Whale. The last two ships encountered, the *Rachel* and the *Delight*, provide a final unheeded warning of the deadly folly of attacking Moby Dick.

While the chapters describing the *Pequod's* encounters with other whalers repeatedly illustrate the theme of failed human communication, they also mirror the larger narrative by appropriating dramatic modes of comedy and tragedy. Thus, we may observe that four of the ships encountered (the *Jungfrau, Rose Bud, Samuel Enderby,* and *Bachelor*) variously exemplify elements of the comic vision including folly, trickery, and festivity while four ships (the *Albatross, Jeroboam, Rachel, Delight*) exhibit features of tragedy in their graphic depictions of isolation, suffering, and catastrophe. Still another extended encounter with the *Town Ho* (first published as a short story in the October 1851 *Harper's New Monthly Magazine*) exemplifies a generic mix of tragedy and comedy together with a complex blend of Christian allegory and myth. "The Town-Ho's Story" in fact differs substantially from the other gams of the *Pequod* in its elaborate frame narrative, its new cast of characters, and multiple sequences of action. Depicting an extended dramatic conflict between the tyrannizing first mate Radney and the charismatic common sailor Steelkilt, the story recalls the brutal struggle between the declining King Saul and the rising young David as God's anointed found in the First Book of Samuel. Like the novel in which it appears, the story is a revenge drama highlighting the ambiguity of good and evil.[26]

In keeping with the division of human experience into comedy and tragedy, we may read the nine encounters of the *Pequod* with other whalers as representative illustrations of major divisions in human attitudes toward the existence of evil, as symbolized by the White Whale. Thus, in the four comic gams we meet individuals who remain psychologically immature because they have no knowledge of the whale (the *Jungfrau, Rose Bud,* and *Bachelor*), or they belittle its existence (the *Samuel Enderby*). Such individuals confirm William James's observation that "systematic healthy-mindedness, failing as it does to accord to sorrow, pain, and death any positive and active attention whatsoever, is formally less complete than systems that try at least to include these elements in their scope." On the other hand, the *Pequod's* encounters with the *Albatross, Jeroboam, Rachel,* and *Delight* convey the traumatic experience of sorrow, pain, and death as existential sources of tragedy, which, as James notes, "may after all be the best key to life's significance, and possibly the only openers of our eyes to the deepest levels of truth."[27]

Two encounters, those with the *Jeroboam* and the *Jungfrau,* exhibit basic elements of tragedy and comedy, respectively, in the larger context of the novel's apocalyptic eschatology while they also exhibit the theme of failed communication. Coded messages and prophetic warning are well-known apocalyptic motifs as seen, for example, in the "writing on the wall" in the midst of Belshazzar's feast (described in the book of Daniel) and in the elaborate punitive warnings of the book of Revelation in the dramatized series of seven seals, trumpets, and vials, with their increasing destructive effects. The use of these symbolic motifs is most explicit in the *Pequod's* encounter with the *Jeroboam,* a dramatic iteration of the tragic potential of Ahab's quest, especially in his persistent Oedipus-like (and Lear-like) blindness to the folly of his actions. The encounter with the *Virgin,* on the other hand, enacts a parody of Christ's apocalyptic parable of the wise and foolish virgins (found in the Gospel of Matthew), thereby acting as a comic complement to the overwrought prophetic atmosphere of madness and moral blindness found ten chapters earlier in the encounter with the *Jeroboam.*

One of the most explicitly apocalyptic scenes in the novel occurs in chapter 71 when the *Pequod* encounters the *Jeroboam,* the third whaler it meets while pursuing the White Whale. The chapter describes how the *Jeroboam* of Nantucket, suffering from an outbreak of epidemic disease among the crew, is dominated by the presence of a sailor named Gabriel, a former Shaker from the original Albany-area settlement at Watervliet Village who has gained ascendancy over the crew as a fanatical prophet. The story of the sailor Gabriel's dominance over the crew of the *Jeroboam* is a case study in a familiar confluence between mental illness and messianic delusion:

> He had been originally nurtured among the crazy society of Neskyeuna [Watervliet Village] Shakers, where he had been a great prophet; in their cracked, secret meetings having several times descended from heaven by way of a trap-door, announcing the speedy opening of the seventh vial, which he carried in his vest-pocket; but, which, instead of containing gunpowder, was supposed to be charged with laudanum. A strange, apostolic whim having seized him, he had left Neskyeuna for Nantucket, where, with that cunning peculiar to craziness, he assumed a steady, common sense exterior, and offered himself as a green-hand candidate for the Jeroboam's whaling voyage. They engaged him; but straightaway upon the ship's getting out of sight of land, his insanity broke out in a freshet. He announced himself as the archangel Gabriel, and commanded the captain to jump overboard. He published his manifesto, whereby he set himself forth as the deliverer of the isles of the sea and vice-general of all Oceanica. The unflinching earnestness with which he declared these things;—the dark, daring play of his sleepless, excited imagination, and the praeternatural terrors of real delirium, united to invest this Gabriel in the minds of the majority of the ignorant crew, with an atmosphere of sacredness. Moreover, they were afraid of him. (314–15)

In its representation of events, chapter 71 draws on a combination of apocalyptic motifs from both Daniel and Revelation. The prophet's assumed name, Gabriel, is based on the name of the prophetic archangel in Daniel who interprets Daniel's vision of various symbolic animals by associating them with future historical events (Dan. 8:16–26) and then postulates a time frame for the redemption of the Jewish people, "to finish the transgression, and to make an end of sins, and to make reconciliation for iniquity" (Dan. 9:24). The mad Shaker prophet has taken on the role of angelic interpreter of political and spiritual liberation in the manner of the Old Testament Gabriel. In the meeting of the *Pequod* and the *Jeroboam*, the latter's Captain Mayhew, keeping his distance in a whaleboat, tells Ahab the story of the ship's encounter with Moby Dick. His tale is punctuated by repeated warnings from Gabriel, who had earlier warned the crew against attacking

Moby Dick, declaring the whale to be the "Shaker god incarnated." When the White Whale was seen a year or two later, the prophet warned the first mate Macey against hunting it, climbing up a masthead "and hurling forth prophecies of speedy doom to the sacrilegious assailants of his divinity" (316). But the captain ignored the warning, and in an attempt to capture the whale, the first mate, who had "burned with ardor to encounter him" (316), was knocked from his whaleboat and sank without a trace.

Captain Mayhew's story of this incident makes no impression on Ahab who remarks that he is bent on hunting the White Whale. This then galvanizes Gabriel into prophetic denunciation: "Think, think of the blasphemer— dead, and down there!—beware of the blasphemer's end!" (317). But Gabriel does not impress Ahab either, and this is significant because it tells us how unable—or disinclined—Ahab is to recognize a grotesquely distorted image of himself in the character of Gabriel. Like the prophet of the *Jeroboam*, Ahab is afflicted with a cunning form of madness. He rules his ship with charismatic but tyrannical authority and, like Gabriel, has assumed the role of a self-righteous redeemer. Moreover, they both give quasi-divine status to Moby Dick. But if both characters view the White Whale as an incarnation of divinity, they interpret the whale from antithetical moral positions— Gabriel announcing vengeance on the whale's attacker and Ahab seeking vengeance on the whale itself. Ahab's failure to be warned off his continued quest for Moby Dick is indicated further in a covert use of the book of Daniel when Ahab attempts to pass on an old letter addressed to one of the officers of the *Jeroboam*:

> Soon Starbuck returned with the letter in his hand. It was sorely tumbled, damp, and covered with a dull, spotted, green mould, in consequence of being kept in a dark locker of the cabin. Of such a letter, Death might well have been the post-boy.
>
> "Can'st not read it?" cried Ahab. Give it me, man. Aye, aye, it's but a dim scrawl;—what's this?" As he was studying it out, Starbuck took a long cutting-spade pole, and with his knife slightly split the end, to insert the letter there, and in that way, hand it to the boat, without its coming any closer to the ship.
>
> Meantime, Ahab holding the letter, muttered, "Mr. Har—yes, Mr. Harry— (a woman's pinny hand,—the man's wife, I'll wager)—Aye—Mr. Harry Macey, Ship Jeroboam;—why it's Macey, and he's dead!"
>
> "Poor fellow! poor fellow! and from his wife," signed Mayhew; "but let me have it."
>
> "Nay, keep it thyself," cried Gabriel to Ahab; "thou art soon going that way." (317–18)

We gain additional insight into this scene when we realize it is based obliquely on the scene in the book of Daniel in which the Old Testament prophet reads the mysterious "writing on the wall" spelling doom for the Chaldean (Babylonian) King Belshazzar as he feasts with his court. When the king's soothsayers are unable to interpret the writing, Belshazzar summons the Hebrew prophet Daniel who assails the impiety of Belshazzar for having "lifted up thyself against the Lord of heaven" (Dan. 5:23) and says that the mysterious writing means that "Mene; God hath numbered thy kingdom and finished it. / Tekel; Thou art weighed in the balances, and art found wanting. / Peres; Thy kingdom is divided, and given to the Medes and Persians" (Dan. 5:26–28). As Daniel predicts, that night Belshazzar is slain, and Darius the Mede seizes Babylon for the Persian empire. Like Daniel reading the writing on the wall Ahab can ostensibly decipher the name on the letter, but like the Babylonian king he is impervious to its deeper spiritual message, which the Shaker prophet is only too willing to reveal. Gabriel's ultimate prediction of Ahab's death and his seizing the letter and throwing it back at Ahab all resonate with the message of the biblical prophet Daniel for the impious Babylonian king.

The name of the ship on which Gabriel has gained control amplifies the biblical symbolism here. Jeroboam was the first king (ca. 922–901 BCE) of the newly divided Northern Kingdom of Israel who allegedly destroyed the religious unity of the Israelites by creating images of golden calves at Bethel and Dan (1 Kings 12:25–33). As the prophet Ahijah tells Jeroboam's wife, when she is sent to inquire about the sickness of the king's son, the Lord condemns her husband because he "hast gone and made thee other gods, and molten images, to provoke me to anger, and hast cast me behind thy back" (1 Kings 14:9). Nathalia Wright has traced the significance of the biblical King Jeroboam in chapter 71 of *Moby-Dick*, and she points out that the biblical prophet Elijah pronounced a curse on King Ahab and forecast for him a similar fate as that suffered by Jeroboam, the head of the dynasty of post-Solomonic kings of Israel, which ended with the conquest of Israel by the Assyrians in 722 BCE.[28] The mad Gabriel of the *Jeroboam* thus has a prototype in the prophet Ahijah, who predicts the death of King Jeroboam's son Abijah just as the Shaker prophet Gabriel views the death of the *Jeroboam*'s mate Macey as punishment for his attempt to kill Moby Dick. The biblical King Jeroboam, like his successor Ahab, was condemned by the harshly judgmental Deuteronomistic historian as an evil monarch who trafficked in foreign idols. Like Belshazzar in the later book of Daniel, Jeroboam is a doomed figure whose royal line will fail and whose kingdom, created through rebellion against Solomon in Jerusalem, will eventually perish (1 Kings 14:14–16). The Danielic context of the encounter between the prophet Gabriel and Captain Ahab and the biblical name of the Shaker prophet's whaleship thus convey a portentous message of tragic doom.

As a patently apocalyptic episode, Ahab's encounter with the mad prophet Gabriel in "The Jeroboam's Story" is predicated on several key motifs from the book of Daniel; yet it also incorporates important symbolic elements from the book of Revelation. In his aggressive denunciation of Ahab, Gabriel thus more nearly approaches one of the angels of wrath in Revelation than the impassive angel Gabriel in Daniel; and in Christian tradition the angel Gabriel traditionally announced the onset of the Last Judgment (1 Corinthians 15:52). The *Jeroboam's* mad prophet gained his apocalyptic apprenticeship originally among his fellow Shakers, in their meetings, when he "descended from heaven by the way of a trap-door, announcing the speedy opening of the seventh vial, which he carried in his vest-pocket" (314). The Shaker prophet has thus cast himself in the role of the angel who pours out the climatic seventh vial of wrath in Revelation. After this angel empties the vial, a heavenly voice announces, "It is done":

> And there were voices, and thunders, and lightnings; and there was a great earthquake, such as was not since men were upon the earth, so mighty an earthquake, and so great.
>
> And the great city was divided into three parts, and the cities of the nations fell: and great Babylon came in remembrance before God, to give unto her the cup of the wine of the fierceness of his wrath.
>
> And every island fled away, and the mountains were not found.
>
> And there fell upon men a great hail out of heaven, every stone about the weight of a talent: and men blasphemed God because of the plague of the hail; for the plague thereof was exceeding great. (Rev. 16:18–21)

Just as the angel with the seventh vial is the agent for a punitive plague (ultimately based on a similar plague of hail against the Egyptians, described in Exodus 9:23), Gabriel has gained his ascendancy onboard the *Jeroboam* because of the outbreak of a malignant epidemic, which the prophet claimed "was at his sole command; nor should it be stayed but according to his pleasure" (315). Earlier in the voyage, the captain had threatened to leave the mad prophet at the nearest port, but "the archangel forthwith opened all his seals and vials—devoting the ship and all hands to unconditional perdition, in case this intention was carried out" (315). Gabriel's credibility as a prophet has since been confirmed by his prescient warning to the deceased mate Macey not to kill Moby Dick.

In view of Gabriel's mastery of texts from the book of Revelation, his identity as a former Shaker is both dramatically and historically appropriate, given the sect's explicit apocalyptic theology. The sect considered its founder, Mother Ann Lee, to be the female incarnation of Christ's Second Coming in spirit, and its celibate cooperative communities were modeled on social arrangements assumed to be characteristic of the Christian millennium. In the late 1830s and early 1840s, the Shaker societies were in the midst of what was then called the Era of Manifestations, or "Mother Ann's Work," a period of recurrent spiritualist revivals in which the charismatic behavior of the sect's origins was spontaneously reasserted. "During the height of the revival, confusion abounded," notes religious historian Stephen Stein. "Everywhere religious excitement rose to fever pitch. . . . Unusual spirit visitors filled the meetinghouses week after week—angels with strange names, natives speaking foreign tongues, biblical figures from ancient times, political figures from America's past. . . . Trances repeatedly interrupted the flow of daily activities, sometimes meetings lasted into the early morning hours, and a few special rituals even took place in the middle of the night."[29] The prophet Gabriel in *Moby-Dick* evokes the Era of Manifestations, which began at the first Shaker community near Albany at Watervliet. Gabriel's act of descending from heaven through a trap door at Shaker meetings evokes the sect's self-consciously theatrical and charismatic modes of worship during the Era of Manifestations. The Shaker prophet's dire message of heavenly retribution similarly accords with the admonitory message found in communications with the spirits of Mother Ann, Mother Lucy Wright, Holy Mother Wisdom, and others at this time.[30]

The character of Gabriel in *Moby-Dick* with his seventh vial of God's wrath in his vest pocket evokes a notable phase of Shaker history spanning the period when Melville's novel was set, in the early 1840s. In keeping with this historical precedent, the *Pequod's* encounter with the *Jeroboam* is suffused with varied motifs from the books of Daniel and Revelation, and the overall message is a warning against Ahab's apocalyptic pursuit of the White Whale and the tragic consequences that will ensue if it is continued. Despite the overt similarities between mad Gabriel and mad Ahab, the latter refuses to recognize the Shaker prophet's admonitions, while the underlying historical similarities between the name *Jeroboam* and Ahab's own biblical namesake are also ignored by the captain of the *Pequod*. As a dramatic episode in the unfolding tragedy of Ahab's career, this chapter operates as a possible—but failed—occasion for tragic recognition in the hero, who refuses to acknowledge, now or hereafter, that his ambition to kill the White Whale may be fatally misguided.

In contrast to the multilayered tragic message of the *Pequod's* encounter with the *Jeroboam*, based on apocalyptic motifs from Daniel and Revelation and on contemporary Shaker history, the *Pequod's* meeting with the German ship *Jungfrau* in chapter 81 ("The Pequod meets the Virgin") is grounded in a parody of a well-known apocalyptic parable from the Gospel of Matthew. This chapter uses its biblical proof text for purposes of comical satire regarding human folly and worldly wisdom, demonstrating a thematic continuity from the earlier chapters describing Stubb's killing and consumption of the whale. The events described in chapter 81 are based on Christ's end-time parable of the wise and foolish virgins, in which Christ reminds his disciples of the need for vigilance regarding his imminent advent, telling the story of the ten virgins who went forth to meet the bridegroom:

> And five of them were wise, and five were foolish.
>
> They that were foolish took their lamps, and took no oil with them:
>
> But the wise took oil in their vessels with their lamps.
>
> While the bridegroom tarried, they all slumbered and slept.
>
> And at midnight there was a cry made, Behold, the bridegroom cometh; go ye out to meet him.
>
> Then all those virgins arose and trimmed their lamps.
>
> And the foolish said unto the wise, Give us of your oil; for our lamps are gone out.
>
> But the wise answered, saying, Not so; lest there be not enough for us and you: but go ye rather to them that sell, and buy for yourselves.
>
> And while they went to buy, the bridegroom came: and they that were ready went in with him to the marriage: and the door was shut.
>
> And afterward came also the other virgins, saying, Lord, Lord, open to us.
>
> But he answered and said, Verily I say unto you, I know you not.
>
> Watch therefore, for ye know neither the day nor the hour wherein the Son of man cometh. (Matt. 25:1–13)

Like the parable of the waiting servants (Mark 13:33–37; Matt. 24:42–51; Luke 12:35–40), the parable of the wise and foolish virgins teaches the unexpectedness of Christ's Second Coming and the need for constant preparedness—unlike a variety of other New Testament prophecies indicating the precise "signs of the times" that will announce the Second Advent. The probable historical backdrop to the biblical lesson of chapter 81 is the experience of the Millerites, whose overeagerness to set a date for the Second Coming led to the "Great Disappointment" in October 1844 just as Melville was returning home from his nautical adventures in the Pacific (see chapter 2 above).

The *Pequod*'s encounter with the *Virgin* in chapter 81 satirizes the eschatological scenario outlined above in the Gospel of Matthew. The *Jungfrau* of Bremen has completely run out of whale oil and its master, Derick De Deer, comes on board the *Pequod* with lamp-feeder and oil can in hand requesting oil to light its lamps. Asked by Ahab about any information about Moby Dick:

> the German soon evinced his complete ignorance of the White Whale; immediately turning the conversation to his lamp-feeder and oil can, with some remarks touching his having to turn into his hammock at night in profound darkness—his last drop of Bremen oil being gone, and not a single flying-fish yet captured to supply the deficiency; concluding by hinting that his ship was indeed what in the Fishery is technically called a *clean* one (that is, an empty one), well deserving the name of Jungfrau or the Virgin. (352)

It is clear that the German whalers of the *Jungfrau*—the foolish virgins of Christ's parable—are unprepared for the apocalyptic arrival of the "bridegroom," and not surprisingly, the ship's master is ignorant of the existence of Ahab's White Whale. And just as the foolish virgins of the parable are unprepared for the bridegroom's midnight advent, the captain of the *Jungfrau* must "turn into his hammock at night in profound darkness." The alliterative German name of the ship's master and his hapless inability to obtain oil both evoke the broad ethnic humor of the comic "Dutchman" of the popular stage.

The comedy here continues after the German captain has obtained his oil from the *Pequod* and is returning back to his ship, for the implicit reliance on the parable of the wise and foolish virgins is again evident after a group of sperm whales is detected just as Derick is reboarding his own vessel. At this point, the crews of both the *Pequod* and the *Virgin* lower their whaleboats to hunt a pod of eight whales, accompanied at some distance behind by an old and infirm male, a "huge, humped old bull, which by his comparatively slow progress, as well as by the unusual yellowish incrustations overgrowing him, seemed afflicted with the jaundice, or some other infirmity" (352). In their hunt for this stricken whale, Derick and his men continue to act as the foolish virgins of the parable who are unable to obtain their oil before the advent of the "bridegroom," while Starbuck, Stubb, Flask, and their respective crews act as the wise virgins, seeking to obtain their oil by showing a great ingenuity in the killing of the old sperm whale. After the *Pequod*'s men have harpooned the whale over the heads of Derick's men (impeded in their chase by a fouled oar of one of the rowers), the grotesquely infirm body of the old whale is made evident from its missing fin, blind eye sockets, and the ulcerous sore on its flank. In the chapter's parodic rewriting of Christ's parable, the old whale is a pathetic stand-in for the apocalyptic bridegroom of Christ's prophecy, while the killing of the old whale is now made into an object lesson in the brutality of whaling, and of human predation generally. Ishmael adduces the ironic reason for the killing of sperm whales in the need to illuminate the weddings and other festivities of humankind—a flagrant violation of the nonviolent ethos of Christianity, and its compassion for the infirm found in Christ's ministry:

> As the boats now more closely surrounded him, the whole upper part of his form, with much of it that is ordinarily submerged, was plainly revealed. His eyes, or rather the places where his eyes had been, were beheld. As strange misgrown masses gather in the knotholes of the noblest oaks when prostrate, so from the points which the whale's eyes had once occupied, now protruded blind bulbs, horribly pitiable to see. But pity there was none. For all his old age, and his one arm, and his blind eyes, he must die the death and be murdered, in order to light the gay bridals and other merry-makings of men, and also to illuminate the solemn churches that preach unconditional inoffensiveness by all to all. Still rolling in his blood, at last he partially disclosed a strangely discolored bunch or protuberance, the size of a bushel, low down on the flank. (357)

In a gratuitously cruel finale to the killing of the old whale, Flask lances the ulcerous wound on the whale's flank (made by an embedded harpoon), inspiring the old whale with a "more than sufferable anguish" (358), and it soon dies from loss of blood.

In its satirical reconfiguration of Christ's parable of the wise and foolish virgins, the killing of the old whale in chapter 81 becomes another object lesson in the unchristian behavior of men as they compete in the modern world of commerce and whaling, with the more aggressive Yankees on the *Pequod* beating out the obtuse Germans of the *Jungfrau* for the prize of the old sperm whale. The crew of the American whaler are thus better prepared, not for the Second Coming of Christ but for the advent of sperm whales and their valuable oil. The implied moral message is underlined by the ironic contrast between Christ, the heavenly bridegroom of the parable, and the decrepit old male whale whose pathetic death is portrayed vividly as it spatters the whaleboats with "showers of gore" and impotently flaps its "stumped fin," while its "last expiring spout" diminishes like the shutting off of "some mighty fountain" (358). Replete with Homeric similes, the killing of the old disabled whale is also a parody of the alleged epic enterprise of whaling.

The ironic rewriting of the apocalyptic New Testament parable here is accompanied by an ironic allusion to chapter 41 of Job, in which God adduces the mighty Leviathan as a reminder of man's limited place in the scale of creation. Ishmael accordingly notes the apparent incongruity between the size and power of a sperm whale and the fact that, after it is harpooned, only three thin ropes attached to three small boats are able to secure him from escape:

> As the three boats there on that gently rolling sea, gazing down into its eternal blue noon; and as not a single groan or cry of any sort, nay, not so much as a ripple or a bubble came up from its depths; what landsman would have thought, that beneath all that silence and placidity, the utmost monster of the seas was writhing and wrenching in agony! Not eight inches of perpendicular rope were visible at the bows. Seems it credible that by three such thin threads the great Leviathan was suspended like the big weight to an eight day clock. Suspended? and to what? To three bits of board. Is this the creature of whom it was once so triumphantly said—"Canst thou fill his skin with barbed irons? or his head with fish-spears? The sword of him that layeth at him cannot hold, the spear, the dart, nor the habergeon: he esteemeth iron as straw; the arrow cannot make him flee; darts are counted as stubble; he laugheth at the shaking of a spear!" This the creature? this he? Oh! that unfulfilments should follow the prophets. For with the strength of a thousand thighs in his tail, Leviathan had run his head under the mountains of the sea, to hide him from the Pequod's fish-spears! (356)

The passage from Job acts as an admonitory subtext for Ahab's doomed pursuit of the White Whale; yet here the same text is challenged by Ishmael's observation of the technical realities of modern whaling. Ishmael's tongue-in-cheek lament that such "unfulfillments should follow the prophets" intentionally misconstrues the book of Job into an example of Old Testament prophecy instead of wisdom literature; the inaccurate prophet here is in fact God in the form of the Voice from the Whirlwind. Ishmael's demythologizing citation of the well-known text from Job draws attention to the disparity between the moral message of Job (humanity's abasement before the power of the creation) and its contemporary mastery of that same creation. Yet there is a New Testament dimension to the passage as well, for the final description of the sickly Leviathan's having "run his head under the mountains of the sea, to hide him from the Pequod's fish-spears," recalls the opening of the sixth seal in the book of Revelation when the kings and "great men" of the earth "hid themselves in the dens and in the rocks of the mountains; / And said to the mountains and rocks, Fall on us, and hide us from the face of him that sitteth on the throne, and from the wrath of the Lamb" (Rev. 6:15–16). Ironically, it is now the wrath of man, not God (in the form of Christ), from which the old whale must hide.[31]

The unexpectedly ironic conclusion to chapter 81 is that the old sperm whale turns out to be a serious hazard to the ship when it starts sinking while tied to the ship's chains. The safety of the *Pequod* is secured by Queequeg, who with a hatchet quickly cuts the chains attaching the whale to the ship, thereby allowing the whale to sink. Not long after this event, the German ship is seen again lowering its whaleboats in order to go after a finback whale—a species with a distinctive spout that looks like a sperm whale's but which cannot be captured because of the speed of its swimming. At the end of the chapter, the foolish virgins of the *Jungfrau* are again fruitlessly going after whale oil while the wise virgins of the *Pequod* have ultimately lost their once secure source of oil because their sickly old whale sinks into the sea. The sinking of the old whale's corpse acts as a climax to the comic bathos of the chapter and its subversion of a number of Old and New Testament proof texts.

In chapter 81, we find a comic inversion of a well-known apocalyptic parable from the Gospel of Matthew, a gospel in which Christ appears as a new Moses updating the moral law in his Sermon on the Mount, including blessings on the merciful and the peacemakers (Matt. 5:7, 9), and the instruction to "resist not evil" (Matt. 5:39) and to love one's enemies (Matt. 5:44). In the actions of both the crew of the *Jungfrau* and those on the *Pequod*, we see Christ's moral laws of mercy and nonviolence flagrantly violated, creating a comic incongruity between New Testament doctrine and the commercial mandates of the whaling industry. Despite his blinded and suffering condition, the old whale is brutally tortured and killed. The sickly old whale becomes a symbol of the violent aggression that underlies modern civilization and its ruthless exploitation of natural resources, as well as the sordid realities underlying the pious pretensions of modern Christianity.

CHAPTER SIX

Hubris and Heroism, Mortality and Immortality

WHEREAS A MIX OF COMIC and tragic motifs informs the larger biblical themes within the middle third of *Moby-Dick*, the development of Ahab's excessive pride, or hubris, appears in tandem with his distinctive traits of heroic courage in the final quarter of the narrative. Both Ishmael and Ahab also speculate in this portion of the novel on the mysterious interrelation of life and death and on the perennial human hope for spiritual immortality—issues that acutely concern Ishmael in his quest for moral wisdom, and Ahab in his quest for divine justice. Biblical themes of heroism and hubris, mortality and immortality, are thus paired in the latter chapters of *Moby-Dick*, and although these themes have appeared before in the narrative, they assume more sustained importance as the drama moves relentlessly toward its tragic climax.

Varying degrees of heroism and hubris are common in the composition of tragic figures, and Melville's Ahab is no exception here. Like a number of his prototypes whether biblical (Job, King Ahab), classical (Prometheus, Oedipus), Renaissance (Faustus, Hamlet, Lear, Macbeth), or Romantic (Faust, Manfred, Cain), Ahab shows outstanding moral strength and resolution when facing adversity. But he also demonstrates the defiant pride, overweening ambition, and delusory infallibility that can contribute to the tragic protagonist's downfall, as we see in the cases of King Ahab, Oedipus, Macbeth, Faustus, and Manfred. The concept of hubris plays a key role in ancient Greek drama and denotes a moral flaw in the tragic hero, which leads him to place himself above others and ignore the warnings of the gods, ultimately releasing the forces of nemesis that cause his downfall.

Aeschylean drama, with its adherence to the traditional pieties of ancient Greek religion, is a particularly fertile territory for examples of hubris. The chorus in the *Agamemnon* early affirms: "'The hand of Zeus has cast / The proud from their high place!' / This we may say, and trace / That hand from first to last."[1] The Old Testament prophet Isaiah had similarly excoriated the proud and lofty who, lifted up like tall trees, mountains, towers, and walls, would be brought low on the impending Day of the Lord:

> For the Day of the Lord of Hosts shall be upon every one that is proud and lofty, and upon every one that is lifted up; and he shall be brought low:
> And upon all the cedars of Lebanon, that are high and lifted up, and upon all the oaks of Bashan.
> And upon all the high mountains, and upon all the hills that are lifted up,
> And upon every high tower, and upon every fenced wall,
> And upon all the ships of Tarshish, and upon all pleasant pictures.
> And the loftiness of man shall be bowed down, and the haughtiness of men shall be made low: and the Lord alone shall be exalted in that day. (2:12–17)

Such presumptuous elevation implies an invasion of the realm of the divine, a prohibited action going back to the story of the Tower of Babel (Gen. 11:1–9) and repeatedly found throughout the books of the Old Testament.

If, in the Old Testament, there is no exact equivalent to the Greek concept of hubris, we still have various terms for "pride," all stemming from a root meaning of physical elevation leading to the sins of arrogance and assumed self-sufficiency. Characteristic of this sinful pride are boastfulness and glorying in an exalted sense of power. Admonitory examples of such behavior can be found in the prophets, Psalms, and Proverbs, the latter text offering the well-known formula "Pride goeth before destruction, and an haughty spirit before a fall" (Prov. 16:18). Donald E. Gowan notes of the Hebrew sense of hubris: "What we would call the proud man is what the Hebrews called the man whose heart, or eyes, or face, or spirit is exalted; i.e., he considers himself above others (said explicitly in Deut. 17:20), to need no one (cf. Jer. 13:15 and the context of Isa. 10:12), and to be responsible to no one." This sense of irresponsibility to others "includes even God, and it is apparent that such an attitude leads one to become insufferably arrogant toward those he considers to be beneath him; to live in disregard of others' feelings and rights."[2]

The figure of Job is in some respects a tragic hero manqué whose questioning of divine justice treads the line between hubristic defiance and chastened acquiescence. Thus, for his friends Job's accusations against God reek of impiety: "Has thou heard the secret of God? and dost thou restrain wisdom to thyself?" asks Eliphaz (Job 15:8). But ironically, it is God in the end who angrily tells the three friends, "ye have not spoken of me the thing that is right, as my servant Job hath" (Job 42:7), and indeed Job himself must intercede with God to spare them their lives. On the other hand, just before his representations of Behemoth and Leviathan to illustrate divine control over the creation, Yahweh sarcastically invites Job to assume the role of regulating the order of the cosmos: "Look on every one that is proud, and bring him low; and tread down the wicked in their place. /.../ Then will I also confess unto thee that thine own right hand can save thee" (Job 40:12, 14). Ultimately, Job's double act of submission (Job 40:3–5, 42:1–5) spares him the fatal punishment that normally accrues to the haughty in spirit in the Old Testament, and his earlier relentless verbal attacks on the deity go unpunished.

Similar motifs of overweening pride and its consequences can be found in the major biblical texts of apocalyptic eschatology. In Daniel, King Belshazzar impiously feasts with the golden vessels taken from the Hebrew temple in Jerusalem and then faces the destruction of his kingdom by the Medes and Persians, as predicted by the Hebrew prophet. In Christ's "little apocalypse," one of the signs of the end-times will be when the "abomination of desolation" stands in the Jewish temple, and Saint Paul similarly taught that during this crisis the "man of sin" and "son of perdition" will appear and "opposeth and exalteth himself above all that is called God, or that is worshipped" (2 Thess. 2:3–4). The last days will thus bring out the Antichrist and his minions, who will recklessly challenge God in his sanctuary but will be destroyed by divine intervention.

In keeping with the aforementioned classical and biblical concepts of hubris, Melville's Ahab provides multiple examples of overweening pride toward both God and man, from his first appearances on the quarterdeck of the *Pequod* to his final confrontation with the White Whale. In chapter 29, for example, Ahab responds with contempt to Stubb's request that he muffle the noise of his wooden leg pacing the decks at night, dismissing the second mate as a dog, donkey, mule, and ass—words that continue to fester in Stubb's mind and even invade his dreams. In chapter 36, in the midst of his blasphemous justification of the hunt for the White Whale, Ahab audaciously tells Starbuck that he would "strike the sun" if it insulted him and expresses his irreverence by demanding, "Who's over me? Truth hath no confines" (164). And in the final chapter of the novel, just before his final confrontation with Moby Dick, Ahab warns his crew: "Down men! The first thing that but offers to jump from this boat I stand in, that thing I harpoon. Ye are not other men, but my arms and my legs; and so obey me" (568). Such arrogant and dehumanizing words and actions throughout the voyage of the *Pequod* invite the fatal power of nemesis, and Ahab is ultimately destroyed by the White Whale, ostensibly acting as a surrogate for the deity.

While signs of Ahab's overweening pride frame his career in the novel, it is mainly in the last quarter of *Moby-Dick* when Ishmael largely drops out of the narrative as active participant that we see questions of epic heroism versus tragic hubris developed to their maximum dramatic intensity. So we find Ahab engaging in several conspicuous acts suitable for an epic hero going into battle, including forging a special harpoon to kill the whale, taking hold of the chains during the typhoon, restoring the proper magnetism to the ship's compass, and in a last act of defiance, confronting the White Whale himself as harpooner. Yet along with these feats of physical and moral courage emerges a fatal spirit of hubris manifested in the captain's arrogance, boastfulness, and moral blindness, the result of his delusory quest for godlike omniscience and omnipotence.

A key sequence of Ahab's heroic and hubristic actions begins in chapter 99 with the well-known dramatic tableau of Ahab and the crew reading the doubloon on the ship's mast. As the *Pequod* is entering the Pacific Ocean where Moby Dick is likely to be found, the captain, followed by the three mates, the Manxman, Queequeg, Fedallah, and Pip, interprets the significance of the Ecuadorian doubloon that Ahab had earlier nailed to the mast (in chapter 36) as a prize for the man who first sighted the White Whale. In order to understand the significance of chapter 99, we must know that the gold doubloon nailed to the mast of the *Pequod* implicitly acts as a symbolic "navel" or omphalos, a pervasive concept in religions and mythologies around the world. Such a cosmic navel was imagined as indicating a central symbolic locale such as those found at the Oracle at Delphi or Mount Zion in Jerusalem, where heaven, earth, and the underworld intersected along an imagined *axis mundi* and where divination was thus possible.[3] Such a symbolic role of omphalos for the doubloon is emphasized by the description of the original mining and minting of the coin in "a country planted in the middle of the world, and beneath the great equator, and named after it; and it had been cast midway up the Andes, in the unwaning clime that knows no autumn" (431). In keeping with the symbolism of this geographical middle, the gold coin located at the ship's symbolic center serves as a self-reflexive medium of oracular pronouncement to the crew of the *Pequod*.

The talismanic doubloon features images of three Andean mountain peaks, at the top of which are placed a lofty tower, an erupting volcano, and a crowing cock, above which is positioned "a segment of the partitioned zodiac, the signs all marked with their usual cabalistics, and the keystone sun entering the equinoctial point at Libra" (431). As Ahab observes, while examining the alluring gold coin, "There's something ever egotistical in mountain-tops and towers, and all other grand and lofty things; look here,— three peaks as proud as Lucifer. The firm tower, that is Ahab; the volcano, that is Ahab; the courageous, the undaunted, and victorious fowl, that, too, is Ahab; all are Ahab" (431). The captain's remarks, like those of the crewmen who follow him, confirm Ishmael's allusion to the myth of Narcissus in the first chapter of the novel as providing a key to human identity. For the coin demonstrates the inescapable subjectivity of human perception, as each character sees himself reflected in its design. In a telling revelation of his ingrained solipsism and instinct for self-assertion, Ahab thus sees in the doubloon's three main figures reflections of his own sovereign self, which, "proud as Lucifer," challenges the heavens like the "three grand and lofty" images—an alternative trinity—on the coin. And while Starbuck may subsequently think that Ahab "seems to read Belshazzar's awful writing" (432) on the doubloon in yet another allusion to this biblical motif of divine warning, the captain sees only rebellious symbols of self-aggrandizement and empowerment, typified by his allusion to Lucifer. By contrast, the orthodox Starbuck finds traditional Christian consolation depicted on the coin, imagining it—in imagery drawn from Psalm 23:4 ("though I walk through the valley of the shadow of death, I will fear no evil") and Malachi 4:2 ("unto you that fear my name shall the Sun of righteousness arise")—as portraying an image of hope: "So in this vale of Death, God girds us round; and over all our gloom, the sun of Righteousness still shines a beacon and a hope" (432). The mate also reluctantly recognizes that the redemptive sun of hope shines only during daylight hours; hence the doubloon only gives him equivocal consolation.

Many commentators have noted that the tableau scene focusing on the doubloon is a multivalent moral, dramatic, and philosophical episode in the novel. Newton Arvin, for example, asserts that the coin for Ahab symbolizes the virility that Moby Dick has destroyed in him, while the image of the sun entering the equinoctial sign of Libra highlights Ahab's lack of a balanced vision of the White Whale. John Seelye draws attention to Pip's final comments on the doubloon as the symbolic navel of the Grand Man of the zodiac, implying the likely disaster that will ensue from "unscrewing" the coin/navel from the ship's mast when the White Whale is sighted. William B. Dillingham argues that Ahab's spiritual identification with the doubloon is symptomatic of his Gnostic tendency toward self-deification; the gold coin thus exemplifies Ahab's belief in the corruption of the material world and the need for rebellion against an evil creator god. Lastly, Randall Bohrer claims that Ahab's identification with the doubloon is representative of a recurrent pattern of microcosm-macrocosm correspondences throughout the novel, repeated here as each character sees himself symbolically reflected in the coin.[4]

While all of these interpretations have merit, we may add that Ahab's remarks on the doubloon set the stage for his coming demonstration of a radical self-assertion that is both hubristic and heroic. Implicit within Ahab's interpretation of the doubloon are thus allusions to Lucifer, the archetypal biblical overreacher, and Achilles, the noblest ancient Greek warrior. We may first note that Ahab's identification with the tower, volcano, and crowing cock on the gold coin graphically demonstrates that he is a man egotistically lifted up like the "high mountains" and "high tower," as denounced by the prophet Isaiah (2:12–17). In his mood of self-aggrandizement, Ahab is similarly "proud as Lucifer" and projects his identity onto the doubloon's three emblems in a manner recalling Isaiah's famous condemnation of the impious Babylonian leader whose mythological name of "light-bringer" (Lucifer), probably based on the planet Venus, would eventually become synonymous with the Christian devil:

> How art thou fallen from heaven, O Lucifer, son of the morning! how art thou cut down to the ground, which didst weaken the nations!
> For thou has said in thine heart, I will ascend into heaven, I will exalt my throne above the stars of God: I will sit also upon the mount of the congregation, in the sides of the north:
> I will ascend above the heights of the clouds; I will be like the most High.
> Yet thou shalt be brought down to hell, to the sides of the pit. (Isa. 14:12–15)

Drawing on the Canaanite myth of a failed pretender to supreme power over the divine assembly on Mount Zaphon in Syria, the biblical author may have been foretelling the demise of the Babylonian King Nebuchadnezzar for his destruction of the Jerusalem temple in 586 BCE.[5]

Like Isaiah's Lucifer, Captain Ahab in his quest for Moby Dick would willfully ascend to heaven in a determined quest for divine omniscience and omnipotence (as a number of subsequent chapters will demonstrate), and again like Lucifer, he will be notably blind to the risks of falling from the celestial realm he wishes to inhabit. Despite his imagined Lucifer-like apotheosis in chapter 99, however, Ahab is still perceptive enough to recognize that his self-aggrandizing interpretation of the doubloon is a psychological projection. After his initial view of the coin, he notes that it resembles an "image of the rounder globe, which, like a magician's glass, to each and every man in turn but mirrors back his own mysterious self" (431). Yet Ahab nevertheless concludes by celebrating the permanent struggle he sees in the coin's symbolism, aligning its meaning with his own heroic vision of life as a quasi-Nietzschean endurance of pain and suffering: "From storm to storm. So be it, then. Born in throes, 'tis fit that man should live in pains and die in pangs" (432).

The heroic spirit of endurance he expresses in chapter 99, combined with the perception of the doubloon as a microcosm of the world, is appropriate for the coin's implicit classical prototype, the shield of Achilles forged by Hephaistos at the request of his mother, Thetis, as found in book 18 of the *Iliad*—one of a number of significant parallels between *Moby-Dick* and Homer's epic, beginning with the signature "wrath" of both Ahab and Achilles.[6] Both coin and shield provide examples of the rhetorical art of *ekphrasis* in which a work of visual art is given detailed verbal representation. Circular in shape and partly or wholly gold in substance, both Ahab's coin and Achilles's shield feature cosmological symbolism based on heavenly constellations (Homer) or astrological signs (Melville); and both provide similar thematic and structural functions in each narrative. Just as Achilles is given his ornamented shield before his final battle with Hector, in the final quarter of Homer's epic, Ahab now reaffirms his heroic, heaven-aspiring spirit and his readiness to do battle with Moby Dick at the same penultimate stage of Melville's narrative. Both coin and shield are represented as talismanic artifacts portending victory. Yet if the shield offers a symmetrical image of the ancient Greek polis and a microcosm of the universe, the image on the doubloon provides a more narrowly focused set of symbols eliciting a diverse range of commentary by other sailors on the *Pequod*.

The varied comments by the crew are ultimately dominated by the comically antiheroic Stubb who, as a dramatic foil to the captain, interprets the coin as a whimsical image of the twelve astrological signs allegedly influencing human life from birth to death. Stubb's attempt to draw a secret meaning out of the doubloon as he had seen Ahab doing suggests the depiction in Marlowe's *Doctor Faustus* of Robin the Clown who, in scene 6, steals Faustus's conjuring book to try to traffic in magic circles and other occult lore. In a similar attempt at conjuring, using the circle of the coin as a symbolic center, Stubb remarks, "I'll get the almanack; and as I have heard devils can be raised with Daboll's arithmetic, I'll try my hand at raising meaning out of these queer curvicues here with the Massachusetts calendar. Here's the book. Let's see now" (432). Following his detailed description of human life as a farcical and fatalistic round of accidents from Aries to Pisces (the new year cycle traditionally beginning in March), Stubb subsequently eavesdrops on the other viewers of the coin, creating an extended verbal portrait of several other representative crew members of the *Pequod*.

The materialistic Flask accordingly sees the coin's substantial value translated into a huge supply of cigars; the superstitious Manxman sees its markings as a confirmation of his astrological predictions; Queequeg the noble savage discovers in it a corresponding symbol to the cosmological tattooing on his thigh; the enigmatic Fedallah finds in it an image of the solar fire he worships; and finally the mad Pip as "wise fool" accurately summarizes the scene as illuminating the conjugations of the verb "to look" while ultimately viewing the coin as a portent of future disaster. Comparing the doubloon to the silver wedding ring found embedded in an old pine tree by his father, Pip asks: "How did it get there? And so they'll say in the resurrection, when they come to fish up this old mast, and find a doubloon lodged in it, with bedded oysters for the shaggy bark" (435). Pip's implied message is that the proud Lucifer commanding the *Pequod* is indeed destined for an oceanic "pit."

Throughout the chapter on "The Doubloon," then, we are given a tragicomic reminder of the universal sway of the human symbolic imagination. As Ishmael asserts at the beginning of the chapter, "some certain significance lurks in all things, else all things are little worth, and the round world itself but an empty cypher" (430). As a symbolic cipher and centralized navel, the *Pequod*'s doubloon is a template for the projection of the crew's collective identity, beginning with the blasphemous captain.

Given his unbridled self-assertions in "The Doubloon," it is appropriately ironic that Ahab's ensuing encounter with the captain of the English whaler *Samuel Enderby*, who has lost his arm to Moby Dick, leads to Ahab's damaging his ivory leg while precipitously escaping the unwelcome humor of the English captain Boomer and his ship's doctor Bunger—an encounter that leads briefly to an experience of cognitive dissonance in the obsessed American captain. It is revealing, too, that immediately after we leave the world of epic heroism indirectly evoked by Ahab's speech in "The Doubloon," we shift to the antiheroic world of a scheming Satan in *Paradise Lost*. For Ahab's humiliating inability to climb the ladder up the side of the *Samuel Enderby* at the start of the scene evokes the comparable humiliation of Satan in his inability to climb the heaven-ascending Jacob's Ladder in book 3 of Milton's epic.[7]

Ahab had impulsively sought an interview with Captain Boomer on the latter's ship after the English captain showed him his missing arm in response to Ahab's initial query about Moby Dick. Boomer and Bunger thereupon take turns in narrating the account of how the former lost his arm following an encounter with the White Whale a year previous, an encounter in which the captain's whaleboat was demolished and a harpoon barb was torn down the length of his arm, which led to a festering wound and eventual amputation. Boomer has thus suffered a dismemberment comparable to Ahab's, but the lesson he takes away from the experience is antithetical to Ahab's—that of avoidance, a common-sense decision that illustrates the national character he typifies. This pragmatic attitude toward the White Whale is reiterated by Doctor Bunger, whose observations on sperm whale anatomy potentially undercut Ahab's view of Moby Dick's deliberate malice: "Do you know, gentlemen, that the digestive organs of the whale are so inscrutably constructed by Divine Providence, that it is quite impossible for him to completely digest a man's arm? And he knows it too. So what you take for the White Whale's malice is only his awkwardness. For he never means to swallow a single limb; he only thinks to terrify by feints" (441). Such practical empirical information, deflating Ahab's mythical view of the White Whale, is anathema to the American captain who is too deeply invested in the notion of the whale's malevolence. Ahab abruptly breaks off the gam, which leads directly to his damaging his ivory leg and a humiliating reminder of his physical impotence.

As we learn for the first time in chapter 106 ("Ahab's Leg"), Ahab had suffered a traumatic injury before the sailing of the *Pequod* when "by some unknown, and seemingly inexplicable, unimaginable casualty, his ivory limb having been so violently displaced, that it had stake-wise smitten, and all but pierced his groin; nor was it without extreme difficulty that the agonizing wound was entirely cured" (463). The fact that Ahab has thus possibly been emasculated by Moby Dick gives new significance to his earlier claim (in chapter 37) that he would dismember his dismemberer. The rationale of Ahab's quest for Moby Dick is not just a lost leg but a damaged sexual potency.[8]

The new information on Ahab's personal history reminds us of the intensity of his physical and psychological pain. The ensuing account of his psychological reactions to the new cause of suffering, and its damage to his narcissistic sense of self, takes us into Ahab's somber meditation on the mythological notion that "both the ancestry and posterity of Grief go further

than the ancestry and posterity of Joy" (464). Such a message initially suggests
the pessimistic teachings of Ecclesiastes, but Ahab's meditation also has an
implied Christian component. Within his brooding mind, the traditional
Judeo-Christian association of guilt with the flesh (found in the canonic
teachings of Christian theologians beginning with Saint Paul, especially in
his Epistle to the Romans) becomes a metaphor for the ascendancy of pain
over pleasure in both this life and the next: "it is an inference from certain
canonic teachings, that while some natural enjoyments here shall have no
children born to them for the other world, but, on the contrary, shall be
followed by the joy-childlessness of all hell's despair; whereas, some guilty
mortal miseries shall still fertilely beget to themselves an eternally progressive
potency of griefs beyond the grave" (464).

Ahab's reasoning seems to imply that, if the physical enjoyments of the
flesh are potential grounds for damnation in Christianity, the sins of the
intellect that result in mental suffering in this life such as Ahab's agonized
disbelief in a benevolent creator god can lead to even greater hellish tortures
in the afterlife. His meditation hints at a heretical blend of theological and
mythological deductions proving the inherent evil of the creation: "To trail
the genealogies of these high mortal miseries, carries us at last among the
sourceless primogenitures of the gods; so that, in the face of all the glad, hay-
making suns, and soft-cyballing, round harvest-moons, we must needs give
in to this: that the gods themselves are not for ever glad. The ineffaceable,
sad birth-mark in the brow of man, is but the stamp of sorrow in the
signers" (464). The sad birthmark in the brow of man here should remind
us of Adam's heritage of original sin, which Saint Paul firmly established
in Christian tradition based on the divine decree in Eden that man must
forever eat his bread in "sorrow" (Gen. 3:17). But Ahab's final assumption
of the gods' sorrow also takes us beyond Christianity into an indefinite
mythological world in which the flaws in human and nonhuman nature
are directly reflected in the flawed creator gods, another likely indication of
Ahab's Gnostic predilections.[9]

Ahab's belief that sorrow outweighs joy in both human and divine worlds
is comparable to Ishmael's own earlier conclusion (in "The Try-Works")
that evil preponderates over good in the universe, and thus suffering is an
inescapable part of the human condition. But Ahab's meditations in chapter
106 have a more subjective bias, based as they are on his damaged virility.
For the whole point of Ahab's thought process here is to rationalize the
pain of his groin injury (which unexpectedly re-creates the original trauma
of his lost leg), by assuming that even the gods suffer pain, a psychological
displacement that puts his own experience on a par with that of the divine.

It is telling that the initial practical result of his grievous groin injury was the "Grand-Lama-like exclusiveness" (464) that marked the initial phase of the *Pequod*'s voyage and that created a fearsome divine aura about the invisible captain—an aura enhanced by the conspiracy of silence among those who knew about Ahab's injury. The information given in chapter 106 thus reinvigorates the revenge plot of the novel by providing an additional motive to Ahab's hunt for the White Whale, which has now entered its semifinal stage of development.

The damage to Ahab's ivory leg sustained during his gam with the captain and ship's doctor of the *Samuel Enderby* means that he must replace his artificial leg, and he orders a new one from the ship's carpenter—a character whose cameo portrait in chapter 107 presents him as a versatile craftsman whose stolid nature presents an unheroic contrast to Ahab's elevated intellectual and moral stature. His dramatically framed encounter with the carpenter (in the next chapter) provides the captain with an opportunity to discuss some key metaphysical questions of mortality and immortality with the uncomprehending carpenter, demonstrating that Ahab's assumed sense of superiority to the general mass of men is indeed justified.[10] Yet the chapter also provides a revealing account of Ahab's ultimately self-destructive ambition to overcome the weaknesses of his body in order to become a being of pure intellect. Ishmael's character portrait begins by depicting the carpenter as embodying a reductive materialism and an indifference to mortality comparable to Hamlet's gravedigger: "Teeth he accounted bits of ivory; heads he deemed top-blocks; men themselves he lightly held for capstans" (467). The character sketch soon modulates into an extended account of the stoical carpenter as a type of indifferent or even nihilistic automaton: "For nothing was this man more remarkable, than for a certain impersonal stolidity as it were; impersonal, I say; for it so shaded off into the surrounding infinite of things, that it seemed one with the general stolidity discernible in the whole visible world; which while pauselessly active in uncounted modes, still eternally holds its peace, and ignores you, though you dig foundations for cathedrals" (467). On one level just a mundane workman, the carpenter can also be viewed as a type of deity—an impersonal mechanical creator in the form of a platonic or Gnostic demiurge or "artificer," to use a term from Plato's *Timaeus*.

The rest of the portrait of the carpenter adds further details to this indifferent "manipulator" of matter. A Shakespearean fool and mechanical in his dramatic role, the carpenter provides an uncomprehending butt to

Ahab's provocative remarks as he makes the captain's prosthetic limb, while the blacksmith (whom Ahab has whimsically dubbed Prometheus) makes the metal fittings for his new leg. Ahab thus addresses the carpenter:

> What's Prometheus about there?—The blacksmith, I mean—what's he about?
>
> He must be forging the buckle-screw, sir, now.
>
> Right. It's a partnership; he supplies the muscle part. He makes a fierce red flame there!
>
> Aye, sir; he must have the white heat for this kind of fine work.
>
> Um-m. So he must. I do deem it now a most meaning thing, that that old Greek, Prometheus, who made men, they say, should have been a blacksmith, and animated them with fire; for what's made in fire must properly belong to fire; and so hell's probable. How the soot flies! This must be the remainder the Greek made the Africans of. Carpenter, when he's through with that buckle, tell him to forge a pair of steel shoulder-blades; there's a pedlar aboard with a crushing pack.
>
> Sir?
>
> Hold; while Prometheus is about it, I'll order a complete man after a desirable pattern. Imprimis, fifty feet high in his socks; then, chest modelled after the Thames Tunnel; then, legs with roots to 'em, to stay in one place; then, arms three feet through the wrist; no heart at all, brass forehead, and about a quarter of an acre of fine brains, and let me see—shall I order eyes to see outwards? No, but put a sky-light on top of his head to illuminate inwards. There, take the order, and away.
>
> Now, what's he speaking about, and who's he speaking to, I should like to know? Shall I keep standing here? (*aside.*) (470)

Ahab's conversation here evokes a sustained mythological play of identities as he explores the implication of his idea that the blacksmith is a potential Prometheus who, according to Ovid and other classical mythographers, created humanity out of mud.[11] Ahab's jesting over the head of the carpenter may remind us of the earlier encounter of Stubb and Fleece, but Ahab's purpose is more serious as he confesses that Prometheus's identity as a blacksmith has a special meaning to him in his theological obsession with evil: "for what's made in fire must properly belong to fire; and so hell's probable" (470). In addition, in his confessed need for steel shoulder blades, he reveals his resemblance to the Titan Atlas, Prometheus's brother, who carried the world on his shoulders. Ahab's ultimate use of the Prometheus myth here is to announce his pattern for an improved version of a man in a description that further demonstrates his hubris arising out of a presumption to improve on the divine creation. Ahab's mechanical giant will thus be invulnerable to emotion or pain since it functions without a heart, its brain will be gigantic (a reminder of Ahab's quest for omniscience), and it will be blind to the outward world except for internal illumination from above, the latter condition providing an oblique confirmation of Ahab's paradoxical endowment of moral insight and willful blindness. As Stephen Ausband notes: "Ahab's pain and insanity are due partly to his ability to 'see outwards' farther than ordinary men. His ideal man would be large enough to absorb the shocks of a malignant universe, would be self-sufficient and immovable, and would have no heart to feel grief and no eyes to see evil."[12] Ahab's superman is in fact an oblique self-portrait for he himself would be the fifty-foot giant with huge brain and no heart, in keeping with his Faustian aspirations to omnipotence and omniscience. The giant embodies a massive psychological compensation for Ahab's humiliating sense of physical and existential powerlessness. Ahab's automaton will thus have legs with "roots to 'em" in order to stay in one place; in other words, its legs cannot be moved or (more appropriately) removed like his own.

Ahab's conversation with the carpenter underlies the captain's anguish over his crippled condition, especially the disparity between his self-sufficient, heaven-ascending mind and his weak dependent body. The conversation ends with Ahab declaring his spiritual kinship with the gods while desiring to reduce his physical form to a minimum, in ironic contrast to his earlier fancy for a fifty-foot giant: "Oh, Life! Here I am, proud as a Greek god, and yet standing debtor to this blockhead for a bone to stand on! Cursed be that mortal inter-indebtedness which will not do away with ledgers. I would be free as air; and I'm down in the whole world's books" (471–72). Aristotle famously wrote in the *Politics* that any creature that can exist without society must either be a god or a beast, and the example of Ahab might be used to confirm this theory. Ahab's desire to be free of all "mortal inter-indebtedness"—the antithesis to Ishmael's earlier message of human interdependence in chapter 72 ("The Monkey-Rope") and elsewhere—is symptomatic of the form his heaven-aspiring hubris will take in the coming chapters as he seeks to transform himself into a quasi-divine figure devoid of any physical, emotional, or psychological vulnerabilities.[13]

The chief focus of Ahab's intolerance for any "mortal inter-indebtedness" will accordingly now be made manifest in a ritualistic sequence of scenes as the captain heroically prepares himself for battle with the White Whale. Thus, in chapter 113 ("The Forge"), Ahab has the blacksmith undertake the forging of a special supernaturally empowered harpoon with which to kill Moby Dick. With a shank made of nails from racehorse shoes and the blade made of his own steel razors, Ahab's custom-made harpoon recalls the myth of the all-powerful magical weapon needed to kill a monstrous or supernatural enemy. The final ritual of forging the harpoon consists of "baptizing" it in the blood of Ahab's three pagan harpooners, punctuated by the captain's blasphemous pronouncement over the ceremony: "'Ego non baptizo te in nomine patris, sed nomine diaboli!' deliriously howled Ahab, as the malignant iron scorchingly devoured the baptismal blood" (489).[14] While the Latin formula here evokes the necromantic ambitions of Doctor Faustus who signed his bond with the devil in blood in scene 5 of Marlowe's play, Ahab's actions also conspicuously subvert Christian doctrine. For if the original purpose of Christian baptism was to exorcize evil spirits and so cleanse the soul of the convert, Ahab is in effect reversing this ritual by invoking the name of the devil and baptizing his weapon in blood, not water. Tempering steel blades in human blood also had a long history in folklore as a means of strengthening the weapon; thus for Ahab the three harpooners' blood will give his harpoon "the true death-temper" (489).[15]

As in the mock Black Mass during which the crew swore eternal vengeance against the whale in chapter 36, the scene in "The Forge" again identifies Ahab as a damned soul and Antichrist figure, but now the ceremony is strategically restricted to the three pagan harpooners, a mock trinity of participants. By baptizing the harpoon in the name of the devil, Ahab—a modern Faustus/Faust—invokes the aid of the demonic to gain the magical power to kill the White Whale. But his reformulated alliance with the devil here is a sign of an increasingly monstrous dehumanization that will become increasingly dangerous for himself and his crew. It is revealing that Ahab "deliriously howled" his blasphemous formula like a wild animal during the forging of the magical harpoon blade. The scene ends with Ahab assembling his harpoon with a wooden shaft and towline, after which "pole, iron, and rope—like the three Fates—remained inseparable, and Ahab moodily stalked away with the weapon; the sound of his ivory leg, and the sound of the hickory pole, both hollowly ringing along every plank" (490). The sense of fatality here is reinforced by the mad laughter of the cabin-bound Pip, whose "strange mummeries not unmeaningly blended with the black tragedy of the melancholy ship, and mocked it!" (490). Placed like a below-stage devil in Elizabethan drama, the mad Pip's laughter recognizes the self-destructive irony of Ahab's forging of the harpoon that will end up killing the captain himself.

A final symptom of Ahab's renunciation of any heavenly connections, and the complement to his formal invocation of the infernal realm in "The Forge," can be found in his smashing his quadrant in chapter 118—a gesture that can be compared to a narcissistic Richard's smashing his mirror because his face no longer "like the sun" makes "beholders wink," in Shakespeare's *Richard II* (IV.i.284). Having reached the region of the equator where he expects to find Moby Dick during the Season-on-the-Line, Ahab uses his quadrant to verify the ship's exact location at sea. But his impatience to know the comparable location of the White Whale leads him to a bitter meditation on the sun's withholding information from him ("Where is Moby Dick? This instant thou must be eyeing him"), and then a curse on the instrument itself for not being able to tell him anything about the future but only the present location of objects: "Curse thee, thou vain toy; and cursed be all the things that cast man's eyes aloft to that heaven, whose live vividness but scorches him, as these old eyes are even now scorched with thy light, O sun! Level by nature to this earth's horizons are the glances of man's eyes; not shot from the crown of his head, as if God had meant him to gaze on his firmament" (501). Although he had earlier depended on scientific instrumentation in his study of oceanic charts, a completely self-reliant Ahab now won't tolerate any power higher than himself; instead of striking the sun, as he threatened in chapter 36, he impulsively destroys the instrument that enabled him to take its measure. Henceforth he will rely on the antiquated method of compass and dead-reckoning by log and line to tell him his location at sea. The infernal light of "The Forge" will replace the natural light of the sun as Ahab's guide, a change that Ishmael warned against in "The Try-Works." In this scene, Ahab demonstrates a Faustian drive to know the future, in a quest for divine omniscience, while his bitter, self-destructive curse on the quadrant evokes Faust's (and before him, Job's) initial curse on the goodness of the creation.

Ahab's soliloquy in "The Quadrant" is also comparable to the Miltonic Satan's renunciation of the heavenly light out of wounded pride; indeed, it is a transformed version of Satan's soliloquy at the start of book 4 of *Paradise Lost*. There the archfiend laments his banishment from heaven, and decrying the catastrophic consequences of his own willful pride he refuses the possibility of repentance and submission; bidding farewell to hope, fear, and remorse, he formally embraces evil as his guiding principle. Like Ahab in "The Quadrant," Satan looks toward the sun as he begins his speech:

> O thou that with surpassing Glory crown'd,
> Look'st from thy sole Dominion like the God
> Of this new World; at whose sight all the Stars
> Hide thir diminisht heads; to thee I call,
> But with no friendly voice, and add thy name

O Sun, to tell thee how I hate thy beams
That bring to my remembrance from what state
I fell, how glorious once above thy Sphere;
Till Pride and worse Ambition threw me down
                              (*Paradise Lost*, IV.32–40)

Satan hates the sun because its beams recall his fall from a higher state; Ahab, because it fails to tell him where Moby Dick is, reflecting his human limitation of knowledge. While Satan curses himself for his decision to rebel, Ahab curses the quadrant for scorching his eyes as they look aloft. In both tragic heroes we find a final rejection of the blessings of heaven because of despair over lost power and felicity. Ahab's countenance is not described during his speech to the quadrant, but we observe in the nearby Parsee "a sneering triumph that seemed meant for Ahab, and a fatalistic despair that seemed meant for himself" (501). The Parsee's expressions may recall those of Milton's Satan as "each passion dimm'd his face, / Thrice chang'd with pale ire, envy, and despair, / Which marr'd his borrow'd visage" (*Paradise Lost*, IV.114–16). If the Parsee's despair stems from Ahab's rejection of the heavenly light (the principle of good in his religion), his sneering triumph mirrors Ahab's overweening, fatalistic resolution to rely on his own (appropriately named) "dead-reckoning" for navigation.

Following "The Doubloon," we find Ahab showing a heroic and fearless spirit in his hunt for the White Whale but engaged, at the same time, in a relentless spiritual corruption through pride and impiety. In "The Candles," we find Ahab demonstrating both heroism and hubris in a climactic cosmic tableau. Motifs from the books of Job, Daniel, and Revelation will provide important thematic touchstones for the chapter, in keeping with other patterns of biblical allusion throughout the narrative.

Chapter 119 ("The Candles") dramatizes a complex amalgam of several thematic strands and symbolic motifs from the Bible. It begins by describing the *Pequod*'s encounter with a raging typhoon, which results in the eerie supernatural appearance of corposants, Saint Elmo's Fire, on the three masts because of the electrically charged atmosphere of the storm. Instead of allowing the ship's lightning rods to be dropped overboard in case lightning strikes the ship's masts, Ahab insists on the ship's receiving the full force of the lightning, thereby showing his own imagined omnipotence and his defiance toward what he considers an intimidating demonstration of heavenly power. In a ritualistic scene imitating the liturgical drama of the

Catholic Easter vigil, Ahab takes hold of the metal "links" to the rods on the mainmast, and with his foot on the fire-worshipping prostrate Parsee, he addresses the "lofty tri-pointed trinity of flames" (507) on the mast in a self-revelatory speech of overweening defiance and tragic pathos—a mock crucifixion featuring a forsaken son attacking a heavenly father.[16]

The scene constitutes a climax in the revelation of Ahab's Romantic Titanism, his willful revolt against the deity, coupled with his paradoxical identification with the heavenly fire and his feeling of betrayal by its punitive might. M. O. Percival notes of the scene: "It is in this grand and tragic speech . . . that the intellectual aspect of Ahab's pursuit of Moby Dick reaches its climax. . . . And yet, as he reaches the height of his nobility, he reaches the height of his self-delusion."[17] The chapter also reaffirms the awed submission of the *Pequod*'s crew to Ahab's absolute power, although Starbuck briefly attempts to point out God's seeming disapproval of Ahab's defiance and later makes a final ineffectual effort in chapter 123 ("The Musket") to oppose the captain's increasingly portentous and dangerous pursuit of the White Whale.

A remarkable number of mythic and literary motifs inform the action of "The Candles." The dramatic sequence has important literary prototypes in *Prometheus Bound*, *King Lear*, *Paradise Lost*, *Manfred*, *Sartor Resartus*, and "Young Goodman Brown." As in Aeschylus's drama, Ahab enacts the symbolic theft of divine fire and suffers the agonizing consequences for doing so, even as he directs that fire back at an oppressive divinity. At the end of the ancient Greek play, the enchained Titan—like Ahab clinging to the chains—anticipates his coming stormy ordeal with Zeus while appealing to his divine mother, Gaia, to witness his wrongs (ll. 1189–204).[18] Like the storm scene on the heath in *Lear*, this chapter in the novel provides a cosmic forum for Ahab's agonized exploration of the divine nature. The mad captain's desire to experience the full force of the typhoon and its thunder functions as an analogue to the old king's mad salute to the destructive power of the storm in *King Lear* (III.ii.2–6). In his ordeal by lightning Ahab also resembles Milton's Satan after his initial ejection from heaven, following an attempt to make war on God:

> Him the Almighty Power
> Hurl'd headlong flaming from th' Ethereal Sky
> With hideous ruin and combustion down
> To bottomless perdition, there to dwell
> In Adamantine Chains and penal Fire,
> Who durst defy th' Omnipotent to Arms.
> (*Paradise Lost*, I.44–49)

A victim of divine lightning like Satan who demonstrates his downwardly mobile affinity here with Isaiah's Lucifer, Ahab hurls verbal defiance at the deity who has exiled him from the skies.

In other respects Ahab is a cousin to Byron's Manfred who lives in proud isolation in the Alps and as a Faust-like figure is visited by a plethora of supernatural spirits. At one point Manfred visits the demonic Hall of Arimanes (a version of the Zoroastrian devil god Ahriman), where he refuses to worship the dark god and is briefly able to evoke the spirit of his lost Astarte. Ahab here is also related to Carlyle's Teufelsdrökh; the captain's "conversion" experience in "The Candles" thus has a partial prototype in the "baphometic fire baptism" of the fictional German philosopher on the rue Saint Thomas d'Enfer in Paris. Finally, Melville borrows extensively from Hawthorne's "Young Goodman Brown" in the framing of Ahab's ordeal as a hallucinatory nocturnal initiation into the demonic, complete with dazzling pyrotechnics and related satanic symbolism.[19]

The events described here accordingly assume the form of a series of dramatic tableaux in which the crew are frozen, mute with fear, at the spectacle of the corposants, which provide a quasi-theatrical illumination as Ahab pronounces an extended soliloquy to the apparently supernatural lights on the mast. The scene performs a combined dramatic function of revelation and admonition. The biblical context of the scene of warning here can be found in the book of Daniel when the Hebrew prophet reads the mysterious writing on the wall to the impious King Belshazzar, a scene that is probably a source for the chapter title "The Candles," for the original description of the writing on the wall is associated with candles. Thus, while Belshazzar and his court are feasting amid the holy vessels taken from the Temple in Jerusalem, "In the same hour came forth fingers of a man's hand, and wrote over against the candlestick upon the plaister of the wall of the king's palace: and the king saw the part of the hand that wrote" (Dan. 5:5). We also find a direct allusion to the book of Daniel when, upon the first eerie appearance of the corposants, Ishmael describes the momentary awe of the crew before this seemingly supernatural warning. Even the carefree Stubb stops his profane banter and begs the corposants to have mercy: "To sailors, oaths are household words; they will swear in the trance of the calm, and in the teeth of the tempest; they will imprecate curses from the topsail-yard-arms, when most they teter over to a seething sea; but in all my voyagings, seldom have I heard a common oath when God's burning finger has been laid on the ship; when His 'Mene, Mene, Tekel, Upharsin' has been woven into the shrouds and the cordage" (506). The Hebrew words constituted a three-part warning of impending doom, which only the prophet Daniel (or in this case, Ishmael) could translate (Dan. 5:26–28); the sailors are thus dumb before the fiery spectacle.

In addition to Daniel, the scene in "The Candles" also draws on imagery from the book of Revelation. The initial description of the corposants compares them to candles at an altar burning in an atmosphere suggestive of a satanic visitation: "each of the three tall masts was silently burning in that sulphurous air, like three gigantic wax tapers before an altar" (505). The description partially mimics the setting of Revelation, in John's throne vision of God surrounded by twenty-four elders: "And out of the throne proceeded lightnings and thunderings and voices: and there were seven lamps of fire burning before the throne, which are the seven Spirits of God" (Rev. 4:5).[20] Yet instead of the sanctified elders surrounding God's throne, in "The Candles" we find the *Pequod*'s three pagan harpooners who now appear intensely savage, or even satanic, in the eerie glow: "Relieved against the ghostly light, the gigantic jet negro, Daggoo, loomed up to thrice his real stature, and seemed the black cloud from which the thunder had come. The parted mouth of Tashtego revealed his shark-white teeth, which strangely gleamed as if they too had been tipped by corpusants; while lit up by the preternatural light, Queequeg's tattooing burned like Satanic blue flames on his body" (506). In a subsequent grotesque freeze-frame we find the crew now appearing in "various enchanted attitudes, like the standing, or stepping, or running skeletons in Herculaneum" (507), while the figure of the Parsee is bowed before the manifestation of light, the symbol of divinity in Zoroastrianism. Ahab himself remains stubbornly resistant to the warning here, perversely taking the corposants as a message of encouragement: "Look up at it; mark it well; the white flame but marks the way to the White Whale" (507). Starbuck, however, recognizes a more symbolic import of the storm when he points out that Ahab's boat has been destroyed by lightning.

We recall that lightning and storm, signifying power and fertility, were the main features of leading gods in several Near Eastern religions, including Zeus (Greek), Baal (Canaanite), and Yahweh (Hebrew). Fire was the principal symbol of the Zoroastrian high god Ormuzd as well. Ahab's address to the corposants may thus be seen as a composite of Zoroastrian, Greek, Gnostic, and Judeo-Christian mythic motifs. Most conspicuously, his dramatic encounter with lightning involves allusions to the Zoroastrianism that he had once espoused as an expression of his sense of the cosmic dualism inherent in the universe.[21]

Melville would have learned from Pierre Bayle's *Historical and Critical Dictionary* that Zoroastrianism interpreted fire as an embodiment of the divine spirit of good, Ahura Mazda (Ormuzd), the god of light, who was locked in prolonged struggle with the evil principle Angra Mainyu (Ahriman), symbolized by darkness. Zoroastrian priests originally maintained fire altars in elevated outdoor places but later built such altars in temples. In his entry on "Zoroaster," Bayle remarked on the legendary prophet's association with lightning. When his mountain retreat was struck by a "celestial fire," Zoroaster allegedly "came out of these flames without being damaged." Moreover, "he wished to be struck with thunder, and consumed by fire from Heaven." The mythical history of Zoroaster is a gloss on Ahab's seemingly suicidal desire to attract the celestial fire of the typhoon in "The Candles."[22]

While the Parsee kneels in veneration before the fire, Ahab assumes a posture of defiance. He holds the lightning rod links in his hand, puts his foot on the kneeling Fedallah, fixes his eyes on the flaming masts, and stands erect with right arm stretched aloft. Ahab addresses the fiery corposants as an embodiment of divine power that earlier had injured him while in the act of worship, teaching him a lesson of defiance:

> "Oh! thou clear spirit of clear fire, whom on these seas I as Persian once did worship, till in the sacramental act so burned by thee, that to this hour I bear the scar; I now know thee, thou clear spirit, and I now know that thy right worship is defiance. To neither love nor reverence wilt thou be kind; and e'en for hate thou canst but kill; and all are killed. No fearless fool now fronts thee. I own thy speechless, placeless power; but to the last gasp of my earthquake life will dispute its unconditional, unintegral mastery in me. In the midst of the personified impersonal, a personality stands here. Though but a point at best; whencesoe'er I came; whencesoe'er I go; yet while I earthly live, the queenly personality lives in me, and feels her royal rights." (507)

Ahab addresses the symbol of the Zoroastrian deity, saying that while engaged in an act of worship he was branded by lightning. Ahab has literally been burned by the god of light and has changed from worshipping the celestial fire to demonizing it. Such an event might explain the sailor Elijah's otherwise enigmatic mention (in chapter 19) of a traumatic injury the captain incurred "off Cape Horn, long ago, when he lay like dead for three days and nights" (92). His branding by lightning is another example of how Ahab has succumbed to the inversion of values Ishmael warned against in "The Try-Works"—letting a demonic vision of fire convince him there was no benign counterpart in the life-giving sun. The first part of Ahab's soliloquy thus indicts the fire as symbol of a deity whose chief manifestation is destructive power and not nurturing love. The "queenly personality" that "feels her royal rights" in him may remind us of the ambitious Jezebel, consort to the biblical King Ahab. Throughout this scene we see parallels with the contest between Jezebel's antagonist, the prophet Elijah, and the priests of Baal over making fire (lightning) come down from heaven (1 Kings 18), a prelude to the fertilizing rains allegedly brought by the storm god Baal. In other respects, the American whaling captain could be invoking a repressed feminine side to his personality to differentiate himself from the tyrannical male realm of power he is addressing.[23]

In his speech to the corposants, Melville's Ahab is ascribing evil to the traditionally benevolent creator god in a subversion of one of the basic tenets of Judeo-Christian theodicy. Ahab thus duplicates the reasoning of Christian Gnostics such as the Paulicians, who were described by Bayle as engaging in a comparable moral inversion: "The Fear which Religion inspires, ought to be attended with Love, Hope, and a great Veneration. When an Object is dreaded only because it has the Power and Will of doing Harm, and exercises that Power cruelly and unmercifully, it must needs be hated and detested: this can be no religious Worship."[24] In like manner, Ahab's address to the corposants expresses a Gnostic belief in an evil creator god who is morally inferior to the possessor of the Gnostic "spark" of divine knowledge such as Ahab himself. Melville expressed a similar sentiment in an April 1851 letter to Hawthorne, in which he praised his friend's new novel *The House of the Seven Gables* and went on to describe its author as gifted with insight into the tragedy of the human condition, which required a fearless commitment to telling the "visible" truth about the world:

> By the visable [*sic*] truth, we mean the apprehension of the absolute condition of present things as they strike the eye of the man who fears them not, though they do their worst to him,—the man who, like Russia or the British Empire, declares himself a sovereign nature (in himself) amid the powers of heaven, hell, and earth. He may perish; but so long as he exists, he insists upon treating with all Powers upon an equal basis. If any of those other Powers choose to withhold certain secrets, let them; that does not impair my sovereignty in myself; that does not make me tributary.

Expressing a remarkable combination of hubris and heroism here, Melville sets forth in this letter a Romantic credo that would not be inappropriate for Byron's Manfred, or Shelley's Prometheus, or his own Ahab in the scene with the corposants—but less obviously true of Hawthorne or his fictional characters. Melville demonstrates that the "ruthless democracy" he espouses politically extends also to the realm of theology, dramatically revealing his independence of traditional Christian dogma.[25]

The scene continues with further flashes of lightning that make the Saint Elmo's fire burn brighter as though a god is responding to Ahab's preceding speech. Indeed, he attributes his failure to be blinded by the light as a vindication of his cosmic challenges:

> (*Sudden, repeated flashes of lightning; the nine flames leap lengthwise to thrice their previous height; Ahab, with the rest, closes his eyes, his right hand pressed hard upon them.*)

> "I own thy speechless, placeless power; said I not so? Nor was it wrung from me; nor do I now drop these links. Thou canst blind; but I can then grope. Thou canst consume; but I can then be ashes. Take the homage of these poor eyes, and shutter-hands. I would not take it. The lightning flashes through my skull; mine eye-balls ache and ache; my whole beaten brain seems as beheaded, and rolling on some stunning ground. Oh, oh! Yet blindfold, yet will I talk to thee. Light though thou be, thou leapest out of darkness; but I am darkness leaping out of light, leaping out of thee! The javelins cease; open eyes; see, or not? There burn the flames! Oh, thou magnanimous! Now I do glory in my genealogy. But thou art but my fiery father; my sweet mother, I know not. Oh, cruel! what hast thou done with her? There lies my puzzle; but thine is greater. Thou knowest not how came ye, hence callest thyself unbegotten; certainly knowest not thy beginning, hence callest thyself unbegun. I know that of me, which thou knowest not of thyself, oh, thou omnipotent. There is some unsuffusing thing beyond thee, thou clear spirit, to whom all thy eternity is but time, all thy creativeness mechanical. Through thee, thy flaming self, my scorched eyes do dimly see it. Oh, thou foundling fire, thou hermit immemorial, thou too hast thy incommunicable riddle, thy unparticipated grief. Here again with haughty agony, I read my sire. Leap! leap up, and lick the sky! I leap with thee; I burn with thee; would fain be welded with thee; defyingly I worship thee."
> (507–8)

After the lightning strikes while he is holding the ship's chains, Ahab is stunned momentarily but still shows his defiance even though temporarily blinded and reeling from the shock, his hands placed like storm shutters over his eyes. While the vivid images of mental torture here evoke the figure of Lear on the heath, the pathos of Ahab's condition is also comparable to two other tragic heroes from Greek drama. In his (temporarily) blind, groping condition, Ahab suggests the figure of the tormented Oedipus, and in his subsequent claim to know a secret unknown to God he recalls the figure of Prometheus who was punished by Zeus for his theft of fire and for possessing the secret of the Olympian's potential overthrow.

In other respects, the second part of Ahab's quasi-liturgical speech to the corposants seems to set forth several Gnostic ideas, especially Ahab's claim that the fiery god he addresses is a mere "mechanical" creator compared to "some unsuffusing thing beyond" it, just as the Gnostic "demiurge" (Plato's term, adapted by Valentinus in the second century) was the corrupt god of the evil physical world, identifiable with Yahweh, beyond whom was the true Gnostic god of eternity. The multiple use of the verb "to know" (the root meaning of "gnostic") in Ahab's speech would seem to confirm this connection as well. Ahab thus criticizes the fire god for its association with the temporal world, claiming it is unaware of how or when it was created. Yet in a subsequent expression of radical ambivalence, he also hails the lightning as his "fiery father" and expresses a sense of bereavement and parental abandonment. Ahab feels sympathy with the divine fire, imputing to it a kindred sense of loss even as he finishes his speech with a reassertion of radical defiance and the fantasy that he has become virtually divine in his survival of the heavenly flashes of lightning from the god of the storm.[26]

The dramatic and mythic elements in the climactic scene in "The Candles" are varied, but there is also a key religious prototype that we have yet to mention. For Ahab's speech is another expression of the captain's archetypal association with Job; more particularly, Ahab's encounter with the raging typhoon and its electrical effects is a symbolic enactment of Job's encounter with the Voice from the Whirlwind. The basic resemblances between Job and Ahab have been noted by Thornton Y. Booth, who contrasts Ahab's defiant reaction to the display of heavenly might in "The Candles" with Job's humble submissiveness:

> In his implacable resentment Ahab reaches one point of heroism that to many modern men appears better than Job's response to essentially the same situation: Ahab will not be cowed by mere power, however great. Job lies prostrate before God in the whirlwind we have noted. He gives up any sense of deserving an answer from God concerning anything, and senses only his own inadequacy and presumption in having questioned at all. Ahab, interpreting a

spectacular burning of St. Elmo's fire on the ship as a display of God's power, forbids the dropping of the rods which would divert the electricity into the sea, and instead seizes the mast chains that he may take the full charge within his own body. Owning the power of the Spirit, he yet defies it; redefies it as the charge builds to even greater intensities; defies it even when he thinks that his hands and eyes may be burned away. Nothing, not even the direct and threatening manifestation of the power of God, can cow Ahab.[27]

Booth notes that the second part of Ahab's speech expresses his un-Job-like modern sense of a more profound reality that extends beyond the divine force he finds in the lightning, a belief that suggests both the basic tenets of Gnosticism and the myth of Prometheus. Yet Ahab's speeches would seem also to echo specific passages from Job's complaints against the deity.

Ahab's address to the divine "spirit of fire" accordingly mimics Job's anguished remarks on God's seeming injustice, as contained in his bitter reply to the first speech of Bildad—a speech that earlier (in "The Quarter-Deck") shaped Ahab's accusations against the deity:

> If I had called, and he had answered me; yet would I not believe that he had harkened unto my voice.
>
> For he breaketh me with a tempest, and multiplieth my wounds without cause.
>
> He will not suffer me to take my breath, but filleth me with bitterness.
>
> If I speak of strength, lo, he is strong: and if of judgment, who shall set me a time to plead? (Job 9:16–19)

As in Job's complaint, Ahab is being "broken" by a tempest in which lightning expresses the god's insuperable strength, and he duly acknowledges the fire's "speechless, placeless power." Job notes that he has been created by a God who is unaccountably trying to destroy him: "Thine hands have made me and fashioned me together round about; yet thou dost destroy me. / Remember, I beseech thee, that thou hast made me as the clay; and wilt thou bring me into dust again?" (Job 10:8–9). Ahab similarly claims to have been fathered by the fire he addresses ("thou art but my fiery father"), which is also, it seems, trying to destroy him as he hangs onto the chains. Job ends his first speech to Bildad by again wishing for death and a return to the darkness of Sheol: "A land of darkness, as darkness itself; and of the shadow of death, without any order, and where the light is as darkness" (Job 10:22). Ahab, on the other hand, associates himself with darkness in a more rebellious manner when he addresses the lightning coming out of the black sky: "Light though thou be, thou leapest out of darkness; but I am darkness leaping out of light, leaping out of thee!" Earlier in his speech to the corposants, he asserted: "I own thy speechless, placeless power; but to the last gasp of my earthquake life will dispute its unconditional, unintegral mastery in me. In the midst of the personified impersonal, a personality stands here" (507). The captain's insistence on human autonomy evokes Job's well-known declaration: "Though he slay me, yet will I trust in him: but I will maintain mine own ways before him" (Job 13:15).

The divine fire that Ahab addresses in "The Candles" is thus the functional equivalent to the divine Voice from the Whirlwind that intimidates Job and asks a litany of rhetorical questions meant to demonstrate God's control over powerful natural forces that Job can not begin to match. Two of God's questions to Job directly pertain to Ahab's defiance of the lightning: "Who hath divided a watercourse for the overflowing of waters, or a way for the lightning of thunder; /. . . / Canst thou send lightnings, that they may go, and say unto thee, Here we are?" (Job 38:25, 35). Contrary to God's sarcastic query, Ahab *does* redirect the path of the lightning, and he holds onto the ship's chains with seeming impunity. God's providential control of the cosmos, as asserted by the Voice from the Whirlwind, is exactly what Ahab is challenging in "The Candles." Furthermore, in his imputation of genealogical ignorance to the divine fire, "Thou knowest not how came ye, hence callest thyself unbegotten; certainly knowest not thy beginning, hence callest thyself unbegun," Ahab also mimicks the taunting queries of the Voice from the Whirlwind while challenging divine omnipotence and identifying a fatal weakness in divine omniscience. Unlike Job after the divine theophany, Ahab is talking back to the Voice from the Whirlwind, risking destruction while claiming his own divine genealogy in "the midst of the personified impersonal."

The climax of Ahab's speech occurs in his act of blowing out the flame burning on his harpoon, thereby demonstrating his seemingly divine power over the heavenly fire but also revealing the extent of his hubris. The act of extinguishing the flames of the corposants shows Ahab potentially mimicking the actions of Christ at his Second Coming, destroying the wicked or "lawless one": "And then shall that Wicked be revealed, whom the Lord shall consume with the spirit of his mouth, and shall destroy with the brightness of his coming" (2 Thess. 2:9). Ahab may be seen here as allying himself with the traditional supernatural evil agents of Antichrist even as he poses as a savior of the crew from the terror of the uncanny corposants.

If the earlier allusions to the book of Daniel in this scene cast Ahab as the blasphemous King Belshazzar, the pyrotechnics of "The Candles" suggest he might also be compared to another agent of Antichrist, the second beast in the book of Revelation, who "doeth great wonders" and "maketh fire come down from heaven on the earth in the sight of men" (Rev. 13:13). Having demonstrated his seemingly magical potency over the elements, Ahab takes advantage of the moment to remind the crew that they are all bound to him on his quest: "All your oaths to hunt the White Whale are as binding as mine; and heart, soul, and body, lungs and life, old Ahab is bound" (508). "The Candles," in sum, incorporates an important restatement of the frequently overlapping themes of theodicy and eschatology while dramatizing a climactic example of Ahab's defiant reaction to his Joban dilemma. This scene thus illustrates Ahab moving ever closer to a final moral judgment on his mission.

If "The Candles" represents a peak moment in the display of Ahab's conjoined heroism and hubris, it has extended repercussions for the crew, as we see in two subsequent chapters. In "The Musket," the conflict between Ahab and Starbuck over the wisdom of the captain's fanatical quest for vengeance comes to a climax, leading to Starbuck's final submission to the authority of his captain, no matter how mad. The scene consists of Starbuck's brief consideration of killing Ahab as a way of saving the ship. The first mate has gone below to tell the sleeping captain about the change in the weather on the night of the typhoon, and as he passes by the ship's gun rack he removes one of the guns. A murderous impulse seizes him (albeit partly in self-defense), and he levels the weapon in the direction of where Ahab is sleeping—a gesture recalling Macbeth's attempt to clutch a hallucinatory dagger as he meditates on whether to murder the sleeping Duncan (*Macbeth* II.i.33–49). Starbuck's interior monologue rehearses the moral case for action against the captain, considering Ahab's reckless disregard for the safety of his ship and crew:

> "Aye and he would fain kill all his crew. Does he not say he will not strike his spars in any gale? Has he not dashed his heavenly quadrant? and in these same perilous seas, gropes he not his way by mere dead reckoning of the error-abounding log? and in this very Typhoon, did he not swear that he would have no lightning-rods? But shall this crazed old man be tamely suffered to drag a whole ship's company down to doom with him?" (514–15)

Starbuck's litany of grievances mixes Ahab's dangerous seamanship with continued alarm at his moral enormities. Yet in the end, the first mate—unlike the Scottish thane in Shakespeare's play—is incapable of such a criminal act as murder. After he hears Ahab cry aloud in his sleep ("Stern all! Oh Moby Dick, I clutch thy heart at last!"), he despairingly puts the gun back in the rack and returns to the deck, telling Stubb that the captain was sleeping and that Stubb should relay the message about the weather. In the end, the scene enacted in "The Musket" demonstrates that a reasonable and virtuous individual such as Starbuck is helpless in dealing with an irrational, demonically driven man such as Ahab who has challenged the cosmos in "The Candles" and has the power to intimidate and manipulate his crew into compliance with his will. Yet if Starbuck can only see the dangerous hubris of Ahab's actions, Stubb and the rest of the crew see only the captain's heroism. As Stubb remarked at the end of "The Quadrant" while endorsing the captain's vision of life as a card game in which one must play one's hand: "And damn me, Ahab, but thou actest right; live in the game, and die in it!" (502).[28]

A final example of Ahab's increasingly extreme hubris in this narrative sequence occurs the day following the scene with the musket. In "The Needle," Ahab now discovers that the magnetism of the ship's compass must have been reversed because of the electric storm the night before. Standing on deck the next morning, Ahab notices that the sun is in the *Pequod*'s stern while it is supposed to be sailing east along the equator. Initially staggered by the discrepancy, Ahab quickly realizes the practical reason for the compass's reversal, telling his first mate who has also seen the reversed direction: "I have it! It has happened before. Mr. Starbuck, last night's thunder turned our compasses—that's all. Thou hast before now heard of such a thing I take it."

Starbuck's muted reply—"Aye: but never before has it happened to me, sir" (517)—has a double meaning in that he has never in his nautical career experienced such a reversal of the compass, but also, on a more private level, he has never had his moral compass so reversed that he would seriously contemplate the act of murder as he did the night before. The whole scene here is in fact meant to suggest that, as a result of the events described in "The Quadrant" and "The Candles," Ahab has indeed suffered a permanent reversal of his moral values. Like Milton's Satan at the start of book 4 of *Paradise Lost*, he has taken evil for his good. Unaware of Starbuck's internal drama or the underlying ethical import of his own actions, Ahab calls for the simple tools—lance, top-maul, and sailmaker's needle—that will enable him to fix the compass by replacing the reversed needles with his own makeshift needle, charged by himself. In the subsequent scene we find Ahab glorying in his apparent magical ability to control the elements:

"Men," said he, steadily turning upon the crew, as the mate handed him the things he demanded, "my men, the thunder turned old Ahab's needles; but out of this bit of steel Ahab can make one of his own, that will point as true as any."

Abashed glances of servile wonder were exchanged by the sailors, as this was said; and with fascinated eyes they awaited whatever magic might follow. But Starbuck looked away. (518)

If thunder was a sign of insuperable divine power for Job and the biblical Ahab, Melville's Ahab will characteristically negate its authority by asserting his own autonomous power over the physical world in an act that combines the technical wizardry of a Franklin and the devilish thaumaturgy of a Faustus. Ahab in fact seems to add a magical component to his relatively simple act of creating the new compass needle when he goes through "some small strange motions with it—whether indispensable to the magnetizing of the steel, or merely intended to augment the awe of the crew, is uncertain" (518). Ahab's magic here (as in "The Candles") is comparable to the miracle-mongering of Saint Paul's end-time "man of sin" and "son of perdition" whose "coming is after the working of Satan with all power and signs and lying wonders" (2 Thess. 2:4, 9). At the end of his technical procedure Ahab unabashedly dubs himself "lord of the level loadstone" and now assumes an explicitly satanic pose: "In his fiery eyes of scorn and triumph, you then saw Ahab in all his fatal pride" (519). Exhibiting a defiant and dehumanizing hubris, Ahab in his "look of fatal pride" evokes not only Milton's arch-rebel but also Isaiah's Lucifer, who said in his heart, "I will ascend into heaven, I will exalt my throne above the stars of God" (Isa. 14:13).

Yet just as Ahab's impious hubris by chapter 124 reaches dangerous heights of self-assertion and delusion, Ahab paradoxically demonstrates a residual humanity and tragic pity in his protective care of the deranged Pip. Such a development is first evident in chapter 125 ("Log and Line") in which Pip appears on deck as the crew are hauling in the snapped line formerly attached to the "log," which since Ahab's destruction of the quadrant (in chapter 118) has been the chief means of the ship's navigation. In response to the mad Pip's disconnected speech, in which the young cabin boy condemns his own cowardice for jumping from his whaleboat, Ahab finds a kindred spirit and object of compassion. He vows to take Pip into his cabin, just as the newly empathic Lear took his court fool out of the storm and into his care. In response to Pip's childlike grasp of Ahab's hand and the cabin boy's imputation of kindness to the captain's grasp ("Ah, now, had poor Pip but felt so kind a thing as this, perhaps he had ne'er been lost!"),

Ahab asserts that the case of Pip shows that human beings can teach the gods a lesson in compassion and humanity: "Lo! ye believers in gods all goodness, and in man all ill, lo you! see the omniscient gods oblivious of suffering man; and man, though idiotic, and knowing not what he does, yet full of the sweet things of love and gratitude" (522). An indictment of divine justice as cogent as any in the last quarter of the narrative, Ahab's speech here (as earlier, in "The Sphinx") shows the heroic compassion for unmerited human suffering still latent in his nature.[29]

In *Democracy in America*, Alexis de Tocqueville noted the importance of religious faith in promoting the belief in spiritual immortality: "Most religions are only general, simple, and practical means of teaching men the doctrine of the immortality of the soul. That is the greatest practical benefit which a democratic people derives from its belief, and hence belief is more necessary to such a people than to all others."[30] In *Moby-Dick*, both Ahab and Ishmael meditate extensively on the moral and metaphysical aspects of death and the afterlife, Ishmael because he is in quest of the philosophical wisdom to understand the complexities of the cosmos and Ahab because the afterlife in Christianity represents an essential component in the problem of theodicy as a compensation for human suffering. If the ideas of heroism and hubris informing the last quarter of *Moby-Dick* are based on a number of biblical precedents, the related issues of mortality and immortality shaping this narrative section are also closely related to several key biblical texts.

The concept of the afterlife was largely absent from the Old Testament, which posited the subterranean realm of Sheol as the location for the inert shades of the dead, the equivalent to Hades or Tartarus in classical mythology. The book of Job is notable for providing several evocations of this ghostly realm, which is a "land of darkness, as darkness itself; and of the shadow of death, without any order, and where the light is as darkness" (Job 10:22). Once someone is in Sheol, moreover, there is no resurrection: "So man lieth down, and riseth not: till the heavens be no more, they shall not awake, nor be raised out of their sleep" (Job 14:12). Similarly, in the book of Ecclesiastes, the "preacher" asserts that at death, "All go unto one place; all are of the dust, and all turn to dust again" (Eccles. 3:20).[31]

Hebrew thought downplayed the fate of the dead as a way of celebrating their god as a divine creator and preventing traditional ancestor worship. Classical Greek thought beginning with Plato in the fourth century BCE postulated the immortality of the soul, a doctrine set forth in its most influential form in the idealist philosopher's *Phaedo*. While late Second

Temple Judaism had extensive contact with Greek ideas and civilization following the conquests of Alexander, the beginnings of a belief in the afterlife may have come from Persia as a result of contact with Zoroastrianism, which pioneered the ideas of bodily resurrection and a last judgment of the dead. The concept of resurrection officially entered the Old Testament only in chapter 12 of the book of Daniel, a late addition to the canon. In Daniel, the idea of resurrection occurs in a passage responding to the martyrdom of Jewish soldiers fighting under the Maccabees against the Hellenizing tyrant Antiochus IV. The angel told Daniel: "many of them that sleep in the dust of the earth shall awake, some to everlasting life [in the form of immortal stars], and some to shame and everlasting contempt" (12:2). Daniel's new doctrine of resurrection probably depended on metaphors of the rebirth of the Israelite nation found in Isaiah 26:19 and Hosea 6:2 and 13:14, the latter prophet likely appropriating imagery from the Canaanite dying and rising fertility god Baal.[32]

In Christianity, the concept of the afterlife became a crucial tenet of the new faith, validated by Christ's apparent resurrection, like the Maccabean martyrs evoked in Daniel 12, on the third day after his martyrdom on the cross. Christ himself may have envisaged immediate ascent to heaven for the faithful (Luke 23:43), but Paul posited the idea of a "spiritual body" that will only rise from the grave at the general resurrection of the dead upon Christ's apocalyptic return to judgment, when he dispenses heavenly redemption or hellish damnation (1 Cor. 15). In the book of Revelation, the same scenario is divided into two resurrections, one before and one after the millennium (Rev. 20–22), at which time Christian martyrs and the souls of the blessed will attain everlasting glory in the New Jerusalem while the damned will descend into a lake of fire. While the early Christian concept of resurrection of the body was different from the Greek idea of the immortality of the soul, the two ideas gradually coalesced in the writings of the early church fathers to create the now well-known Christian idea of the afterlife.

Ishmael's quest for a whaling vessel in the early chapters of the novel is, as we have seen, saturated with allusions to Christian eschatology, and the ensuing narrative touches periodically on such concerns, before the final sequence of events beginning with chapter 99. In chapter 92, which discusses the precious ambergris found in the whale's intestines, Ishmael explores the paradox that the fragrant secretion, used as a fixative in perfumes, is formed in the putrid bowels of the whale: "Now that the incorruption of this most fragrant ambergris should be found in the heart of such decay; is this nothing? Bethink thee of that saying of St. Paul in Corinthians, about corruption and incorruption; how that we are sown in dishonor, but raised in glory [1 Cor. 15:43]" (409). The reference does not imply Ishmael's conversion to Saint Paul's teachings on the Christian afterlife but is, rather, a provocative allusion meant to suggest the philosophical notion of paradoxical truths, all set within a humorous disquisition debunking the "odious stigma" that "all whales always smell bad" (409).

Ishmael more extensively shares his thoughts on the mysteries of mortality and immortality in four chapters of natural history on the sperm whale. He accordingly describes a Polynesian skeletal whale used as a chapel (chapter 102), the scientific measurement of the whale's skeleton (chapter 103), the whale's remarkable prehistoric antiquity (chapter 104), and the question of whether the whale might ever become extinct (chapter 105). Significantly, his visit to the whale temple at Tranque in chapters 102 and 103 represents a dramatic and thematic antithesis to the theophany of Moby Dick at the end of the novel, for Ishmael's seriocomic philosophical visit to the temple explores the metaphysical mysteries of life while Ahab's tragic confrontation with the White Whale predictably results in disaster and death.

The start of Ishmael's meditations in chapter 102 ("A Bower in the Arsacides") describes his visit to the remote, semi-mythical kingdom of Tranque in the atoll islands of the Arsacides, the southern tip of the Solomon group in the southwestern Pacific—the name of the islands here being appropriate to Ishmael's acquisition of Solomonic wisdom during his visit. Invited by the king to survey his domain, Ishmael visits the skeleton of a large sperm whale that has washed ashore and then been converted into a chapel by the island's priests, a Polynesian equivalent to the contemporary popularity in Europe and America of articulated whale skeletons as curiosities of natural history. In its multivalent symbolism, the whale skeleton chapel has both biblical and literary prototypes. Mario L. D'Avanzo has thus argued that the description of the skeletal temple in chapter 102 is partially modeled on the description of the construction of Solomon's temple near the beginning of the First Book of Kings, while the description of King Tranquo's love of "barbaric virtue" suggests the rare and beautiful objects that filled the temple. Carole Moses, on the other hand, has noted that the visit to the whale temple constitutes Melville's version of the generative Garden of Adonis of book 3 of Spenser's *Faerie Queene*, except that Ishmael's depiction of the cycles of life and death here is infused with the pessimism evident in the earlier destruction of the Bower of Bliss in book 2, with its corrupt pleasures hiding spiritual death.[33]

If Ahab's final confrontation with the White Whale is a tragic, self-destructive attempt to solve the metaphysical mystery of an allegedly evil creator god, Ishmael's exploration of the whale temple is a seriocomic antithesis, a disinterested intellectual quest to probe the mysterious interrelationship of life and death within a skeletal cetacean body. By literally entering into the body of the whale Ishmael is enacting a satirical version of Jonah's descent into the belly of the "great fish." Yet the parody of Jonah is supplemented by implicit allusions to Ezekiel's vision of the Valley of the Dry Bones, in which God predicts the miraculous revivification of the disorderly pile of bones as a model for the restoration of the Hebrew people to their homeland after their Babylonian captivity. In his penetration into and measurement of the skeleton Ishmael is parodying both Jonah and Ezekiel, two Old Testament prophets obsessed with death and spiritual rebirth, while demonstrating God's ultimate silence and invisibility.[34]

At the beginning of chapter 102 Ishmael compares himself to Jonah for his unusual opportunity to investigate the anatomy of a young sperm whale that had been caught for his "poke or bag" to make harpoon sheaths. His visit to the whale chapel will expand on this initial experience: "I confess, that since Jonah, few whale men have penetrated very far beneath the skin of the adult whale; nevertheless, I have been blessed with an opportunity to dissect him in miniature" (448–49). We recall that in the episode of Jonah's engulfment in the whale's belly, the prophet looks toward God's temple in Jerusalem for redemption (Jonah 2:4). In Ishmael's visit to the whale skeleton temple in the Arsacides, by contrast, the sailor is not at all concerned with his spiritual state, for he wanders freely in and out of a protected cetacean "bower," not a hell-like "belly" (Jonah 2:1–2). The skeletal temple is noticeably devoid of any living god, even as the priests who guard the temple are embodiments of primitive superstition. Ishmael comically deflates the image of the whale skeleton as sacred precinct modeled on the Jewish temple, while reinscribing the whale skeleton as an imagined personification of a cosmic creator god.

Ishmael's association with the prophet Ezekiel during his visit to the whale skeleton chapel also rewrites the meaning of the sacred text. As the Lord tells Ezekiel: "Prophecy upon these bones, and say unto them, O ye dry bones, hear the word of the Lord. / Thus said the Lord God unto these bones; Behold, I will cause breath to enter into you, and ye shall live" (Ezek. 37:4–5). In order for the bones to live, the body must be reconstituted and wind (*nephesh* or soul) blown into it to reanimate the body. Following the Lord's command, Ezekiel describes the process of reanimation: "So I prophecied as I was commanded; and as I prophecied, there was a noise, and behold a shaking and the bones came together, bone to his bone" (Ezek.

37:7). Like the biblical prophet, Ishmael's vision of the whale bones leads to a meditation on the divine role in the creation of life and death. But instead of Ezekiel's Valley of the Dry Bones, we are now in a tropical landscape of lush vegetation. The skeletal chapel is interlaced with verdure from the abundant plant life in a manner that suggests the actions of an anonymous pantheistic "weaver-god," who refuses to answer Ishmael's questions about the ultimate meaning of life and death. The scene here contrasts the primitive temple in which the priests cannily manipulate symbols of the sacred within the larger metaphysical meaning of the huge skeleton and its living decor:

> The ribs were hung with trophies; the vertebrae were carved with Arsacidean annals, in strange hieroglyphics; in the skull, the priests kept up an unextinguished aromatic flame, so that the mystic head again sent forth its vapory spout; while, suspended from a bough, the terrific lower jaw vibrated over all the devotees, like the hair-hung sword that so affrighted Damocles.
>
> It was a wondrous sight. The wood was green as mosses of the Icy Glen; the trees stood high and haughty, feeling their living sap; the industrious earth beneath was as a weaver's loom, with a gorgeous carpet on it, whereof the ground-vine tendrils formed the warp and woof, and the living flowers the figures. All the trees, with all their laden branches; all the shrubs, and ferns, and grasses; the message-carrying air; all these unceasingly were active. Through the lacings of the leaves, the great sun seemed a flying shuttle weaving the unwearied verdure. Oh, busy weaver! unseen weaver!—pause!—one word!—whither flows the fabric? what palace may it deck? wherefor all these ceaseless toilings? Speak, weaver!—stay thy hand!—but one single word with thee! (449–50)

Just as there is an unextinguished aromatic flame in the whale temple, the Hebrew tabernacle and temple were required to have a perpetual oil lamp burning there (Exod. 27:20; 30:8). So, too, the terrific lower jaw of the whale creates an aura of fear in keeping with the threatening reality of the Hebrew god as found within the temple (Deut. 32; 1 Kings 9:6–9, 11:11). Ironically, the deity of the whale temple is a vegetative nature god of a kind the Hebrew god would have abominated. Melville adapted the image of his incommunicative god from Carlyle's *Sartor Resartus* (book 1, chapter 8), in which the divine creator is depicted as weaving the world "on the roaring Loom of Time," a metaphor Carlyle borrowed from the speech of the Earth Spirit at the start of Goethe's *Faust*.[35] We recall that Ishmael also used a weaving metaphor to figure the interaction of necessity, free will, and chance on the "Loom of Time" in "The Mat-Maker." Ishmael's eloquent portrait in chapter 102 of the creation as the product of a loom, spinning the vegetative fabric of life into a "gorgeous carpet," envisages the sun as a "flying shuttle weaving the unwearied verdure" of organic compounds. Yet as Ishmael plaintively expresses, the process of creation remains a metaphysical mystery for, unlike Ezekiel's or Jonah's communicative Old Testament deity, the Arsacidean weaver god is deaf to the questions Ishmael is posing. The ultimate nature and purpose of life remain an apocalyptic secret, only to be divulged—if at all—when we are removed from the physical universe. Unlike the imagery of the lethal Joban Leviathan, which characterizes the deadly White Whale, the image of the Leviathanic skeleton here is an enigmatic blending of life and death, confirming Ishmael's growing perception of the inextricable blending of good and evil in the cosmos.

The scene at the whale chapel continues with a suggestion of the identity of the weaver god who is now imagined to be an incongruous combination of lazy giant and active artificer—a platonic demiurge creating life out of death in an allegorized conjugal embrace:

> Now, amid the green, life-restless loom of that Arsacidean wood, the great, white, worshipped skeleton lay lounging—a gigantic idler! Yet, as the ever-woven verdant warp and woof intermixed and hummed around him, the mighty idler seemed the cunning weaver; himself all woven over with the vines; every month assuming greener, fresher verdure; but himself a skeleton. Life folded Death; Death trellised Life; the grim god wived with youthful Life, and begat him curly-headed glories. (450)

This evocation presents us with a striking set of paradoxes. The lounging skeletal idler, a *deus otiosus*, is also the busy artificer, the inert white bones mysteriously producing the bright green vegetation. Death and Life have the conjoined identity of a married couple such as Hades and Persephone in Greek, Isis and Osiris in Egyptian, Ishtar and Tammuz in Mesopotamian, and Kali and Shiva in Indian mythology, or Freud's conjunction of Eros and Thanatos in modern psychoanalytic theory. The whale skeleton here is an active but silent partner in the process of creation and procreation—a partner who, like the biblical patriarchs, begets endless vegetative life and makes planetary life possible by combining solar energy and organic compounds.

Ishmael's vision of the integral interrelation of life and death in the whale chapel will turn out to be prophetic. We later witness the metaphorical resurrection of the *Pequod*'s coffin–life buoy that will save Ishmael from the wreck. But for now, his experience of the skeletal whale merges into theological satire as he wanders "long amid its many winding, shaded colonnades and arbors" using a ball of twine, like Theseus in the Cretan labyrinth, to make sure he doesn't get lost. His ultimate report is that the inside of the skeletal temple is empty despite the abundant verdure that surrounds it, confirming that this is a *deus absconditus*, or hidden god (Isa. 45:15): "I saw no living thing within; naught was there but bones" (450). Ishmael's view of the emptiness of the divine body anticipates the modern scientific view of god and religion as an evolutionary adaptation of human consciousness projected onto the world—a faith or belief instinct.[36]

Still bent on measuring the size of the skeleton, Ishmael cuts a measuring rod and begins his calculations but is interrupted by the temple priests who do not want an outsider measuring their "god." When Ishmael asks the priests what their measurements are, "a fierce contest rose among them, concerning feet and inches; they cracked each other's sconces with their yard-sticks—the great skull echoed—and seizing that lucky chance, I quickly concluded my own admeasurements" (450–51). The scene at the whale chapel thus transmutes from metaphysical inquiry in the manner of Sir Thomas Browne to theological satire in the manner of Jonathan Swift, as we witness the priests of Tranque fighting over the measurements of their silent and empty "god," just as various sects and faiths have recurrently fought each other over the exact metaphysical dimensions of their gods— including Protestants and Catholics in America in the 1830s and '40s after the first large influx of Catholic immigrants into the country.

Ishmael's measurement of the skeletal whale continues his mimicry of the prophet Ezekiel who, after his vision of the Valley of the Dry Bones (Ezek. 37), went on to have a vision of the measurements of the restored temple in Jerusalem (Ezek. 40–43). Led by an angel with a "measuring reed" (a ten-foot measure), Ezekiel goes on an exhaustive tour of the imaginary temple while learning the exact dimension of its architecture, a project parodied in Ishmael's attempt to get the exact measurements of the skeletal whale. Ishmael's subsequent calculations of the whale skeleton are set forth in chapter 103 ("Measurement of the Whale's Skeleton") and confirm the formidable size of the whale; but he ultimately rejects the reductive results of the scientific study of anatomy for the more accurate, if more dangerous, experience of the living body—a valorization of Romantic-era organicism at the expense of Enlightenment-era scientific rationalism: "How vain and foolish, then, thought I, for timid untravelled man to try to comprehend aright this wondrous whale, by merely poring over his dead attenuated skeleton, stretched in this peaceful wood. No. Only in the heart of quickest perils; only when within the eddyings of his angry flukes; only on the profound unbounded sea, can the fully invested whale be truly and livingly found out" (453–54). Unlike the biblical prophet Ezekiel, then, Ishmael's measurements constitute a futile endeavor. Indeed, in his conclusions here, Ishmael duplicates the example of Job who was resigned to remain ignorant of the mysteries of nature that he could not rationally understand.

As is made clear in the next two chapters of natural history, the whale as a representative "king of creation" may be said to be synonymous with life on earth, both in its primordial and its future ages when humans may no longer populate the planet. Thus, in "The Fossil Whale" Ishmael adduces fossil evidence for the existence of whales in the early ages of creation when ice sheets covered much of the earth according to the recent geological theories of Louis Agassiz and before even humankind was created, in keeping with the current theory of successive creations and cataclysms set forth by the naturalist Georges Cuvier: "Then the whole world was the whale's; and, king of creation, he left his wake along the present lines of the Andes and the Himmalehs. Who can show a pedigree like Leviathan?" (457). The question leads directly to Ishmael's sublime terror at the antiquity of the whale: "I am horror-struck at this antemosaic, unsourced existence of the unspeakable terrors of the whale, which, having been before all time, must needs exist after all humane ages are over" (457).

In an era when dinosaurs were first being formally identified by the British paleontologist Richard Owen and others, Ishmael contemplates the primeval antiquity and theoretical immortality of the whale as species and comes close to characterizing it as an embodiment of primordial terror like the Leviathan of Job—except that the terms of his analysis are based on modern science, not biblical myth. Unlike Ahab's quest for immortality in his denial of human corporeality and interdependence, Ishmael here envisages geological ages both before the creation and after the extinction of the human race, ages when the whale was—and might still be—the dominant species on the planet. Such a naturalistic vision, which replaces the Christian god with the whale, is allegedly confirmed by the images of the whale in the ancient Egyptian "great temple of Denderah" (457) and in a whale-bone temple with a legendary connection to the prophets Mahomet and Jonah, noted by the sixteenth-century Arabian traveler John Leo Africanus.

In chapter 105 ("Does the Whale's Magnitude Diminish?—Will He Perish?") Ishmael completes his discussion of the quasi-divine antiquity of the whale by examining the question of how long whales will continue in the future if they continue to be hunted in such large numbers as at the present. Despite the evidence that whale populations have suffered significant declines, Ishmael nevertheless argues that they will in fact outlive human civilization since they have a vast oceanic domain in which to flee their predators, and at one hundred years they also have a longer life expectancy than humans. To gain an idea of what the latter fact means, Ishmael tells us to imagine "all the graveyards, cemeteries, and family vaults of creation yielding up the live bodies of all the men, women, and children who were alive seventy-five years ago; and adding this countless host to the present human population of the globe" (462). Such a mock rehearsal of the Resurrection and the Last Judgment shows, in the end, that humans have no divinely sanctioned privileges to dominate the life of the planet. He confidently concludes that "for all these things [reasons], we account the whale immortal in his species, however perishable in his individuality" (462). Immortality, whether for humans or for whales, is not to be found in the individual but in the species, and whales according to Genesis have been on earth longer than humans and will probably outlive them. This strikingly non-anthropocentric view of the cosmos makes Ishmael a prescient protoenvironmentalist, even as he midjudges the vulnerability of whale species to human predation and human-induced climate change. Ishmael ends the chapter by ironically postulating that "if ever the world is to be again flooded, like the Netherlands, to kill off its rats, then the eternal whale will still survive, and rearing upon the top-most crest of the equatorial flood, spout his frothed defiance to the skies" (462). Subversively rewriting the account of the Flood in Genesis, Ishmael envisages the whales—not Noah and his family—as survivors of God's apocalyptic extermination of a sinful humanity.

Ishmael's four-chapter excursus on the whale's skeleton and its larger biblical significance, the coda to his extended discussion of cetology, is enmeshed in questions of mortality and immortality regarding the whale, which now assumes the symbolic role of primordial divinity. As in his earlier discussions of cetology, Ishmael blends a wide array of scientific fact, history, and legendary lore to demonstrate the whale's unprecedented nature, concluding that since it existed before all human ages it will probably outlive humanity. Such a conclusion largely accords with the meaning of Leviathan to Job, even as it envisages the living Leviathan as the dominant creature in the future of planetary life. When we return to the drama on the *Pequod* after Ishmael's excursus on whale skeletons, however, we return to issues of life and death on a more recognizably human scale.

One main symptom of Ahab's perilously growing hubris, beginning with his solipsistic view of the doubloon in chapter 99, is his self-serving, increasingly delusional belief in his own immortality and powers of self-deification, even as the *Pequod's* steadily growing proximity to the White Whale gives increasing grim reminders of human mortality. For this reason, the last quarter of *Moby-Dick* frequently evokes the subject of death and, with it, the related ideas of spiritual immortality and the afterlife.

In his discussion with the carpenter making him a new whalebone leg in chapter 108 ("Ahab and the Carpenter"), Ahab speculates on death and spiritual immortality in a series of jocular exchanges that evoke the probing metaphysical wit of Hamlet interrogating the gravedigger preparing Ophelia's grave. Some of Ahab's remarks to the dull-witted carpenter exhibit the flippant black humor of the melancholy Dane, as Ahab questions the carpenter about his trade:

> Carpenter? Why that's—but no;—a very tidy, and, I may say, an extremely gentlemanlike sort of business thou art in here, carpenter;—or would'st thou rather work in clay?
>
> Sir?—Clay? clay, sir? That's mud; we leave clay to ditchers, sir.
>
> The fellow's impious! What art thou sneezing about?
>
> Bone is rather dusty, sir.
>
> Take the hint, then; and when you art dead, never bury thyself under living people's noses. (471)

Ahab initially pretends here that the carpenter might aspire to be a sculptor of clay like the divine fabricator (Job 10:9, 13:12, 33:6; Ps. 40:2; Isa. 45:9, 64:8). But he then expresses mock outrage at the carpenter's impiety when the latter identifies working in clay—the substance out of which God made human beings—as the occupation of "ditchers." As the carpenter continues to work on his artificial leg, Ahab mentions the mystery of his still having feeling within his missing limb, a phenomenon now called a "phantom limb" sensation and explicated by modern medical research.[37]

The strange phenomenon of sensation without ostensible cause leads Ahab to suggest to the carpenter that invisible spiritual bodies may exist in a parallel world to our own: "How dost thou know some entire, living, thinking thing may not be invisibly and uninterpenetratingly standing precisely where thou now standest; aye, and standing there in thy spite?" (471). He suggests a revealing analogy between his own strange physical condition of bodiless sensations and the carpenter's postmortem condition: "And if I still feel the smart of my crushed leg, though it now be so long dissolved; then, why mayst not thou, carpenter, feel the fiery pains of hell for ever, and without a body? Hah!" (471). Ahab's reasoning here evokes the Cartesian divide between matter and spirit, but his purpose is not so much disinterested metaphysical speculation as sardonic provocation of the carpenter with the apparent reality of hell. Ahab's conversation with the carpenter exhibits his absorbing interest in death and the fate of the soul, which forms part of his radical ambivalence toward the idea of having a bodily identity.[38]

As a believer in a malicious creator god, Ahab views nature as a cosmic manifestation of evil and uses that knowledge to validate his hunt for Moby Dick. So in chapter 116 ("The Dying Whale") Ahab meditates on the habit of sperm whales who allegedly turn their heads to the sun prior to their death, which he interprets as a sign of religious homage to the source of all life: "He turns and turns him to it,—how slowly, but how steadfastly, his homage-rendering and invoking brow, with his last dying motions. He too worships fire; most faithful, broad, baronial vassal of the sun!" (496–97). Yet Ahab interprets this act as an archetypal example of the creator's betrayal of the creature; for the whale's sun-worshipping act of dying faith leads only to the darkness of physical annihilation: "here, too, life dies sunwards full of faith, but see! no sooner dead, than death whirls round the corpse, and it heads some other way.—" (497). Ahab's remarks may remind us again of Job's complaints against the deity: "What is the Almighty that we should serve him? and what profit should we have, if we pray unto him?" (Job 21:15). The answer, repeated throughout Job's lamentations, is that spiritual annihilation ultimately overtakes us: "As the cloud is consumed and vanisheth way: so he that goeth down to the grave shall come up no more" (Job 7:9).

More demonically than Job, Ahab in chapter 116 goes so far as to identify the ruthless destructiveness of the sea as the realm of the Hindu goddess Kali, the Destroyer: "Oh, thou dark Hindoo half of nature, who of drowned bones hast builded thy separate throne somewhere in the heart of these unverdured seas; thou art an infidel, thou queen, and too truly speakest to me in the wide-slaughtering typhoon, and the hushed burial of its after calm" (497). A goddess of death seems, for Ahab, appropriate to the destructive chaos of the oceans. He accordingly declares his spiritual allegiance not to the life-giving sun but to the death-dealing sea, the source of a "prouder, if a darker faith" that recognizes the existence of universal amoral annihilation. Ahab's oath of allegiance (with its continuing hints of Milton's Satan) is yet another symptom of Ahab's ongoing reversal of moral values from light to dark and from life to death, as he approaches the final phase of his hunt for the White Whale.

Ahab's meditations on death continue in the next chapter ("The Whale-

Watch"), in which he and his Asiatic crew keep overnight watch on a dead whale that has not been tied to the side of the *Pequod* and is now surrounded by hungry sharks. The chapter title evokes Job's earlier-cited complaint against the deity that he is being treated like one of the elements of primordial chaos that must be checked: "Am I a sea, or a whale, that thou settest a watch over me?" (Job 7:12). But the key association with Job is to the next few lines of biblical text when a beleaguered Job claims that God has been afflicting him with nightmares: "When I say, My bed shall comfort me, my couch shall ease my complaint; / Then thou scarest me with dreams, and terrifiest me through visions" (Job 7:13–14). Dozing in his whaleboat with the Parsee, Ahab wakes from a dream of hearses, which has already occurred in his sleep more than once. He goes over the ambiguous prophecies that Fedallah has previously explained to him—prophetic equivocations implicitly related to the "lying spirit" that fatally misled the biblical King Ahab, as well as Melville's more immediate source, *Macbeth*. In a scene modeled on the witches' predictions to Macbeth in Shakespeare's play, the Parsee sets forth the strange and seemingly impossible preconditions for Ahab's death, causing Ahab momentarily to exult in his own sense of invulnerability and immortality. First, "two hearses must verily be seen by thee on sea; the first not made by mortal hands; and the visible wood of the last one must be grown in America"; second, "Though it come to the last, I shall still go before thee thy pilot"; and third, "Hemp only can kill thee" (499). Such predictions remind us of the witches' prophecies, which Macbeth could "laugh to scorn / The power of man; for none of woman born / Shall harm Macbeth"; indeed, "Macbeth shall never vanquish'd be until / Great Birnam wood to high Dunsinane hill / Shall come against him" (*Macbeth*, IV.i.79–81, 92–94). In both *Macbeth* and *Moby-Dick*, the aura of supernatural and oracular doom that initiates and concludes each tragedy is in part a projection of the hero's divided mind, with the witches and Fedallah acting as both quasi-supernatural characters and personifications of a pathologically fragmented subconscious.[39]

The cultural context of the Parsee's predictions is not just Shakespearean, however, but also biblical. For the hearse not made by mortal hands (which will turn out to be the body of Moby Dick) recalls the prophet Daniel's well-known interpretation of the Babylonian King Nebuchadnezzar's dream, in which a "stone cut out of the mountain without hands" breaks apart a giant idol with head of gold, breast and arms of silver, belly and thighs of brass, legs of iron, and feet of clay—a symbol of four world empires (Dan. 2:31–45). The stone cut out without hands was an image of divine vengeance against a series of historical enemies of the Jews, anticipating the arrival of God's kingdom. The hearse not made by mortal hands in *Moby-Dick* will similarly be an agent of quasi-divine vengeance, the White Whale. The Parsee's prediction that he will go before Ahab in death makes him, in turn, a demonic John the Baptist or false prophet to Ahab's Antichrist. Finally, the prediction that only hemp can kill Ahab, which the latter assumes to be the gallows (it will be his own whale line attached to Moby Dick) recalls the "scandal" of the cross for early Christians whose messiah was executed as a common criminal (1 Cor. 1:23). The Parsee's predictions—all of which will turn out to be true in a sense not anticipated by Ahab—are encoded by biblical subtexts that reinforce the captain's increasingly reckless impiety and his usurpation of divine prerogatives in the final sequences of the narrative. Deluded into thinking he has the potential to be immortal, Ahab has reached a spiritual state antithetical to that of Job who foresees his own annihilation: "And why dost thou not pardon my transgression, and take away my iniquity? for now I shall sleep in the dust; and thou shalt seek me in the morning, but I shall not be" (Job 7:21).

Death is a palpable presence in several of the novel's later chapters, and salient questions of mortality and immortality accordingly become the focus of interest for characters other than Ahab as well. One of the most pathos-laden crewmen on the *Pequod* is the blacksmith described in chapter 112, whose nautical career illustrates the living death that characterizes the life of many whalemen. As Ishmael recounts in his extended character sketch, the blacksmith's career as a sailor began in advanced age because of the fatal influence of intemperance on his household, blighting his family and sending him to sea in a kind of posthumous condition. The blacksmith in his catastrophic loss of family and property is thus another Job figure on the *Pequod*; but unlike the archetypal biblical victim, the blacksmith is himself responsible for these losses because of his experience with what Ishmael evocatively describes as the "Bottle Conjurer." The sketch of the blacksmith superficially resembles an antebellum temperance tract, preaching that the wages of sin is death, but Ishmael's final message is more ambiguous. Meditating on the blacksmith's career, Ishmael describes the allure of the ocean as a kind of seductive death-in-life realm: "Death seems the only desirable sequel for a career like this; but Death is only a launching into a region of the strange Untried; it is but the first salutation to the possibilities of the immense Remote, the Wild, the Watery, the Unshored" (486). Since life after death is a metaphysical unknown, for those men who don't want to be guilty of suicide, shipping out as a sailor represents a more alluring if comparable fate. Thus does the ocean "alluringly spread forth his whole plain of unimaginable, taking terrors, and wonderful, new-life adventures; and from the hearts of infinite Pacifics, the thousand mermaids sing to them" (486). As in Tennyson's "Ulysses," the sea represents a seductive and sublime realm of posthumous life for sailors like the blacksmith whose choice of going to sea is, as it was for Ishmael, a substitute for suicide and an opportunity to escape disaster or depression on land.

Beyond the inset character sketch of the blacksmith, the most sustained depiction of interrelated questions of mortality and immortality informing the final movement of the novel involves the coffin–life buoy that will eventually save Ishmael after its conversion from funerary to nautical use.[40] In chapter 110 ("Queequeg in His Coffin"), Queequeg assists in moving cargo in the *Pequod's* hold in order to investigate a possible leak, and in the process catches a fever that first prostrates him and then puts his life at risk. As he wastes away in his hammock, the Polynesian "savage" seems to show mystic signs of his approaching death:

> And like circles on the water, which, as they grow fainter, expand; so his eyes seemed rounding and rounding, like the rings of Eternity. An awe that cannot be named would steal over you as you sat by the side of this waning savage, and saw as strange things in his face, as any beheld who were bystanders when Zoroaster died. For whatever is truly wondrous and fearful in man, never yet was put into words or books. And the drawing near of Death, which alike levels all, alike impresses all with a last revelation, which only an author from the dead could adequately tell. (477)

In antebellum religious culture, scenes of dying were occasions for the living to gain an understanding of the fate of the soul after death, as reflected in the countenance and behavior of the dying—especially the traditional questions of eschatology involving the likelihood of heaven or hell. James P. Grove has cogently argued that in Queequeg's deathbed scene, Melville reproduces this sentimental cultural convention.[41] During the assumed death of Queequeg, however, the living witnesses can gain no understanding of the afterlife. Indeed, as a pagan, Queequeg can have no concept of the spiritual resurrection promised to Christians, but his notions of the immortality of the soul conform instead to the religious ideas of his Polynesian forebears, who launched the dead on the ocean, suitably provisioned and embalmed, in the belief that the soul will be assimilated into the cosmos; "and so [they] left him to be floated away to the starry archipelagoes; for not only do they believe that the stars are isles, but that far beyond all visible horizons, their own mild, uncontinented seas, interflow with the blue heavens; and so form the white breakers of the milky way" (478). In this beautiful image of interblending firmaments of sea and heaven, Ishmael seems to imply that Polynesian and Western notions of death and the afterlife may be poetic fables that suit their respective cultural milieus, being designed to provide consolation for the living.

Unwilling to be buried in the ocean in just a shroud made of his hammock, Queequeg asks the carpenter to make him a coffin so he can follow his own native funerary customs, and once the coffin is constructed he asks it to be provisioned for his journey into the afterlife. However, after he is fully prepared for his launch into eternity, Queequeg inexplicably and anticlimactically thinks of something he still needs to accomplish ashore and decides he can't die yet. In the meantime, he will use his coffin as a sea chest and spends his time carving his coffin to match the figures on his own body.

> Many spare hours he spent, in carving the lid with all manner of grotesque figures and drawings; and it seemed that hereby he was striving, in his rude way, to copy parts of the twisted tattooing on his body. And this tattooing had been the work of a departed prophet and seer of his island, who, by those hieroglyphic marks, had written out on his body a complete theory of the heavens and the earth, and a mystical treatise on the art of attaining truth; so that Queequeg in his own proper person was a riddle to unfold; a wondrous work in one volume; but whose mysteries not even himself could read, though his own live heart beat against them; and these mysteries were therefore destined in the end to moulder away with the living parchment whereon they were inscribed, and so be unsolved to the last. (480–81)

Queequeg's coffin thus becomes a kind of physical double to the pagan harpooner, covered with hieroglyphic marks that constitute a theory of cosmology and a treatise on philosophy. In its duplicative identity, the coffin can accordingly be viewed as a parodic Pauline "spiritual body" (1 Cor. 15:44) that will double as his physical body after death. Queequeg's act of transcription similarly draws on the traditional Christian metaphor of the "book" of nature, as Ishmael once again underlines the futility of any attempt to grasp the mysteries of human life and death since the tattooed writing on the "volume" of Queequeg's body—the creation of a "departed prophet and seer"—is unreadable by Queequeg himself and the "living parchment" of the text will disintegrate with his death. The sight of Queequeg carving on the coffin becomes a part of Ahab's indictment against heavenly injustice.

Frustrated by his own limitations of knowledge and power Ahab remarks, "Oh, devilish tantalization of the gods!" (481), seeing confirmation here that the secrets of the cosmos are provocatively suggested but never fully revealed to human beings.

Not used for its original purpose because Queequeg spontaneously recovers from his illness, the coffin is converted later into a life preserver when the original one sinks into the ocean while the crew is trying to rescue a man who has fallen overboard in chapter 126. As the *Pequod* approaches the Season-on-the-Line where Ahab expects to find Moby Dick, a drowsy sailor falls from the masthead and disappears underwater, along with the ship's defective life buoy. "And thus the first man of the Pequod that mounted the mast to look out for the White Whale, on the White Whale's own peculiar ground; that man was swallowed up in the deep. But few, perhaps, thought of that at the time" (524). For most of the crew, the sailor's death is only a confirmation of the portentous message heard the night before: "a cry so plaintively wild and unearthly—like half-articulated wailings of the ghosts of all Herod's murdered innocents," the humanlike sounds of seals on a "cluster of rocky islets," interpreted by the Manxman as "the voices of newly drowned men at sea" (523). In the meantime, at Queequeg's suggestion, Starbuck orders the coffin to be converted into a replacement life buoy; and the carpenter with some reluctance prepares it for its new function by sealing it up and attaching a set of rope lines.

In the next chapter ("The Deck"), Ahab interviews the carpenter about the coffin–life buoy, again in the manner of Hamlet and gravedigger, with the same combination of ironic humor and metaphysical suggestiveness.[42] For Ahab, the carpenter's seemingly indifferent manufacture of articles for both death and life, in his conversion of the coffin to a life preserver suggests the amorality of the divine creator (or the gods, in this case): "Then tell me; art thou not an arrant, all-grasping, intermeddling, monopolizing, heathenish old scamp, to be one day making legs, and the next day coffins to clap them in, and yet again life-buoys out of those same coffins? Thou art as unprincipled as the gods, and as much of a jack-of-all-trades" (527). When the carpenter responds in his own defense, "I do not mean anything, sir. I do as I do," Ahab is quick to note a parallel to the impersonal workings of the universe: "The gods again" (528). Ahab's response to the carpenter's "I do as I do" probably also plays on the enigmatic name of the Hebrew deity revealed to Moses at the burning bush: "I AM THAT I AM" (Exod. 3:14).[43]

In a further exchange, Ahab, alluding to the singing gravedigger in *Hamlet*, notes that the carpenter's calking mallet is full of music: "the lid there's a sounding-board; and what in all things makes the sounding-board is this—there's naught beneath. And yet, a coffin with a body in it rings pretty much the same, Carpenter" (528). In other words, with or without a body, the coffin implies that death is a condition of spiritual annihilation.

Ahab demonstrates a similar point when he elicits from the carpenter that his frequent use of the verbal expletive "faith" is merely a "sort of exclamation-like—that's all, sir" (528). The ultimate result of Ahab's interview with the carpenter is a newly confirmed skepticism concerning the possibilities of an afterlife. For though he savors the grim humor of a coffin converted into a life buoy, he cannot believe in the potentially hopeful message of spiritual resurrection that this conveys: "Can it be that in some spiritual sense the coffin is, after all, but an immortality-preserver! I'll think of that. But no. So far gone am I in the dark side of earth, that its other side, the theoretic bright one, seems but uncertain twilight to me" (528). Like Job, Ahab can imagine only spiritual annihilation at death and demonstrates his adherence to antichristian beliefs by refusing to put faith in a spiritual resurrection. In the meantime, the coffin–life buoy is hung at the stern of the *Pequod*, an ambiguous symbol of the inextricable unity—and paradoxical mystery—of life and death.

CHAPTER SEVEN

Combat and Catastrophe

IN THE PREVIOUS CHAPTER, we have seen how Ahab's exemplary heroism blends with self-destructive hubris, while related questions of mortality and immortality raised by both Ahab and Ishmael in the last quarter of the novel contribute to the development of important religious and philosophical ideas. We now follow the *Pequod* to Ahab's final disastrous confrontation with the White Whale and explore its implications for the novel's interrelated themes of theodicy and eschatology. In the combat of Ahab and the whale, and the ensuing catastrophe, we witness the captain's defeat by a creature exhibiting all the features of the archetypal chaos monster Leviathan in the book of Job. Ahab's defeat effectively demonstrates the presumption and futility of his mad attempt to eliminate evil in the world and implicitly confirms Yahweh's evocation to Job of the inscrutable mysteries of the creation. In the end, Ahab remains in the role of the rebellious Job of the poetic dialogues, while Ishmael plays the part of the patient, submissive Job of the folktale frame story. By the same token, the novel's conclusion shows that the messianic zealotry and metaphysical dualism of Judeo-Christian apocalyptic are ultimately self-defeating, for only Ishmael—who has accepted the mysteriously linked relationship between good and evil in the world and the need for human solidarity— survives the wreck.

While the novel's conclusion draws heavily on the biblical motifs that have governed its thematic and dramatic development, the climactic account of Ahab's combat with the whale also conforms to comparable archetypal patterns of conflict from other influential mythic traditions. Joseph Fontenrose has made a comprehensive study of a common combat myth involving an order-creating hero and a chaos-creating monster in five ancient cultures: Greece (Apollo versus Python/Dragon; Zeus versus Typhon), Canaan (Baal versus Mot), Mesopotamia (Marduk versus Tiamat), Egypt (Horus versus Set), and India (Indra versus Vritra). Citing a broad range of examples, Fontenrose has identified in this class of myths a recurrent sequence of ten basic narrative components: (1) the monstrous antagonist is of divine origin, with a primordial father or mother; (2) it has a distinctive habitation, often in a body of water; (3) it has an extraordinary appearance, often marked by a huge size, and typically takes the form of a snake, lizard, crocodile, or fish; (4) it shows a vicious nature, making war in its particular domain; (5) it has conspired against heaven, sometimes in quest of world rule; (6) the god or hero as divine champion appears to face the monstrous antagonist; (7) the champion goes out to fight his formidable adversary; (8) the champion nearly loses the battle against his adversary; (9) the monstrous antagonist is eventually outwitted or deceived and then destroyed; (10) the champion disposes of the body of his antagonist and celebrates his victory.[1]

It is immediately apparent that *Moby-Dick* conforms to many of these mythic components, especially in the legendary characterization of its cetacean monster, with its huge size, oceanic domain, ostensibly vicious nature, and seemingly omnipotent power. But the mythic parallels go awry with the appearance of the hero to fight the monster for Ahab is hardly a virtuous exemplar of moral heroism. Unlike the archetypal pattern of the hero's ultimate victory over the monster, moreover, Melville's novel ends with Ahab's defeat. In effect, the polarity of order and chaos, good and evil, in the contest between hero and monster is here replaced by the moral ambiguity of both the enraged American whaling captain and his (allegedly) vindictive monstrous antagonist. The Old Testament version of the combat myth postulated Yahweh as the exclusive warrior-champion who defeated the primordial antagonist Leviathan; hence Captain Ahab, as a presumptuous Faustian overreacher, must be defeated.[2] On the other hand, Ahab's messianic mission is fueled partly by legitimate outrage at his own—and humanity's—gratuitous suffering, and his death accordingly bears traces of a Christlike aura of crucifixion.

The divergence of Ahab's story from the traditional combat myth of order-creating hero and chaos-creating monster is partly explained by the merging in Melville's novel of the mythic model of primordial combat with another influential mythic tradition. Neil Forsyth in *The Old Enemy: Satan and the Combat Myth* presents this pattern as featuring a "satanic" adversary, or oppositional figure, in combat with a messianic or divine hero. In effect, the Judeo-Christian Satan was the necessary creation of mythic narrative structures before he became the metaphysical embodiment of the devil. With its origins in the same Near Eastern mythological context of divine combat with a chaos monster (as analyzed by Fontenrose and others), this tradition had a pervasive impact on the development of Judeo-Christian canonical and noncanonical scripture, and on Christian tradition generally. The development of Christian theology included a recurrent retelling and reinterpretation of various forms of the Near Eastern and Hebrew "satanic" myths. Melville's novel, like Milton's epic, is yet another formulation of this tradition, as Melville's Ahab assumes the role of the satanic adversary whose cause is based on a doomed protest or rebellion against the divine order.[3]

To this archetypal tradition Melville would add the element of tragedy, a dramatic form originating in classical Greece but implicitly present as a category of human experience in the Hebrew Bible. For our present purposes, we may divide the influence of biblical tragedy to its Old and New Testament dimensions. In an examination of tragedy in the Hebrew Bible, J. Cheryl Exum has focused on the figures of Saul, his children, Jepthah and David as exemplary tragic personalities.[4] Missing from this list are the figures of Job and King Ahab, who provided the chief Old Testament models for Melville's whaling captain, as we have seen. Indeed, it took Melville's conflation of these two biblical figures to create a viable tragic hero in Captain Ahab; for King Ahab alone was too morally reprehensible to serve as a tragic figure, and Job was ultimately rewarded for his grievous suffering despite his outspoken protests against the deity. But the biblical Ahab shares several characteristics with at least two of Exum's tragic figures. Like Saul he exhibits a melancholic, paranoid mind-set and is deliberately destroyed by Yahweh for his violations of the national covenant. Like David he blends charismatic leadership with moral failings that are highlighted by an outspoken prophet (Nathan, Elijah). Despite his condemnation by the Deuteronomistic historian for having angered Yahweh more than any other Israelite king, King Ahab, like Melville's whaling captain, has his humanities. Much of his evil-doing grows out of his dynastic alliance with the Tyrian Jezebel, whose Canaanite gods alienate the Hebrew deity and whose overweening ambitions, as in the appropriation of Naboth's vineyard, may remind us of a ruthless and ambition-driven Lady Macbeth.[5]

Yet Melville's Ahab also seems comparable to several other well-known enemies of the Hebrew god. In his blindness to the obvious signs of impending disaster, for example, Ahab is similar not only to Belshazzar of the book of Daniel but also to the prototypical example of Pharaoh, whose heart is "hardened" by Yahweh to refuse Moses's demands to free the Israelite people and who, with his army, is drowned in the Red Sea (Exod. 5–14). Like Pharaoh, Ahab and most of his crew will drown for the captain's inability to reconsider the wisdom of his scheme of revenge. Ahab similarly enacts the fall of at least two well-known targets of prophetic denunciation in Isaiah and Ezekiel, the King of Babylon and the Prince of Tyre.

In addition to its pervasive Old Testament background, Ahab's final tragedy is steeped also in a number of New Testament texts. Several decades ago, Roger L. Cox demonstrated the fallacy of the common critical assumption that Christian tragedy was by definition impossible given the optimistic tenor of Christian faith in the Resurrection, in contrast to the fatalism of the classical world in which Greek tragedy first developed. Examining three tragedies of Shakespeare (*Hamlet, King Lear,* and *Macbeth*) and three novels of Dostoevsky (*Crime and Punishment, The Idiot,* and *The Brothers Karamazov*), Cox has identified the largely Pauline moral and intellectual matrix of the Shakespearean texts he examines, as compared to the more mystical dualistic Johannine writings (the gospel, letters, and Apocalypse of John) that shaped Doestoevsky's fiction.[6]

When examining *Moby-Dick* as a "Christian" tragedy, we can readily discern the salient apocalyptic symbolism of the narrative, with its basis in the "little apocalypse" of the synoptic gospels, in the letters of Saint Paul, and especially in the book of Revelation—writings setting forth the basic New Testament doctrines of the immortality of the soul, the end-time combat of the forces of good and evil, and the allegedly redemptive direction of history. What should also be mentioned here is the relevance of a passage from Saint Paul's Epistle to the Romans, the central statement of Paul's theology, in the contrast between Ahab's destruction and Ishmael's survival. In chapter 12 of his letter, Paul sets forth some of the most important principles for living a Christian life, including humility, compassion, charity, honesty, benevolence, and nonviolence:

> Let love be without dissimilation. Abhor that which is evil; cleave to that which is good.
>
> Be kindly affectioned one to another with brotherly love; in honour preferring one another ...
>
> Rejoice with them that do rejoice, and weep with them that weep.
>
> Be of the same mind one toward another. Mind not high things, but condescend to men of low estate. Be not wise in your own conceits.
>
> Recompense no man evil for evil. Provide things honest in the sight of all men.
>
> If it be possible, as much as lieth in you, live peaceably with all men.
>
> Dearly beloved, avenge not yourselves, but rather give place unto wrath; for it is written, Vengeance is mine; I will repay, saith the Lord.

Therefore, if thine enemy hunger, feed him; if he thirst, give him drink; for in so doing thou shalt heap coals of fire on his head.

Be not overcome of evil, but overcome evil with good. (Rom. 12:9–10, 15–21)

If there is one New Testament text that defines the moral and ideological divide between Ishmael and Ahab, it is undoubtedly this well-known statement of Pauline ethics. This is not to say that either Ishmael or Ahab are Christians in any conventional sense of the term, although both are products of Protestant American religious cultures, Ishmael of Presbyterianism and Ahab of Quakerism. Nonetheless, Paul's famous prohibition on vengeance in the temptation to be "overcome with evil" goes to the heart of Ahab's tragedy, which exemplifies the potentially self-destructive cycle of violence that revenge can generate, as illustrated by the long tradition of revenge tragedy that begins with Aeschylus's *Oresteia* and reaches a major milestone with Shakespeare's *Hamlet*.[7]

As an antichristian avenger, Ahab repeatedly fails to show brotherly love, arrogantly refuses to "condescend to men of low estate," and is "wise" in his own philosophical conceits, contrary to Paul's injunctions in Romans 12. He refuses to "rejoice" with those aboard the *Samuel Enderby* and the *Bachelor* and to "weep" with those aboard the *Rachel*. He fails to "give place to wrath" in the justification of his apocalyptic quest. By the same token, Ahab violates the Pauline admonition to "Provide things honest in the sight of men" when he engages in acts of subterfuge in his quest for the White Whale, including smuggling aboard a demonic crew of Asian sailors, concealing the true nature of his voyage from his owners, and manipulating the loyalty of his crew with antichristian rituals of communion, baptism, and miracles. Collective destruction is the price for Ahab's path of vengeance.

On the other hand, Paul's injunctions in Romans 12 may be said to describe many of Ishmael's salient moral virtues, which illustrate the benefits of humane reciprocity rather than self-destructive revenge. Throughout the novel, Ishmael is "kindly affectioned" with Queequeg, despite the cultural divide that separates them, and is able unself-consciously to "condescend to men of low estate" in his identification with the crew of the *Pequod*. So, too, his self-deprecating humor shows that he is not "wise" in his own conceits. Highlights of these redeeming traits are especially evident in chapter 10 ("A Bosom Friend"), chapter 72 ("The Monkey-Rope"), and chapter 94 ("A Squeeze of the Hand"), chapters in which we have seen him drawing on, or even parodying, other well-known Pauline and New Testament texts. And despite the fact that Ishmael swears allegiance to his captain's vengeful vision of the White Whale, he is not "overcome with evil" to the same extent as it warps the personality of Ahab, as demonstrated in chapter 96 ("The Try-Works"). In order to assess these biblical motifs and the intensification of the tragedy in the final chapters of the novel, we must trace Ahab's fate as he nears the completion of his relentless quest for the White Whale.

Ever since the *Pequod's* arrival in the Pacific Ocean in chapter 111, it has been drawing ever closer to the targeted feeding grounds of Moby Dick during the Season-on-the-Line, but it is only after the ship's encounter with the *Rachel* in chapter 128 that the near proximity of the White Whale is first established. The *Rachel* encountered the legendary whale the day before hailing the *Pequod*, and its chief officer, Captain Gardiner, has lost his own young son since the encounter, among the crew of a whaleboat that has gone missing. Gardiner pleads for Ahab to help him for two days in seeking his lost son, but Ahab impatiently rejects the request and pushes off in quest of his long-anticipated prey. The rejection here confirms Ahab's chilling indifference to the basic principles of Christian charity and the Golden Rule of reciprocity (Matt. 7:12). As Captain Gardiner notes, during his request, "Do to me as you would have me do to you in the like case. For *you* too have a boy, Captain Ahab" (532). Ahab's rejection is also an egregious violation of nautical etiquette. Denied the aid of the *Pequod*, the *Rachel* continues with its task of searching for its missing crew and at the end of the chapter is transformed into a symbol of inconsolable grief and mourning, for "by her still halting course and winding, woeful way, you plainly saw that this ship that so wept with spray, still remained without comfort. She was Rachel, weeping for her children, because they were not" (533). The final sentence here evokes the biblical Rachel, the wife of Jacob and mother of Joseph, who served as a type of the Jewish people and their repeated historical disasters, whether referring to the sixth-century destruction of Jerusalem and resulting exile as interpreted by the prophet Jeremiah (Jer. 31:15) or its later echo in Herod's Slaughter of the Innocents according to the Gospel of Matthew (Matt. 2:18). The whale ship *Rachel* thus becomes representative of maternal grief that can presumably only be overcome at the apocalyptic end-time.[8]

If Ahab is so fixated on revenge that he refuses to help Captain Gardiner look for his lost son, this does not mean Ahab is absolutely bereft of compassion for his own crew at this point. For in the next chapter ("The Cabin") we find him telling Pip to remain in his cabin because of the upcoming confrontation with the White Whale. His pathos-laden presence might weaken Ahab's resolve to fight, and Pip's madness might cure Ahab's own, according to the contemporary homeopathic principle that "like cures like." Although he has denied Captain Gardiner the chance to search for his lost son, Ahab shows renewed concern for his own surrogate child, Pip, who is lost in mind, if not in body.

The same compassionate concern makes Ahab tell Starbuck in chapter 132 ("The Symphony") not to put out to sea in his whaleboat during the forthcoming hunt for Moby Dick. In this, the last chapter before the chase begins, Ahab in an unprecedented act of confession reveals his loneliness and suffering to his first mate, showing an eloquent capacity to grieve and demonstrating the lack of feminine or domestic influence on his life. Yet the chapter ends with Ahab's renewed commitment to revenge and the triumph of intellectual obsession over domestic affection.[9]

The scene begins when the beauty of the sea and sky is evoked in richly metaphorical language: "It was a clear steel-blue day. The firmaments of air and sea were hardly separable in that all-pervading azure; only, the pensive air was transparently pure and soft, with a woman's look, and the robust and man-like sea heaved with long, strong, lingering swells, as Samson's chest in his sleep" (542). In this evocative description, the firmaments of air and ocean appear united in an apocalyptic marriage, superseding their division at the creation (Gen. 1:6–8), but the allusion to Samson, emasculated in his sleep by Delilah (Judges 16), strikes a potentially ominous note. Indeed Ahab now appears like the blinded, captive strongman of Milton's tragedy as well as the sublimely tortured Satan of book 4 of *Paradise Lost*: "Tied up and twisted; gnarled and knotted with wrinkles; haggardly firm and unyielding; his eyes glowing like coals, that still glow in the ashes of ruin; untottering Ahab stood forth in the clearness of the morn; lifting his splintered helmet of a brow to the fair girl's forehead of heaven" (542–43). The extraordinary atmospheric beauty softens Ahab's heart, however, as though the earth in the role of affectionate mother were able to express love for her wayward son:

> that glad, happy air, that winsome sky, did at last stroke and caress him; the step-mother world, so long cruel—forbidding—now threw affectionate arms round his stubborn neck, and did seem to joyously sob over him as if over one, that however willful and erring, she could yet find it in her heart to save and to bless. From beneath his slouched hat Ahab dropped a tear into the sea; nor did all the Pacific contain such wealth as that one wee drop. (543)

Momentarily shedding his tragic Old Testament identity, Ahab figuratively experiences the world of New Testament redemption. While the tearful return of the errant son to the "step-mother world" evokes the parable of the prodigal son (Luke 15:11–24), the teardrop that Ahab lets fall is equivalent to the widow's mite in Christ's parable of exemplary charity (Mark 12:42–44; Luke 21:2–4).

The allusively rich pathos of "The Symphony" in fact combines biblical, classical, Shakespearean, Miltonic, and Hawthornean elements in an eloquent depiction of regret before the final catastrophe. In Ahab's speech to Starbuck, we find the captain regretting the spiritual bereavement and emotional deprivation he has undergone through so many years of whaling: "Forty—forty—forty years ago!—ago! Forty years of continual whaling! forty years of privation, and peril, and storm-time! forty years on the pitiless sea! forty years has Ahab forsaken the peaceful land, for forty years to make war on the horrors of the deep!" (543). The number forty here evokes the forty years that the Israelites wandered in the wilderness for their sins against Yahweh (Num. 14:33); its reiteration implies the general biblical sense of forty being an indefinitely large number. Lamenting his tragic burden of isolation, Ahab exhibits the spiritual desiccation of a Macbeth before his final battle: "for forty years I have fed upon dry salted fare—fit emblem of the dry nourishment of my soul!" (543–44). The passage also seems to recall the weary age-conscious Lear: "Here, brush this old hair aside; it blinds me, that I seem to weep. Locks so grey did never grow but from out some ashes!" (544). Even though Ahab married in his fifties, his "girl-wife" is a virtual widow since he has been away from her so much at sea: "Aye, I widowed that poor girl when I married her, Starbuck" (544). Like Hawthorne's Roger Chillingsworth, Ahab has made a grass widow of his young wife and traded domestic comforts for the loneliness of the ocean and the pursuit of a sterile scheme of revenge. Just as Chillingsworth tells Hester in chapter 14 of *The Scarlet Letter* that his actions, together with Hester's and Dimmesdale's, have all been determined by a "dark necessity," so Ahab claims to Starbuck that all his actions have been determined by fate.[10]

In his confession to Starbuck, Ahab laments the loss of his leg, his gray hair, and his advancing age (fifty-eight), which makes him feel like "Adam, staggering beneath the piled centuries since Paradise" (544). Looking into Starbuck's eyes, Ahab even thinks he sees his wife and child in this "magic glass." He tells Starbuck he should stay onboard when they encounter Moby Dick, and as a result Starbuck excitedly tries to convince him to give up the chase. In the chapter's classical dramatic context, the first mate acts as the admonitory chorus of *Prometheus Unbound*, which evokes an image of the Titan's wife, Hesione, in the attempt to end his defiance of Zeus.[11] But despite the first mate's best efforts, Ahab is immune to such pleading and averts his glance, for "like a blighted fruit tree he shook, and cast his last, cindered apple to the soil" (545). Like the barren fig tree cursed by Christ (Mark 11:12–14), Ahab can offer no further emotional sustenance to Starbuck. Indeed, he figuratively becomes the potential source for bitter disillusionment, symbolized by the ashen Apples of Sodom that the rebel angels ate as they were transformed into serpents in Milton's *Paradise Lost* (X.547–70).

Attaining a rare moment of self-scrutiny, however, Ahab questions the source of his compulsion for revenge while still protesting the hidden forces that have driven him on. Momentarily oblivious of Starbuck's presence, a now chastened Ahab recognizes that, in a deterministic universe, a single prime mover is theoretically responsible for all actions, rendering his individual identity problematic: "Is Ahab, Ahab? Is it I, God, or who, that lifts this arm? But if the great sun move not of himself; but is an errand-boy in heaven; nor one single star can revolve, but by some invisible power; how then can this one small heart beat; this one small brain think thoughts; unless God does that beating, does that thinking, does that living, and not I" (545). Ahab's speculation about the ultimate causality of events in a theistic universe suggests Pierre Bayle's similar speculation concerning the possible divine origins of evil in his article on the Gnostic sect of Paulicians:

> It is impossible to comprehend, that God did not only permit sin; for a bare permission of sin added nothing to free-will, and was not a means to foresee, whether Adam would persevere in his innocence or fall from it. Besides according to the idea we have of a created Being, we cannot comprehend that it can be a principle of action, that it can move itself, and that receiving in every moment of its duration its existence and the existence of its faculties, wholly from another cause, it should create in itself any modalities by a power peculiar to itself. . . . Seeing therefore a creature cannot be moved by a bare permission of acting, and has not in itself a principle of motion, it is absolutely necessary that God should move it; he must therefore do something else than barely permit man to sin.[12]

Ahab's perception of absolute human and cosmic dependence on God may also remind us of the creation theology in Job: God "alone spreadeth out the heavens, and treadeth upon the waves of the sea" (Job 9:8). But Ahab's inquiry nevertheless hovers between a tragic fatalism and an incipient self-deification. For Ahab's cogent case for determinism ends with an accusation against the god of the universe who not only permits the act of murder in humans and animals but must also be implicated in the act: "Where do murderers go, man! Who's to doom when the judge himself is dragged to the bar?" (545). The ultimate rationale for Ahab's actions, then, remains the problem of theodicy that he first outlined to Starbuck, and as in the earlier chapter "The Quarter-Deck," the agonized cries of Job against divine injustice form the implicit backdrop here: "The earth is given into the hand of the wicked: he covereth the faces of the judges thereof; if not, where, and who is he?" (Job 9:24). By this time, however, a "blanched" Starbuck has left Ahab's side; such talk of murder can only have been unnerving for the man who recently was tempted to kill his captain. The only eyes that Ahab now sees are the "two reflected, fixed eyes in the water" (545) belonging to Fedallah. By reminding himself of his rationale for revenge, Ahab has in effect dismissed his good and invoked his bad angel. Unlike the hallowed tear in Ahab's eye or the "magic glass" of Starbuck's eye in which the sacred ties of family appear, the demonic eyes of Fedallah are reflected off the sea, a realm of death and destruction in the novel and the place from which Moby Dick will soon emerge.

The increasingly visible presence of Fedallah as the *Pequod* approaches the known location of Moby Dick has already been made evident in chapter 130 ("The Hat"), for the Parsee is always present on deck even though his appearance gives the crew additional doubts about his ultimate identity: "Such an added, gliding strangeness began to invest the thin Fedallah now; such ceaseless shudderings shook him; that the men looked dubious at him; half uncertain, as it seemed, whether indeed he were a mortal substance, or else a tremulous shadow cast upon the deck by some unseen being's body" (537). Such "shudderings" confirm Fedallah's multiform oracular and prophetic identity. A "lying spirit" like the one commissioned by God to destroy King Ahab in the First Book of Kings, or like the prosecutorial satan who tests Job, the Parsee is also Ahab's demonic familiar, his prophetic guide in the apocalyptic quest for Moby Dick. A religious figure in his own right, the Parsee embraces the cosmic dualism that has enabled Ahab to demonize the White Whale. In his nervous excitement he seems increasingly aware of the approaching battle between Ahab and the whale, a form of climactic eschatological battle between the forces of light and darkness like that found in his native Zoroastrian religion. The description of Fedallah's relationship with Ahab plays on the unspoken intimacy between the two, as though they are the shadow and substance of one driven being:

> But though his whole life was now become one watch on deck; and though the Parsee's mystic watch was without intermission as his own; yet these two never seemed to speak—one man to the other—unless at long intervals some

passing unmomentous matter made it necessary. Though such a potent spell seemed secretly to join the twain; openly, and to the awestruck crew, they seemed pole-like asunder. If by day they chanced to speak one word; by night, dumb men were both, so far as concerned the slightest verbal interchange. At times, for longest hours, without a single hail, they stood far parted in the starlight; Ahab in his scuttle, the Parsee by the mainmast; but still fixedly gazing upon each other; as if in the Parsee Ahab saw his forethrown shadow, in Ahab the Parsee his abandoned substance.

And yet, somehow, did Ahab—in his own proper self, as daily, hourly, and every instant, commandingly revealed to his subordinates,—Ahab seemed an independent lord; the Parsee but his slave. Still again both seemed yoked together, and an unseen tyrant driving them; the lean shade siding the solid rib. For be this Parsee what he may, all rib and keel was solid Ahab. (537–38)

The ambiguity of the relationship here reflects the ambiguity of Fedallah's role in Ahab's quest, for the Parsee is both a demonic manifestation of Ahab's madness (thus a slave of the captain's will) and the prophetic bearer of a predetermined fate (the unseen tyrant) whose life is inextricably linked to Ahab's end.

While the presence of Fedallah now prefigures the long-awaited appearance of Moby Dick, the key action of chapter 130 is the loss of Ahab's hat while he is hoisted aloft on his watch for the White Whale. Not trusting that his mates will inform him of a possible sighting of Moby Dick, Ahab has decided to keep watch himself and perhaps even claim the reward of the doubloon when the legendary whale is finally sighted. And so it is while he is stationed in the rigging that "one of those red-billed savage sea-hawks" that haunt these latitudes descends on his aerial lookout and carries off Ahab's slouched hat. As Ishmael notes, the omen might have been good if the hat was put back on Ahab's head, according to a legendary incident concerning Tarquin, the first king of ancient Rome, recorded by the historian Livy. But the hawk flies off with the hat "and at last disappeared; while from the point of that disappearance, a minute black spot was dimly discerned, falling from that vast height into the sea" (539). The loss of Ahab's hat conveys several prophetic meanings. As a symbolic "discrowning," it constitutes the undoing of the captain's self-coronation in chapter 37, while it also anticipates his defeat in the coming battle, just as the biblical King Ahab lost his crown and kingdom with his death at the battle of Ramosh-gilead. Prefiguring the appearance of the biblical Leviathan, the loss of his hat reiterates Ahab's association with the suffering Job who at one point complains of the deity: "He hath stripped me of my glory, and taken the crown from my head"

(Job 19:9). Finally, in the novel's apocalyptic frame, the hat falling into the Pacific Ocean prefigures Ahab's forthcoming "fall" in dubious battle with the whale, an event reminiscent of the fates of such biblical overreachers as the King of Babylon (Lucifer) in Isaiah 14, the Prince of Tyre in Ezekiel 28, and the Dragon in Revelation 12, all of whom, like Ahab, have recklessly aspired to divine status.

The likely outcome of Ahab's engagement with the White Whale is made even clearer in chapter 131, when the *Pequod* encounters the *Delight*, which is in the process of sea burial for one of its crew, the only recovered occupant of a whaleboat that has recently been attacked and destroyed by Moby Dick. Bearing a name that is grimly ironic in relation to the funeral taking place on deck (and to Father Mapple's use of the word in his sermon on Jonah), the *Delight* is the last of the nine whale ships to be encountered by the *Pequod*. The encounter with the *Delight* would seem to verify the invincible malignity of Moby Dick, yet in answer to the captain's claim that "The harpoon is not yet forged" that will kill Moby Dick, Ahab proudly boasts that *his* harpoon has the magical properties to do so: "Tempered in blood, and tempered by lightning are these barbs" (540–41). As in previous gams with other whalers, the encounter with the *Delight* here reiterates the folly of attacking the White Whale, a message that Ahab, like his Old Testament prototypes, arrogantly refuses to hear, repeating a pattern seen in his previous encounters with the *Jeroboam* and *Rachel*. But in the act of sailing away from the other ship, "the strange life-buoy hanging at the Pequod's stern came into conspicuous relief" (541), and a "foreboding voice" from the *Delight* confirms that their flight from death is futile; for they too will go down to defeat before the White Whale: "In vain, oh, ye strangers, ye fly our sad burial; ye but turn us your taffrail to show us your coffin!" (541). Yet before Ahab glimpses Moby Dick arising from the sea in chapter 133, he experiences his final regrets and reexamines his rationale for revenge in "The Symphony," a meditative pause before the combat proper begins. According to the Aristotelian principles of tragedy this chapter acts as kind of opening choral ode to the final sequence of the tragedy—an exhibition of pity for the hero before the terror of the final chase begins.[13]

The dramatic climax, initiated by the long-awaited appearance of the White Whale, takes the form of an enthralling three-day chase recounted in the final three chapters of the novel.[14] Beyond its rich metaphysical and symbolic dimensions, the three-day chase provides a vivid depiction of a nineteenth-century whaler's ultimately disastrous encounter with an aggressive bull sperm whale. The male's powerful tail flukes and toothed lower jaw could inflict significant injury on his pursuers in their whaleboats, while in rare cases the encounter could lead to the ramming and sinking of the ship itself, the ultimate fate of the *Pequod*. As Ishmael describes in chapter 45 ("The Affidavit") while affirming the factual basis for his narrative, "The Sperm Whale is in some cases sufficiently powerful, knowing, and judiciously malicious, as with direct aforethought to stave in, utterly destroy, and sink a large ship; and what is more, the Sperm Whale *has* done it" (206). He then cites the experience of the American whale ship *Essex*, sunk by an aggressive sperm whale in November 1820, as recounted in Owen Chase's *Narrative of the Wreck of the Whaleship Essex* (1821).[15] Sailing out of Nantucket in 1819, the *Essex* was officered by Chase as first mate and by George Pollard, Jr., as captain. While cruising the Central Pacific just below the equator over two thousand miles from the South American coast, the *Essex* was twice rammed by a large bull sperm whale, first on the side and then in the bow. Chase described the second deadly onset of the whale in a manner that suggested the intelligent malignity of its actions, thereby providing an important precedent for the conclusion of *Moby-Dick*:

> He [the angry whale] was enveloped in the foam of the sea, that his continual and violent thrashing about in the water had created around him, and I could distinctly see him smite his jaws together, as if distracted with rage and fury. He remained a short time in this situation, and then started off with great velocity, across the bows of the ship, to windward. . . . I turned around, and saw him about one hundred rods directly ahead of us, coming down apparently with twice his ordinary speed, and to me at that moment, it appeared with tenfold fury and vengeance in his aspect. The surf flew in all directions about him, and his course towards us was marked by a white foam of a rod in width, which he made with the continual violent thrashing of his tail; his head was about half out of water, and in that way he came upon, and again struck the ship.[16]

The twenty crewmen from the *Essex* who succeeded in abandoning the ship before it sank faced a deadly ordeal at sea in three whaleboats; after resorting to cannibalism, only Chase, Pollard, and a few others survived after sailing two thousand miles east to the coast of South America. Ironically, despite the prevailing winds to the west, they shunned the accessible islands of the Marquesas and Tahiti as a destination because of their fears of cannibalism. During a visit to Nantucket with his father-in-law in July 1852, Melville met and talked to the former captain of the *Essex*, George Pollard, Jr., who was working as a night watchman after his premature retirement from the sea because of another whaler lost under his command. As Melville later noted of Pollard in his annotated copy of Owen Chase's *Narrative*: "To the islanders he was a nobody—to me, the most impressive man, tho' wholly unassuming, even humble—that I ever encountered." Melville's intense interest in this unlucky captain doubtless had something to do with the latter's Job-like identity following his traumatic encounter with the deadly Leviathan, and the stoic humility that seemed to mark Pollard's demeanor was suggestive of the humbled Job at the end of the Old Testament book.[17]

Curiously enough, Melville heard another account of a deadly attack of a sperm whale on an American whaler from his New York friend Evert Duyckinck, in Pittsfield in early November 1851, shortly before publication of the American edition of *Moby-Dick* that month. Duyckinck sent an article, probably from the *New York Daily Tribune*, recounting the sinking of the *Ann Alexander* in the Pacific the previous August after being attacked by a sperm whale. In his reply to his friend, Melville hypothesized that the whale that sank the *Ann Alexander* was in fact Moby (or Mocha) Dick; he also noted this unexpected confirmation of the credibility of his narrative and speculated whether his soon-to-be-published novel might magically have evoked the disaster: "Ye Gods! What a Commentator is this Ann Alexander whale. What he has to say is short & pithy & very much to the point. I wonder if my evil art has raised this monster."[18]

While the final chapters of *Moby-Dick* are consistent with the recorded disasters of nineteenth-century American whaling, which included the sinking of at least three whaling vessels by angry bull sperm whales, the three-day chase also contains a rich biblical subtext. Indeed, it is here that the novel's dramatization of its chief biblical sources reaches a climax. The long-awaited appearance of the White Whale is in part a theophany often associated with the punitive intervention of Yahweh on the Day of the Lord; and it is Ahab who hopes to be the divine redeemer described in Isaiah: "In that day the Lord with his sore and great and strong sword shall punish leviathan the piercing serpent, even leviathan that crooked serpent; and he shall slay the dragon that is in the sea" (Isa. 27:1). The three-day chase reveals the fact that the White Whale is an embodiment of the archetypal chaos monster informing the image of Leviathan in the book of Job, Psalms, and Isaiah—and in transmuted form (as beast from the sea or dragon) in Daniel and Revelation. Just as the portrait of Leviathan marks the climax to the prolonged debate over divine justice in Job so, too, the long-awaited appearance of the White Whale provides the stunningly dramatic conclusion to *Moby-Dick*. And just as the initial evocation of the White Whale in chapter 41 relied heavily on the image of Leviathan from

Job so, too, the three chapters of the three-day chase draw extensively on the same source, which provides a detailed backdrop to the epic struggle between Ahab and the White Whale.

For all the dramatic buildup to the whale's murderous power in the final chapters, the first full view of Moby Dick ironically conveys an impression of majestic, godlike beauty: "A gentle joyousness—a mighty mildness of repose in swiftness, invested the gliding whale. . . . not Jove, not that great majesty Supreme! did surpass the glorified White Whale as he so divinely swam" (548). Moby Dick's initially majestic appearance accords with God's description in the book of Job of the "comely proportion" and "joy" that Leviathan embodies in his appearance: "I will not conceal his parts, nor his power, nor his comely proportion. . . . In his neck remaineth strength, and sorrow is turned to joy before him" (41:12, 22). As Perdue notes, "Beauty as well as power is a significant feature of Leviathan's appearance. While the descriptions of Leviathan in art and language normally picture a terrifying, horribly ugly monster, Yahweh uncharacteristically glories in the beauty of this divine being."[19] In addition, the White Whale is accompanied by "hundreds of gay fowl softly feathering the sea" (548) like the angels that accompanied an Old Testament theophany. The sea fowls are thus seen "to and fro skimming like a canopy over the fish" (548) as though engaged in a royal progress.

In a previous image, the whale is seen swimming through the ocean like a semi-divine potentate before whom nature unrolls a carpet and makes musical accompaniment: "Before it, far out on the soft Turkish-rugged waters, went the glistening white shadow from his broad, milky forehead, a musical rippling playfully accompanying the shade," while on either side behind him "bright bubbles arose and danced by his side" (548). The whale's divine majesty in which nature joyfully participates now hints at the celebration of the deity found in a series of "enthronement" psalms (Pss. 93, 96–99) featuring imagery of the storm god Yahweh's triumphant control of the elements, especially the unruly seas. In Psalm 93, for example, the psalmist exults: "The floods have lifted up, O Lord, the floods have lifted up their voice; the floods lift up their waves. / The Lord on high is mightier than the noise of many waters, yea, than the mighty waves of the sea" (Ps. 93:3–4). A comparable injunction is found in Psalm 98 in another celebration of divine kingship: "Let the sea roar, and the fullness thereof; . . . / Let the floods clap their hands: let the hills be joyful together / Before the Lord; for he cometh to judge the earth: with righteousness shall he judge the world, and the people with equity" (Ps. 98:7–9).[20] The pathetic fallacy of waves clapping their hands informs the ensuing description of the combined beauty and terror that characterize the White Whale's appearance: "And thus, through the serene tranquillities of the tropical sea, among waves whose hand-clappings were suspended by exceeding rapture, Moby Dick moved on, still withholding from sight the full terrors of his submerged trunk, entirely hiding the wrenched hideousness of his jaw" (548). At the first appearance of the White Whale, we gain a paradoxical impression of celebration and dread, majesty and terror, life and death—a divided moral identity in keeping with the image of Leviathan in the book of Job and in the Old Testament generally.[21]

Moby Dick's sublime, godlike identity is similarly suggested by a mythological comparison to the "white bull Jupiter swimming away with ravished Europa clinging to his graceful horns; his lovely, leering eyes sideways intent upon the maid; with smooth bewitching fleetness, rippling straight for the nuptial bower in Crete" (548). A foreshadowing of Ahab's eventual "ravishment" (both literal and figurative) by the White Whale, the image of sexual abduction here also typifies the traditionally amoral behavior of the chief god of the classical pantheon while demonstrating the polymorphous forms of the gods generally. Both a divine monarch of the seas and a magnificent sperm whale, Moby Dick also reveals himself an avatar of the natural sublime: "But soon the fore part of him slowly rose from the water; for an instant his whole marbleized body formed a high arch, like Virginia's Natural Bridge, and warningly waving his bannered flukes in the air, the grand god revealed himself, sounded, and went out of sight" (548–49). Moby Dick's initial theophany as "grand god" is distinctive for its melding of Hebraic and classical religious allusions in an iconic evocation of wonder and terror.[22]

The sublime terrors of the White Whale are soon on full display as Ahab begins the hunt following the whale's extended dive, at which time "there were plainly revealed two long crooked rows of white, glistening teeth, floating up from the undiscoverable bottom. It was Moby Dick's open mouth and scrolled jaw; his vast, shadowed bulk still half blending with the blue of the sea. The glittering mouth yawned beneath the boat like an open-doored marble tomb" (549). A creature from the chaotic depths of the ocean, Moby Dick—like the mythic Leviathan—is identified as blending with the elemental realm of the sea while manifesting the hideous jaws and teeth of a dragon-like monster, its mouth a symbolic tomb, as in the book of Job: "Who can open the doors of his face? his teeth are terrible round about" (Job 41:14).

Meeting Ahab's strategy of evasion "with that malicious intelligence ascribed to him," the White Whale then lies obliquely on its back under

Ahab's whaleboat, "slowly and feelingly taking its bows full within his mouth, so that the long, narrow, scrolled lower jaw curled high up into the open air, and one of the teeth caught in a row lock. The bluish pearl-white of the inside of the jaw was within six inches of Ahab's head, and reached higher than that. In this attitude the White Whale now shook the slight cedar as a mildly cruel cat her mouse" (549–50). The image of cat and mouse here evokes God's taunting of Job by asking him if he thinks he can treat Leviathan like a tame pet: "wilt thou play with him as with a bird? or wilt thou bind him for thy maidens?" (Job 41:5). When an enraged Ahab attempts manually to push the whale's clamped jaws off the whaleboat's gunwales (as God told Job, "Lay thine hand upon him, remember the battle, do no more" [Job 41:8]), then "both jaws, like an enormous shears, sliding further aft, bit the craft completely in twain, and locked themselves fast again in the sea, midway between the two floating wrecks" (550). In the midst of his failed attempt to grapple with the whale's jaws Ahab has been thrown from his boat and "fell flat-faced upon the sea" (550), an action that suits God's warning of the power of Leviathan: "Behold, the hope of him is in vain: shall not one be cast down even at the sight of him" (Job 41:9).

After snapping Ahab's boat in two, the whale withdraws a short distance and engages in an up-and-down movement called pitchpoling, "so that when his vast wrinkled forehead rose—some twenty or more feet out of the water—the now rising swells, with all their confluent waves, dazzlingly broke against it; vindictively tossing their shivered spray still high into the air. So, in a gale, the but half baffled [English] Channel billows only recoil from the base of the Eddystone [Lighthouse], triumphantly to overleap its summit with their scud" (550–51). Moby Dick's agitation of the ocean here corresponds to the foamy seas created by Leviathan. As God tells Job: "He maketh the deep to boil like a pot: he maketh the sea like a pot of ointment" (Job 41:31). Moby Dick's final action on this first day of the chase is to swim around the wrecked crew of Ahab's whaleboat, "sideways churning the water in his vengeful wake, as if lashing himself up to still another and more deadly assault" until Ahab, "half smothered in the foam of the whale's insolent tail, and too much of a cripple to swim" (551), is able to call to the *Pequod* to sail directly upon the White Whale and so drive him off.

The first day of the chase, Moby Dick is revealed as presenting many features of the archetypal sea monster Leviathan of the book of Job. The next two days of the chase exemplify other aspects of the same biblical text. When Moby Dick initially appears on the second day of the chase, he exhibits the "wondrous phenomenon of breaching" (557), leaping diagonally out of the water in a dazzling display of force. No harpoons were thrown at the whale during the first day of the chase, but the second day is characterized by a full-scale assault involving all three whaleboats, with their harpoons and lances. The whale "offered appalling battle on every side; and heedless of the irons darted at him from every boat, seemed only intent on annihilating each separate plank of which those boats were made" (558). By means of his "untraceable evolutions" (558), the whale manages to tangle all the whale lines together, at which point Ahab tries to disentangle his own line by loosening and then jerking on it. The unexpected result of this gesture is that a deadly-looking collection of "loose harpoons and lances, with all their bristling barbs and points, came flashing and dripping up to the chocks in the bows of Ahab's boat" (559). An agile maneuver allows Ahab to remove the dangerous cluster of irons and to reaffix his line—but the whale nonetheless then smashes the boats of Stubb and Flask together and sends Ahab's boat high in the air by surfacing rapidly and knocking it from beneath. The prominence of harpoons, lances, and boat knives in this scene shows that another aspect of the Joban chaos monster is dramatized here, God's assertion that swords, spears, darts, and other weapons will fail to injure Leviathan (Job 41:26–29).

Like the mythical Leviathan, during the second day of the chase Moby Dick easily dislodges most of the barbs thrown at him. The only line that hasn't dislodged is Ahab's own, which has somehow dragged Fedallah to his death as Ahab discovers to his horror after the *Pequod* has come to his rescue, and he counts the men of his whaleboat on deck. Earlier Ahab had boasted of his quasi-divine invulnerability because he noted only his whalebone leg had splintered in the day's encounter with the whale: "Nor white whale, nor man, nor fiend, can so much as graze old Ahab in his own proper and inaccessible being" (560). When he realizes that his specially forged harpoon is useless against the White Whale, however, and that his own line has killed Fedallah, Ahab shows his first momentary sign of fear. As Stubb reports that the Parsee is missing and that he was in fact dragged under by Ahab's line, the captain reacts with enraged disbelief, like Macbeth hearing of the uncanny movement of Birnam Wood. "*My* line! *my* line? Gone?—gone? What means that little word?—What death-knell rings in it, that Old Ahab shakes as if he were the belfry. The harpoon, too!—toss over the litter there,—d'ye se it?—the forged iron, men, the white whale's—no, no, no,—blistered fool! this hand did dart it!—'tis in the fish!" (561). Ahab's momentary panic inadvertently confirms God's assertion to Job: "Upon earth there is not his [Leviathan's] like, who is made without fear" (Job 41:33). The captain's dismay also incorporates the traditional recognition (*anagnorisis*) and reversal of fortune (*peripeteia*) of the Aristotelian analysis of Greek tragedy and adds to the aura of terror and pity that distinguish Ahab's fatal combat with the whale.[23] Aristotle cites as a prime example of reversal the messenger's speech from *Oedipus the King*, which is comparable to Stubb's messenger speech concerning the Parsee—implying that the prophecies are indeed being fulfilled but not in the way that Ahab understood them.

Ahab's tragic recognition quickly yields to heroic self-assertion in the face of possible death. When Starbuck makes a desperate last attempt to show that his captain's course is calamitous, surrounded with divine warnings of doom and damnation, Ahab responds with the claim that his actions have the divine certitude of fate:

> "Great God! but for one single instant show thyself," cried Starbuck; "never, never wilt thou capture him, old man—In Jesus' name no more of this, that's worse than devil's madness. Two days chased; twice stove to splinters; thy very leg once more snatched from under thee; thy evil shadow gone—all good angels mobbing thee with warnings:—what more wouldst thou have?—Shall we keep chasing this murderous fish till he swamps the last man? Shall we be dragged by him to the bottom of the sea? Shall we be towed by him to the infernal world? Oh, oh,—Impiety and blasphemy to hunt him more!"
>
> "Starbuck, of late I've felt strangely moved to thee; ever since that hour we both saw—thou know'st what, in one another's eyes. But in this matter of the whale, be the front of thy face to me as the palm of this hand—a lipless, unfeatured blank. Ahab is for ever Ahab, man. This whole act's immutably decreed. 'Twas rehearsed by thee and me a billion years before this ocean rolled. Fool! I am the Fates' lieutenant; I act under orders. Look thou, underling! that thou obeyest mine." (561)

Starbuck's Christian pieties fall on deaf ears. In a final demonstration of self-delusion, Ahab asserts the deterministic nature of his mission while deflecting ultimate responsibility for his actions onto the Fates. The momentary cognitive dissonance created by the death of the Parsee yields to the indelible conviction that Ahab's actions cannot be questioned because of the emotional and psychological investment he has made in the quest to kill the whale. Like Pharaoh in his confrontation with Yahweh, Ahab's heart is hardened in his hubris, so that any course besides vengeance becomes unthinkable. It is significant that Starbuck in this scene calls Moby Dick a "fish," using the language of the book of Jonah (Jon. 1:17)—and indeed,

Starbuck's fears of drowning and damnation suggest Jonah's cry from the belly of the monster. But Ahab will not repent like the reluctant prophet who served as Father Mapple's model of Christian humility nor even like the Job who submitted when confronted with Yahweh's overwhelming evocation of Leviathan.

The third and final day of the chase results in Ahab's last attack on Moby Dick and the subsequent sinking of the *Pequod* after it is rammed by the enraged whale. Ironically enough, the day of catastrophe dawns beautiful and fair, inspiring Ahab with an uncharacteristically rhapsodic vision: "What a lovely day again! were it a new-made world, and made for a summer-house to the angels, and this morning the first of its throwing open to them, a fairer day could not dawn upon that world" (563). Yet in the ensuing dramatic monologue, Ahab laments that he can't *think* about the beauty of the day but can only *feel* the intensity of his passions: "our poor brains beat too much" (563) for the calm reflection that only a divine being can enjoy.

Feeling the strong breeze blowing in his hair, Ahab launches into an ambivalent meditation on the wind, first considering it tainted for having blown through prisons and hospitals while on land, then praising it as a noble and heroic thing, unconquerable by quixotic mortals like himself: "In every fight it has the last and bitterest blow. Run tilting at it, and ye but run through it" (564). It soon becomes apparent that the wind he is referring to is a manifestation of divine spirit. Ahab here recapitulates his Job-like complaints (in chapters 36 and 37) against the unfair play of the "gods" when he exclaims against the wind: "Ha! a coward wind that strikes stark naked men, but will not stand to receive a single blow. Even Ahab is a braver thing—a nobler thing than *that*. Would now the wind but had a body; but all the things that most exasperate and outrage mortal man, all these things are bodiless, but only bodiless as objects, not agents. There's a most special, a most cunning, oh, a most malicious difference!" (564). In other words, malicious agents like Ahab's God are often bodiless in form and so cannot be attacked physically, even though they visibly cause human hardship. Ahab's argument here implicitly recapitulates Job's bitter complaints against the wind-like elusiveness of the deity: "Lo, he goeth by me, and I see him not: he passeth on also, but I perceive him not. / Behold, he taketh away, who can hinder him? who will say unto him, What doest thou?" (Job 9:11–12).

Interrupting his meditation on the wind, Ahab resumes his command of the ship, taking up his position again in the raised hempen basket from which he keeps watch for the whale. When eventually lowered by the first mate, Ahab says his final farewell to the grieving Starbuck, who (as in "The

Symphony") again pleads with him, in a scene of similarly marked pathos, not to pursue the hunt for Moby Dick. Again Ahab is impervious. The scene of parting is in fact shadowed by the threat of Ahab's death. The captain emphasizes his readiness for this possibility, in the tragic accents of Brutus's farewell to Cassius before the battle of Philippi (*Julius Caesar*, V.i.92–125), Hamlet's final assertions to Horatio on his readiness for events (*Hamlet*, V.ii.19–24), or Macbeth's remarks to Seward before his final battle that he has lived long enough (*Macbeth*, V.ii.19–29). Ahab now tells his first mate: "Some men die at ebb tide; some at low water; some at the full of flood;— and I feel now like a billow that's all one crested comb, Starbuck. I am old;—shake hands with me, man" (566). Ahab then enters his whaleboat with his Asiatic crew (with Ishmael to replace Fedallah) as a group of sharks suddenly appears from the depths and "maliciously snapped at the blades of the oars, every time they dipped in the water" (566), portending the violent disaster to come. In an ironic contrast of dramatic roles, Starbuck on the decks of the *Pequod* is overwhelmed with forebodings of catastrophe despite his stubborn faith in God: "Is my journey's end coming? My legs feel faint; like his who has footed it all day" (567). The blasphemous Ahab, however, quickly resumes his former role as enraged unholy warrior against the whale.

Ahab's fight against Moby Dick on this last day is characterized by a final show of hubris in the mad captain as he reiterates, like an overconfident Macbeth, the Parsee's final two predictions: "Drive, drive in your nails, oh ye waves! to their uttermost heads drive them in! ye but strike a thing without a lid; and no coffin and no hearse can be mine:—and hemp only can kill me! Ha! ha!" (567). Yet Moby Dick's ensuing appearance demonstrates an overwhelming show of force as the huge whale shoots diagonally from the water: "Shrouded in a thin drooping veil of mist, it hovered for a moment in the rainbowed air; and then fell swamping back into the deep. Crushed thirty feet upwards, the waters flashed for an instant like heaps of fountains, then brokenly sank in a shower of flakes, leaving the circling surface creamed like new milk round the marble trunk of the whale" (567). Like the Old Testament god who created the Flood when "the fountains of the great deep [were] broken up, and the windows of heaven were opened," and who later identified the rainbow as its "token of a covenant" (Gen. 7:11, 9:12), the White Whale here makes a show of divine majesty and power, its creamy wake again suggesting God's image of Leviathan that "maketh the deep to boil like a pot" (Job 41:31).

The White Whale's role in undermining Ahab's overweening pride in this last encounter is suitable to God's final words to Job about Leviathan: "he is a king over all the children of pride" (Job 41:34). For the most outstanding feature of the whale on this last day is its malicious behavior, either because of its exasperation at being hunted the previous two days or (as Ahab would believe) the natural malignity instilled in its very being. When the whale breaches on this third day, it appears to be demonically set on revenge against its attackers: "maddened by yesterday's fresh irons that corroded in him, Moby Dick seemed combinedly possessed by all the angels that fell from heaven. The wide tiers of welded tendons overspreading his broad white forehead, beneath the transparent skin, looked knitted together; as head on, he came churning his tail among the boats" (567). The allusion here to the Judeo-Christian combat myth of a war in heaven reinforces Moby Dick's archetypal identity as a latter-day version of the chaos monster that underlies the image of the dragon-serpent-devil of the book of Revelation and of the Leviathan of Job.

The description of Moby Dick's "knitted" forehead accordingly anticipates his climactic ramming of the *Pequod* while evoking still another aspect of the invincible Leviathan: "The flakes of his flesh are joined together: they are firm in themselves; they cannot be moved. / His heart is as firm as a stone; yea, as hard as a piece of the nether millstone" (Job 41:23–24). In a final, grotesque, yet tragic recognition for the captain, Ahab discovers the body of the dead Parsee fastened to the whale: "Lashed round and round to the fish's back; pinioned in the turns upon turns in which, during the past night, the whale had reeled the involutions of the lines around him, the half torn body of the Parsee was seen; his sable raiment frayed to shreds; his distended eyes turned full upon old Ahab" (568). The body of the Parsee completes his symbolic role as prosecutorial satan of Job, lying prophet to King Ahab, and demonic John the Baptist to Ahab's Antichrist. As in the opening of the fourth seal in Revelation, the body of Fedallah now appears as a type of Death on a pale horse (Rev. 6:8). But although he recognizes with dismay that two of the Parsee's prophecies are now fulfilled, Ahab still insists on the evidence of a "second hearse" before he will fully believe the predictions of his own mortality are true.

Ahab's subsequent attempt to harpoon the whale results only in a snapped line and an ominous movement of the enraged whale toward the advancing *Pequod*: "catching sight of the nearing black hull of the ship; seemingly seeing in it the source of all his persecutions; bethinking it—it may be—a larger and nobler foe; of a sudden, he bore down upon its advancing prow, smiting his jaws amid fiery showers of foam" (570). The final oxymoronic image of "fiery showers" implicitly subsumes the dragon-like breath of Job's Leviathan: "Out of his mouth go burning lamps, and sparks of fire leap out. / . . . / His breath kindleth coals, and a flame goeth out of his mouth"

(Job 41:19, 21). The White Whale then rams the *Pequod*, an act conveying a combination of vengeance and malice in its "predestinating head": "Retribution, swift vengeance, eternal malice were in his whole aspect, and spite of all that mortal man could do, the solid white buttress of his forehead smote the ship's starboard bow, till men and timbers reeled" (571). Despite the whale's act of destruction, Ahab refuses to admit defeat and is ultimately pulled to his death by a final harpoon line he hurls, after vowing holy war against the creature to whom he has imputed an eternal malice. This is again the antithesis to Job's final submission to God after the intimidating display of power in the evocation of Leviathan. Ahab's last words before he darts his harpoon—"*Thus*, I give up the spear" (572)—instead find their echo in God's words to Job concerning the invincible Leviathan: "he laugheth at the shaking of a spear" (41:29).[24]

In addition to its Joban matrix of references, the scene of Ahab's death has a variety of other biblical associations. As a final demonstration that vengeance belongs to the Lord, not to human beings (Lev.19:18; Prov. 20:22; Rom. 12:19–20), he dies when the whale line running out from the tub gets fouled and he stoops to free it: "the flying turn caught him round the neck, and voicelessly as Turkish mutes bowstring their victims, he was shot out of the boat, ere the crew knew he was gone" (572). The violent manner of his death confirms the assertion in Ecclesiastes that "the sons of men [are] snared in an evil time, when it falleth suddenly upon them" (Eccles. 9:12). It also recalls Job's complaint to God that he would prefer strangling and death to continued suffering (Job 7:15). Significantly, Ahab's manner of death evokes the earlier description of how he lost his leg to the White Whale in the first place, when Ishmael claims that no Turkish, Venetian, or Malay assassin "could have smote him with more seeming malice" (184). His death may seem to provide final proof of malicious cruelty in his eschatological adversary, but the captain's violent end is implicitly the result of his misguided attempt, like Milton's Satan and other biblical overreachers, to usurp divine prerogatives of power and authority. Ahab's fate accordingly resembles that of other prominent figures denounced in Old Testament prophecy, beginning with his biblical model in the First Book of Kings.

The captain's final encounter with Moby Dick parallels several key aspects of the biblical King Ahab's divinely ordained defeat and death in battle against the Syrians. Ahab was bowstrung in the manner of Turkish mutes and shot out of his boat, which recalls the death of the biblical king who was killed when "a certain man [a Syrian soldier] drew a bow at a venture, and smote the king of Israel between the joints of the harness" (1 Kings 22:34). After the king dies, "the dogs licked up his blood" in his chariot, as earlier predicted by the prophet Elijah (1 Kings 21:19: 22:38). The doglike sharks that accompany Ahab's chariot-like whaleboat on the third and final day of the chase, which "maliciously snapped at the blades of the oars" (566), is an analogous image.

The account of King Ahab's death is given no overt apocalyptic emphasis in the Old Testment, but it represents a divine judgment on his crimes of impiety and the Syrians who defeat him act as agents of divine retribution. In the same way, the death of Melville's captain recalls the Judeo-Christian traditions of the fall of Lucifer/Satan from heaven, which provided Milton with a key model for his epic hero. The prophet Isaiah announced the fall into Sheol of the King of Babylon, who was given the ironic name of Lucifer or "light bringer": "I will ascend above the heights of the clouds; I will be like the most High. / Yet thou shalt be brought down to hell, to the sides of the pit" (Isa. 14:14–15). So, too, the prophet Ezekiel denounced the hubris of the Prince of Tyre, who was ironically described as possessing a superior wisdom that has allowed him to become an aspirant to divine honors: "Because thine heart is lifted up, and thou hast said, I am a God, in the midst of the seas; yet thou art a man, and not God, though thou set thine heart as the heart of God: / . . . / Wilt thou yet say before him that slayeth thee, I am God? but thou shalt be a man, and no God, in the hand of him that slayeth thee" (Ezek. 28:2, 9). Like the kings of Babylon and Tyre, Melville's Ahab, through pride and false wisdom, has exalted himself into the realm of the divine. His ultimate fate will be that of the "pit," condemned to destruction through moral blindness and overweening pride.

In addition to such well-known Old Testament prophetic warnings, the finale to Ahab's climactic encounter with the White Whale also has a New Testament dimension, for the scene of his death bears an oblique resemblance to Christ's Passion on the cross. The captain's heart-stricken reaction to the sight of the sinking *Pequod*—"death-glorious ship! must ye then perish, and without me? . . . Oh, lonely death on lonely life!" (571)—is comparable to Christ's final cry of despair on the cross: "My God, my God, why hast thou forsaken me?" (Matt. 27:46). So, too, Ahab's paradoxical claim—"Oh, now I feel my topmost greatness lies in my topmost grief" (571)—encapsulates the latent significance of Christ's martyrdom. The paradox of Christ's spiritual exaltation through the ignominy of crucifixion is a commonplace of Saint Paul's writings, especially his well-known explication of Christ's exaltation through self-humbling or *kenosis* ("emptying out") in the Epistle to the

Philippians. On the other hand, Ahab's last words—"*Thus*, I give up the spear!" (572)—make an aggressive, potentially punning counterstatement ("give up" here means "hurl" rather than "renounce") to Christ's peacefully yielding up his spirit while dying on the cross (Matt. 27:50).[25]

The allusively dense description of Ahab's combat with the White Whale in the last three chapters of *Moby-Dick* has important links to the book of Revelation, especially the war in heaven depicted in chapter 12, and the epic tradition in English poetry influenced by this mythic combat, notably in book 1 of *The Faerie Queene* and book 6 of *Paradise Lost*.[26] As the dramatization of an armed epic hero confronting a legendary dragon with seemingly supernatural power, Ahab's three-day fight with Moby Dick is comparable to the three-day battle of Redcrosse Knight with the dragon in book 1, canto 11, of Spenser's *Fairie Queene*. The winged dragon that Redcrosse Knight fights is, like the White Whale of Melville's novel, a huge and intimidating opponent, unlike the more lizard-like dragons of many medieval depictions of Saint George, the prototype of Spenser's knight:

> By this the dreadfull beast drew nigh to hand,
>   Halfe flying, and halfe footing in his hast,
>   That with his largenesse measured much land,
>   And made wide shadow under his huge wast;
>   As mountaine doth the valley overcast.
>   Approaching nigh, he reared high afore
>   His body monstrous, horrible, and vaste,
>   Which to increase his wondrous greatnesse more,
> Was swolne with wrath & poyson, & with bloudy gore.
>   (*Faerie Queene* I.xi.8)

Despite this intimidating opponent, the knight of pure Protestant faith nevertheless succeeds in vanquishing the monster on the third day of combat through a very un-Ahab-like access to Christian grace after receiving a near lethal wound from the dragon. In his final defeat in combat with the White Whale, Captain Ahab is more akin to Milton's Satan in the rebel angel's unsuccessful three-day combat against the heavenly host led by Christ the Messiah in book 6 of *Paradise Lost*, which ends with Satan and his associates' final descent into the hellish abyss. Leslie E. Sheldon notes that the final attack of the White Whale partly evokes Milton's portrait of the Messiah in final combat with the archfiend and rebel.[27] So, for example, following his speech to the heavenly host just before the final engagement, the Messiah changes countenance: "So spake the Son, and into terror chang'd / His count'nance too severe to be beheld / And full of wrath bent on his Enemies" (*Paradise Lost*, VI.824–26). Moby Dick's final assault on the *Pequod* is described in similar terms of quasi-divine wrath, except for its final hint of satanic evil: "Retribution, swift vengeance, eternal malice were in his whole aspect" (571).

In terms that evoke the disastrous end of the chase in *Moby-Dick*, the angel Raphael describes the final rout of Satan and his rebel angels, and their free fall into the "wasteful Deep" as they succumb to the overwhelming force of the Son:

> headlong themselves they threw
> Down from the verge of Heav'n, Eternal wrath
> Burn'd after them to the bottomless pit.
>   Hell heard th' unsufferable noise, Hell saw
> Heav'n ruining from Heav'n, and would have fled
> Affrighted; but strict Fate had cast too deep
> Her dark foundations, and too fast had bound.
> Nine days they fell; confounded *Chaos* roar'd,
> And felt tenfold confusions in thir fall
> Through his wild Anarchy, so huge a rout
> Incumber'd him with ruin: Hell at last
> Yawning receive'd them whole, and on them clos'd,
> Hell thir fit habitation fraught with fire
> Unquenchable, the house of woe and pain.
>   (*Paradise Lost*, VI.864–77)

Spenser, Milton, and Melville's ultimate prototype for these epic combats was, of course, the battle of the angel Michael with the heavenly dragon-serpent-devil in chapter 12 of Revelation, a combat myth transferred from a primordial to an eschatological event. Defeated in heaven, the dragon-serpent-devil and his followers will only have a short time on earth before the divine warrior Christ routs them permanently. The war in heaven found in Revelation 12:7–9, which Milton incorporated as a central event in *Paradise Lost*, is replayed at the end of the last chapter of *Moby-Dick*, when the sinking *Pequod* evokes the apocalyptic fall of the rebel angels from heaven. In Ahab's last speech to the White Whale, he identifies himself as an enraged, chariot-driven rebel against his insuperable adversary: "Towards thee I roll, thou all-destroying but unconquerable whale; to the last I grapple with thee; from hell's heart I stab at thee; for hate's sake I spit my last breath at thee" (571–72). Following Ahab's precipitous death, the crew of his whaleboat see the sinking *Pequod*'s "fading phantom" with only its masts still above water, "while fixed by infatuation, or fidelity, or fate, to their once lofty perches, the pagan harpooners still maintained their sinking lookouts on the sea" (572).

The sinking of the *Pequod* is characterized by a final apocalyptic image, as Tashtego in the act of nailing the ship's flag to a sinking spar catches the wing of a sky-hawk under his hammer; "and so the bird of heaven, with archangelic shrieks, and his imperial beak thrust upwards, and his whole captive form folded in the flag of Ahab, went down with his ship, which, like Satan, would not sink to hell till she had dragged a living part of heaven along with her, and helmeted herself with it" (572). According to traditions of Intertestamental Judaism followed by Milton, Satan brought a third of the heavenly host along with him in his rebellion against the deity.[28] The sinking *Pequod* topped by its rebellious captain's flag is also a displaced representation of the satanic forces overthrown by the angel Michael in Revelation: "And the great dragon was cast out, that old serpent, called the Devil, and Satan, which deceiveth the whole world: he was cast out into the earth and his angels were cast out with him" (Rev. 12:9). In the climactic combat of Melville's novel, then, the White Whale subsumes the forms of Leviathan as chaos monster in Job, Christ as messianic nemesis in Milton's epic, and Michael the avenging angel in Revelation, while Ahab, who aspires to the role of holy warrior against cosmic evil, ends his career as a vanquished satanic rebel against divine order.[29]

If the voyage of the *Pequod* began on Christmas Day in accordance with Ahab's quasi-messianic identity, Ishmael's mock resurrection after the three-day chase may be associated symbolically with Easter.[30] And just as Ahab's final encounter with Moby Dick is steeped in biblical allusions pertaining to the themes of theodicy and eschatology, the ensuing epilogue, which depicts Ishmael's survival of the wreck, evokes the Old Testament types of Job, Noah, Jonah, and Ishmael, as well as apocalyptic passages from Isaiah, 1 Corinthians, and Revelation. Following Ahab's death it is now Ishmael who inherits the mantle of Joban suffering; and his solitary condition, as described in the somber epilogue, is appropriately prefaced with a quotation that occurs four times at the beginning of the book of Job, in which a series of messengers report a string of catastrophes involving the loss of his possessions and his children: "And I only am escaped alone to tell thee" (Job 1:15–17, 19). While the lines from Job suggest Ishmael's physical situation as sole survivor of the destruction of the *Pequod*, Ishmael's moral and spiritual condition is akin to that of the chastened Job at the end of his ordeal. For just as Job learned the mysterious interrelation of good and evil in both the creator and the creation, Ishmael now experiences the mysterious intertwining of life and death as he undergoes a symbolic death and rebirth when the *Pequod's* coffin–life buoy rises to the surface after the wreck and provides him with a life-saving flotation device.

In like manner, the whirlpool of the wreck may also be viewed as a naturalistic duplicate of the theophanic Voice from the Whirlwind, in which God sets forth the insuperable might of his primeval adversary and surrogate, Leviathan. Like Job, Ishmael has been punished with the loss of all possessions but then inexplicably rewarded with the means of survival. And like Job, Ishmael has apparently learned to accept the existence of evil as part of the mystery of creation. Yet unlike Job, Ishmael has no personal god to thank for his preservation and can only view his survival as an accident, or the action of "the Fates."[31]

The only other character with whom Ishmael is explicitly identified in the epilogue is the Lapith King Ixion, who was bound by Zeus to a fiery wheel in the sky for his attempt to rape Hera: "Round and round, then, ever contracting towards the button-like black bubble at the axis of the slowly wheeling circle, like another Ixion I did revolve. Till, gaining that vital centre, the black bubble upward burst; and now, liberated by reason of its cunning spring, and, owing to its great buoyancy, rising with great force, the coffin life-buoy shot lengthwise from the sea, fell over, and floated by my side" (573). While it conforms to the repeated interplay of biblical and classical motifs in the novel, the allusion here to Ixion probably implies Ishmael's residual guilt for participating in Ahab's Promethean crime of assault on the deity.[32]

Ishmael's symbolic punishment is soon terminated by his ostensibly providential resurrection, which blends the imagery of the sinking ship with the mysterious symbiosis of life and death. The sonorously evocative "button-like black bubble" at the axis or "vital center" of the turning wheel, the vortex of the sinking *Pequod*, is the same navel-like source for the coffin–life buoy that ultimately saves Ishmael. The "cunning spring" of the life buoy is the "snap-spring" that the carpenter used to attach the coffin–life buoy to the ship (described at the end of chapter 126), but the phrase also hints at the resurrection symbolism of the epilogue.[33] The conclusion of *Moby-Dick* thus implies the intertwining of life and death (seen earlier in "A Bower in the Arsacides"), as the novel comes full circle from its first paragraph in which Ishmael joked about "pausing before coffin warehouses, and bringing up the rear of every funeral" (3) he met. By the same token, Ishmael's survival by means of the coffin–life buoy fulfills Queequeg's early claim (in chapter 10) that he would gladly die for his friend as a result of their sworn friendship—this perhaps being related to the unexplained "little duty ashore, which he was leaving undone" (480), for which Queequeg chooses not to die in chapter 110, thereby allowing for the conversion of his coffin into the *Pequod's* life buoy.[34]

In his survival of Ahab's fight with his eschatological adversary, Ishmael is the sole representative of the traditional "remnant" to be saved from Old Testament apocalyptic destruction as well as a type of Noah and Jonah.[35] In addition to the divinely sanctioned chaos monster that has killed Ahab and sunk the *Pequod*, the agent of end-time destruction here is water: "the great shroud of the sea rolled on as it rolled five thousand years ago" (572), referring to the era of the Flood (Gen. 7–8) according to older traditions of biblical chronology that were still given credence despite advances in contemporary geology.[36]

Within this model, Ishmael's survival on his coffin–life buoy also evokes the survival of Noah in his "ark," which in the original Hebrew simply meant "chest." As a Jonah figure, Ishmael escapes death from a possibly divinely sanctioned "great fish," although he has experienced no conversion except that of becoming a literary prophet. As though the beneficiary of a special providence, Ishmael on his sanctified coffin–life buoy is thus mysteriously protected, and his remark that no creatures harmed him during his abandonment at sea—"The unharming sharks, they glided by as if with padlocks on their mouths; the savage sea-hawks sailed with sheathed beaks" (573)—accords with the fate of his biblical namesake who, though exiled from Abraham's patrimony because of his illegitimacy, was still to be protected by God (Gen. 21:14–21) and was ultimately to receive God's blessing as the future father of a "great nation" (Gen. 17:20, 21:18).[37] The characterization of harmless sharks and hawks here also suggests the well-known image of millennial transformation evoked in the prophet Isaiah:

> The wolf also shall dwell with the lamb, and the leopard shall lie down with the kid; and the calf and the young lion and the fatling together; and a little child shall lead them. . . .
> And the sucking child shall play on the hole of the asp, and the weaned child shall put his hand on the cockatrice' den.
> They shall not hurt nor destroy in all my holy mountain: for the earth shall be full of the knowledge of the Lord, as the waters cover the sea. (Isa. 11:6, 8–9)

Despite his apparently miraculous protection, however, there is no other overt sign that Ishmael has a special blessing from the deity; and indeed, the final association with millennial transformation is personal, not universal, and lasts only one day, not a thousand years. There is no redemptive, universal millennium following the enacted apocalypse at the end of the novel. Evil and suffering have not been eliminated as in the famous vision of the new heaven and earth in Revelation: "And God shall wipe away all tears from their eyes; and there shall be no more death, neither sorrow, nor crying, neither shall there be any more pain: for the former things are passed away" (Rev. 21:4). The words from Revelation echo those found in the apocalyptic section of Isaiah describing a comparable victory of the Lord: "He will swallow up death in victory, and the Lord God will wipe away tears from off all faces" (Isa. 25:8). Unlike the end of pain, sorrow, and death promised in Isaiah and Revelation, at the end of *Moby-Dick* we encounter only the whaleship *Rachel*, an emblem of inconsolable grief, looking for its lost children.

In its ironic rewriting of Christian typology and eschatology, the epilogue of *Moby-Dick* similarly undermines another key passage from Revelation describing the universal resurrection that takes place at the Last Judgment: "And the sea gave up the dead which were in it; and death and hell delivered up the dead which were in them: and they were judged every man according to their works" (Rev. 20:13). Contrary to this mythic scenario, at the end of *Moby-Dick*, the sea—a traditional symbol of chaos—does *not* give up its dead; neither is there any spiritual resurrection to new life or scene of heavenly judgment. In Judeo-Christian apocalyptic, resurrection was the reward given to martyrs of the faith for their premature mortality, but in no sense does Ishmael suit this role at the end of Melville's novel. We have already suggested the idea that the coffin–life buoy with its design scheme corresponding exactly to Queequeg's body is a probable parody of the "spiritual body" that Saint Paul envisages as a corporeal envelope for the dead (1 Cor. 15:44). The image of the life buoy's rapid rise to the surface of the ocean would also seem to parody the general resurrection at the Last Judgment as well as Saint Paul's description of the transformation of natural to spiritual body in 1 Corinthians 15—except that there is no vanquishing of death here as there is in Saint Paul's teaching that "Death is swallowed up in victory" (1 Cor. 15:54).

In the end, Ishmael's rescue on the second day by "the devious-cruising Rachel, that in her retracing search after her missing children, only found another orphan" (573) suggests a death motif carried over from the *Pequod*'s earlier encounter with the *Rachel*, for ultimately God enigmatically both takes life and preserves it—a dual role in keeping with the mixed moral identity of the Old Testament deity. The image of the Old Testament Rachel searching for her lost children is a type of the suffering of the Hebrew people amid historical disaster, notably their sixth-century exile, about which the prophet Jeremiah invoked the image of Rachel mourning for her "children." Ishmael's rescue by the *Rachel* cruising for the captain's lost child thus typifies the repetitive trauma of human bereavement, which Ishmael carries away from the wreck and which the conclusion to the novel implies is a part of the human condition. Although the name is based on a well-known Nantucket whaling family, it is nevertheless ironic that a Captain *Gardiner* rescues Ishmael, since, in the gospel of John, Mary Magdalene mistakes the figure of the risen Christ for a "gardener" (John 20:15). The Nantucket captain is accordingly a figure of physical—not spiritual—salvation.

Ishmael ends the novel as he began it, alone, dispossessed, and haunted by death. The last chapter and epilogue of *Moby-Dick* thus resemble the traumatic ending of *King Lear*, in which, as Frank Kermode notes, "tragedy assumes the figuration of apocalypse, of death and judgment, heaven and hell; but the world goes forward in the hands of exhausted survivors." With the tragic loss of the *Pequod*, Ishmael has gained an incomparable wisdom on the complex and contradictory ways of history, nature, God, and humanity. And if Ishmael's accidental rescue and return to civilization do not suggest the biblical Ishmael's status as the promised father of a great nation of descendents, he will instead become the father of a great nation of readers by magisterially reconfiguring the Bible to dramatize enduring questions of theodicy and eschatology for the modern world.[38]

Epilogue

AT THE START OF HIS DISCUSSION of "How Religion in the United States Avails Itself of Democratic Tendencies" in *Democracy in America*, Alexis de Tocqueville noted the importance of having "fixed ideas" to support one's religious beliefs and also the challenges that the power of private judgment, as fostered by democracy, could present to a properly ordered view of the universe:

> There is hardly any human action, however particular it may be, that does not originate in some very general idea men have conceived of the Deity, of his relation to mankind, of the nature of their own souls, and of their duties to their fellow creatures. Nor can anything prevent these ideas from being the common spring from which all the rest emanates.
>
> Men are therefore immeasurably interested in acquiring fixed ideas of God, of the soul, and of their general duties to their Creator and their fellow men; for doubt on these first principles would abandon all their actions to chance and would condemn them in some way to disorder and impotence.
>
> This, then, is the subject on which it is most important for each of us to have fixed ideas; and unhappily it is also the subject on which it is most difficult for each of us, left to himself, to settle his opinions by the sole force of his reason. None but minds singularly free from the ordinary cares of life, minds at once penetrating, subtle, and trained by thinking, can, even with much time and care, sound the depths of these truths that are so necessary.[1]

Tocqueville's formulation here provides a revealing backdrop to *Moby-Dick*, for both Ahab and Ishmael are men of penetrating and subtle intellect, but both are also characterized by antithetical first principles about God, the soul, and their duties to their fellow men. Ahab suffers from a condition of traumatic physical impotence and assumes the role of tragic hero by adopting a heretically fixed idea of the deity as the creator and perpetrator of evil. This leads to his tyrannical control of the crew and their destruction in his self-centered quest for vindication. Ishmael, on the other hand, remains in a constant (often comic) condition of intellectual flux and disorder and ultimately espouses a radically "unfixed" idea of the deity, which leads to his fluid evaluations of cosmos and creation and his redemptive acknowledgment of solidarity with his fellow man. Tocqueville's observation reminds us how central Christian beliefs were to the very fabric of life in nineteenth-century America and the potential radical permutations of those beliefs that were possible in the religious and intellectual ferment of the first half of the century.

The quest for moral and metaphysical first principles in *Moby-Dick* is, as we have seen, primarily focused on the issues of theodicy and eschatology. Melville dramatized these issues by drawing on key books of the Bible to highlight varying responses to the problem of evil and human suffering. In keeping with conventional morality, the "classical" view of suffering as divine punishment for sin, as found in the Hebrew prophets and Saint Paul, is illustrated in the fatal career of Melville's whaling captain, whose hatred of the whale and its creator along with his self-aggrandizing personality and tryannical actions results in the unleashing of a cetacean chaos monster as a divine nemesis, just as the biblical King Ahab was defeated by divine intervention. The poetic dialogues of the book of Job, on the other hand, provide Ahab with rhetorical ammunition for his eloquent assault on divine justice, which casts him as a champion of human dignity against cosmic malice. As a Romantic hero-villain, then, Ahab is given an inextricably mixed moral identity based on the biblical roles he plays.

In Ishmael's case, the conclusion to the book of Job ultimately reinforces the ultimate mystery of human suffering following Ahab's defeat and death. Ishmael similarly learns that natural and moral evil are grounded in the ineluctable metaphysical laws of the universe as depicted in the book of Ecclesiastes. As in the apocalyptic books of the Bible, moreover, the universe of *Moby-Dick* is one of human suffering and oppression climaxed by all-out battle and final judgment, which leads both to Ahab's death and symbolic damnation and to Ishmael's mysterious survival and his philosophical, if not theological, redemption. Consistent with Christian tradition and Old Testament wisdom literature, Ishmael learns that opportunistic evil and educative suffering are necessary parts of an enigmatic and ambiguous moral universe. Finally, as an essential element of his homiletic style, Ishmael frequently adapts many of the well-known doctrines of Saint Paul, both parodying the apostle's orthodox metaphysics and endorsing his humanistic ethics in a series of lay sermons to the reader.

Such a mixed representation of the "problem of evil" in *Moby-Dick* potentially accords with the most extended discussion of *Moby-Dick* as a text shaped by the traditions of Judeo-Christian theodicy, Richard Forrer's *Theodicies in Conflict: A Dilemma in Puritan Ethics and Nineteenth-Century Literature.* In this work Forrer has argued that Melville's novel constitutes an unorthodox pluralistic theodicy that critiques both the Calvinistic vision of Puritan America and the more benign vision of liberal nineteenth-century theology—a conclusion that complements the examination of biblical theodicy that has shaped the argument of the present study.[2]

Steeped in the Bible while he was writing *Moby-Dick*, Melville was, throughout his fiction, long concerned with the injustices of the human condition and the problematic nature of modern Christianity. Yet he was hardly alone in these concerns; indeed, in his preoccupation with evil we may class him in company with some of the leading philosophical and creative minds of his time. In her study of *Evil in Modern Philosophy*, Susan Nieman has traced, in a number of eighteenth- and nineteenth-century philosophers and writers, two general attitudes toward evil: the "rationalist" and the "empiricist." The rationalist attitude (in Leibniz, Rousseau, Kant, Hegel, and Marx) attempts to explain the existence of moral and natural evil by referring to various secondary causes and theoretical justifications that ultimately make evil intelligible according to rationalistic norms. So, for example, Leibniz viewed evil as a necessary foil to the good, Rousseau saw it as originating in the corruptions of society, Kant posited evil as a sufficient reason for the moral imperative to do good, and Hegel and Marx envisaged the realm of history as a setting for overcoming human suffering. The empiricist attitude toward evil, on the other hand (in Bayle, Voltaire, Hume, Sade, and Schopenhauer), seeks no mitigation of the harsh reality of evil but acknowledges the unintelligibility of its existence. So Bayle envisaged the incompatibility of faith and reason, Voltaire encouraged the modest goal of "cultivating one's garden" in defiance of this worst of all possible worlds, Hume questioned the very laws of causality, Sade advocated violent and obsessive revolt against the divine creator, and finally, Schopenhauer promoted withdrawal from a universe dominated by evil and suffering.

At the start of her discussion of the empiricist group of thinkers, Nieman notes that the rationalism of the first group could potentially lead, as it did in the twentieth century, to a catastrophic displacement of God as the presumed author of evil. But the overreaching hazards of such an ambition were also apparent to some in the empiricist group of thinkers:

The wish to displace God that is contained in every attempt to re-create the world is the very essence of the sin of pride. It's pride that can lead to rebellion caused by the contemplation of all the evil in Creation. If God failed to get it right, why don't we do without Him and take over the job ourselves? The urge to humility is a product of acquiescence, if not terror: we agree not to understand why there is evil. . . . But even those who view humility as an old-fashioned, slavish virtue have a simpler problem with the wish to be God. We are so conspicuously lacking in His major virtues, benevolence and omnipotence, that even imitation is probably out of reach.[3]

Such a dichotomy is in fact well suited as a description of the characters of Ahab and Ishmael in *Moby-Dick*. Ishmael acquiesces to his own ignorance about the ultimate sources of evil and so exemplifies the virtues of limiting his metaphysical revolt. Ahab's attempt to re-create the moral and metaphysical world by slaying the White Whale, on the other hand, magnifies the intellectual sin of pride and compromises his ability to rectify the divine injustices of creation, leading to the morally corrosive doctrine that the ends justify the means. Yet if Ahab is patently guilty of the sin of pride, the trajectory of his moral career is not so simple for he can be viewed as both tragically limited by his human fallibility and heroically reacting to a greater theistic culpability in the universe. By relying on the biblical models of both King Ahab and Job—the first guilty of sinfulness according to the canons of the Deuteronomistic historian, and the second largely innocent of the suffering inflicted on him according to the wisdom writer of Job— Melville implied that his whaling captain was both legitimately punished for his sins and also *not* fully deserving of the evil inflicted on him by God. *Moby-Dick* thus dramatizes what might be called both the rationality and the irrationality of evil.

In 1791 Immanuel Kant published "On the Miscarriage of All Philosophical Trials in Theodicy," in which he refuted all previous attempts to reconcile the wisdom of the creator with the existence of what he characterized as the "counterpurposive," namely, the experience of sin, pain, and injustice. Kant systematically considered each of these evils to be balanced by divine holiness, goodness, and justice, but he found an insuperable flaw in the logical application of each compensatory virtue— confirmation for his general skepticism about the validity of religion within the limits of reason. Couching his argument in the language of a legal proceeding, Kant concluded that by their very nature all such rational attempts at theodicy were unable to vindicate the "moral wisdom of the world-government against the doubts raised against it on the basis of what the experience of this world teaches." Kant's main textual confirmation for such a conclusion was the book of Job. Commenting on the contrast between the candor of Job's complaints against divine injustice and the formulaic moralism of his three friends, Kant noted God's ultimate commendation of Job and his criticism of Job's friends: "Hence only sincerity of heart and not distinction of insight; honesty in openly admitting one's doubts; repugnance to pretending conviction where one feels none, especially before God (where this trick is pointless enough)—these are the attributes which, in the person of Job, have decided the preeminence of the honest man over the religious flatterer in the divine verdict." Unlike the failure of the "science" of theodicy, Job represents an "authentic" theodicy grounded not in the authority of religious tradition but, instead, in honest doubt.[4]

We can assume that the appeal of the book of Job to Melville was its evident "sincerity" in openly acknowledging doubts about the wisdom of divine governance, unlike the many mid-nineteenth-century Christians who rested their faith on an unquestioned acceptance of religious doctrine and authority. Such fundamental sincerity was, in fact, ultimately what Melville sought with his readers. Writing from Boston to his friend Evert Duyckinck in March 1849, while he was reading Shakespeare in depth for the first time, Melville expressed a desire to meet the dramatist in contemporary New York since the playwright would then be able to drop the "muzzle" that men wore on their speech in Elizabethan times. For even Shakespeare "was not a frank man to the uttermost. And, indeed, who in this intolerant Universe is, or can be? But the Declaration of Independence makes a difference." As a nineteenth-century American, Melville believed he had a better opportunity to tell the truth to his audience because of the nation's founding principles of democracy and freedom of speech. Writing from London in December 1849, Melville later struck a more pessimistic note, however. In another letter to Duyckinck, he commented on the conflict between his financial needs and his creative ambitions, as seen in the recent commercial failure of *Mardi*: "What a madness & anguish it is, that an author can never—under no conceivable circumstances—be at all frank with his readers.—Could I, for one, be frank with them—how would they cease their railing."[5]

Almost two years later, Melville's ambitious whaling novel would in fact test the limits of the author's attempt to be "frank" with his readers about the problematic nature of divine governance in the world, beginning with his own friend Duyckinck. For if the story of Ahab's hunt for the White Whale was steeped in the language and symbolism of Job, the pious Episcopalian Duyckinck inadvertently assumed the moralistic tone of one of Job's three false "friends" at the end of his November 1851 review of the novel in the *Literary World*. Despite his astute analysis of the generically mixed nature of the narrative, Duyckinck was also conscious of the potential dangers of his writer friend's religious and philosophical skepticism: "This piratical running down of creeds and opinions, the conceited indifferentism of Emerson, or the run-a-muck style of Carlyle is, we will not say dangerous in such cases, for there are various forces at work to meet more powerful onslaught, but it is out of place and uncomfortable. We do not like to see what, under any view, must be to the world the most sacred associations of life violated and defaced." Duyckinck also had disapproving words for the character of Ishmael as "a self-dependent, self-torturing agency of a mind driven hither and thither as a flame in a whirlwind." He went on to note "the strong powers with which Mr. Melville wrestles in this book. It would be a great glory to subdue them to the highest uses of fiction." With such a pompous indictment of Melville's religious heterodoxy, which vitiated the reviewer's qualified endorsement of his greatest work of fiction, we can well understand why Melville would shortly go on to break off relations with this friend and to caricature Duyckinck in his satire on the New York literary scene in his next novel, *Pierre*.[6]

If Duyckinck's *Moby-Dick* review reminded Melville of the moralistic disapproval of one of Job's indignant friends, he did not have to contend with such criticisms from his more latitudinarian friend and fellow novelist Nathaniel Hawthorne, who would tell Duyckinck in a letter of 1 December 1851: "What a book Melville has written! It gives me an idea of much greater power than his preceding ones. It hardly seemed to me that the review of it, in the Literary World, did justice to its best points."[7] In a letter from November 1851 expressing gratitude for Hawthorne's generous praise of *Moby-Dick* (in a now lost letter), Melville had revealingly written: "A sense of unspeakable security is in me this moment, on account of your having understood the book. I have written a wicked book, and feel spotless as the lamb."[8] Melville's ecstatic sense that Hawthorne had understood his novel leads him here to express a paradoxical feeling of creative catharsis and awareness of the moral challenges posed by his book's irreligious themes. To orthodox readers such as Duyckinck, Melville's novel was indeed dangerously free-thinking on moral and religious grounds (the English edition of the novel had in fact been bowdlerized by his publisher Bentley); but to his more discerning readers such as Hawthorne, Melville felt himself innocent of any gratuitous immorality because of his adherence to the truth of his own experience, the divinely sanctioned virtue of Job.

Finally, it is grimly ironic that, just as Melville had performed a modern recasting of the book of Job in *Moby-Dick*, he would himself undergo an equivalent Joban ordeal following its publication—an ordeal that included mixed reviews and lackluster sales of the novel; the departure of his friend Hawthorne from the Berkshires in November 1851; the angry rupture in his friendship with Duyckinck, in early 1852, over the subversive content of his new novel, *Pierre*; the near termination of his career as a writer with the publication of the scandalous *Pierre* the following summer; and the first default, that fall, on the interest on a $2,050 loan dating from 1851 from a family friend, Tertullus D. Stewart. A year after the publication of *Moby-Dick*, the parallels between Melville's life and the sufferings of Job continued with the onset of an incapacitating depressive breakdown in the spring of 1853; the rejection by his publisher of his lost novel, *The Isle of the Cross*, that June; the concurrent failure of his attempt to obtain a foreign consulship despite the presumed influence of his friend Hawthorne with the new president, Franklin Pierce; and the disastrous fire at the Harper Brothers' New York warehouse in December 1853, which cost Melville a thousand dollars of much-needed lost royalties. The Joban parallels reached a head when arthritis and sciatica incapacitated him in 1855, and when his continued default on his loan from Tertullus D. Stewart threatened the loss of his Pittsfield farm when the loan matured in the spring of 1856. Yet Melville's Joban fate uncannily climaxed when the loss of his property was averted through the intervention of his wealthy father-in-law, Massachusetts Supreme Court judge Lemuel Shaw, who now acted in the role of the deus ex machina who restored Job's property and family.[9]

Just as his dramatization of the question of theodicy in *Moby-Dick* drew heavily on the book of Job, Melville's use of apocalyptic symbolism in the novel also largely relied on Daniel and Revelation. The latter has in fact served as a key source for a number of prominent literary works in English and American literature, some of which had a decisive impact on the author's whaling novel, as we have seen. For example, Ishmael's seriocomic journey to join the crew of the *Pequod* re-created aspects of Bunyan's well-known allegory of Christian's journey to the Celestial City (New Jerusalem), while Ahab's challenge to divine justice during the ensuing voyage followed the tragic model of *King Lear*, with its pervasive eschatological themes of end-time evil and final judgment. So, too, the captain's long-anticipated combat with the White Whale looked back to similar physical and metaphysical combats in books 1 and 2 of *The Faerie Queene* and book 6 of *Paradise Lost*.

All these well-known literary prototypes necessarily concluded with the vanquishing of satanic evil by a human or quasi-human agent of holiness and virtue, just as this occurs at the end of the book of Revelation. But *Moby-Dick* offers a more equivocal ending in the simultaneous defeat of its overreaching hero and the amoral triumph of a divinely empowered White Whale.

In its secularized apocalyptic ideology, Melville's novel also draws on various eighteenth- and nineteenth-century religious, literary, and cultural traditions. In *Natural Supernaturalism*, M. H. Abrams explains how Romantic writers displaced their political hopes for the French Revolution into a theory of the imagination where the mind of the poet unites with nature in an apocalyptic "holy marriage."[10] Such an ambitious program anticipates Ishmael's extended attempts to "know" the whale epistemologically (in the many chapters on cetology), and it is given a tour de force of sublime terror in Ishmael's meditation on "The Whiteness of the Whale." The novel's conclusion exemplifies a biblical model of apocalyptic combat and judgment without the sequel of millennial redemption—except (as we have seen) in the survival of the solitary Ishmael. Such a recasting of biblical apocalyptic can also be associated with the English Romantic poets, as Morton Paley has demonstrated, for a prominent strain of apocalyptic symbolism in the work of Wordsworth, Coleridge, Byron, Shelley, and Keats excluded the traditional pattern of millennial transformation after end-time judgment.[11]

In addition to the sublime terrors of apocalyptic destruction that he experiences, Ishmael as the sole survivor at the end of *Moby-Dick* evokes the early nineteenth-century literary tradition of the "last man," best-known from Mary Shelley's 1826 novel *The Last Man*, a tradition adapted by Poe in a number of his tales including *The Narrative of Arthur Gordon Pym*.[12] Related to this tradition was the popularity in both England and America of fiction and poetry depicting the pathos of human extinction among both individuals and marginalized human groups, starting with Milton's representation of Noah in *Paradise Lost* and reaching a terminus in the mid-nineteenth century with the evolutionary theories of Darwin. According to Fiona Stafford, this literary depiction of human and racial extinction grew out of the temporalization of the classical concept of the Great Chain of Being in the seventeenth and eighteenth centuries, creating the necessary conditions for a theory of progressive creation and destruction of species.[13]

Such secularized ideas of biological decline eventually challenged the moral underpinnings of biblical apocalyptic. The gradual yielding of biblical to scientific concepts of catastrophe in the nineteenth century was popularized in the theories of the "catastrophist" school of geology pioneered by the French zoologist and paleontologist Georges Cuvier (1769–1832) who postulated a series of multiple creations and extinctions in the fossil record that seemed to supersede the account of the creation in Genesis—a sign of the ongoing conflict of Genesis and geology in an era that saw the assumed age of the earth expand from a few thousands to untold millions of years. In his blending of biblical creationism with modern scientific theories of catastrophe and extinction in *Moby-Dick*, Melville reflects the transitional intellectual milieu of his mid-nineteenth-century world.[14]

Whatever its general European literary and cultural background, however, the apocalyptic eschatology of *Moby-Dick* was rooted firmly in the biblical foundations of American culture and the ingrained belief in America as a covenanted nation with the historical task of bringing about a millennial future. While such views contributed to both the original Puritan errand and the later revolutionary founding of the nation, they were also a key tenet of American national identity in the era of Manifest Destiny with its overweening confidence in the country's divinely sanctioned expansive missions of democracy and Christianity. It hardly needs repeating that Melville was a wary skeptic toward such an optimistic faith, as were his fellow novelists Cooper and Hawthorne. As a result, their fiction often reflects the latent ironies of the American attempt to restore Paradise by precipitating the millennium.[15]

On a more immediately topical level, Melville's use of apocalyptic symbolism in *Moby-Dick* was also conditioned by some of the allegorical tales and sketches in Hawthorne's *Mosses from an Old Manse*, a work reflecting the atmosphere of millennial social reform and Millerite Adventism of the early 1840s that Melville read in the summer of 1850 while he was composing his whaling novel. Sketches such as "Earth's Holocaust," "The New Adam and Eve," and "The Celestial Railroad" contributed to the moral background of Ahab's embattled attempt to extirpate evil from the cosmos and of his repeated failure to heed the prophetic warnings against his moral presumptions and messianic delusions.[16]

Following the publication of *Moby-Dick*, Melville went on to dramatize a detailed satirical enactment of the Second Coming in *The Confidence-Man*, which would formally end his career as a published novelist in 1857.[17] With the silencing of Melville as a writer of fiction and his shift to the more marginal role of poet, we must look to the writings of other, more prominent Europeans for his peers in the fictional representation of questions of theodicy and eschatology. In the work of Dostoevsky, above all, we find the same anguished witness to the spiritual crises of the nineteenth century and to the moral dramas of Job and the apocalyptic writings of the New Testament. Dostoevesky's *The Idiot* (1868), like Melville's *Pierre*, depicts the melodramatic career of a modern-day Christ whose fatal history is steeped in the details of the book of Revelation and its contemporary Russian interpreters. Dostoevsky's *The Brothers Karamazov* (1879–1880), like *Moby-Dick*, constitutes a grand fictional summa of Joban theodicy, especially in its well-known parable of the Grand Inquisitor. In his clear perception of the unspeakable evils of the world, the ostensibly mad Ivan Karamazov duplicates Ahab's outrage at cosmic injustice and repeats the whaling captain's death in the midst of a heroically sustained metaphysical revolt.[18]

Literary apocalyptic would experience a rapid growth in the twentieth century, with its unrivaled global horrors and catastrophes duplicating the violent cosmic warfare of the book of Revelation; but these developments are beyond the scope of this study. Suffice it to say that in his representations of biblical theodicy and eschatology, Melville has reformulated a rich philosophical and theological tradition with both ancient roots and continuing contemporary relevance. As T. Walter Herbert has aptly remarked, "*Moby-Dick* is a consummate work of religious imagination, standing at the threshold of the modern world and articulating our distinctive religious perplexities; yet the power and authority with which it fashions a modern tradition follows from the mastery with which it brings our ancient inheritance to life."[19] Reading *Moby-Dick* as a work of religious imagination thus allows us both to acknowledge the dominant place of the Bible and Judeo-Christian tradition in Melville's thought and to appreciate the novel's probing investigation into the "inscrutable malice" of the cosmos and creation.

Notes

Preface

1. Herman Melville, *Correspondence*, ed. Lynn Horth (Evanston and Chicago: Northwestern University Press and the Newberry Library, 1993), 219.

2. Ibid., 212.

3. Stephen Prickett, *Origins of Narrative: The Romantic Appropriation of the Bible* (New York: Cambridge University Press, 1996), 102, 221. On the cultural enshrinement of the King James Bible and its literary consequences, see David Norton, *A History of the English Bible as Literature* (New York: Cambridge University Press, 2000).

1—Joban Theodicy and Apocalyptic Eschatology

1. See William James, *The Varieties of Religious Experience*, in *Writings, 1902–1910* (New York: Library of America, 1987), Lectures 6–7 (quotations, pages 124, 152). On Henry James, Sr., and William James's depressive crises ("vastations"), see R. W. B. Lewis, *The Jameses: A Family Narrative* (New York: Farrar, Straus, and Giroux, 1991), 37–57, 183–206, 508–15.

2. James, *Writings 1902–1910*, 152, 153, 154.

3. See William Braswell, *Melville's Religious Thought* (Durham, NC: Duke University Press, 1943); Nathalia Wright, *Melville's Use of the Bible* (Durham, NC: Duke University Press, 1949); Lawrance Thompson, *Melville's Quarrel with God* (Princeton, NJ: Princeton University Press, 1952); H. Bruce Franklin, *The Wake of the Gods: Melville's Mythology* (Stanford: Stanford University Press, 1963); William H. Shurr, *The Mystery of Iniquity: Melville as Poet, 1857–1891* (Lexington: University Press of Kentucky, 1972); T. Walter Herbert, Moby-Dick *and Calvinism: A World Dismantled* (New Brunswick, NJ: Rutgers University Press, 1977).

4. On the novel's language, style, allegory, and narrative techniques see for example Sharon Cameron, *The Corporeal Self: Allegories of the Body in Melville and Hawthorne* (Baltimore: Johns Hopkins University Press, 1981), 15–75; Bainard Cowan, *Exiled Waters:* Moby-Dick *and the Crisis of Allegory* (Baton Rouge: Louisiana State University Press, 1982); Gayle L. Smith, "The Word and the Thing: *Moby-Dick* and the Limits of Language," *ESQ* 31 (1985): 260–71; Carolyn Porter, "Call Me Ishmael, or How to Make Double-Talk Speak," in *New Essays on* Moby-Dick, ed. Richard H.

Brodhead (New York: Cambridge University Press, 1986), 73–108; Paul Lukacs, "The Abandonment of Time and Place: History and Narrative, Metaphysics and Exposition in *Moby-Dick*," *CLIO* 20 (1991): 139–55; Bryan C. Short, *Cast by Means of Figures: Herman Melville's Rhetorical Development* (Amherst: University of Massachusetts Press, 1992), ch. 8. On European Romanticism and Western philosophical traditions, see Leon Chai, *The Romantic Foundations of the American Renaissance* (Ithaca: Cornell University Press, 1987), 74–88; John Wenke, *Melville's Muse: Literary Creation and the Forms of Philosophical Fiction* (Kent, OH: Kent State University Press, 1995), chs. 5–6; Bernhard Radloff, *Will and Representation: The Philosophical Foundations of Melville's Theatrum Mundi* (New York: Peter Lang, 1996); Christopher S. Durer, *Herman Melville: Romantic and Prophet: A Study of His Romantic Sensibility and His Relationship to European Romantics* (Fredericton, NB, Canada: York Press, 1996), ch. 3. On American democratic ideals and national ideologies, see Leo Bersani, *The Culture of Redemption* (Cambridge, MA: Harvard University Press, 1990), ch. 6; Russ Castronovo, *Fathering the Nation: American Genealogies of Slavery and Freedom* (Berkeley and Los Angeles: University of California Press, 1995), ch. 2; Timothy B. Powell, *Ruthless Democracy: A Multicultural Interpretation of the American Renaissance* (Princeton, NJ: Princeton University Press, 2000), ch. 6; Peter Coviello, *Intimacy in America: Dreams of Affiliation in Antebellum Literature* (Minneapolis: University of Minnesota Press, 2005), ch. 3; John Michael, *Identity and the Failure of America: From Thomas Jefferson to the War on Terror* (Minneapolis: University of Minnesota Press, 2008), ch. 2.

5. On humor, popular culture, and the literary marketplace in *Moby-Dick*, see for example Jane Mushabac, *Melville's Humor: A Critical Study* (Hamden, CT: Archon Books, 1981), 79–110; David S. Reynolds, *Beneath the American Renaissance: The Subversive Imagination in the Age of Emerson and Melville* (New York: Knopf, 1988), 151–59, 541–61; Stephen Railton, *Authorship and Audience: Literary Performance in the American Renaissance* (Princeton, NJ: Princeton University Press, 1991), ch. 8; Sheila Post-Lauria, *Correspondent Colorings: Melville in the Marketplace* (Amherst: University of Massachusetts Press, 1996), ch. 5; John Evelev, *Tolerable Entertainment: Herman Melville and Literary Professionalism in Antebellum New York* (Amherst: University of Massachusetts Press, 2006), chs. 3–4. On epic and dramatic principles and prototypes, see John P. McWilliams, Jr., *The American Epic: Transforming a Genre, 1770–1860* (New York: Cambridge University Press, 1989), ch. 7; Christopher Sten, *The Weaver God, He Weaves: Melville and the Poetics of the Novel* (Kent, OH: Kent State University Press, 1996), ch. 6; Alan L. Ackerman, *The Portable Theater: American Literature and the Nineteenth-Century Stage* (Baltimore: Johns Hopkins University Press, 1999), ch. 3. On the visual arts and aesthetics, see Richard S. Moore, *That Cunning Alphabet: Melville's Aesthetics of Nature* (Amsterdam: Rodopi, 1982); Robert K. Wallace, *Melville and Turner: Spheres of Love and Fright* (Athens: University of Georgia Press, 1992), chs. 7–10; Douglas Robillard, *Melville and the Visual Arts: Ionian Form, Venetian Tint* (Kent, OH: Kent State University Press, 1997), ch. 4.

6. On the body, gender, and sexuality, see for example Robert K. Martin, *Hero, Captain, Stranger: Male Friendship, Social Critique, and Literary Form in the Sea Novels of Herman Melville* (Chapel Hill: University of North Carolina Press, 1986), ch. 3; Peter J. Bellis, *No Mysteries out of Ourselves: Identity and Textual Form in the Novels of Herman Melville* (Philadelphia: University of Pennsylvania Press, 1990), 35–44, 61–69, 102–44; Leland S. Person, Jr., "Melville's Cassock: Putting on Masculinity in

Moby-Dick," *ESQ* 40 (1994): 1–26; Clark Davis, *After the Whale: Melville in the Wake of* Moby-Dick (Tuscaloosa: University of Alabama Press, 1995), ch. 1; Rita Bode, "'Suckled by the Sea': The Maternal in *Moby-Dick*," in Elizabeth A. Schultz and Haskell Springer, eds., *Melville and Women* (Kent, OH: Kent State University Press, 2006), 181–98. On mourning, trauma, and disaster, see Neal Tolchin, *Mourning, Gender, and Creativity in the Art of Herman Melville* (New Haven: Yale University Press, 1988), ch. 6; Janet Reno, *Ishmael Alone Survived* (Lewisburg, PA: Bucknell University Press, 1990); Joseph Adamson, *Melville, Shame, and the Evil Eye: A Psychoanalytic Reading* (Albany: State University of New York Press, 1997). On science, pseudoscience, and environmentalism, see Richard Dean Smith, *Melville and Science: "Devilish Tantalization of the Gods!"* (New York: Garland, 1993), ch. 4; Joseph Andriano, "Brother to Dragons: Race and Evolution in *Moby-Dick*," *ATQ* 10 n.s. (1996): 141–53; Eric Wilson, *Romantic Turbulence: Chaos, Ecology, and American Space* (New York: St. Martin's Press, 2000), ch. 3; Elizabeth Schultz, "Melville's Environmental Vision in *Moby-Dick*," *Interdisciplinary Studies in Literature and the Environment* 7 (Winter 2000): 97–113; John F. Birk, *Tracing the Round: The Astrological Framework of "Moby-Dick"* (Xlibris, 2004); Philip Armstrong, *What Animals Mean in the Fiction of Modernity* (New York: Routledge, 2008), ch. 3.

7. On Melville biography and biographical criticism of *Moby-Dick*, see for example Hershel Parker, *Herman Melville: A Biography*, vol. 1, *1819–1851* (Baltimore: Johns Hopkins University Press, 1996), chs. 33–40; Wilson Heflin, *Herman Melville's Whaling Years* (Nashville: Vanderbilt University Press, 2004); Robert Milder, *Exiled Royalties: Melville and the Life We Imagine* (New York: Oxford University Press, 2006), chs. 4–5. On the composition of *Moby-Dick*, see James Barbour, "'All My Books Are Botches': Melville's Struggle with *The Whale*," in James Barbour and Tom Quirk, eds., *Writing the American Classics* (Chapel Hill: University of North Carolina Press, 1990); Peter L. Shillingsberg, "The Three *Moby-Dicks*," *American Literary History* 2 (1990): 199–30; Robert Sattelmeyer, "'Shanties of Chapters and Essays': Rewriting *Moby-Dick*," *ESQ* 49 (2003): 213–47. On recognition and influence, see Kingsley Widmer, "Melville and the Myths of Modernism," in John Bryant, ed., *A Companion to Melville Studies*, (New York: Greenwood Press, 1986), ch. 22; Sanford E. Marovitz, "Herman Melville: A Writer for the World," in Bryant, *Companion*, ch. 24; Elizabeth A. Schultz, *Unpainted to the Last:* Moby-Dick *and Twentieth-Century Art* (Lawrence: University of Kansas Press, 1995); Clare L. Spark, *Hunting Captain Ahab: Psychological Warfare and the Melville Revival* (Kent, OH: Kent State University Press, 2001); David Dowling, *Chasing the White Whale: The* Moby-Dick *Marathon; or What Melville Means Today* (Iowa City: University of Iowa Press, 2010); George Cotkin, *Dive Deeper: Journeys with* Moby-Dick (New York: Oxford University Press, 2012).

8. See Ilana Pardes, *Melville's Bibles* (Berkeley and Los Angeles: University of California Press, 2008); Robert Alter, *Pen of Iron: American Prose and the King James Bible* (Princeton, NJ: Princeton University Press, 2010), ch. 2; Jamie Lorentzen, *Sober Cannibals, Drunken Christians: Melville, Kierkegaard, and Tragic Optimism in Polarized Worlds* (Macon, GA: Mercer University Press, 2010); Hubert Dreyfus and Sean Dorrance Kelly, *All Things Shining: Reading the Western Classics to Find Meaning in a Secular Age* (New York: Free Press, 2011), ch. 6. I have discussed the strengths and weaknesses of Pardes's book in a review in *Christianity and Literature* 59 (Autumn 2009): 143–47. Critics who have continued to examine the religious themes in *Moby-Dick* over

the past few decades include T. Walter Herbert, Jr., "Calvinist Earthquake: *Moby-Dick* and Religious Tradition," in Brodhead, *New Essays*, 109–44; John T. Matteson, "The Little Lower Layer: Anxiety and the Courage to Be in *Moby-Dick*," *Harvard Theological Review* 81 (1988): 97–116; Herbert N. Schneider and Homer B. Pettey, "Melville's Ithyphallic God," *Studies in American Fiction* 26 (1998): 193–212; Elisa New, "Bible Leaves! Bible Leaves! Hellenism and Hebraism in Melville's *Moby-Dick*," *Poetics Today* 19 (1998): 281–303; Catherine Keller, *Face of the Deep: A Theology of Becoming* (New York: Routledge, 2003), ch. 8; Zachary Hutchins, "*Moby-Dick* as Third Testament: A Novel 'Not Come to Destroy but to Fulfill' the Bible," *Leviathan* 13 (June 2011): 18–37. Recent critics who have continued to note the importance of religion in Melville's writing include Rowland A. Sherrill, "Melville and Religion," in Bryant, *Companion*, ch. 15; Gail H. Coffler, *Melville's Allusions to Religion: A Comprehensive Index and Glossary* (Westport, CT: Praeger, 2004); Emory Elliott, "'Wandering To-and-Fro': Melville and Religion," in *A Historical Guide to Herman Melville*, ed. Giles Gunn (New York: Oxford University Press, 2005), 167–204; Brian Yothers, "One's Own Faith: Melville's Reading of *The New Testament and Psalms*," *Leviathan* 10 (October 2008): 39–59.

9. See for example Carolyn Karcher, *Shadow over the Promised Land: Slavery, Race, and Violence in Melville's America* (Baton Rouge: Louisiana State University Press, 1980), ch. 3; Michael Paul Rogin, *Subversive Genealogy: The Politics and Art of Herman Melville* (New York: Knopf, 1983), ch. 4; James Duban, *Melville's Major Fiction: Politics, Theology, and Imagination* (DeKalb: Northern Illinois University Press, 1983), 82–148; Andrew Delbanco, *Melville: His World and Work* (New York: Knopf, 2005), ch. 6; Nathaniel Philbrick, *Why Read Moby-Dick?* (New York: Viking, 2011). Delbanco's summary is representative of this school of criticism: "As the American political system went to pieces before his eyes, Melville saw in Calhoun one model for his haunted captain; but more than that, he turned the *Pequod* into a sort of Democratic Party death convention—a ship of political fools sailing headlong for disaster" (*Melville*, 164). The pioneering article on *Moby-Dick* and the slavery crisis, associating Ahab with Calhoun, is Allen Heimert, "*Moby-Dick* and American Political Symbolism," *American Quarterly* 15 (1963): 498–534.

10. Calling Ahab "for his time and place, the noblest and most complete embodiment of the tragic hero," Newton Arvin noted: "About Ahab's moral largeness there can be no uncertainty; the cleansing effect of *Moby-Dick* depends vitally upon that." Arvin, *Herman Melville* (New York: William Sloane, 1950), 176. On the importance of the heroic in Melville's creative vision, see Stanley Geist, *Herman Melville: The Tragic Vision and the Heroic Ideal* (Cambridge, MA: Harvard University Press, 1939).

11. On Melville and the Bible, see Braswell, *Melville's Religious Thought*; Wright, *Use of the Bible*; Mark Heidmann, "Melville and the Bible: Leading Themes in the Marginalia and the Major Fiction, 1850–1856" (PhD dissertation, Yale University, 1979), and "The Markings in Herman Melville's Bibles," in *Studies in the American Renaissance, 1990*, ed. Joel Myerson (Charlottesville: University Press of Virginia, 1990).

12. David Hume, *Writings on Religion*, ed. Anthony Flew (La Salle, IL: Open Court 1992), 261; Bart D. Ehrman, *God's Problem: How the Bible Fails to Answer Our Most Important Question—Why We Suffer* (New York: HarperOne, 2008).

13. On the history of theodicy as a theological and philosophical problem in the Judeo-Christian tradition, see John Hick, *Evil and the God of Love* (New York: Harper and Row, 1966); Jeffrey Burton Russell, *The Devil: Perceptions of Evil from*

Antiquity to Primitive Christianity (Ithaca: Cornell University Press, 1977); Joseph F. Kelly, *The Problem of Evil in the Western Tradition: From the Book of Job to Modern Genetics* (Collegeville, MN: Liturgical Press, 2002); Timothy K. Beal, *Religion and Its Monsters* (New York: Routledge, 2002); James L. Crenshaw, *Defending God: Biblical Responses to the Problem of Evil* (New York: Oxford University Press, 2005).

14. On Augustine's theories of evil, see Hick, *God of Love*, chs. 3–5 (on Calvin and evil, 123–32). On Milton and theodicy, see Dennis Danielson, *Milton's Good God: A Study in Literary Theodicy* (New York: Cambridge University Press, 1982).

15. See Elmar J. Kremer and Michael J. Latze, eds., *The Problem of Evil in Early Modern Philosophy* (Toronto: University of Toronto Press, 2001); Susan Neiman, *Evil in Modern Thought: An Alternative History of Philosophy* (Princeton, NJ: Princeton University Press, 2002).

16. Section F, "Paulicians," in Pierre Bayle, *The Dictionary Historical and Critical of Mr. Peter Bayle*, 5 vols. (1734–1738; rpt. New York: Garland, 1984), 4:518. On Bayle, see Howard Robinson, *Bayle the Sceptic* (New York: Columbia University Press, 1931); Karl C. Sandberg, *At the Crossroads of Faith and Reason: An Essay on Pierre Bayle* (Tucson: University of Arizona Press, 1966); D. Anthony Lariviere and Thomas M. Lennon, "Bayle on the Moral Problem of Evil," in Kremer and Latze, *Problem of Evil*, 101–18; Neiman, *Evil in Modern Thought*, 113–28.

17. "Explanatory Notes" in Herman Melville, *Moby-Dick; or, The Whale*, ed. Luther S. Mansfield and Howard P. Vincent (New York: Hendricks House, 1952), 699.

18. Ibid., 699–703; Thompson, *Melville's Quarrel*, ch. 7; C. Hugh Holman, "The Reconciliation of Ishmael: *Moby-Dick* and the Book of Job," *South Atlantic Quarterly* 57 (1958): 477–90; Thornton Y. Booth, "*Moby-Dick*: Standing Up to God," *Nineteenth-Century Fiction* 17 (1962): 33–43; Nathalia Wright, "*Moby-Dick*: Jonah's or Job's Whale?" *American Literature* 37 (1965): 190–95; Janis Stout, "Melville's Use of the Book of Job," *Nineteenth-Century Fiction* 25 (1970): 69–83; Heidmann, "Melville and the Bible," 58–83; William A. Young, "Leviathan in the Book of Job and *Moby-Dick*," *Soundings* 65 (1982): 388–401; L. Joseph Kreitzer, *The Old Testament in Fiction and Film* (Sheffield, England: Sheffield Academic Press, 1994), ch. 2; Pardes, *Melville's Bibles*, ch. 1. My argument in the present study confirms and extends Holman's pioneering claim that the influence of Job in *Moby-Dick* was "pervasive and controlling, basic and thematic, the most informing single principle of the book's composition" ("Reconciliation of Ishmael," 477).

19. See R. E. Watters, "Melville's Metaphysics of Evil," *University of Toronto Quarterly* 9 (1940): 170–82; Joseph Thomas Ward, "Herman Melville: The Forms and Forces of Evil" (PhD dissertation, Notre Dame, 1959); Grant Edgar McMillan, "Nature's Dark Side: Herman Melville and the Problem of Evil" (PhD dissertation, Syracuse University, 1973); Herbert, *Moby-Dick and Calvinism*; Richard Forrer, *Theodicies in Conflict: A Dilemma in Puritan Ethics and Nineteenth-Century American Literature* (Westport, CT: Greenwood Press, 1986), ch. 10.

20. See Dayton Grover Cook, "The Apocalyptic Novel: *Moby-Dick* and *Doctor Faustus*" (PhD dissertation, University of Colorado, 1974); Michael T. Gilmore, *The Middle Way: Puritanism and Ideology in American Romantic Fiction* (New Brunswick, NJ: Rutgers University Press, 1977): 136–51; Lakshmi Mani, *The Apocalyptic Vision in Nineteenth-Century Fiction: A Study of Cooper, Hawthorne, and Melville* (Washington, DC: University Press of America, 1981), 211–35; Douglas Robinson, *American*

Apocalypses: The Image of the End of the World in American Literature (Baltimore: Johns Hopkins University Press, 1985), 127–42, 154–62.

21. See Richard Chase, *Herman Melville: A Critical Study* (New York: Macmillan, 1949), 43–65; James Baird, *Ishmael* (Baltimore: Johns Hopkins University Press, 1956); Franklin, *Wake of the Gods*, ch. 3; H. B. Kulkarni, *Moby-Dick: A Hindu Avatar: A Study of Hindu Myth and Thought in Moby-Dick* (Logan: Utah State University Press, 1970); Mario L. D'Avanzo, "Ahab, the Grecian Pantheon, and Shelley's *Prometheus Unbound*: The Dynamics of Myth in *Moby-Dick*," *Books at Brown* 24 (1971): 19–44; Gerard M. Sweeney, *Melville's Use of Classical Mythology* (Amsterdam: Rodopi, 1975), chs. 2–4; Robert D. Richardson, Jr., *Myth and Literature in the American Renaissance* (Bloomington: Indiana University Press, 1978), 210–26; William H. Shurr, *Rappaccini's Children: American Writers in a Calvinist World* (Lexington: University of Kentucky Press, 1981), ch. 8; Michael Vannoy Adams, "Ahab's Jonah and the Whale Complex: The Fish Archetype in *Moby-Dick*," *ESQ* 28 (1982): 167–82; Arnold M. Hartstein, "Myth and History in *Moby-Dick*," *American Transcendental Quarterly* 57 (July 1985): 31–43; Gabriele Schwab, *Subjects without Selves: Transitional Texts in Modern Fiction* (Cambridge, MA: Harvard University Press, 1994), ch. 3.

22. On *Moby-Dick*'s form as an epic, see David Ketterer, "The Time-Break Structure of *Moby-Dick*," *Canadian Review of American Studies* 19 (1988): 299–323; George de Forest Lord, *Trials of the Self: Heroic Ordeals in the Epic Tradition* (Hamden, CT: Archon Books, 1983), ch. 7; Christopher Sten, "Threading the Labyrinth: *Moby-Dick* as Hybrid Epic," in *A Companion to Herman Melville*, ed. Wyn Kelley (New York: Wiley-Blackwell, 2006). On *Moby-Dick* as anatomy, see A. Robert Lee, "*Moby-Dick* as Anatomy," in *Herman Melville: Reassessments*, ed. A. Robert Lee (Totowa, NJ: Barnes and Noble, 1984). On *Moby-Dick* as romance, see Richard Chase, *The American Novel and Its Tradition* (Garden City, NY: Doubleday, 1957), ch. 5; Helen P. Trimpi, "Conventions of Romance in *Moby-Dick*," *Southern Review* 7 (1971): 115–29.

23. According to John Wenke, "Ahab's cosmological focus needs to be approached through his Promethean-Messianic complex. He aspires not merely to vengeance; he wishes to redefine the basic human condition. Thus, his Prometheanism informs his cosmic millennialism. A single act will eradicate 'all evil.' . . . Ahab's tragedy derives from a fundamental misapprehension of his cosmological condition. He believes that his fiction actually expresses the truth of creation" (*Melville's Muse*, 160, 161). For David Morse, on the other hand, "Ahab is an anachronistic hero—a man who seeks a direct confrontation with God in a return to the manner of the Old Testament, when Moses, Abraham and the prophets parleyed with Yahweh on strangely intimate terms." *American Romanticism, Volume 2, From Melville to James: The Enduring Excessive* (Houndmills, Basingstoke: Macmillan, 1987), 55.

24. Leo G. Perdue, *Wisdom in Revolt: Metaphorical Theology in the Book of Job* (Sheffield, England: Almond Press, 1991), 74. Perdue's insightful analysis of Job is repeated in *Wisdom and Creation: The Theology of Wisdom Literature* (Nashville: Abingdon, 1994), ch. 4. Job has been the subject of a formidable body of theological, philosophical, and literary commentary. Modern examples include Carl Jung, *Answer to Job*, in *The Portable Jung*, ed. Joseph Campbell (1960; New York: Penguin, 1976), 519–650; Robert Gordis, *The Book of God and Man: A Study of Job* (Chicago: University of Chicago Press, 1965); Rivkah Schärf Kluger, *Satan in the Old Testament*, trans. Hildegard Nagel (Evanston, IL: Northwestern University Press, 1967), 79–136;

David Robertson, "The Book of Job: A Literary Study," *Soundings* 56 (1973), 446–69; Jack Kahn, *Job's Illness: Loss, Grief, and Integration: A Psychological Interpretation* (New York: Pergamon Press, 1975); James L. Crenshaw, *Whirlpool of Torment* (Philadelphia: Fortress, 1984), ch. 3; Peggy L. Day, *An Adversary in Heaven: Satan in the Hebrew Bible* (Atlanta: Scholars Press, 1988), ch. 5; Harold Bloom, ed., *Modern Critical Interpretations of the Book of Job* (New York: Chelsea House, 1988); John T. Wilcox, *The Bitterness of Job: A Philosophical Reading* (Ann Arbor: University of Michigan Press, 1989); Leo G. Perdue and W. Clark Gilpin, eds., *The Voice from the Whirlwind: Interpreting the Book of Job* (Nashville: Abingdon, 1992); Philippe Nemo, *Job and the Excess of Evil*, trans. Michael Kigel (Pittsburgh, PA: Duquesne University Press, 1998); J. William Whedbee, *The Bible and the Comic Vision* (New York: Cambridge University Press, 1998), ch. 5; Carol A. Newsom, *The Book of Job: A Contest of Moral Imaginations* (New York: Oxford University Press, 2003); Keller, *Face of the Deep*, ch. 7.

25. Newsom, *Book of Job*, 251 (on Leviathan and the sublime, see ch. 9). For an informative close reading of the description of Leviathan in Job 41, see Perdue, *Wisdom in Revolt*, 227–32.

26. Rudolph Otto, *The Idea of the Holy: An Inquiry into the Non-rational Factor in the Idea of the Divine and Its Relation to the Rational* (New York: Oxford University Press, 1958), 80.

27. On Calvin's interpretation of Job, see Susan E. Schreiner, "Exegesis and Double Justice in Calvin's Sermons on Job," *Church History* 58 (1989): 322–38; Schreiner, *Where Shall Wisdom Be Found? Calvin's Exegesis of Job from Medieval and Modern Perspectives* (Chicago: University of Chicago Press, 1994).

28. Newsom, *Book of Job*, 31. Whedbee similarly notes: "[Job's] language of attack against God is probably the most searing in the Hebrew Bible. God often emerges as a grotesque, demonic deity, a cosmic bully and tyrant" (*Comic Vision*, 237).

29. On Job's influence on a selection of twentieth-century writers, see Schreiner, *Where Shall Wisdom Be Found*, ch. 5; Harold Fisch, *New Stories for Old: Biblical Patterns in the Novel* (New York: St. Martin's Press, 1998), chs. 5–7. On Job and *King Lear*, see Harold Fisch, *The Biblical Presence in Shakespeare, Milton, and Blake: A Comparative Study* (Oxford: Clarendon Press, 1999), ch. 4; Steven Marx, *Shakespeare and the Bible* (New York: Oxford University Press, 2000), ch. 4. On Job and *The Brothers Karamazov*, see Predag Cicovacki, "The Trial of Man and the Trial of God: Job and Dostoevsky's 'Grand Inquisitor,'" in Predag Cicovacki, ed., *Destined for Evil? The Twentieth-Century Responses* (Rochester, NY: University of Rochester Press, 2005).

30. Jung, *Answer to Job*, 548. In keeping with his larger psychological theories of psychic integration, Jung attributes the existence of evil in Job to the "shadow" side of God. For insightful ironic readings of Job, see Robertson, "Book of Job"; Day, *Adversary in Heaven*, ch. 5.

31. On Job and Prometheus, see W. A. Irwin, "Job and Prometheus," *Journal of Religion* 30 (1950): 91–108. On *Moby-Dick* and Prometheus, see especially Sweeney, *Classical Mythology*, chs. 2–4; Shurr, *Rappaccini's Children*, ch. 8.

32. On Thomas Roscoe's translation of "Doctor Faustus" as the newly identified source for Melville's notes on the devil in the back of the seventh volume of his edition of Shakespeare, see Scott Norsworthy, "Melville's Notes from Thomas Roscoe's *The German Novelists*," *Leviathan* 10 (October 2008): 7–37. On *Moby-Dick* and *Faust Part 1*, see William W. Betts, "*Moby-Dick*: Melville's *Faust*," *Lock Haven Review* 1 (1959):

31–44; Gustaaf Van Cromphout, "*Moby-Dick*: The Transformation of the Faustian Ethos," *American Literature* 51 (1979): 17–32; James McIntosh, "Melville's Use and Abuse of Goethe: The Weaver Gods in *Faust* and *Moby-Dick*," *Amerikastudien* 25 (1980): 158–73. Martin Bidney argues for Melville's acquaintance with part 2 of Goethe's poetic drama, in "Character Creation as Intensive 'Reading': Ahab and the Sea in *Faust* and *Moby-Dick*," *ESQ* 36 (1990): 295–313. On *Moby-Dick* and Marlowe's *Doctor Faustus*, see James S. Leonard, "Melville's Ahab as Marlovian Hero," *American Transcendental Quarterly* 62 (December 1986): 47–58.

33. Millicent Bell, "Pierre Bayle and *Moby-Dick*," *PMLA* 66 (1951): 626–48; Thomas Vargish, "Gnostic Mythos in *Moby-Dick*," *PMLA* 81 (1966): 272–77; William B. Dillingham, *Melville's Later Novels* (Athens: University of Georgia Press, 1986), ch. 4; Etsuko Taketani, "*Moby-Dick*: Gnostic Re-writing of History," *ATQ* 8 n.s. (1994): 119–35. Bell was the first to demonstrate Melville's extensive use of Bayle's multivolume dictionary, which he purchased in 1849. Vargish attempted to show Melville's likely indebtedness to Andrews Norton's *Evidences of the Genuineness of the Gospels* (1844). Dillingham has questioned Melville's acquaintance with Norton's study and instead adduced another possible source in Ephraim Chambers's two-volume *Cyclopaedia; or An Universal Dictionary of Arts and Sciences* (London: Knapton, 1728), which Melville received as a gift from his uncle Herman in 1846. Taketani expands the range of Melville's possible sources to include contemporary periodical literature.

34. For comprehensive overviews of apocalyptic and millennialist ideology in Western history, see Bernard J. McGinn, John J. Collins, and Stephen J. Stein, eds., *The Continuum History of Apocalypticism* (New York: Continuum, 2003). For useful studies of literary representations of apocalyptic ideology, see Frank Kermode, *The Sense of an Ending: Studies in the Theory of Fiction* (New York: Oxford University Press, 1967); M. H. Abrams, *Natural Supernaturalism: Tradition and Revolution in Romantic Literature* (New York: Norton, 1971); C. A. Patrides and Joseph Wittreich, eds., *The Apocalypse in English Renaissance Thought and Literature: Patterns, Antecedents, and Repercussions* (Ithaca, NY: Cornell University Press, 1984); Morton Paley, *Apocalypse and Millennium in English Romantic Poetry* (Oxford: Clarendon Press, 1999).

35. See Bernhard Lang, *The Hebrew God: Portrait of an Ancient Deity* (New Haven: Yale University Press, 2002), chs. 6–8.

36. On the historical development of apocalyptic eschatology in the Bible, see Norman Cohn, *Cosmos, Chaos, and the World to Come: The Ancient Roots of Apocalyptic Faith*, 2nd ed. (New Haven: Yale University Press, 2001); Stephen L. Cook, *Prophecy and Apocalypticism: The Postexilic Social Setting* (Minneapolis: Fortress Press, 1995); Donald E. Gowan, *Eschatology in the Old Testament* (Edinburgh: T&T Clark, 2000).

37. Stephen D. O'Leary, *Arguing the Apocalypse: A Theory of Millennial Rhetoric* (New York: Oxford University Press, 1994), 34. On the development of apocalypse as a genre in late Judaism, see D. S. Russell, *The Method and Message of Jewish Apocalyptic, 200 BC–AD 100* (Philadelphia: Westminster, 1964); John J. Collins, *The Apocalyptic Imagination: An Introduction to the Jewish Matrix of Christianity* (New York: Crossroad, 1984).

38. See John J. Collins, *The Apocalyptic Vision of the Book of Daniel* (Missoula, MT: Scholars Press, 1977); John J. Collins, *Daniel: A Commentary on the Book of Daniel* (Minneapolis: Fortress Press, 1993); Alan F. Segal, *Life after Death: A History of the*

Afterlife in the Religions of the West (New York: Doubleday, 2004), ch. 7.

39. See E. P. Sanders, *The Historical Figure of Jesus* (New York: Penguin, 1995); Dale C. Allison, *Jesus of Nazareth: Millenarian Prophet* (Minneapolis: Fortress Press, 1998); Bart D. Ehrman, *Jesus: Apocalyptic Prophet of the New Millennium* (New York: Oxford University Press, 1999).

40. On the eschatology of Paul, see Larry J. Kreitzer, *Jesus and God in Paul's Eschatology* (Sheffield, England: JSOT Press, 1987); Martinus C. de Boer, *The Defeat of Death: Apocalyptic Eschatology in 1 Corinthians 15 and Romans 5* (Sheffield, England: JSOT Press, 1988); Segal, *Life after Death*, ch. 10. On the origins and development of the Antichrist myth, see Bernard McGinn, *Anti-Christ: Two Thousand Years of Human Fascination with Evil* (San Francisco: Harper and Row, 1994).

41. Religious historians still debate the circumstances that inspired book of Revelation. See, for example, Adela Yarbro Collins, *The Combat Myth in the Book of Revelation* (Missoula, MT: Scholars Press, 1977); Adela Yarbro Collins, *Crisis and Catharsis: The Power of the Apocalypse* (Philadelphia: Westminster Press, 1984); Paul B. Duff, *Who Rides the Beast? Prophetic Rivalry and the Rhetoric of Crisis in the Churches of the Apocalypse* (New York: Oxford University Press, 2001); Elaine Pagels, *Revelations: Visions, Prophecy, and Politics in the Book of Revelation* (New York: Viking, 2012).

42. On the influence of archetypal combat and creation myths on the Hebrew Bible, see Bernhard W. Anderson, *Creation versus Chaos: The Reinterpretation of Mythical Symbolism in the Bible* (1967; rpt., Philadelphia: Fortress, 1987); John Day, *God's Conflict with the Dragon and the Sea: Echoes of Canaanite Myth in the Old Testament* (New York: Cambridge University Press, 1985); Neil Forsyth, *The Old Enemy: Satan and the Combat Myth* (Princeton: Princeton University Press, 1987); Jon Levenson, *Creation and the Persistence of Evil: The Jewish Doctrine of Divine Omnipotence* (San Francisco: Harper and Row, 1988); Bernard Batto, *Slaying the Dragon: Mythmaking in the Biblical Tradition* (Louisville: Westminster/John Knox Press, 1992); K. William Whitney, *Two Strange Beasts of the Bible: Leviathan and Behemoth in Second Temple and Early Rabbinic Judaism* (Winona Lake, IN: Eisenbrauns, 2006); Gregory Mobley, *The Return of the Chaos Monsters: And Other Backstories of the Bible* (Grand Rapids, MI: Eerdmans, 2012). For a wide-ranging comparative study of combat myths in ancient Greek, Near Eastern, and Indian cultures, see Joseph Fontenrose, *Python: A Study of the Delphic Myth and Its Origins* (Berkeley and Los Angeles: University of California Press, 1959). For an earlier review of the biblical background to the mythical Leviathan in *Moby-Dick*, see David H. Hirsch, *Reality and Idea in the Early American Novel* (The Hague: Mouton, 1971), 203–19.

43. See *Myths from Mesopotamia*, trans. Stephanie Dalley (New York: Oxford University Press, 1989), 247, 251.

44. See Batto, *Slaying the Dragon*, ch. 3.

45. Michael D. Coogan, *Stories from Ancient Canaan* (Philadelphia: Westminster Press, 1978), 89. On Canaanite myth and the Old Testament, see Frank Moore Cross, *Canaanite Myth and Hebrew Epic* (Cambridge, MA: Harvard University Press, 1973); John Day, *Yahweh and the Gods and Goddesses of Canaan* (Sheffield, England: Sheffield Academic Press, 2000).

46. Coogan, *Stories from Ancient Canaan*, 106.

47. Anderson, *Creation versus Chaos*, 132.

48. For a fuller exposition of the relation between Psalm 104 and Genesis 1–2:3,

see Levenson, *Persistence of Evil*, ch. 5; see also Batto, *Slaying the Dragon*, 83–84.

49. On the different depictions of Leviathan here, see Beal, *Religion and Its Monsters*, 25–32.

50. According to Marvin Pope, "The supernatural character of Leviathan is abundantly clear. . . . If the author of the present composition wished merely to exercise his poetic abilities on the power and ferocity of the crocodile, he surpassed his goal at the start with the use of the term Leviathan." *Job*, Anchor Bible 15, 3rd ed. (Garden City, NY: Doubleday, 1973), 331. On Leviathan's mythical nature, see also Day, *God's Conflict*, 62–72; Perdue, *Wisdom in Revolt*, 121–32; Perdue, *Wisdom and Creation*, 176–80. On the probable mythical origins of Behemoth, see Pope, *Job*, 320–22. John Day more speculatively adduces the source in an oxlike creature, Ars, mentioned in conjunction with Leviathan in the Ugaritic texts; see *God's Conflict*, 80–84.

51. Collins, *Apocalyptic Vision of the Book of Daniel*, ch. 4.

52. See Collins, *Combat Myth*, chs. 2–3.

53. Beal, *Religion and Its Monsters*, 81.

54. Collins, *Combat Myth*, ch. 4.

55. See especially Whitney, *Two Strange Beasts*.

56. Richardson, *Myth and Literature*, 195.

57. Yvonne Sherwood, *A Biblical Text and Its Afterlives: The Survival of Jonah in Western Culture* (New York: Cambridge University Press, 2000), 157.

58. On the background of the biblical Ishmael and his symbolic identity, see Jon D. Levenson, *The Death and Resurrection of the Beloved Son: The Transformation of Child Sacrifice in Judaism and Christianity* (New Haven: Yale University Press, 1993), ch. 10. For other discussions of the significance of Ishmael's name in *Moby-Dick*, see Wright, *Use of the Bible*, 47–51; *Moby-Dick*, ed. Mansfield and Vincent, 586–92; Reno, *Ishmael Alone*, 57–59; Maria Ujhazy, *Herman Melville's World of Whaling* (Budapest: Akadémiai Kiadó, 1982), 78–81. On the nineteenth-century exegetical background to the biblical Ishmael, see Pardes, *Melville's Bibles*, ch. 3.

59. On the biblical Ahab, see Jerome T. Walsh, *Ahab: The Construction of a King* (Collegeville, MN: Liturgical Press, 2006). On the anti-imperial political uses of the biblical Ahab in the era of the Mexican War, see Rogin, *Subversive Genealogy*, ch. 4; Pardes, *Melville's Bibles*, ch. 4. For a useful review of the biblical and cultural background to Melville's use of the name Ahab, see *Moby-Dick*, ed. Mansfield and Vincent, 637–52.

60. Walsh, *Construction of a King*, 22.

2—Pilgrimage and Prophecy

1. See John Harmon McElroy, "The Dating of the Action in *Moby-Dick*," *Papers on Language and Literature* 13 (1977): 420–23. Two essays on the structure of *Moby-Dick* have divided it into six parts, a number consonant with the novel's epic structure and its one-year chronological frame. See Herbert G. Eldridge, "'Careful Disorder': The Structure of *Moby-Dick*," *American Literature* 39 (1967): 145–62; Henry Golemba, "The Shape of *Moby-Dick*," *Studies in the Novel* 5 (1973): 197–210. On the biographical basis for Ishmael's engagement as a whaleman, see Hershel Parker,

Herman Melville, 1819–1851 (Baltimore: Johns Hopkins University Press, 1996), ch. 10; Wilson Heflin, *Herman Melville's Whaling Years*, ed. Mary K. Bercaw Edwards and Thomas Farel Heffernan (Nashville, TN: Vanderbilt University Press, 2004), chs. 1–7.

2. Alexis de Tocqueville, *Democracy in America*, 2 vols. (New York: Vintage, 1945), 1:314; Mark A. Noll, *America's God: From Jonathan Edwards to Abraham Lincoln* (New York: Oxford University Press, 2002); Tocqueville, *Democracy in America*, 2:6.

3. On the antebellum "benevolent empire," see Timothy L. Smith, *Revivalism and Social Reform in Mid-Nineteenth-Century America* (Nashville: Abingdon, 1957); Clifford S. Griffin, *Their Brothers' Keepers: Moral Stewardship in the United States, 1800–1865* (New Brunswick, NJ: Rutgers University Press, 1960); Ronald G. Walters, *American Reformers, 1815–1860* (New York: Hill and Wang, 1978); Robert H. Abzug, *Cosmos Crumbling: American Reform and the Religious Imagination* (New York: Oxford University Press, 1994); Steven Mintz, *Moralists and Modernizers: America's Pre–Civil War Reformers* (Baltimore: Johns Hopkins University Press, 1995).

4. On varieties of nineteenth-century American millennialist belief, see Ernest Lee Tuveson, *Redeemer Nation: The Idea of America's Millennial Role* (Chicago: University of Chicago Press, 1968); Ernest R. Sandeen, *The Roots of Fundamentalism: British and American Millenarianism, 1800–1930* (Chicago: University of Chicago Press, 1970).

5. James H. Moorhead, "Apocalypticism and Mainstream Protestantism," in Bernard J. McGinn, John J. Collins, and Stephen J. Stein, eds., *The Continuum History of Apocalypticism* (New York: Continuum, 2003), 473.

6. On the history of William Miller and his movement, see Michael Barkun, *Crucible of the Millennium: The Burned-over District of New York in the 1840s* (Syracuse: Syracuse University Press, 1986); George R. Knight, *Millennial Fever and the End of the World* (Boise, ID: Pacific Press, 1993); Stephen D. O'Leary, *Arguing the Apocalypse: A Theory of Millennial Rhetoric* (New York: Oxford University Press, 1994), chs. 4–5; David L. Rowe, *God's Strange Work: William Miller and the End of the World* (Grand Rapids, MI: Eerdmans, 2008).

7. See Herman Melville, *Correspondence*, ed. Lynn Horth (Evanston and Chicago: Northwestern University and the Newberry Library, 1993), 27. Allan Melville wrote his mother on 21 October 1844: "Herman has arrived & you may expect him every hour after tomorrow" (ibid.). News of the Millerite movement was pervasive in the press at the time, especially in Boston where Melville was discharged from the Navy in October 1844. See Ira V. Brown, "The Millerites and the Press," *New England Quarterly* 16 (1943): 592–614. Melville's return from the sea coincided also with the final days of the Polk-Clay presidential campaign, in which his brother Gansevoort would play a significant role. See Parker, *Herman Melville, 1819–1851*, ch. 16.

8. See T. Walter Herbert, *Moby-Dick and Calvinism: A World Dismantled* (New Brunswick, NJ: Rutgers University Press, 1977), chs. 1–4; Parker, *Herman Melville, 1819–1851*, chs. 1–9.

9. Herman Melville, *The Piazza Tales and Other Prose Pieces, 1839–1860* (Evanston and Chicago: Northwestern University Press and the Newberry Library, 1987), 243. For an overview of the Melville–Hawthorne relationship and an analysis of Melville's *Mosses* review, see Jonathan A. Cook, "Introduction to Melville's Marginalia in Nathaniel Hawthorne's *Mosses from an Old Manse*," in *Melville's*

Marginalia Online, http://melvillesmarginalia.org. On Melville's ascription of a "messianic" role to Hawthorne, see Jonathan A. Cook, "Melville's *Mosses* Review and the Proclamation of Hawthorne as America's Literary Messiah," *Leviathan* 10 (October 2008): 62–70. For informative surveys of the impact of Calvinism on *Moby-Dick*, see Thomas Werge, "*Moby-Dick* and the Calvinist Tradition," *Studies in the Novel* 1 (1969): 484–506; Herbert, Moby-Dick *and Calvinism*, chs. 5–10; William H. Shurr, *Rappaccini's Children: American Writers in a Calvinist World* (Lexington: University Press of Kentucky, 1981), ch. 8.

10. Thomas D. Hamm, *The Transformation of American Quakerism: Orthodox Friends, 1800–1907* (Bloomington: Indiana University Press, 1988), 27. On the Quakers of Nantucket, see Robert J. Leach and Peter Gow, *Quaker Nantucket: The Religious Community behind the Whaling Empire* (Nantucket, MA: Mill Hill Press, 1997). On the rise of whaling in America, see Eric Jay Dolin, *Leviathan: The History of Whaling in America* (New York: Norton, 2007).

11. For useful comments on the Quaker background of the owners and two officers of the *Pequod*, see Gerhard Friedrich, *In Pursuit of Moby-Dick: Melville's Image of Man* (Wallingford, PA: Pendle Hill, 1958). As Friedrich notes, Melville unsparingly probes "the nature of Quakerism or rather of Quaker conduct, as if it epitomized much that is characteristic of Christianity and of civilization at large" (9).

12. See Merrel D. Clubb, Jr., "The Second Personal Pronoun in *Moby-Dick*," *American Speech* 35 (1960): 252–60.

13. Leach and Gow, *Quaker Nantucket*, 153. Ahab's name would not look out of place among some of the other Old Testament first names used by Nantucket Quakers such as Abishai, Barzillai, Eleaser, Elihu, Enoch, Ephraim, Ichabod, Jabez, Jedidiah, Jethro, Job, Josiah, Kezia, Micajah, Obed, Peleg, Shubael, and Zachariah. See the names listed in the index (ibid.).

14. See Priscilla J. Brewer, *Shaker Communities, Shaker Lives* (Hanover, NH: University Press of New England, 1986); Stephen J. Stein, *The Shaker Experience in America: A History of the United Society of Believers* (New Haven: Yale University Press, 1992).

15. Merton M. Sealts, Jr., "Melville and the Shakers," *Studies in Bibliography* 2 (1949–1950): 105–14 (114).

16. On the sources of the "Etymology" and "Extract" sections, see *Moby-Dick; or, The Whale*, ed. Luther S. Mansfield and Howard P. Vincent (New York: Hendricks House, 1952), 578–86. On the "late consumptive usher" as partially suggested by the schoolmaster in Thomas Hood's well-known poem "The Dream of Eugene Aram," see Edward Stone, "Melville's Late Pale Usher," *English Language Notes* 9 (September 1971): 51–53. On the thematic and symbolic significance of the "Extracts" section, see Frank Shuffelton, "Going through the Long Vaticans: Melville's 'Extracts' in *Moby-Dick*," *Texas Studies in Literature and Language* 25 (1983): 528–40. On the death theme in *Moby-Dick*, see James P. Grove, "Melville's Vision of Death in *Moby-Dick*: Stepping away from the 'Snug Sofa,'" *New England Quarterly* 52 (1979): 177–86.

17. For an overview of Pauline theology, see Bart D. Ehrman, *Peter, Paul, and Mary Magdalene: The Followers of Jesus* (New York: Oxford University Press, 2006), chs. 7–12. On Bunyan's influence on American literature, see David E. Smith, *John Bunyan in America* (Bloomington: Indiana University Press, 1966). In chapter 26 of *Moby-Dick*, in his invocation of the "great democratic God," Ishmael salutes the "swart convict, Bunyan" as having been endowed by God with the "pale, poetic pearl"

(117). In chapter 27, Ishmael evokes Bunyan's allegory in his description of Stubb's pipe, which "made Stubb such an easy-going, unfearing man, so cheerily trudging off with the burden of life in a world full of grave pedlars, all bowed to the ground with their packs" (118–19). In chapter 108, Ahab banteringly tells the carpenter that, when the blacksmith is "through with that buckle, tell him to forge a pair of steel shoulder-blades; there's a pedlar aboard with a crushing pack" (470).

18. On the background of *Moby-Dick* in antebellum folklore and popular culture, see Daniel E. Hoffman, *Form and Fable in American Fiction* (New York: Oxford University Press, 1961), ch. 11; David S. Reynolds, *Beneath the American Renaissance: The Subversive Imagination in the Age of Emerson and Melville* (New York: Knopf 1988). On Ishmael as a version of the New York b'hoy, see Reynolds, *American Renaissance*, 543–44. On Ishmael's obsession with death, the void, and universal "sharkishness," see Robert Zoellner, *The Salt-Sea Mastodon: A Reading of* Moby-Dick (Berkeley and Los Angeles: University of California Press, 1973), ch. 7. For an overview of Ishmael and Romantic irony, see Robert Milder, *Exiled Royalties: Melville and the Life We Imagine* (New York: Oxford University Press, 2006), 92–96. For an insightful brief examination of Ishmael as Romantic-era hero, see James D. Wilson, *The Romantic Heroic Ideal* (Baton Rouge: Louisiana State University Press, 1982), 88–95.

19. On the pervasive influence of the sublime in *Moby-Dick*, see Barbara Glenn, "Melville and the Sublime in *Moby-Dick*," *American Literature* 48 (1976): 165–82; Bryan Wolf, "When Is a Painting most like a Whale? Ishmael, *Moby-Dick*, and the Sublime," in Richard H. Brodhead, ed., *New Essays on* Moby-Dick (New York: Cambridge University Press, 1986), 141–79; Nancy Fredricks, *Melville's Art of Democracy* (Athens: University of Georgia Press, 1995), ch. 3.

20. For an informative analysis of Ahab and Ishmael in relation to modern theories of narcissistic personality disorder, see Joseph Adamson, *Melville, Shame, and the Evil Eye: A Psychoanalytic Reading* (Albany: State University of New York Press, 1997).

21. John Bunyan, *The Pilgrim's Progress* (New York: Oxford University Press, 1984), 51–52.

22. On the Spouter Inn picture and the sublime, see Fredricks, *Art of Democracy*, 29–30. Robert K. Wallace has argued that the painting (along with the character of Bulkington) is a tribute to the art of J. M. W. Turner (1775–1851), whom Melville learned about from Ruskin's *Modern Painters* and the various Turner connoisseurs he met in London in late 1849. See "Bulkington, J. M. W. Turner, and 'The Lee Shore,'" in Christopher Sten, ed., *Savage Eye: Melville and the Visual Arts* (Kent, OH: Kent State University Press, 1991), 55–76; also Wallace, *Melville and Turner: Spheres of Love and Fright* (Athens: University of Georgia Press, 1992), 318–30, 453–69. For further comments on the Spouter Inn painting and Ishmael's aesthetic sensibilities, see Douglas Robillard, *Melville and the Visual Arts: Ionian Form, Venetian Tint* (Kent, OH: Kent State University Press, 1997), 71–75. On the painting as a possible paradigm for the interpretation of *Moby-Dick*, see Manfred Putz, "The Narrator as Audience: Ishmael as Reader and Critic in *Moby-Dick*," *Studies in the Novel* 19 (1987): 161–64.

23. On the larger literary history of the noble savage ideal, see Hoxie N. Fairchild, *The Noble Savage: A Study in Romantic Naturalism* (New York: Columbia University Press, 1928). On Queequeg as a model natural man who has learned to govern his inner shark, see Zoellner, *Salt-Sea Mastodon*, ch. 11. On racial equality

generally in *Moby-Dick*, see Edward S. Grejda, *The Common Continent of Man: Racial Equality in the Writings of Herman Melville* (Port Washington, NY: Kennikat Press, 1974), ch. 6. Carolyn Karcher argues that, in his portrait of Queequeg, Melville has blurred racial lines in order to address the issue of anti-Negro prejudice; see *Shadow over the Promised Land: Slavery, Race, and Violence in Melville's America* (Baton Rouge: Louisiana State University Press, 1980), 63–74.

24. On Apollyon, see Bunyan, *Pilgrim's Progress*, 46–50 (47); on Faithful, see ibid., 55–80.

25. Geoffrey Sanborn, *Whipscars and Tattoos:* The Last of the Mohicans, Moby-Dick, *and the Maori* (New York: Oxford University Press, 2011), chs. 3–4. For Sanborn's previous, more theoretical discussion of this historical source, see "Whence Come You, Queequeg?" *American Literature* 77 (2005): 227–57. Te Pehi Kupe eventually returned to his tribe in New Zealand in 1828 to exact revenge for the earlier killing and cannibalizing of his son by an enemy tribe but went on to suffer the same fate. See Sanborn, *Whipscars and Tattoos*, 85–88. On Queequeg and the contemporary discourse of cannibalism, see Sanborn, *The Sign of the Cannibal: Melville and the Making of the Post-colonial Reader* (Durham, NC: Duke University Press, 1998), ch. 3. In a Jungian analysis of the novel, John Halverson, "The Shadow in *Moby-Dick*," *American Quarterly* 15 (1963): 436–46, notes that Queequeg fulfills the role of a repressed shadow figure, whose acceptance by Ishmael leads to the latter's fully integrated personality.

26. A number of critics interpret the friendship between Ishmael and Queequeg as a sexualized relationship; see, for example, Robert K. Martin, *Hero, Captain, Stranger: Male Friendship, Social Critique, and Literary Form in the Sea Novels of Herman Melville* (Chapel Hill: University of North Carolina Press, 1986), 77–79. T. Walter Herbert, Jr., "Homosexuality and Spiritual Aspiration in *Moby-Dick*," *Canadian Review of American Studies* 6 (1975): 50–58, argues that the allegedly homosexual aspects of Ishmael's friendship with Queequeg constitute a comic critique of Calvinist traditions associating homosexuality and idolatry.

27. Modern psychological research has identified sleep paralysis as occurring while waking from the deepest, or REM (rapid eye movement), sleep in which dreaming occurs and bodily movements are suspended to protect the dreamer from acting out his or her dream. The sleeper then experiences a momentary paralysis, in which dream images are still generated although the eyes are open—creating, in effect, a waking dream. See David J. Hufford, *The Terror that Comes in the Night: An Experience-Centered Study of Supernatural Assault Traditions* (Philadelphia: University of Pennsylvania Press, 1982); J. A. Cheyne, S. D. Rueffer, and I. R. Newby-Clark, "Hypnogogic and Hypnopompic Hallucinations during Sleep Paralysis: Neurological and Cultural Construction of the Nightmare," *Consciousness and Cognition* 8 (1999): 39–57.

28. See Edward F. Edinger, *Melville's* Moby-Dick: *A Jungian Commentary* (New York: New Directions, 1978), 34–35.

29. See Merton M. Sealts, Jr., "Melville and the Platonic Tradition," in *Pursuing Melville, 1940–1980* (Madison: University of Wisconsin Press, 1982), 301–4 (Plato, 301–2; *Phaedo,* 109c–e).

30. On these two traditions, see Alan F. Segal, *Life after Death: A History of the Afterlife in the Religions of the West* (New York: Doubleday, 2004), chs. 5, 7–13.

31. Tocqueville, *Democracy in America*, 1:321.

32. On the source for the hymn sung in the Whaleman's Chapel, see David H. Battenfield, "The Source for the Hymn in *Moby-Dick*," *American Literature* 27 (1955): 393–96. Steven Olsen-Smith has clarified the hymn's exact provenance and developed its larger thematic implications in "The Hymn in *Moby-Dick*: Melville's Adaptation of 'Psalm 18,'" *Leviathan* 5 (March 2003): 29–47. For overviews of the significance of the book of Jonah in *Moby-Dick*, see Nathalia Wright, "*Moby-Dick*: Jonah or Job's Whale?" *American Literature* 37 (1965): 190–95; Yvonne Sherwood, *A Biblical Text and Its Afterlives: The Survival of Jonah in Western Culture* (New York: Oxford University Press, 2000), 152–62. In *Melville's Bibles* (Berkeley and Los Angeles: University of California Press, 2008), ch. 2, Pardes examines the exegesis of Jonah in John Kitto's *Cyclopedia of Biblical Literature* (1845) in relation to Melville's use of the prophet in *Moby-Dick*.

33. For discussions of Father Mapple's sermon and its significance, see Nathalia Wright, *Melville's Use of the Bible* (Durham, NC: Duke University Press, 1949), 82–93, 146–51; Zoellner, *Salt-Sea Mastodon*, 58–62; Reynolds, *American Renaissance*, 27–30; Janet Reno, *Ishmael Alone* (Lewisburg, PA: Bucknell University Press, 1990), 59–76; Adamson, *Melville, Shame, and the Evil Eye*, 101–6; Giorgio Mariani, "'Chiefly Known by His Rod': The Book of Jonah, Mapple's Sermon, and Scapegoating," in John Bryant, Mary K. Bercaw Edwards, and Timothy Marr, eds., *"Ungraspable Phantom": Essays on* Moby-Dick (Kent, OH: Kent State University Press, 2006), 37–57; James Duban, "Level Dead-Reckoning': Father Mapple, Goethe, and Ahab," *Leviathan* 11 (March 2009): 74–79.

34. See Herbert, *Moby-Dick and Calvinism*, 106–19; Herbert, "Calvinist Earthquake: *Moby-Dick* and Religious Tradition," in Richard H. Brodhead, ed., *New Essays on* Moby-Dick (New York: Cambridge University Press, 1986). On Father Taylor, see Allan Macdonald, "A Sailor among the Transcendentalists," *New England Quarterly* 8 (1935): 307–19 (Emerson, 316n); R. E. Watters, "Boston's Salt Water Preacher," *South Atlantic Quarterly* 45 (1946): 350–61. Adding to the evidence of Melville's use of Taylor for Father Mapple is the picture of a ship off a lee shore in Taylor's Boston chapel, which is partially replicated in the picture of the ship behind Father Mapple's pulpit. Taylor preached in New Bedford, Martha's Vineyard, and other Massachusetts port towns while a Methodist circuit rider in the 1820s, before his assumption of duties at the Boston Seaman's Bethel in 1833.

35. See J. William Whedbee, *The Bible and the Comic Vision* (New York: Cambridge University Press, 1998), ch. 4.

36. For useful discussions of biblical motifs in Mapple's sermon, see Wright, *Use of the Bible*, 146–51; Vasanth Joseph, "Some Biblical Nuances in *Moby-Dick*," *Osmania Journal of English Studies* (India) 8 (1971): 70–71; David H. Hirsch, "*Hamlet, Moby-Dick*, and Passional Thinking," in *Shakespeare: Aspects of Influence*, ed. G. B. Evans (Cambridge, MA: Harvard University Press, 1976), 135–62. Mapple's invocation of "woe to him whose good name is more to him than goodness" (48) directly restates Luke 6:26: "Woe unto you, when all men shall speak well of you! for so did their fathers to the false prophets." Mapple's claim that "Delight is to him, who gives no quarter in the truth, and kills, burns, and destroys all sin though he pluck it out from under the robes of Senators and Judges" (48) reformulates Jeremiah 1:10: "See, I have this day set thee over the nations and over the kingdoms, to root out, and to pull

down, and to destroy, and to throw down, to build, and to plant." It is telling that Edmund Burke's well-known treatise on the sublime and beautiful posits the word *delight* "to express the sensation which accompanies the removal of pain or danger." If Father Mapple's sermon on Jonah is designed to arouse sublime terror in the auditor, avoidance of such terror through obedience to God produces delight. See Edmund Burke, *A Philosophical Enquiry into the Origin of Our Ideas of the Sublime and Beautiful*, ed. James T. Boulton (Notre Dame, IN: University of Notre Dame Press, 1968), 36–37, also 45–48, 51, 134–36.

37. See Perry Miller, "The Marrow of Puritan Divinity," in *Errand into the Wilderness* (Cambridge, MA: Harvard University Press, 1956).

38. See Susan VanZanten Gallagher, "The Prophetic Narrator of *Moby-Dick*," *Christianity and Literature* 36 (1987): 11–25. On the value of "truth" in relation to Ishmael's narrative technique, see A. Robert Lee, "*Moby-Dick*: The Tale and the Teller," in Faith Pullin, ed., *New Perspectives on Melville* (Kent, OH: Kent State University Press, 1978), 86–127. Bruce L. Grenberg, *Some Other World to Find: Quest and Negation in the Works of Herman Melville* (Urbana: University of Illinois Press, 1989), ch. 4, argues that Ishmael's quest for truth is characterized by futility.

39. On Queequeg and the ritual of the tayo, see James Baird, *Ishmael* (Baltimore: Johns Hopkins University Press, 1956), 230–41. On Queequeg as a Christ figure, see Wilson, *Romantic Heroic Ideal*, 92–95.

40. See David H. Hirsch, *Reality and Idea in Early American Literature* (The Hague: Mouton, 1971), 199–219.

41. Bunyan, *Pilgrim's Progress*, 93, 94.

42. The discussion here draws on Jonathan A. Cook, "*Moby-Dick*, Myth, and Classical Moralism: Bulkington as Hercules," *Leviathan* 5 (March 2003): 15–28. On Bulkington as a possible tribute to the painter J. M. W. Turner, see Wallace, "Bulkington."

43. Ishmael's evocation of the lee shore here conforms closely to Burke's well-known analysis of the sublime in terms of terror, obscurity, power, vastness, and infinity, in *Philosophical Enquiry*, 57–74. Burke's remarks on the appeal of tragedy (ibid., 43–48) also provide grounds for the emotional appeal of Bulkington's confrontation with overwhelming terror and disaster. On Bulkington and Emerson, see Sealts, "Melville and Emerson's Rainbow," in *Pursuing Melville*, 264–65. On the larger Emersonian context of "The Lee Shore," see S. A. Cowan, "In Praise of Self-Reliance: The Role of Bulkington in *Moby-Dick*," *American Literature* 38 (1967): 547–56.

3—Chaos Monster and Unholy Warrior

1. See T. Walter Herbert, Jr., Moby-Dick *and Calvinism: A World Dismantled* (New Brunswick, NJ: Rutgers University Press, 1977), 117.

2. See Kurt Gray and Daniel M. Wegner, "Blaming God for Our Pain: Human Suffering and the Divine Mind," *Personality and Social Psychology Review* 14 (2010): 7–16. For an overview of Job's varied physical and psychological afflictions, see Philippe Nemo, *Job and the Excess of Evil*, trans. Michael Kigel (Pittsburgh, PA: Duquesne University Press, 1998), ch. 1. On Ahab's hinted emasculation and its blasphemous results, see Herbert N. Schneider and Homer B. Pettey, "Melville's Ithyphallic God,"

Studies in American Fiction 26 (1998): 193–212.

3. On *Moby-Dick* and Shakespearean tragedy, see F. O. Matthiessen, *American Renaissance: Art and Expression in the Age of Emerson and Whitman* (New York: Oxford University Press, 1941), 409–59; Julian C. Rice, "*Moby-Dick* and Shakespearean Tragedy," *Centennial Review* 14 (1970): 444–68; David H. Hirsch, "*Hamlet, Moby-Dick*, and Passional Thinking," in G. B. Evans, ed., *Shakespeare: Aspects of Influence* (Cambridge, MA: Harvard University Press, 1976), 135–62; Julian Markels, *Melville and the Politics of Identity: From* King Lear *to* Moby-Dick (Urbana: University of Illinois Press, 1993).

4. On *Moby-Dick* and classical tragedy, see T. R. Dale, "Melville and Aristotle: The Conclusion of *Moby-Dick* as Classical Tragedy," *Boston University Studies in English* 3 (1957): 45–50; Gerard M. Sweeney, *Melville's Use of Classical Mythology* (Amsterdam: Rodopi, 1975), ch. 2. On *Moby-Dick* and tragedy generally, see Richard B. Sewall, *The Vision of Tragedy* (1959; New Haven: Yale University Press, 1980), ch. 10; Leon Howard, "Melville and the American Tragic Hero," in *Four Makers of the American Mind: Emerson, Thoreau, Whitman, and Melville*, ed. Thomas Edward Crawley (Durham, NC: Duke University Press, 1976), 65–82. On the tradition of revenge tragedy, see John Kerrigan, *Revenge Tragedy: Aeschylus to Armageddon* (Oxford: Clarendon Press, 1996).

5. On Ahab as Romantic hero-villain, see especially Christopher S. Durer, *Herman Melville: Romantic and Prophet. A Study of His Romantic Sensibility and His Relationship to European Romantics* (Fredericton, NB, Canada: York Press, 1996), 118–41.

6. For an examination of the pervasive imagery linking Ahab and the White Whale, interpreted as a form of psychological projection, see Sister Mary Ellen, "Duplicate Imagery in *Moby-Dick*," *Modern Fiction Studies* 8 (1962–1963): 252–64.

7. On Platonic analogues to Ahab's speech here, see Michael Levin, "Ahab as Socratic Philosopher: The Myth of the Cave Inverted," *ATQ* 41 (Winter 1979): 61–73. On the echoes of Carlyle, see *Sartor Resartus* (New York: Oxford University Press, 1987), 56. For background on Melville's use of Carlyle in *Moby-Dick*, see Linden Peach, *British Influence on the Birth of American Literature* (New York: St. Martin's Press, 1982), ch. 5.

8. Leo G. Perdue, *Wisdom in Revolt: Metaphorical Theology in the Book of Job* (Sheffield, England: Almond Press, 1991), 148 (see generally 32–56, 91–106, 131–48). On Job's use of legal language, see also Carol A. Newsom, *Book of Job: A Contest of Moral Imaginations* (New York: Oxford University Press, 2003), 150–61. Ilana Pardes discusses Ahab's famous quarterdeck speech in the context of Job's "blasphemous wrath" as expressed in chapter 3 of the book of Job; see *Melville's Bibles* (Berkeley and Los Angeles: University of California Press, 2008), 33–38.

9. Alexis de Tocqueville, *Democracy in America*, 2 vols. (New York: Vintage, 1945), 2:3.

10. As Perdue notes, "Humanity, including Job, is no royal figure or exalted creature, chosen to rule over God's creation and confident in a gracious providence. Rather humans are slaves, victimized by the destiny allotted them and the terrors wrought by a cruel and suspicious sovereign" (*Wisdom in Revolt*, 130–31; also 90–91, 125–31).

11. James Crenshaw, *Whirlpool of Torment* (Philadelphia: Fortress Press, 1984), 61.

12. Jack Kahn, *Job's Illness: Loss, Grief, and Integration: A Psychological*

Interpretation (New York: Pergamon Press, 1975), ch. 3.

13. For a different analysis of Ahab's rhetorical powers over Starbuck, see Anthony Fassano, "The Power of Ahab's Speech," *Milton and Melville Review* 1, no. 2, at www.miltonandmelville.org.

14. On the structural and thematic function of the novel's thirteen explicitly "dramatic" chapters in the consolidation of Ahab's power over the crew beginning with "The Quarter-Deck," see Dan Vogel, "The Dramatic Chapters of *Moby-Dick*," *Nineteenth-Century Fiction* 13 (1958): 239–47; also Fred E. H. Schroeder, "*Enter Ahab, Then All*: Theatrical Elements in Melville's Fiction," *Dalhousie Review* 46 (1966): 223–32. Glauco Cambon views the novel's shifts to dramatic form as the creation of a historical present to intensify certain episodes in the narrative; see "Ishmael and the Problem of Formal Discontinuities in *Moby-Dick*," *Modern Language Notes* 76 (1961): 516–23.

15. See E. Bruce Kirkham, "The Iron Crown of Lombardy," *ESQ* 58 (1970): 127–29.

16. On Melville's use of Milton's Satan, see Henry F. Pommer, *Milton and Melville* (Pittsburgh: University of Pittsburgh Press, 1950), ch. 6; Leslie E. Sheldon, "Messianic Power and Satanic Decay: Milton in *Moby-Dick*," in *Melville and Milton*, ed. Robin Grey (Pittsburgh, PA: Duquesne University Press, 2004).

17. Nemo, *Excess of Evil*, 134.

18. Foster Rhea Dulles, *Lowered Boats: A Chronicle of American Whaling* (New York: Harcourt Brace, 1933), 23, 22. On the seeming malevolence of some sperm whales, see ibid., chs. 2, 12, 13.

19. See Janez Stanonik, *Moby-Dick: The Myth and the Symbol: A Study in Folklore and Literature* (Ljubljana, Yugoslavia: Ljubljana University Press, 1962); H. Bruce Franklin, *The Wake of the Gods: Melville's Mythology* (Stanford, CA: Stanford University Press, 1963), 54–63. For a brief summary of the influence of legendary nautical lore in the novel, see Kevin J. Hayes, *Melville's Folk Roots* (Kent, OH: Kent State University Press, 1999), ch. 7.

20. As David H. Hirsch notes, "What Melville's use of these materials suggests is that in writing *Moby-Dick* he did not naively create the symbolic leviathan out of the naturalistic whale, but that he combined two levels of fiction—the quasi-biographical whaling voyage and the quasi-mythical Leviathanic literature which was already traditionally problematic." *Reality and Idea in the Early American Novel* (The Hague: Mouton, 1971), 213.

21. See J. N. Reynolds, "Mocha Dick," in *Moby-Dick; or, The Whale*, ed. Hershel Parker and Harrison Hayford, 2nd ed. (New York: Norton, 2002); ensuing page citations to "Mocha Dick" will be to this edition.

22. Helen P. Trimpi theorizes that Melville's transformation of Mocha to Moby Dick was meant to suggest the West African–Caribbean magical religion of obi, or Obeah; see "Melville's Use of Demonology and Witchcraft in *Moby-Dick*," *Journal of the History of Ideas* 30 (1969): 558–61.

23. Melville may well have begun his description of Moby Dick "with the Leviathan of Job xli." *Moby Dick; or, The Whale*, ed. Luther S. Mansfield and Howard P. Vincent (New York: Hendricks House, 1952), 694. See also Michael T. Gilmore, *The Middle Way: Puritanism and Ideology in American Romantic Fiction* (New Brunswick, NJ: Rutgers University Press, 1977), 148; Michael Paul Rogin, *Subversive Genealogy: The Politics and Art of Herman Melville* (New York: Knopf, 1983), 121.

24. Joseph Adamson, *Melville, Shame, and the Evil Eye: A Psychoanalytic Reading* (Albany: State University of New York Press, 1997), 75–89.

25. Joseph Fontenrose, *Python: A Study of the Delphic Myth and Its Origins* (Berkeley and Los Angeles: University of California Press, 1959), 219.

26. For useful discussions of Ahab's madness in the context of contemporary understanding of "monomania," see Henry Nash Smith, "The Madness of Ahab," in *Democracy and the Novel: Popular Resistance to Classic American Writers* (New York: Oxford University Press, 1978); Paul McCarthy, *"The Twisted Mind": Madness in Herman Melville's Fiction* (Iowa City: University of Iowa Press, 1990), 67–73. Sanford E. Marovitz draws attention to Melville's encounter with George J. Adler, an incipiently monomaniacal New York University lexicographer and professor of German, during his trip to England in the fall of 1849 as a possible influence on the conception of Ahab. See "Correspondences: Paranoiac Lexicographers and Melvillean Heroes," in John Bryant, Mary K. Bercaw Edwards, and Timothy Marr, eds., *Ungraspable Phantom: Essays on* Moby-Dick (Kent, OH: Kent State University Press, 2006), 100–113; also Sanford E. Marovitz, "More Chartless Voyaging: Melville and Adler at Sea," in *Studies in the American Renaissance, 1986*, ed. Joel Myerson (Charlottesville: University Press of Virginia, 1986), 373–84. Michael J. Hoffman, "The Anti-transcendentalism of *Moby-Dick*," *Georgia Review* 33 (1969): 3–16, interprets Ahab as an Emersonian "great man" whose self-centered delusional mythmaking and "passion without compassion" lead to collective disaster for the *Pequod*. For other views of Ahab's Emersonian mindset, see Gene Bluestein, "Ahab's Sin," *Arizona Quarterly* 41 (1985): 101–16; Michael McLoughlin, *Dead Letters to the New World: Melville, Emerson, and American Transcendentalism* (New York: Routledge, 2003), ch. 4. Finally, Wendy Stallard Flory provides an insightful examination of the various means by which the three mates and Queequeg overcome the depressive mind that afflicts Ahab; see "Melville, *Moby-Dick*, and the Depressive Mind: Queequeg, Starbuck, Stubb, and Flask as Symbolic Characters," in Bryant, Edwards, and Marr, *Ungraspable Phantom*, 81–99.

27. Joan Burbick, *Healing the Republic: The Language of Health and the Culture of Nationalism in Nineteenth-Century America* (New York: Cambridge University Press, 1994), 163–75.

28. John T. Wilcox, *The Bitterness of Job: A Philosophical Reading* (Ann Arbor: University of Michigan Press, 1989), 109.

29. See Harrison Hayford, "Melville's Prisoners," in *Melville's Prisoners* (Evanston, IL: Northwestern University Press, 2003), ch. 1. Robert Milder has also related the "captive king" motif to the Enceladus myth in *Pierre*, noting of Ahab: "Like his ancestral archetype, the captive king whose spiritual exile he shares, Ahab craves recognition that he is heaven-born and, if not heaven-destined, then at least, by nature and bearing, heaven-worthy." *Exiled Royalties: Melville and the Life We Imagine* (New York: Oxford University Press, 2006), 98.

30. Dillingham, *Melville's Later Novels* (Athens: University of Georgia Press, 1986), 97–98. See also Etsuko Taketani, "*Moby-Dick*: Gnostic Re-writing of History," *ATQ* 8 n.s. (1994): 119–35.

31. See Perdue, *Wisdom in Revolt*, 166–67; Dexter E. Callender, Jr., *Adam in Myth and History: Ancient Israelite Perspectives on the Primal Human* (Winona Lake, IN: Eisenbrauns, 2000).

32. Writing to Nathaniel Hawthorne in April 1851, Melville irreverently speculated on the alleged divine "secret" of the creation: "And perhaps, after all, there is *no* secret. We incline to think that the Problem of the Universe is like the Freemason's mighty secret, so terrible to all children. It turns out, at last, to consist in a triangle, a mallet, and an apron,—nothing more! We incline to think that God cannot explain His own secrets, and that He would like a little information upon certain points Himself. We mortals astonish Him as much as He us." *Correspondence*, ed. Lynn Horth (Evanston and Chicago: Northwestern University Press and the Newberry Library, 1993), 186.

33. For a survey of the literature of devil lore that may have contributed to the novel's thematics of evil, see Trimpi, "Demonology and Witchcraft," 543–62. On Ahab's paradoxical representation as both messianic Christ figure and satanic tyrant, see Gilmore, *Middle Way*, 140–44. As Daniel Hoffman notes: "A Faust who commands and enchants his followers becomes, as Ahab does, a Satan, a sorcerer, an Antichrist." *Form and Fable in American Fiction* (New York: Oxford University Press, 1961), 234.

34. See Herbert Rothschild, Jr., "The Language of Mesmerism in 'The Quarter-Deck' Scene in *Moby-Dick*," *English Studies* 53 (1972): 235–38; Bernhard Radloff, *Will and Representation: The Philosophical Foundations of Melville's Theatrum Mundi* (New York: Peter Lang, 1996), 90–98.

35. See James E. Miller, Jr., "Hawthorne and Melville: The Unpardonable Sin," in *Quests Surd and Absurd: Essays in American Literature* (Chicago: University of Chicago Press, 1967), 209–38. On Ahab's moral corruption, see also Charles H. Cook, Jr., "Ahab's 'Intolerable Allegory,'" *Boston University Studies in English* 1 (1955–1956), 45–52. For useful discussions of the philosophical grounds for Ahab's revolt, see John D. Reeves, *Windows on Melville* (Danbury, CT: Rutledge Books, 2001), part 1; Burton F. Porter, *The Head and the Heart: Philosophy in Literature* (Amherst, NY: Humanity Books, 2006), ch. 1.

36. On the evolution of the identity of the satan/Satan in the Old and New Testament, see Rivkah Schärf Kluger, *Satan in the Old Testament*, trans. Hildegard Nagel (Evanston, IL: Northwestern University Press, 1967); Peggy L. Day, *An Adversary in Heaven: Satan in the Hebrew Bible* (Atlanta: Scholars Press, 1988); Jeffrey Burton Russell, *The Devil: Perceptions of Evil from Antiquity to Primitive Christianity* (Ithaca: Cornell University Press, 1977). On Goethe's Mephistopheles and the modern devil, see Jeffrey Burton Russell, *Mephistopheles: The Devil in the Modern World* (Ithaca, NY: Cornell University Press, 1986).

37. Bainard Cowan aptly notes: "If the image of Christ is suggested as a play on the word 'nails' here, it marks Ahab as a Romantic antitype, the would-be harrower of heaven rather than of hell, who nonetheless has his own agony in the garden. His suffering is staged within him, however, largely hidden from the conscious Ahab, revealing itself only at the threshold between sleep and waking, a continually fruitful moment for allegory in that it suggests two parallel worlds both conjoined and disjoined, able to bring out the disjunctures, and doublings within the supposedly integral self." *Exiled Waters:* Moby-Dick *and the Crisis of Allegory* (Baton Rouge: Louisiana State University Press, 1982), 105. On the philosophical basis of Ahab's will in "The Chart," see Radloff, *Will and Representation*, 135–45.

38. *Prometheus Bound*, in Elizabeth Barrett Browning, *"Prometheus Bound" and Other Poems* (New York: C. S. Francis, 1854), 52.

39. Johann Wolfgang von Goethe, *Faust, The First Part of the Tragedy*, trans.

David Constantine (New York: Penguin, 2005), 39.

40. See Sweeney, *Classical Mythology*, ch. 3.

41. For more on *Moby-Dick* and *Frankenstein*, see Chris Baldick, *In Frankenstein's Shadow: Myth, Monstrosity, and Nineteenth-Century Writing* (Oxford: Clarendon Press, 1987), 75–84.

42. See Scott Norsworthy, "Melville's Notes in Thomas Roscoe's *The German Novelists*," *Leviathan* 10 (October 2008): 7–37.

43. In a discussion of the Islamic and "Eastern" origins of Fedallah, Dorothee Metlitsky Finkelstein argues that silent and ancient-looking Fedallah is a modern version of the legendary leader (the "old man of the mountain") of an ancient band of Islamic assassins; Fedallah's Malay associates are evil spirits, called *divas* or *jinns*. See *Melville's Orienda* (New Haven: Yale University Press, 1961), 229–34. Ali Mukhtar Isani, in "The Naming of Fedallah in *Moby-Dick*," *American Literature* 40 (1968): 380–85, traces Fedallah's name to Melville's early reading of Tom Moore's *Lalla Rookh*. The frame story of this famous compilation of Romantic Orientalism included the characters of Fadladeen and Abdalla and contained a Zoroastrian tale entitled "The Fire-Worshippers." For Fedallah as an exemplar of the Jungian shadow, see John Halverson, "The Shadow in *Moby-Dick*," *American Quarterly* 15 (1963): 436–46. For Fedallah's role as oracular prophet comparable to the witches in *Macbeth*, see Jeffrey M. Jeske, "Macbeth, Ahab, and the Unconscious," *American Transcendental Quarterly* 31 (Summer 1976): 8–12.

44. Elizabeth Schultz explores the cultural sources of Fedallah and his Malay crewmen in nineteenth-century American prejudices against Asians; see "'The Subordinate Phantoms': Melville's Conflicted Response to Asia in *Moby-Dick*," in *"Whole Oceans Away": Melville and the Pacific*, ed. Jill Barnum, Wyn Kelley, and Christopher Sten (Kent, OH: Kent State University Press, 2007), ch. 14. On Fedallah and crew as versions of contemporary Japanese shipwrecked "sea drifters," see Ikuno Saiki, "'Strike through the Unreasoning Masks': *Moby-Dick* and Japan," in Barnum, Kelley, and Sten, *"Whole Oceans Away,"* ch. 13.

45. On the doctrines and history of the Zoroastrian religion, see Mary Boyce, *Zoroastrians: Their Religious Beliefs and Practices* (New York: Routledge, 2001); Norman Cohn, *Cosmos, Chaos, and the World to Come: The Ancient Roots of Apocalyptic Faith*, 2nd ed. (New Haven: Yale University Press, 2001), ch. 4.

46. On the historical and mythical background of the fall of the watcher angels, see George W. E. Nickelsburg, "Apocalypse and Myth in 1 Enoch 6–11," *Journal of Biblical Literature* 96 (1977): 383–405.

47. Ishmael's remark in chapter 51 that the Cape of Good Hope were better named "Cape Tormentoso" (234), or Cape of Torments, is similarly directly drawn from Camoëns's epic poem, which provided a model itinerary for the *Pequod* around the coast of Africa instead of South America, the more traditional route for whaling vessels leaving the northeast United States. On *Moby-Dick* and *The Lusiads*, see Norwood Andrews, Jr., *Melville's Camões* (Bonn, Germany: Bouvier, 1989), ch. 3. Sailing around Africa was also the itinerary taken by J. Ross Browne in his non-fiction *Etchings of a Whaling Cruise* (1846), which Melville reviewed for his friend Evert Duyckinck's *Literary World* in March 1847.

48. See Howard P. Vincent, *The Trying-Out of Moby-Dick* (Boston: Houghton, Mifflin, 1949), 210–11. Richard Gravil, in *Romantic Dialogues: Anglo-American Continuities, 1776–1862* (New York: St. Martin's, 2000), ch. 7, discusses Melville's use

of Coleridge and the *Rime* throughout *Moby-Dick*, noting that Ahab "is a demonic potentiation of the Ancient Mariner: a mariner who would knowingly and willingly transgress against his shipmates, against the albatross, and against the Polar Spirit" (160). Oddly, Gravil does not discuss the Coleridgean implications of Melville's chapter on "The Spirit Spout."

49. For a full account of the natural history and cultural impact of the giant squid, see Richard Ellis, *The Search for the Giant Squid: The Biology and Mythology of the World's Most Elusive Sea Creature* (New York: Penguin, 1998). Ishmael's ascription of furlongs (one furlong equals 220 yards) to the squid's size is presumably a mistake for fathoms (one fathom equals six feet). The giant squid, like other squid species, is not naturally white but a transparent silvery gray; like other cephalopods it can change its color and create body patterns with remarkable agility. The squid has eight arms and two longer tentacles, all with variously sized suckers, radiating out from its main tubular body; a large parrot-like beak at its "mouth" allows it to shred its food.

4—Cetology, Cosmology, Epistemology

1. See Howard P. Vincent, *The Trying-Out of* Moby-Dick (Boston: Houghton Mifflin, 1949), part 4. On Melville's extensive use of Bayle in *Moby-Dick*, see Millicent Bell, "Pierre Bayle and *Moby-Dick*," *PMLA* 66 (1951): 636–48. On the influence of Calvinism on Ishmael's cetology, see Thomas Werge, "*Moby-Dick* and the Calvinist Tradition," *Studies in the Novel* 1 (1969): 484–506. Robert M. Greenberg, in *Splintered Worlds: Fragmentation and the Ideal of Diversity in the Work of Emerson, Melville, Whitman, and Dickinson* (Boston: Northeastern University Press, 1993), argues that "the aesthetic and philosophical goal of the cetological material is to convey a sense of epistemological fragmentation and disarray" (84). Elizabeth Duquette, "Speculative Cetology: Figuring Philosophy in *Moby-Dick*," *ESQ* 47 (2001): 33–57, also comments on Ishmael's skeptical outlook in the cetology chapters of the novel. On Ishmael's cetology in relation to contemporary ethnological literature, see Samuel Otter, *Melville's Anatomies* (Berkeley and Los Angeles: University of California Press, 1999), 132–56.

2. In a letter to Hawthorne dated June 1851, Melville wrote, "I read Solomon [Ecclesiastes] more and more, and every time see deeper and deeper and unspeakable meanings in him." *Correspondence*, ed. Lynn Horth (Evanston and Chicago: Northwestern University Press and the Newberry Library, 1993), 193. On wisdom traditions in the Old Testament, see Leo G. Perdue, *Wisdom Literature: A Theological History* (Louisville, KY: Westminster John Knox, 2007). Perdue notes of Ecclesiastes: "The cosmological rendering of a world of goodness in which moral action led to desired consequences could no longer sustain itself in an enigmatic and fearful reality that gave no appearance of responding at all to human behavior. 'The God' was hidden in darkness and could not be known. There was no evidence of divine retribution, and what occurred seemed to be the result of mere divine caprice. . . . The philosophical tradition most akin to Qoheleth's [Ecclesiastes'] worldview was that of Greek Skepticism developed and transmitted at the time in which he lived and wrote [late third-century BCE]" (*Wisdom Literature*, 179, 184).

3. Robert Zoellner, *The Salt-Sea Mastodon: A Reading of* Moby-Dick (Berkeley and Los Angeles: University of California Press, 1973), 154 (chs. 8–9 in general); J. A.

Ward, "The Function of the Cetological Chapters in *Moby-Dick*," *American Literature* 28 (1956): 164–83. John Seelye notes: "The cetology chapters, with their relatively static, discursive movements, act to block and impede the forward movement of the narrative, much as the ideas which they contain qualify Ahab's absolutism." *Melville: The Ironic Diagram* (Evanston: Northwestern University Press, 1970), 63. For more on Ishmael's epistemological dilemmas, see John Wenke, *Melville's Muse: Literary Creation and the Forms of Philosophical Fiction* (Kent, OH: Kent State University Press, 1995), 146–59. On Ishmael's homiletic style in the cetology chapters, see Robert Alter, *Pen of Iron: American Prose and the King James Bible* (Princeton, NJ: Princeton University Press, 2010), ch. 2. On the interrelationship between the description of the whale killings and the evolution of Ishmael's cetological knowledge, see Barbara Meldrum, "Structure in *Moby-Dick*: The Whale Killings and Ishmael's Quest," *ESQ* 21 (1975): 162–68.

4. On Melville's whaling sources, see Vincent, *Trying-Out*; Steven Olsen-Smith, "Melville's Copy of Thomas Beale's *The Natural History of the Sperm Whale* and the Composition of *Moby-Dick*," *Harvard Library Bulletin* 21 (Fall 2010): 1–77. The relevant texts and other works on nineteenth-century whaling are available online at www.mysite.du.edu/~ttyler/ploughboy.

5. Nancy Fredricks, *Melville's Art of Democracy* (Athens: University of Georgia Press, 1995), 30.

6. Randall Bohrer, "Melville's New Witness: Cannibalism and the Microcosm-Macrocosm Cosmology of *Moby-Dick*," *Studies in Romanticism* 22 (1983): 65–91 (68–69, 66). For another discussion of Ishmael's dialectical vision, see A. D. Van Nostrand, *Everyman His Own Poet: Romantic Gospels in American Literature* (New York: McGraw Hill, 1968), ch. 6.

7. For a discussion of the influence of Rabelais, Burton, Sterne, De Quincey, Lamb, and Irving on *Moby-Dick*, see Jane Mushabac, *Melville's Humor: A Critical Study* (Hamden, CT: Archon Books, 1961), 89–104. On the influence of Sir Thomas Browne's *Vulgar Errors* on the cetological chapters, see Brian Foley, "Herman Melville and the Example of Sir Thomas Browne," *Modern Philology* 81 (1984): 265–77. On *Moby-Dick* and Sterne, see Carol Fabricant, "*Tristram Shandy* and *Moby-Dick*: A Cock and Bull Story and a Tale of a Tub," *Journal of Narrative Technique* 7 (1977): 57–69. For Carlyle's influence, see James Barbour and Leon Howard, "Carlyle and the Conclusion to *Moby-Dick*," *New England Quarterly* 49 (1976): 215–24; Linden Peach, *British Influence on the American Renaissance* (New York: St. Martin's Press, 1982), ch. 5; Wenke, *Melville's Muse*, 106–11.

8. Otter, *Melville's Anatomies*, 156.

9. Daniel Hoffman, *Form and Fable in American Fiction* (New York: Oxford University Press, 1961), 250; Alexis de Tocqueville, *Democracy in America*, 2 vols. (New York: Vintage, 1945), 2:42. For a study of the 1818 New York lawsuit *Maurice v. Judd* and the general dispute over the whale's identity as mammal or fish, see D. Graham Burnett, *Trying Leviathan: The Nineteenth-Century New York Case That Put the Whale on Trial and Challenged the Order of Nature* (Princeton: Princeton University Press, 2007).

10. As Carlyle wrote, "We speak of the Volume of Nature: and truly a Volume it is,—whose Author and Writer is God. To read it! Dost thou, does man, so much as well know the Alphabet thereof? With its Words, Sentences, and grand descriptive Pages, poetical and philosophical, spread out through Solar Systems, and Thousands

of Years, we shall not try thee. It is a volume written in celestial hieroglyphs, in the true Sacred-writing; of which even Prophets are happy that they can read here a line and there a line." *Sartor Resartus* (New York: Oxford University Press, 1987), 195. On Melville's use of the article on "Whales" in the *Penny Cyclopaedia*, see Kendra H. Gaines, "A Consideration of an Additional Source for Melville's *Moby-Dick*," *Melville Society Extracts* no. 29 (January 1977): 6–12.

11. On the Romantic ethos of incompletion, see Thomas McFarland, *Romanticism and the Forms of Ruin: Wordsworth, Coleridge, and the Modalities of Fragmentation* (Princeton: Princeton University Press, 1981), ch. 1.

12. Melville described this pantheistic feeling to Hawthorne as the ability to "get out of yourself, spread and expand yourself, and bring to yourself the tinglings of life that are felt in the flowers and the woods, that are felt in the planets Saturn and Venus, and the Fixed Stars" (*Correspondence*, 193). For more on the sources and philosophical significance of the masthead chapter, see Vincent, *Trying-Out*, 146–59.

13. See David Charles Leonard, "The Cartesian Vortex in *Moby-Dick*," *American Literature* 51 (1979): 105–10. Matthew Mancini, "Melville's 'Descartian Vortices,'" *ESQ* 36 (1990): 315–27, argues that the allusion to Descartian vortices, which Melville apparently found in Bayle's *Dictionary* (article on Ovid, note F), evokes a philosophy rooted in a rationalized solipsism. On Melville's larger criticism of Transcendentalism, see Michael J. Hoffman, "The Anti-transcendentalism of *Moby-Dick*," *Georgia Review* 33 (1969): 3–16.

14. John Bunyan, *The Pilgrim's Progress* (New York: Oxford University Press, 1984), 32.

15. Tocqueville, *Democracy in America*, 2:33.

16. For a review of interpretations of chapter 42 through the early 1970s, see Khalil Husni, "The Whiteness of the Whale: A Survey of Interpretation, 1851–1970," *College Language Association Journal* 20 (1976): 210–21. On the sources for Ishmael's multiple allusions in the chapter, see "Explanatory Notes," in *Moby-Dick; or, The Whale*, ed. Luther S. Mansfield and Howard P. Vincent (New York: Hendricks House, 1952), 704–17. For discussions of Melville's use of the sublime, see Barbara Glenn, "Melville and the Sublime," *American Literature* 48 (1976): 165-82; Richard S. Moore, *That Cunning Alphabet: Melville's Aesthetics of Nature* (Amsterdam: Rodopi, 1982), 156–76; Bryan Wolf, "When Is a Painting Most Like a Whale? Ishmael, *Moby-Dick*, and the Sublime," in Richard H. Brodhead, ed., *New Essays on* Moby-Dick (New York: Cambridge University Press, 1986); Fredricks, *Art of Democracy*, ch. 3. Janet Reno notes of chapter 42: "The psychological purpose of the chapter seems to be to establish that Ishmael's enthusiastic participation in the whale hunt was morally innocent." *Ishmael Alone Survived* (Lewisburg, PA: Bucknell University Press, 1990), 59.

17. Moore, *That Cunning Alphabet*, 159.

18. Edmund Burke, *A Philosophical Enquiry into the Original of Our Ideas of the Sublime and Beautiful*, ed. James T. Boulton (Notre Dame, IN: University of Notre Dame Press, 1968), 57.

19. See Bell, "Bayle and *Moby-Dick*," 647–48.

20. "Pyrrho," Note B, in Pierre Bayle, *The Dictionary Historical and Critical of Mr. Peter Bayle*, 5 vols. (1734–1738; rpt. New York: Garland, 1984), 4:654.

21. On Melville's adaptation of the weaving metaphor in Goethe, see James McIntosh, "Melville's Use and Abuse of Goethe: The Weaver Gods in *Faust* and

Moby-Dick,"Amerikastudien 25 (1980): 158–73. For a discussion of some philosophic and linguistic implications of the weaving metaphor in this chapter, see Reuben J. Ellis, "The Interiority of the Weave: Raising the Shed in Melville's Incomplete 'Mat-Maker,'" *ATQ* 2 n.s. (1988): 111–24.

22. For a useful review of these sequential events, see Michael J. Hoffman, "Anti-Transcendentalism," 12–13. For a perceptive discussion of the role of chance in "The Mat-Maker" and elsewhere in the novel, see Maurice S. Lee, *Uncertain Chances: Science, Skepticism, and Belief in Nineteenth-Century American Literature* (New York: Oxford University Press, 2012), ch. 2.

23. On the biblical stylistics of this passage, see Alter, *Pen of Iron*, 53–55. Ishmael's message here contradicts his earlier celebration of intellectual and spiritual freedom on the open sea (in "The Lee Shore"), but this is but one of many paradoxes and dialectical representations of truth that characterize Ishmael's vision. See Van Nostrand, *Everyman His Own Poet*, 121–22.

24. See Foley, "Sir Thomas Browne," 274.

25. Stuart M. Frank, *Herman Melville's Picture Gallery: Sources and Types of the "Pictorial" Chapters of* Moby-Dick (Fairhaven, MA: Edward J. Lefkowicz, 1986).

26. Merton M. Sealts, "Melville and the Platonic Tradition," in *Pursuing Melville 1940–1980* (Madison: University of Wisconsin Press, 1982), 302–3.

27. Lawrance Thompson, *Melville's Quarrel with God* (Princeton, NJ: Princeton University Press, 1952), 214; Ilana Pardes, *Melville's Bibles* (Berkeley and Los Angeles: University of California Press, 2008), 24. On Ishmael as a Romantic interpreter of nature, see Kerry McSweeney, *"Moby-Dick": Ishmael's Mighty Book* (Boston: Twayne, 1986), ch. 5. For useful comments on the novel's many binary oppositions, see Edward J. Rose, "Annihilation and Ambiguity: *Moby-Dick* and 'The Town-Ho's Story,'" *New England Quarterly* 45 (1972): 541–58.

28. Bert Bender, "The Allegory of the Whale's Head," *Renascence* 32 (1980): 152–66.

29. As Greenberg observes, the whale's "helpless perplexity of vision" also suggests "implications about the possible predicament of a Deity who might be caught between clashing powers of vision, one benign, the other malevolent, so that they tend to cancel each other out or to reduce Him to helplessness" (*Splintered Worlds*, 99).

30. Zoellner notes of Tashtego's plunge into the whale's case: "This death-and-rebirth sequence marks a major turning-point. Tashtego's accident makes Ishmael see that death and birth are but the dualities of a unity, the two sides of a single coin. For the first time, he is able to apprehend death as a beginning, rather than an ending." *Salt-Sea Mastodon*, 160. James D. Wilson notes that the act of saving Tashtego is one "in a series of incidents in which Queequeg, like Christ, becomes in his love an agent of rebirth." *The Romantic Heroic Ideal* (Baton Rouge: University of Louisiana Press, 1982), 92.

31. See Harold Aspiz, "Phrenologizing the Whale," *Nineteenth-Century Fiction* 23 (1968): 18–27.

32. Marius Bewley, *Eccentric Design: Form in the Classic American Novel* (New York: Columbia University Press, 1959), 201–5.

33. Bainard Cowan notes of this scene: "Nature reveals itself in a timeless moment which in itself seems to have no dependency on death. Death lies at the extremity of experience, this revelation seems to say, but what maintains nature in

existence is love. Sexuality, birth, and nursing all find their home in a feminine world whose characteristics have been conspicuously absent on the *Pequod*." *Exiled Waters: Moby-Dick and the Crisis of Allegory* (Baton Rouge: Louisiana State University Press, 1982), 154. See also the remarks of Zoellner, *Salt-Sea Mastodon*, 179–84; Reno, *Ishmael Alone*, 92–96. On the literary source for "The Grand Armada" in Frederick Debell Bennett's *Narrative of a Whaling Voyage around the World*, see Vincent, *Trying-Out*, 299–310.

34. Bruce Grenberg notes: "Pip's two misadventures in Stubb's whaleboat prefigure precisely what happens to Ahab and Ishmael on the fatal third day of the chase." *Some Other World to Find: Quest and Negation in the Works of Herman Melville* (Urbana: University of Illinois Press, 1989), 115. For Grenberg, "The Castaway" is central to the novel's philosophical vision (114–15).

35. On Pip's relation to the biblical Jonah, see Pardes, *Melville's Bibles*, 57–71.

36. See, for example, G. J. Barker-Benfield, *The Horrors of the Half-Known Life: Male Attitudes toward Women and Sexuality in Nineteenth-Century America* (New York: Harper and Row, 1976), ch. 14.

37. William M. Davis, *Nimrod of the Sea; or, The American Whaleman* (New York, 1874), 86. On the philosophical virtues of physical touch in Ishmael's world, see Lisa Ann Robertson, "'Universal Thump': The Redemptive Epistemology of Touch in *Moby-Dick*," *Leviathan* 12 (June 2010): 5–20.

38. Dayton Grover Cook notes that "on more than one occasion, Ishmael sings the praises of democracy in a way which might lead one to assume that a new Jerusalem of sorts had already arrived. Another echo of this feature is contained in the chapter called 'A Squeeze of the Hand,' where the illusion of a perfect community is temporarily achieved." "The Apocalyptic Novel: *Moby-Dick* and *Doctor Faustus*" (PhD dissertation, University of Colorado, 1974), 193.

39. On the biographical implications of chapter 94 concerning Melville's new residence in Pittsfield, Massachusetts, see Hershel Parker, "Melville and Domesticity," in *Critical Essays on Herman Melville's* Moby-Dick, ed. Brian J. Higgins and Hershel Parker (New York: G. K. Hall, 1992), 545–62.

40. McSweeney argues that the scene here "is the parodic apotheosis of the squeezing of sperm, as the celestial ejaculations of the seraphim mirror in a finer tone the masturbatory and exhibitionistic excesses of the description of the sailors at the sperm vat" (*Ishmael's Mighty Book*, 97). For Lee Person, Melville in this chapter "revises the prominent nineteenth-century belief in a spermatic economy, the male's fear that his supply of sperm is limited and that its expenditure has to be severely restricted." "Melville's Cassock: Putting on Masculinity in *Moby-Dick*," *ESQ* 40 (1994): 19. For more on Ishmael's inversion of Job here, see Pardes, *Melville's Bibles*, 29–32.

41. Vincent, *Trying-Out*, 329–36.

42. Dante Alighieri, *The Vision; or Hell, Purgatory, and Paradise of Dante Alighieri*, trans. Rev. Henry Francis Cary (1814; New York: E. P. Dutton, 1908), 90.

43. We may recall that only two months after *Moby-Dick* was published, Melville and Duyckinck experienced a break in their friendship, almost certainly in connection with Duyckinck's reaction to the religious heresies of Melville's new novel, *Pierre*. See Hershel Parker, *Herman Melville: A Biography*, vol. 2, *1851–1991* (Baltimore: Johns Hopkins University Press, 2002), ch. 4. The relevance of Hawthorne to this passage in "The Try-Works" is confirmed by Melville's use of a scene from

"Rappaccini's Daughter" in Ishmael's insistence on the need for daylight to make a proper judgment of appearances. As Hawthorne wrote of Giovanni's morning view of Beatrice Rappaccini, after seeing her interacting with the toxic flowers of the garden the night before: "But there is an influence in the light of morning that tends to rectify whatever errors of fancy, or even of judgment, we may have incurred during the sun's decline, or among the shadows of the night, or in the less wholesome glow of moonshine." Hawthorne, *Tales and Sketches*, 980–81. On Melville and Hawthorne in comparative perspective as writers of prose romance, see Richard Brodhead, *Hawthorne, Melville, and the Novel* (Chicago: University of Chicago Press, 1976).

44. In his *Mosses* review, Melville wrote of Hawthorne that "there is no man, in whom humor and love, like mountain peaks, soar to such a rapt height as to receive the irradiation of the upper skies"—but, as an "indispensable complement," Hawthorne also possessed "a great, deep intellect, which drops down into the universe like a plummet." Melville continued: "For spite of all the Indian-summer sunlight on the hither side of Hawthorne's soul, the other side—like the dark half of the physical sphere—is shrouded in blackness, ten times black. But this darkness but gives more effect to the ever-moving dawn, that forever advances through it, and circumnavigates his world." *The Piazza Tales and Other Prose Pieces, 1839–1860*, ed. Harrison Hayford, Alma A. MacDougall, and G. Thomas Tanselle (Evanston and Chicago: Northwestern University Press and the Newberry Library, 1987), 242, 243. For an insightful examination of Ishmael's "unorthodox theodicy" based on his vision of radical pluralism, see Richard Forrer, *Theodicies in Conflict: A Dilemma in Puritan Ethics and Nineteenth-Century American Literature* (Westport, CT: Greenwood Press, 1986), ch. 10.

45. Zachary Hutchins, "*Moby-Dick* as Third Testament: A Novel 'Not Come to Destroy but to Fulfill' the Bible," *Leviathan* 13 (June 2011): 18–37.

5—Comic and Tragic Variations

1. For useful background on comic and tragic elements in the world's leading religions, see John Morreall, *Comedy, Tragedy, and Religion* (Albany: State University of New York Press, 1999). On comedy and tragedy in the Old Testament generally, see J. William Whedbee, *The Bible and the Comic Vision* (New York: Cambridge University Press, 1998); J. Cheryl Exum, *Tragedy and Biblical Narrative: Arrows of the Almighty* (New York: Cambridge University Press, 1992). On Lowth and Herder's views of Job as tragedy, see Ilana Pardes, *Melville's Bibles* (Berkeley and Los Angeles: University of California Press, 2008), 20–21; also Horace M. Kallen, *The Book of Job as a Greek Tragedy* (New York: Moffat, Yard, 1918). On Job as comedy, see Whedbee, *Comic Vision*, ch. 5; but see the critique of Whedbee's argument in Morreall, *Comedy, Tragedy, and Religion*, 97–99. On the book of Revelation as tragicomedy, see Stephen D. O'Leary, *Arguing the Apocalypse: A Theory of Millennial Rhetoric* (New York: Oxford University Press, 1994), ch. 3.

2. On *King Lear* and Job, see Harold Fisch, *The Biblical Presence in Shakespeare, Milton, and Blake: A Comparative Study* (Oxford: Clarendon Press, 1999), ch. 4; Steven Marx, *Shakespeare and the Bible* (New York: Oxford University Press, 2000), ch. 4. On *Samson Agonistes* and the book of Revelation, see Barbara K. Lewalski, "*Samson Agonistes* and the Tragedy of the Apocalypse," *PMLA* 85 (1970): 1050–62. On

Hawthorne's use of apocalyptic symbolism, see Lakshmi Mani, *The Apocalyptic Vision in Nineteenth-Century American Fiction: A Study of Cooper, Hawthorne, and Melville* (Washington, DC: University Press of America, 1981), ch. 3; Jonathan A. Cook, "New Heavens, 'Poor Old Earth': Satirical Apocalypse in Hawthorne's *Mosses from an Old Manse*," *ESQ* 39 (1993): 209–51.

3. Mark Heidmann, "Melville and the Bible: Leading Themes in the Marginalia and Major Fiction, 1850–1856" (PhD dissertation, Yale University, 1979), 61. Pardes argues that "There are many Jobs aboard the *Pequod* (there is no need to limit the scope to Ahab and Ishmael. . . . The splitting of Job among the various crew members allows Melville to explore the different genres that intersect in Job—theophany (the whirlwind poem), dialogues, tragedy, folkloric tales, and sermons" (*Melville's Bibles*, 25).

4. As Joseph Adamson notes, "*Moby-Dick* is full of images of wounding, striking, and sundering, of dismemberment and tearing to pieces. The humorous counterpart of this violent imagery would seem to be the verbal alternatives of knocking, thrashing, punching, or thumping, imagery that suggests the countertragic, carnivalesque spirit of a communal comic beating or drubbing." *Melville, Shame, and the Evil Eye: A Psychoanalytic Reading* (Albany: State University of New York Press, 1987), 81.

5. For the theological implications of the castration motif here, see Herbert N. Schneider and Homer B. Pettey, "Melville's Ithyphallic God," *Studies in American Fiction* 26 (1988): 193–212. On *Moby-Dick's* phallic humor in this scene and elsewhere in the novel, see Robert Schulman, "The Serious Function of Melville's Phallic Jokes," *American Literature* 33 (1961): 179–94; Terry Roberts, "Ishmael as Phallic Narrator," *Studies in American Fiction* 20 (1992): 99–109.

6. On Asherah in the Old Testament, see John Day, *Yahweh and the Gods and Goddesses of Canaan* (Sheffield, England: Sheffield Academic Press, 2000), ch. 2. The Vulgate version of 1 Kings 15:13 reads: "Maacham matrem suam amovit ne esset princeps in sacris Priapi et in luco eius quem consecraverat" ([Asa] removed his mother Maachah from being the princess in the sacrifices of Priapus, and in the grove she had consecrated to him).

7. See Mario L. D'Avanzo, "'The Cassock' and Carlyle's 'Church Clothes,'" *ESQ* 50 supplement (First Quarter, 1968): 74–76. The alleged power residing in official vestments, or "canonicals," would be especially relevant to the controversy in the Episcopalian church in the 1840s concerning the importance of vestments and ritual in the Protestant service—a controversy originating in the Tractarian (or Oxford) Movement in England, which sought to restore lost ecclesiastical traditions within the Anglican church. It is likely that, on a topical level, "The Cassock" was intended as a covert jibe at Melville's orthodox friend Evert Duyckinck, who was heavily involved in the Episcopal church in New York City and with whom Melville shared a fondness for Rabelaisian humor.

8. See the discussion in Howard P. Vincent, *The Trying-Out of* Moby-Dick (Boston: Houghton Mifflin, 1949), 269–86.

9. See Brian Foley, "Herman Melville and the Example of Sir Thomas Browne," *Modern Philology* 81 (1984), 275. On Perseus and Hercules as heroes of combat myths in the chaos monster tradition, see Joseph Fontenrose, *Python: A Study of the Delphic Myth and Its Origins* (Berkeley and Los Angeles: University of California Press, 1959), chs. 11–12. As Fontenrose notes, "Perseus' encounter with a sea monster was referred in the earliest extant records to the very regions where Baal fought Yam and Yahweh

fought Leviathan, and . . . seems to be a Greek reflection of the Canaanite myth" (279). Moreover, "Hercules' killing of the Trojan sea monster and rescue of Hesione is almost an exact replica of the Andromeda story" (347).

10. On the linguistic relation of whales and dragons here, see David H. Hirsch, *Reality and Idea in the Early American Novel* (The Hague: Mouton, 1971), 210–13.

11. On Melville's use of Indian mythology here, see Vincent, *Trying-Out*, 277–80. On Indian traditions of the divine combat with the chaos monster, see Fontenrose, *Python*, 194–216 (on St. George and the Dragon, 515–20).

12. On Bayle, see Vincent, *Trying-Out*, 283–86; Millicent Bell, "Pierre Bayle and *Moby-Dick*," *PMLA* 66 (1951): 631–36. On Kitto, see Pardes, *Melville's Bibles*, ch. 2.

13. Alexis de Tocqueville, *Democracy in America*, 2 vols. (New York: Vintage, 1945), 2:42.

14. The only critic to notice this parody is Hirsch, *Reality and Idea*, 206n.

15. K. William Whitney, *Two Strange Beasts: Leviathan and Behemoth in Second Temple and Early Rabbinic Judaism* (Winona Lake, IN: Eisenbrauns, 2006), chs. 2 and 3 (quotations from 4 Ezra, 2 Apocalypse of Baruch, and 1 Enoch at 32, 38, 44–45).

16. For other comments on this celebrated comic scene, see Vincent, *Trying-Out*, 233–36; Robert Zoellner, *The Salt-Sea Mastodon: A Reading of* Moby-Dick (Berkeley and Los Angeles: University of California Press, 1973), 221–25; Kerry McSweeney, *Ishmael's Mighty Book* (Boston: Twayne, 1986), 88–89; Robert T. Tally, Jr., "Whale as Dish: Culinary Rhetoric and the Discourse of Power in *Moby-Dick*," in *Culinary Aesthetics and Practices in Nineteenth-Century American Literature*, ed. Monika Elbert and Marie Drews (New York: Palgrave Macmillan, 2009), 82–85.

17. David S. Reynolds, *Beneath the American Renaissance: The Subversive Imagination in the Age of Emerson and Melville* (New York: Knopf, 1988), 547.

18. Mary K. Bercaw Edwards notes of the ironic reversals in this scene: "Stubb wants Fleece to be born again to serve him, *not* Christ. Fleece replies by blessing himself, but his blessing is far from sacred: it is at best just an expression, and at worst a curse. Stubb follows this exchange with an inversion of the sacrament of Communion when he forces Fleece to taste the cooked whale then asks him the question Bildad posed of Queequeg: 'Do you belong to the church?'" *Cannibal Old Me: Spoken Sources in Melville's Early Work* (Kent, OH: Kent State University Press, 2009), 194.

19. For historical background on the consumption of whale meat, see Nancy Shoemaker, "Whale Meat in American History," *Environmental History* 10 (2005): 269–94. As Shoemaker notes, "At some point in their whaling careers, every American whaleman seems to have eaten some part of a whale. . . . The flesh of larger whales— 'whale lean,' 'tenderloin,' and whale steaks—also found its way into whalemen's stomachs as did assorted whale body parts, such as sperm-whale tongues. . . . American whalemen considered sperm whale meat the least desirable of any; by one account, a single sperm whale steak in a lifetime was enough" (278).

20. For a discussion of Stubb as a more astute philosopher than critics are generally disposed to recognize, see Alan Dagovitz, "*Moby-Dick*'s Hidden Philosopher: A Second Look at Stubb," *Philosophy and Literature* 32 (2008): 330–46.

21. Pardes discusses this scene in relation to the folkloric opening of the book of Job (*Melville's Bibles*, 40–43).

22. See Fisch, *Biblical Presence*, ch. 4; Marx, *Shakespeare and the Bible*, ch. 4.

23. As was common at the time, the sphinx here conflates Greek and Egyptian exemplars of the mythical beast. The Greek sphinx of Thebes had the face of a woman, the body of a lion, and the wings of a bird and posed the famous riddle. The giant Egyptian sphinx, over 140 feet in length, had the body of a lion and the head of a man and represented the sun god Ra. Emerson, like Melville, would conflate the two antique sphinxes in his poem "The Sphinx" (1841). For an insightful comparison of each writer's representation of this figure, see E. J. Rose, "Melville, Emerson, and the Sphinx," *New England Quarterly* 36 (1963), 249–58. On Ahab and Oedipus in this scene, see Gerard M. Sweeney, *Melville's Use of Classical Mythology* (Amsterdam: Rodlopi, 1975), 72–77.

24. Walter E. Bezanson, "*Moby-Dick*: Work of Art," in *Moby-Dick; or, The Whale*, ed. Hershel Parker and Harrison Hayford, 2nd ed. (New York: Norton, 2002), 655; Edward Stone, "The Function of the Gams in *Moby-Dick*," *College Literature* 2 (1975): 171–81. John O. Rees, Jr., "Spenserian Analogues in *Moby-Dick*," *ESQ* 18 (1972): 174–78, notes the parallels between "a pattern of omens, exemplary contrasts, and attempts to deflect Ahab from his quest" (175) in several of the gams, and the approach to Acrasia's deadly Bower of Bliss in book 2, canto 12, of Spenser's *Fairie Queene*.

25. See James Dean Young, "The Nine Gams of the *Pequod*," *American Literature* 25 (1954): 449–63.

26. On Christian allegory in "The Town-Ho's Story," see especially Allen C. Austin, "The Other Side of Steelkilt: The Town-Ho's Satire," *American Transcendental Quarterly* 52 (Fall 1981): 237–53; Marcia Reddick, "Something, Somehow like Original Sin: Striking the Uneven Balance in 'The Town-Ho's Story' and *Moby-Dick*," *ATQ* 10 n.s. (1996): 181–89.

27. James, *The Varieties of Religious Experience*, in *Writings, 1902–1910* (New York: Library of America, 1987), 154, 152.

28. See Nathalia Wright, *Melville's Use of the Bible* (Durham, NC: Duke University Press, 1949), 66–69.

29. Stephen J. Stein, *The Shaker Experience in America: A History of the United Society of Believers* (New Haven: Yale University Press, 1992), 185. See also Priscilla J. Brewer, *Shaker Communities, Shaker Lives* (Hanover, NH: University Press of New England, 1986), chs. 7–8.

30. One young woman at Watervliet, for example, reported a five-hour vision during which the Shaker foundress spoke at length of an impending day of judgment. A visitor from a western Shaker settlement reported in a letter on the recent happenings in the East: "Powerful *shakings* & *quakings*, testimonies, promises, threatenings, warnings, predictions, prophecies, *trances*, revelations, visions, songs, and dances" (quoted in Stein, *Shaker Experience*, 171).

31. In his commentary on this passage in relation to the Bible, Robert Alter adduces the lines from Job here as paradoxically both undermining biblical credibility and foreshadowing the destructive power of Moby Dick at the end of the novel. Alter, however, neglects to cite the subsequent allusion to Revelation, thereby rendering this interpretation incomplete. *Pen of Iron: American Prose and the King James Bible* (Princeton, NJ: Princeton University Press, 2010), 66–70.

6—Hubris and Heroism, Mortality and Immortality

1. Aeschylus, *The Oresteian Trilogy*, trans. Philip Vellacott (New York: Penguin, 1956), 55. On the idea of the heroic in the Western literary tradition of the epic, with a chapter on *Moby-Dick*, see George de Forest Lord, *Trials of the Self: Heroic Ordeals in the Epic Tradition* (Hamden, CT: Archon Books, 1983).

2. Donald E. Gowan, *When Man Becomes God: Humanism and Hybris in the Old Testament* (Pittsburgh: Pickwick Press, 1975), 22. Gowan's analysis focuses on Isaiah 14, Ezekiel 28 and 31, and Daniel 4.

3. See Samuel Terrien, "The Omphalos Myth and Hebrew Religion," *Vetus Testamentum* 20 (1970): 315–38; Mircea Eliade, "Symbolism of the 'Centre,'" in *Images and Symbols*, trans. Philip Mairet (Princeton: Princeton University Press, 1991), 27–56.

4. See Newton Arvin, *Herman Melville* (New York: William Sloane, 1950), 150, 190–91; John Seelye, "The Golden Navel: The Cabalism of Ahab's Doubloon," *Nineteenth-Century Fiction* 14 (1960): 350–55; William Dillingham, *Melville's Later Novels* (Athens: University of Georgia Press, 1986), 97–110; Randall Bohrer, "New Witness: Cannibalism and the Microcosm-Macrocosm Cosmology of *Moby-Dick*," *Studies in Romanticism* 22 (1983): 65–91.

5. See John Day, *Yahweh and the Gods and Goddesses of Canaan* (Sheffield, England: Sheffield Academic Press, 2000), 166–84.

6. See Daniel H. Garrison, "Melville's Doubloon and the Shield of Achilles," *Nineteenth-Century Fiction* 26 (1971): 171–84.

7. See Leslie E. Sheldon, "Messianic Power and Satanic Decay: Milton in *Moby-Dick*," in Robin Grey, ed., *Milton and Melville* (Pittsburgh, PA: Duquesne University Press, 2004), 35–39. For an incisive analysis of Ahab's sense of shame in this scene, see Joseph Adamson, *Melville, Shame, and the Evil Eye: A Psychoanalytic Reading* (Albany: State University of New York Press, 1997), 81–83.

8. See Herbert N. Schneider and Homer B. Pettey, "Melville's Ithyphallic God," *Studies in American Fiction* 26 (1998): 193–212.

9. On the possible Gnostic associations here, see Thomas Vargish, "Gnostic Mythos in *Moby-Dick*," *PMLA* 81 (1966): 274.

10. See the discussion of the carpenter in John Evelev, *Tolerable Entertainment: Herman Melville and Literary Professionalism in Antebellum New York* (Amherst: University of Massachusetts Press, 2006), 105–7.

11. For an insightful discussion of these identities, see Mario D'Avanzo, "Ahab, the Greek Pantheon, and Shelley's *Prometheus Unbound*: The Dynamics of Myth in *Moby-Dick*," *Books at Brown* 24 (1971): 19–32. Etsuko Taketani demonstrates that the carpenter is comparable to the mechanical creativity of the Demiurge in Greek mythology; see "*Moby-Dick*: Gnostic Re-writing of History," *ATQ* 8 n.s. (1994): 130–31.

12. Stephen C. Ausband, "The Whale and the Machine: An Approach to *Moby-Dick*," *American Literature* 47 (1975): 197–211 (203).

13. See especially the analysis in Adamson, *Melville, Shame, and the Evil Eye*, ch. 2.

14. On Melville's source for this blasphemous formula in a review article by Francis Palgrave on the history of witchcraft in the *Quarterly Review* (July 1823),

see Geoffrey Sanborn, "The Name of the Devil: Melville's Other 'Extracts' for *Moby-Dick*," *Nineteenth-Century Literature* 47 (1992): 212–35.

15. See Joseph Jones, "Ahab's 'Blood-Quench': Theater or Metallurgy?" *American Literature* 18 (1946): 35–37.

16. On the associations with the Catholic Easter vigil here, see R. H. Winnick, "Melville's 'The Candles' and the Easter Vigil," *Nineteenth-Century Literature* 53 (1998): 171–87.

17. M. O. Percival, *A Reading of* Moby-Dick (Chicago: University of Chicago Press, 1950), 84–95 (94–95). See also the discussion in Peter Bellis, *No Mysteries out of Ourselves: Identity and Textual Form in the Novels of Herman Melville* (Philadelphia: University of Pennsylvania Press, 1990), 66–69.

18. On Ahab and Aeschylus's Prometheus, see William H. Shurr, *Rappaccini's Children: American Writers in a Calvinist World* (Lexington: University of Kentucky Press, 1981), 127–33.

19. On the associations in chapter 119 with Carlyle's *Sartor Resartus*, see James Barbour and Leon Howard, "Carlyle and the Conclusion of *Moby-Dick*," *New England* Quarterly 49 (1976): 215–24. On the scene's relation to Hawthorne's short story, see Larry J. Reynolds, "Melville's Use of 'Young Goodman Brown,'" *American Transcendental Quarterly* 31 (Summer 1976): 12–14.

20. See Lakshmi Mani, *The Apocalyptic Vision in Nineteenth-Century American Fiction: A Study of Cooper, Hawthorne, and Melville* (Washington, DC: University Press of America, 1981), 223.

21. See Vargish, "Gnostic Mythos"; Mukhtar Ali Isani, "Zoroastrianism and the Fire Symbolism in *Moby-Dick*," *American Literature* 44 (1972): 385–97. For other discussions of the fire symbolism in *Moby-Dick*, see Charles C. Walcutt, "The Fire Symbolism in *Moby-Dick*," *Modern Language Notes* 59 (1944): 304–10; Paul W. Miller, "Sun and Fire in Melville's *Moby-Dick*," *Nineteenth-Century Fiction* 13 (1958): 139–44.

22. See Pierre Bayle, *The Dictionary Historical and Critical of Mr. Peter Bayle*, 5 vols. (1734–1738; rpt. New York: Garland, 1984), 5:630–38 (632).

23. On the association of Ahab's "queenly personality" with Jezebel, see Sanford E. Marowitz, "Ahab's 'Queenly Personality' and Melville's Art," *Melville Society Extracts* no. 65 (February 1986): 6–9.

24. Quoted in Isani, "Zoroastrianism," 395.

25. Melville, *Correspondence*, ed. Lynn Horth (Evanston and Chicago: Northwestern University Press and the Newberry Library, 1993), 186. Melville expressed his belief in a "ruthless democracy" in a June 1851 letter to Hawthorne (ibid., 190). On Melville's belief in Hawthorne's metaphysical revolt, see James E. Miller, Jr., "Hawthorne and Melville: No! in Thunder," in *Quests Surd and Absurd: Essays in American Literature* (Chicago: University of Chicago Press, 1967), 186–208.

26. For an informative discussion of the pervasive Gnostic background to "The Candles," see Robert Milder, *Exiled Royalties: Melville and the Life We Imagine* (New York: Oxford University Press, 2006), 203–9.

27. Thornton Y. Booth, "*Moby-Dick*: Standing Up to God," *Nineteenth-Century Fiction* 17 (1962): 39; see also the comments in Percival, *A Reading of* Moby-Dick, 86–88.

28. For an insightful discussion of Starbuck's predicament in the context of

contemporary legal theory contrasting "positive" with "natural" law, see Kathryn Mudgett, "'I Stand Alone upon an Open Sea': Starbuck and the Limits of Positive Law," in John Bryant, Mary K. Bercaw Edwards, and Timothy Marr, eds., *"Ungraspable Phantom": Essays on* Moby-Dick (Kent: Ohio: Kent State University Press, 2006), 132–44. On the shifting direction of the *Pequod* as a symptom of the conflict between Ahab and Starbuck, see Sumner W. D. Scott, "Some Implications of the Typhoon Scenes in *Moby-Dick*," *American Literature* 12 (1940): 91–98.

29. See Edward F. Edinger, *Melville's* Moby-Dick: *A Jungian Commentary* (New York: New Directions, 1978), 131–32.

30. Alexis de Tocqueville, *Democracy in America*, 2 vols. (New York: Vintage, 1945), 2:154.

31. On the idea of the afterlife in Hebrew, Greek, Zoroastrian, and Christian thought, see Alan F. Segal, *Life after Death: A History of the Afterlife in the Religions of the West* (New York: Doubleday, 2004). For an insightful discussion of Ahab's and Ishmael's attitudes on the interrelation of life and death in general philosophical terms, see Robert Zoellner, *The Salt-Sea Mastodon: A Reading of* Moby-Dick (Berkeley and Los Angeles: University of California Press, 1973), ch. 10. On the pervasive death theme in *Moby-Dick*, see James P. Grove, "Melville's Vision of Death: Stepping Away from the 'Snug Sofa,'" *New England Quarterly* 52 (1979): 177–96.

32. See Day, *Yahweh and the Gods and Goddesses of Canaan*, 116–27. As Day notes, "we must assume that the resurrection imagery had its ultimate origin in Canaanite Baal mythology, that it was 'demythologized' in prophets such as Hosea and in the 'Isaiah apocalypse' as a way of referring to Israel's restoration after exile, and then 'remythologized' in the book of Daniel, where it again refers to literal life after death" (ibid., 125).

33. See Mario D'Avanzo, "'A Bower in the Arsacides' and Solomon's Temple," *Arizona Quarterly* 34 (1978): 317–26; Carole Moses, *Melville's Use of Spenser* (New York: Peter Lang, 1989), 90–92. Howard P. Vincent notes that Melville is partly parodying Thomas Beale's account of the articulated whale skeleton of Sir Clifford Constable in Yorkshire, England; see *The Trying-Out of* Moby-Dick (Boston: Houghton Mifflin, 1949), 352–64.

34. Anne Baker proposes that Ishmael's measurement of the whale's skeleton conflates allusions to the prophets Ezekiel, Zechariah, and St. John the Divine, as well as to the account of the visit of the US Exploration Expedition to newly named Bowditch Island in the South Pacific. See "Mapping and Measurement in *Moby-Dick*," in Bryant, Edwards, and Marr, *"Ungraspable Phantom,"* 182–96.

35. See D'Avanzo, "Bower in the Arsacides," 320; James McIntosh, "Melville's Use and Abuse of Goethe: The Weaver Gods in *Faust* and *Moby-Dick*," *Amerikastudien* 25 (1980): 158–73.

36. See, for example, Nicholas Wade, *The Faith Instinct: How Religion Evolved and Why It Endures* (New York: Penguin, 2009); Jesse Bering, *The Belief Instinct: The Psychology of Souls, Destiny, and the Meaning of Life* (New York: Norton, 2011).

37. See V. S. Ramachandran and Sandra Blakeslee, *Phantoms in the Brain: Probing the Mysteries of the Human Mind* (New York: William Morrow, 1998), chs. 2–3, 12. As Ramachandran has discovered, the sensation of a phantom limb arises when nerve cells in the somatosensory cortex, which contains a complete "body map" on the parietal lobes of the brain, are stimulated in the absence of the missing limb.

On the psychological and philosophical consequences of Ahab's dismemberment, see Bellis, *No Mysteries*, 37–44.

38. See Sharon Cameron, *The Corporeal Self: Allegories of the Body in Melville and Hawthorne* (Baltimore: Johns Hopkins University Press, 1981), 60–66.

39. See Jeffrey M. Jeske, "Macbeth, Ahab, and the Unconscious," *American Transcendental Quarterly* 31 (Summer 1976): 8–12.

40. For discussions of the religious and metaphysical meanings of the coffin–life buoy, see Louis Leiter, "Queequeg's Coffin," *Nineteenth-Century Fiction* 13 (1958): 249–54; William Rosenfeld, "Uncertain Faith: Queequeg's Coffin and Melville's Use of the Bible," *Texas Studies in Literature and Language* 7 (1966): 317–27; Gordon V. Boudreau, "Herman Melville, Immortality, St. Paul, and the Resurrection: From *Rose-Bud* to *Billy Budd*," *Christianity and Literature* 52 (2003): 343–64.

41. Grove, "Vision of Death," 185–88.

42. David R. Eastwood suggests that the carpenter's remarks on the conversion of the coffin to life-buoy reflect Melville's own hidden commentary on the improvisational composition of the novel; see "Melville's 'Aristotelian' Carpenter," *Arizona Quarterly* 37 (1981): 310–16.

43. Maria Ujhazy, *Herman Melville's World of Whaling* (Budapest: Akadémiai Kiadó, 1982), 138.

7—Combat and Catastrophe

1. Joseph Fontenrose, *Python: A Study of the Delphic Myth and Its Origins* (Berkeley and Los Angeles: University of California Press, 1959), 9–11, and passim.

2. On Ahab's resemblance to Marlowe's dramatic overreachers Faustus and Tamerlaine, see James S. Leonard, "Ahab as Marlovian Hero," *American Transcendental Quarterly* 62 (December 1986), 47–58.

3. Neil Forsyth, *The Old Enemy: Satan and the Combat Myth* (Princeton: Princeton University Press, 1987).

4. J. Cheryl Exum, *Tragedy and Biblical Narrative: Arrows of the Almighty* (New York: Cambridge University Press, 1992).

5. See Jerome T. Walsh, *Ahab: The Construction of a King* (Collegeville, MN: Liturgical Press, 2006); Lesley Hazleton, *Jezebel: The Untold Story of the Bible's Harlot Queen* (New York: Doubleday, 2007). On Jezebel and Lady Macbeth, see Hazleton, *Jezebel*, 113.

6. Roger L. Cox, *Between Earth and Heaven: Shakespeare, Dostoevsky, and the Meaning of Christian Tragedy* (New York: Holt, Rinehart, and Winston, 1969).

7. See John Kerrigan, *Revenge Tragedy: Aeschylus to Armageddon* (Oxford: Clarendon Press, 1996).

8. On the nineteenth-century exegetical and cultural background to the biblical figure of Rachel, see Ilana Pardes, *Melville's Bibles* (Berkeley and Lost Angeles: University of California Press, 2008), ch. 5. For a perceptive examination of the motif of mourning throughout *Moby-Dick*, see Neal L. Tolchin, *Mourning, Gender, and Creativity in the Art of Herman Melville* (New Haven: Yale University Press, 1988), ch. 6.

9. For an extended discussion of the chapter, see P. Adams Sitney, "Ahab's Name: A Reading of 'The Symphony,'" in *Modern Critical Interpretations: Herman Melville's*

"Moby-Dick," ed. Harold Bloom (New York: Chelsea House, 1986), 131–45. On the larger implications of the absence of the feminine in *Moby-Dick*, see Elizabeth A. Schultz, "The Sentimental Subtext of *Moby-Dick*: Melville's Response to the 'World of Woe,'" *ESQ* 42 (1996): 29–49.

10. For an insightful discussion of Ahab's age, see Sanford E. Marovitz, "Old Man Ahab," in *Artful Thunder: Versions of the Romantic Tradition in American Literature in Honor of Howard P. Vincent*, ed. Robert J. DeMott and Sanford E. Marovitz (Kent, OH: Kent State University Press, 1975), 139–61.

11. See Gerard M. Sweeney, *Melville's Use of Classical Mythology* (Amsterdam: Rodopi, 1975), 48–49.

12. Pierre Bayle, *The Dictionary Historical and Critical of Mr. Peter Bayle*, 5 vols. (1734–1738; rpt. New York: Garland, 1984), 4:517.

13. For a perceptive analysis of the last four chapters of *Moby-Dick* as exhibiting Aristotle's formal components of Greek tragedy, see T. R. Dale, "Melville and Aristotle: The Conclusion of *Moby-Dick* as a Classical Tragedy," *Boston University Studies in English* 3 (1957): 45–50.

14. For another interpretation of the final chase for Moby Dick, see Robert M. Greenberg, *Splintered Worlds: Fragmentation and the Ideal of Diversity in the Work of Emerson, Melville, Whitman, and Dickinson* (Boston: Northwestern University Press, 1993), 101–11. On the apocalyptic symbolism of the end of the novel, see also Michael T. Gilmore, *The Middle Way: Puritanism and Ideology in American Romantic Fiction* (New Brunswick, NJ: Rutgers University Press, 1977), 147–51.

15. See Thomas F. Heffernan, *Stove by a Whale: Owen Chase and the "Essex"* (Middletown, CT: Wesleyan University Press, 1981); Nathaniel Philbrick, *In the Heart of the Sea: The Tragedy of the Whaleship Essex* (New York: Penguin, 2000).

16. Heffernan, *Stove by a Whale*, 26–27.

17. Melville's notes on Pollard in his copy of Owen Chase's *Narrative* can be found in Heffernan, *Stove by a Whale*, 184–209, and Melville, *Moby-Dick*, ed. Hayford, Parker, and Tanselle, 971–95 (987–88). For discussions of Melville's familiarity with the *Essex* disaster and the influence of the disaster and Pollard's character on *Moby-Dick* and later *Clarel*, see Henry F. Pommer, "Herman Melville and the Wake of the *Essex*," *American Literature* 20 (1948): 290–304. Neither Heffernan nor Pommer mentions Pollard's possible association with Job in Melville's mind. Heffernan, *Stove by a Whale*, 160–71, cites Bartleby and the figure of Nehemiah in *Clarel* as influenced by Melville's view of Pollard. In *Moby-Dick; or, The Whale*, ed. Hershel Parker and Harrison Hayford, 2nd ed. (New York: Norton, 2002), 571, in a note to Melville's "Manuscript Notes on Owen Chase," the editors trace Melville's interest in Pollard mainly to the latter's experience of cannibalism.

18. Melville, *Correspondence*, ed. Lynn Horth (Evanston and Chicago: Northwestern University Press and the Newberry Library, 1993), 209.

19. Leo G. Perdue, *Wisdom in Revolt: Metaphorical Theology in the Book of Job* (Sheffield, England: Almond Press, 1991), 230n. Greenberg asserts that, in depicting the beauty and grace of Moby Dick, "Melville is trying to convey through this spell of poetic vision the wonder of the men as they finally approach the object of so much rumored divinity . . . trying to dramatize for the questing consciousness of Ishmael, the story-teller, the mythopoeic ecstasy of arriving at the central symbol of the work—the White Whale himself" (*Splintered Worlds*, 103).

20. On the imagery of Psalms 93 and 98, see Mitchell Dahood, ed., *Psalms II: 51–100* Anchor Bible 17 (Garden City, NY: Doubleday, 1968), 339–44, 364–70. Both psalms celebrated Yahweh's enthronement after subduing the chaotic powers of the sea; both were possibly recited at the Hebrew New Year celebration and share many similarities to Canaanite and Mesopotamian mythologies.

21. John O. Rees, in "Spenserian Analogues in *Moby-Dick*," *ESQ* 18 (1972): 174–78, notes that the paradoxical combination of seductive allure and extreme danger in the novel's final chase scenes draws on the depiction of Guyon's attack on Acrasia and the Bower of Bliss as described in book 2, canto 12, of Spenser's *Fairie Queene*. For other comments on the Spenserian nature of Ahab's quest, see Carole Moses, *Melville's Use of Spenser* (New York: Peter Lang, 1989), ch. 4.

22. Thomas Jefferson noted of the famous Virginia Natural Bridge: "It is impossible for the emotions, arising from the sublime, to be felt beyond what they are here: so beautiful an arch, so elevated, so light, and springing, as it were, up to heaven, the rapture of the Spectator is really indescribable!" *Notes on the State of Virginia*, ed. William Peden (New York: Norton, 1982), 25.

23. See Dale, "Melville and Aristotle," 47–49.

24. Lawrance Thompson notes of Ahab's final words: "In effect, Ahab is saying that even though God may be invulnerable, the defiance behind that spear-hurling gesture is more significant than the futility of the gesture." *Melville's Quarrel with God* (Princeton, NJ: Princeton University Press, 1952), 235.

25. For other comments on Ahab's resemblances to Christ here, see also Gilmore, *Middle Way*, 147–48; Thompson, *Melville's Quarrel*, 235–36.

26. On Spenser's use of Revelation in book 1 (especially canto 12) of the *Faerie Queene*, see John Erskine Hankins, *Source and Meaning in Spenser's Allegory: A Study of "The Faerie Queene"* (Oxford: Oxford University Press, 1971), ch. 5. On Milton's use of Revelation in *Paradise Lost* (especially book 6), see Austin C. Dobbins, *Milton and the Book of Revelation: The Heavenly Cycle* (Tuscaloosa: University of Alabama Press, 1975).

27. See Sheldon, "Messianic Power and Satanic Decay: Milton in *Moby-Dick*," in Robin Grey, ed., *Milton and Melville* (Pittsburgh, PA: Duquesne University Press, 2004), 43–50.

28. See Forsyth, *The Old Enemy*, chs. 6–10.

29. For useful reviews of the White Whale as a polyvalent symbol of God, the devil/evil, and fate, see R. E. Watters, "The Meanings of the White Whale," *University of Toronto Quarterly* 20 (1951): 155–68; Leonard A. Slade, Jr., *Symbolism in Herman Melville's* Moby-Dick: *From the Satanic to the Divine* (Lewiston, NY: Edwin Mellen Press, 1998).

30. James E. Mulqueen, "Ishmael's Voyage: The Cycle of Everyman's Faith," *Arizona Quarterly* 31 (1975): 57–68.

31. T. Walter Herbert asserts that Ishmael's accidental survival serves a metaphysical purpose: "Ishmael is not 'saved' because he has discovered the ground of a triumphant Goodness which overcomes Ahab's triumphant Evil. He is rescued by chance, escaping alone to tell us of a catastrophe in which divine Truth is struck down as a moral standard." Moby-Dick *and Calvinism: A World Dismantled* (New Brunswick, NJ: Rutgers University Press, 1977), 169.

32. See Sweeney, *Classical Mythology*, 97–98.

33. Janet Reno notes of the means of Ishmael's survival: "The coffin, released from the ship by means of a 'cunning' spring, also relates back to the Carpenter, who demonstrated his 'cunning life principle' in converting it." *Ishmael Alone Survived* (Lewisburg, PA: Bucknell University Press, 1990), 158. Reno associates the coffin in *Moby-Dick* with all of the crew of the *Pequod* (ibid., 158–59).

34. For insightful remarks on the images of the wheel and the vortex as cyclical symbols of life in the Epilogue, see H. B. Kulkarni, *Moby-Dick: A Hindu Avatar: A Study of Hindu Myth and Thought in* Moby-Dick (Logon: Utah State University Monograph Series,1970), 48–51. According to Catherine Keller, "The vortex sends Ishmael forward and the reader backward to the novel's beginning. Even as it belies the linearity of time, the trope of the spiraling waters inverts life into death and death into life, ship into coffin and coffin into raft. The sign of the Vortex mirrors the final, all-encompassing vantage point of the book of Job: the divine whirlwind." *The Face of the Deep: A Theology of Becoming* (New York: Routledge, 2003), 143.

35. See Amos 5:14–15; Isa. 7:3, 10:20–22, 11:10–16, 17:5–8, 28:5, 30:17–19, 37:4, 31–32; Joel 2:32, 3:5; Micah 4:6–7, 5:2–8. Dayton Grover Cook notes that "the manner in which Ishmael is rescued suggests that he is the apocalyptic 'remnant' which traditionally enters the new Jerusalem, although it is equally obvious that he will do no such thing." "The Apocalyptic Novel: *Moby-Dick* and *Doctor Faustus*," (PhD dissertation, University of Colorado, 1974), 193–94. Cook goes on to note the resemblance between Ishmael's description of his safety from sharks and sea hawks in the Epilogue and the protomillennial vision of Isaiah 65:25. Gilmore similarly remarks: "It is a common theme in the Old Testament, as well as in the millennial writings of divines such as Edwards, that in the kingdom to come the beasts of prey will be transformed into peaceable creatures. By virtue of his redemption, in short, Ishmael figures as the saving remnant, a concept that the emigrant Puritans were wont to apply to themselves" (*Middle Way*, 149).

36. On the pervasive influence of the Flood myth in Western culture through the early nineteenth century, see Norman Cohn, *Noah's Flood: The Genesis Story in Western Thought* (New Haven: Yale University Press, 1996).

37. As Gilmore notes, "Only Ishmael, the outcast son of Abraham, escapes with his life in the demonic apocalypse that engulfs the *Pequod*. Since the ship itself is said to resemble its prey, and since Ahab is accounted 'a great lord of Leviathans' [129], Ishmael's survival on the third day of the chase may be seen as a symbolic rebirth from the belly of the whale. In this respect he invites comparison to Jonah, and he may be regarded as a type of the Savior himself, a detail which imparts special meaning to his eventual rescue by the *Rachel*. For Melville's objective in *Moby-Dick* is nothing less than to rewrite the covenant that God was presumed to have made with the American people as the heirs of the biblical Hebrews" (*Middle Way*, 148).

38. Frank Kermode, *The Sense of an Ending: Studies in the Theory of Fiction* (New York: Oxford University Press, 1967), 82. Douglas Robinson notes of the conclusion of *Moby-Dick*: "The end of the *Pequod* is an image of the end of the world—but it is a cautionary image, an allegorical image that displaces apocalyptic images in the *world* metonymically into the iconic mediations of the *word*." *American Apocalypses: The Image of the End of the World in American Literature* (Baltimore: Johns Hopkins University Press, 1985), 162. For Milder, on the other hand, "The sinking of the *Pequod* is Melville's rendering of a cultural apocalypse, represented by the death

and birth of an avatar, or center of cultural energy, or 'god.' The old god (Ahab) had defined himself by his relation to God; the new god (Ishmael) is humanity itself as it assumes the task of reconstituting social and spiritual life in the wreckage of the Christian promise." *Exiled Royalties: Melville and the Life We Imagine* (New York: Oxford University Press, 2006), 95.

Epilogue

1. Alexis de Tocqueville, *Democracy in America*, 2 vols. (New York: Vintage, 1945), 2:21.

2. See Forrer, *Theodicies in Conflict: A Dilemma in Puritan Ethics and Nineteenth-Century Literature* (Westport, CT: Greenwood Press, 1986), ch. 10.

3. Susan Neiman, *Evil in Modern Thought: An Alternative History of Philosophy* (Princeton, NJ: Princeton University Press, 2002), 114.

4. Immanuel Kant, "On the Miscarriage of All Philosophical Trials in Theodicy," in *Religion and Rational Theology*, trans. Allen W. Wood and George di Giovanni (New York: Cambridge University Press, 1996), 21–37 (30, 33).

5. Melville, *Correspondence*, ed. Lynn Horth (Evanston and Chicago: Northwestern University Press and the Newberry Library, 1993), 122, 149.

6. Brian Higgins and Hershel Parker, *Herman Melville: The Contemporary Reviews* (New York: Cambridge University Press, 1995), 385, 386. For a full record of the contemporary reception of *Moby-Dick*, see ibid., 353–415.

7. "Historical Note," in *Moby-Dick, or The Whale*, ed. Harrison Hayford, Hershel Parker, and G. Thomas Tanselle (Evanston and Chicago: Northwestern University and the Newberry Library, 1988), 691–92.

8. Melville, *Correspondence*, 212. The "lamb" referred to here is, of course, Christ, whose blood was sacrificed "as of a lamb without blemish and without spot" (1 Peter 1:19).

9. See Hershel Parker, "Damned by Dollars: *Moby-Dick* and the Price of Genius," in *Moby-Dick; or, The Whale*, ed. Hershel Parker and Harrison Hayford, 2nd ed. (New York: Norton, 2002), 713–24. For a more extensive account of Melville's troubled life in the early and mid 1850s, see Parker, *Herman Melville: A Biography, Vol. 2, 1851–1891* (Baltimore: Johns Hopkins University Press, 2002) chs. 1–13.

10. M. H. Abrams, *Natural Supernaturalism: Tradition and Revolution in Romantic Literature* (New York: Norton, 1971).

11. Morton Paley, *Apocalypse and Millennium in English Romantic Poetry* (Oxford: Clarendon Press, 1999).

12. See Grace Lee Farrell, "*Pym* and *Moby-Dick*: Essential Connections," *American Transcendental Quarterly* 37 (Winter 1978): 73–86.

13. Fiona J. Stafford, *The Last of the Race: The Growth of a Myth from Milton to Darwin* (Oxford: Clarendon Press, 1994).

14. See Charles Coulston Gillispie, *Genesis and Geology: A Study of the Relations of Scientific Thought, Natural Theology, and Social Opinion in Great Britain* (Cambridge, MA: Harvard University Press, 1951).

15. See, for example, Lakshmi Mani, *The Apocalyptic Vision in Nineteenth-Century*

American Fiction: Cooper, Hawthorne, and Melville (Washington, DC: University Press of America, 1981).

16. See Jonathan A. Cook, "New Heavens, 'Poor Old Earth': Satirical Apocalypse in Hawthorne's *Mosses from an Old Manse*," *ESQ* 39 (1993): 209–51. For an annotated edition of Melville's copy of Hawthorne's *Mosses from an Old Manse*, see Cook, "Introduction to Melville's Marginalia in Nathaniel Hawthorne's *Mosses from an Old Manse*," *Melville's Marginalia Online*, http://melvillesmarginalia.org.

17. See Jonathan A. Cook, *Satirical Apocalypse: An Anatomy of Melville's* The Confidence-Man (Westport, CT: Greenwood Press, 1996).

18. On *The Idiot* and the book of Revelation, see Robert Hollander, "The Apocalyptic Framework of Dostoevsky's *The Idiot*," *Mosaic* 7 (1974): 123–39. On *The Brothers Karamazov* and Job, see Predag Cicovacki, "The Trial of Man and the Trial of God: Job and Dostoevsky's 'Grand Inquisitor,'" in *Destined for Evil? The Twentieth-Century Responses*, ed. Predag Cicovacki (Rochester, NY: University of Rochester Press, 2005). For an insightful comparative study of Melville, Dostoevsky, and other modern "existential" writers, see Maurice Friedman, *Problematic Rebels: Melville, Dostoevsky, Kafka, Camus* (Chicago: University of Chicago Press, 1970).

19. Herbert, "Calvinist Earthquake: *Moby-Dick* and Religious Tradition," in Richard H. Brodhead, ed., *New Essays on* Moby-Dick (New York: Cambridge University Press, 1986), 115.

Selected Bibliography of
Melville and *Moby-Dick* Studies

Ackerman, Alan L. *The Portable Theater: American Literature and the Nineteenth-Century Stage*. Baltimore: Johns Hopkins University Press, 1999.

Adams, Michael Vannoy. "Ahab's Jonah and the Whale Complex: The Fish Archetype in *Moby-Dick*." *ESQ* 28 (1982): 167–82.

Adamson, Joseph. *Melville, Shame, and the Evil Eye: A Psychoanalytic Reading*. Albany: State University of New York Press, 1997.

Alter, Robert. *Pen of Iron: American Prose and the King James Bible*. Princeton, NJ: Princeton University Press, 2010.

Andrews, Norwood, Jr. *Melville's Camões*. Bonn, Germany: Bouvier, 1989.

Andriano, Joseph. "Brother to Dragons: Race and Evolution in *Moby-Dick*." *ATQ* 10 n.s. (1996): 141–53.

Armstrong, Philip. *What Animals Mean in the Fiction of Modernity*. New York: Routledge, 2008.

Arvin, Newton. *Herman Melville*. New York: William Sloane, 1950.

Aspiz, Harold. "Phrenologizing the Whale." *Nineteenth-Century Fiction* 23 (1968): 18–27.

Ausband, Stephen. "The Whale and the Machine: An Approach to *Moby-Dick*." *American Literature* 47 (1975): 197–211.

Austin, Allen C. "The Other Side of Steelkilt: The Town-Ho's Satire." *American Transcendental Quarterly* 52 (Fall 1981): 237–53.

Baird, James. *Ishmael*. Baltimore: Johns Hopkins Press, 1956.

Baker, Anne. "Mapping and Measurement in *Moby-Dick*." In Bryant, Edwards, and Marr, "*Ungraspable Phantom*," 182–96.

Baldick, Chris. *In Frankenstein's Shadow: Myth, Monstrosity, and Nineteenth-Century Writing*. Oxford: Clarendon Press, 1987.

Barbour, James. "'All My Books Are Botches': Melville's Struggle with *The Whale*." In *Writing the American Classics*, edited by James Barbour and Tom Quirk. Chapel Hill: University of North Carolina Press, 1990.

Barbour, James, and Leon Howard. "Carlyle and the Conclusion of *Moby-Dick*." *New England Quarterly* 49 (1976): 215–24.

Barnum, Jill, Wyn Kelley, and Christopher Sten, eds. *"Whole Oceans Away": Melville and the Pacific*. Kent, OH: Kent State University Press, 2007.

Battenfield, David H. "The Source for the Hymn in *Moby-Dick*." *American Literature* 27 (1955): 393–96. Rpt. in *Moby-Dick*, ed. Parker and Hayford, 574–77.

Bell, Millicent. "Pierre Bayle and *Moby-Dick*." *PMLA* 66 (1951): 626–48.

Bellis, Peter J. *No Mysteries out of Ourselves: Identity and Textual Form in the Novels of Herman Melville.* Philadelphia: University of Pennsylvania Press, 1990.

Bender, Bert. "The Allegory of the Whale's Head." *Renascence* 32 (1980): 152–66.

Bersani, Leo. *The Culture of Redemption.* Cambridge, MA: Harvard University Press, 1990.

Betts, William W. "*Moby-Dick*: Melville's *Faust.*" *Lock Haven Review* 1 (1959): 31–44.

Bewley, Marius. *Eccentric Design: Form in the Classic American Novel.* New York: Columbia University Press, 1959.

Bezanson, Walter E. "*Moby-Dick*: Work of Art." In Tyrus Hillway and Luther S. Mansfield, eds., *Moby-Dick Centennial Essays.* Dallas: Southern Methodist University Press, 1953. Rpt. in *Moby-Dick*, ed. Parker and Hayford, 641–57.

Bidney, Martin. "Character Creation as Intensive 'Reading': Ahab and the Sea in *Faust* and *Moby-Dick.*" *ESQ* 36 (1990): 295–313.

Birk, John F. *Tracing the Round: The Astrological Framework of* Moby-Dick. Xlibris, 2004.

Bluestein, Gene. "Ahab's Sin." *Arizona Quarterly* 41 (1985): 101–16.

Bode, Rita. "'Suckled by the Sea': The Maternal in *Moby-Dick.*" In *Melville and Women*, edited by Elizabeth A. Schultz and Haskell Springer, 181–98. Kent, OH: Kent State University Press, 2006.

Bohrer, Randall. "Melville's New Witness: Cannibalism and the Microcosm-Macrocosm Cosmology of *Moby-Dick.*" *Studies in Romanticism* 22 (1983): 65–91.

Booth, Thornton Y. "*Moby-Dick*: Standing Up to God." *Nineteenth-Century Fiction* 17 (1962): 33–43.

Boudreau, Gordon V. "Herman Melville, Immortality, St. Paul, and the Resurrection: From *Rose-Bud* to *Billy Budd.*" *Christianity and Literature* 52 (2003): 343–64.

Braswell, William. *Melville's Religious Thought.* Durham, NC: Duke University Press, 1943.

Brodhead, Richard H. *Hawthorne, Melville, and the Novel.* Chicago: University of Chicago Press, 1976.

———, ed. *New Essays on* Moby-Dick. New York: Cambridge University Press, 1986.

Bryant, John, ed. *A Companion to Melville Studies.* Westport, CT: Greenwood, 1986.

Bryant, John, Mary K. Bercaw Edwards, and Timothy Marr, eds. "*Ungraspable Phantom*": *Essays on* Moby-Dick. Kent, OH: Kent State University Press, 2006.

Burbick, Joan. *Healing the Republic: The Language of Health and the Culture of Nationalism in Nineteenth-Century America.* New York: Cambridge University Press, 1994.

Cambon, Glauco. "Ishmael and the Problem of Formal Discontinuities in *Moby-Dick.*" *Modern Language Notes* 76 (1961): 516–23.

Cameron, Sharon. *The Corporeal Self: Allegories of the Body in Melville and Hawthorne.* Baltimore: Johns Hopkins University Press, 1981.

Castronovo, Russ. *Fathering the Nation: American Genealogies of Slavery and Freedom.* Berkeley and Los Angeles: University of California Press, 1995.

Chai, Leon. *The Romantic Foundations of the American Renaissance.* Ithaca: Cornell University Press, 1987.

Chase, Richard. *The American Novel and Its Tradition.* Garden City, NY: Doubleday, 1957.

———. *Herman Melville: A Critical Study.* New York: Macmillan, 1949.

Clubb, Merrel D., Jr. "The Second Personal Pronoun in *Moby-Dick*." *American Speech* 35 (1960): 252–60.

Coffler, Gail H. *Melville's Allusions to Religion: A Comprehensive Index and Glossary.* Westport, CT: Praeger, 2004.

Cook, Charles H., Jr. "Ahab's 'Intolerable Allegory.'" *Boston University Studies in English* 1 (1955–1956): 45–52. Rpt. in *Discussions of* Moby-Dick, ed. Milton Stern, 60–65. Boston: Heath, 1960.

Cook, Dayton Grover. "The Apocalyptic Novel: *Moby-Dick* and *Doctor Faustus*." PhD diss., University of Colorado, 1974.

Cook, Jonathan A. "Introduction to Melville's Marginalia in Nathaniel Hawthorne's *Mosses from an Old Manse*." In *Melville's Marginalia Online*, edited by Steven Olsen-Smith, Peter Norberg, and Dennis C. Marnon. http://melvillesmarginalia.org.

———. "Melville's *Mosses* Review and the Proclamation of Hawthorne as America's Literary Messiah." *Leviathan* 10 (October 2008): 62–70.

———. "*Moby-Dick*, Myth, and Classical Moralism: Bulkington as Hercules." *Leviathan* 5 (March 2003): 15–28.

———. Review of Ilana Pardes, *Melville's Bibles*. *Christianity and Literature* 59 (Autumn 2009): 143–47.

———. *Satirical Apocalypse: An Anatomy of Melville's* The Confidence-Man. Westport, CT: Greenwood Press, 1996.

Cotkin, George. *Dive Deeper: Journeys with* Moby-Dick. New York: Oxford University Press, 2012.

Coviello, Peter. *Intimacy in America: Dreams of Affiliation in Antebellum Literature.* Minneapolis: University of Minnesota Press, 2005.

Cowan, Bainard. *Exiled Waters:* Moby-Dick *and the Crisis of Allegory*. Baton Rouge: Louisiana State University Press, 1982.

Cowan, S. A. "In Praise of Self-Reliance: The Role of Bulkington in *Moby-Dick*." *American Literature* 38 (1967): 547–56.

Dagovitz, Alan. "*Moby-Dick*'s Hidden Philosopher: A Second Look at Stubb." *Philosophy and Literature* 32 (2008): 330–46.

Dale, T. R. "Melville and Aristotle: The Conclusion of *Moby-Dick* as a Classical Tragedy." *Boston University Studies in English* 3 (1957): 45–50.

D'Avanzo, Mario L. "Ahab, the Grecian Pantheon, and Shelley's *Prometheus Bound*: The Dynamics of Myth in *Moby-Dick*." *Books at Brown* 24 (1971): 19–44.

———. "'A Bower in the Arsacides' and Solomon's Temple." *Arizona Quarterly* 34 (1978): 317–26.

———. "'The Cassock' and Carlyle's 'Church-Clothes.'" *ESQ* 50 supplement (First Quarter 1968): 74–76.

Davis, Clark. *After the Whale: Melville in the Wake of* Moby-Dick. Tuscaloosa: University of Alabama Press, 1995.

Delbanco, Andrew. *Melville: His World and Work*. New York: Knopf, 2005.

Dillingham, William B. *Melville's Later Novels*. Athens: University of Georgia Press, 1986.

Dowling, David. *Chasing the White Whale: The* Moby-Dick *Marathon; or, What Melville Means Today*. Iowa City: University of Iowa Press, 2010.

Dreyfus, Hubert, and Sean Dorrance Kelly. *All Things Shining: Reading the Western Classics to Find Meaning in a Secular Age*. New York: Free Press, 2011.

Duban, James. "'Level Dead Reckoning': Father Mapple, Goethe, and Ahab." *Leviathan* 11 (March 2009): 74–79.

———. *Melville's Major Fiction: Politics, Theology, and Imagination.* DeKalb: Northern Illinois University Press, 1983.

Duquette, Elizabeth. "Speculative Cetology: Figuring Philosophy in *Moby-Dick.*" *ESQ* 47 (2001): 33–57.

Durer, Christopher S. *Herman Melville: Romantic and Prophet. A Study of His Romantic Sensibility and His Relationship to European Romantics.* Fredericton, NB, Canada: York Press, 1996.

Eastwood, David R. "Melville's 'Aristotelian' Carpenter." *Arizona Quarterly* 37 (1981): 310–16.

Edinger, Edward F. *Melville's* Moby-Dick: *A Jungian Commentary.* New York: New Directions, 1978.

Edwards, Mary K. Bercaw. *Cannibal Old Me: Spoken Sources in Melville's Early Work.* Kent, OH: Kent State University Press, 2009.

Eldridge, Herbert G. "'Careful Disorder': The Structure of *Moby-Dick.*" *American Literature* 39 (1967): 145–62.

Ellen, Sister Mary. "Duplicate Imagery in *Moby-Dick.*" *Modern Fiction Studies* 8 (1962–1963): 252–64.

Elliott, Emory. "'Wandering To-and-Fro': Melville and Religion." In *A Historical Guide to Herman Melville,* edited by Giles Gunn, 167–204. New York: Oxford University Press, 2005.

Ellis, Reuben J. "The Interiority of the Weave: Raising the Shed in Melville's Incomplete 'Mat-Maker.'" *ATQ* 2 n.s. (1988): 111–24.

Evelev, John. *Tolerable Entertainment: Herman Melville and Literary Professionalism in Antebellum New York.* Amherst: University of Massachusetts Press, 2006.

Fabricant, Carole. "*Tristram Shandy* and *Moby-Dick*: A Cock and Bull Story and a Tale of a Tub." *Journal of Narrative Technique* 7 (1977): 57–69.

Farrell, Grace Lee. "*Pym* and *Moby-Dick*: Essential Connections." *American Transcendental Quarterly* 37 (Winter 1978): 73–86.

Fassano, Anthony. "The Power of Ahab's Speech." *Milton and Melville Review.* Vol. 1, No. 2. www.miltonandmelville.org.

Finkelstein, Dorothee Metlitsky. *Melville's Orienda.* New Haven: Yale University Press, 1961.

Flory, Wendy Stallard. "Melville, *Moby-Dick,* and the Depressive Mind: Queequeg, Starbuck, Stubb, and Flask as Symbolic Characters." In Bryant, Edwards, and Marr, "*Ungraspable Phantom,*" 81–99.

Foley, Brian. "Herman Melville and the Example of Sir Thomas Browne." *Modern Philology* 81 (1984): 265–77.

Forrer, Richard. *Theodicies in Conflict: A Dilemma in Puritan Ethics and Nineteenth-Century American Literature.* Westport, CT: Greenwood Press, 1986.

Frank, Stuart M. *Herman Melville's Picture Gallery: Sources and Types of the "Pictorial" Chapters of* Moby-Dick. Fairhaven, MA: Edward J. Lefkowicz, 1986.

Franklin, H. Bruce. *The Wake of the Gods: Melville's Mythology.* Stanford, CA: Stanford University Press, 1963.

Fredricks, Nancy. *Melville's Art of Democracy.* Athens: University of Georgia Press, 1995.

Friedman, Maurice. *Problematic Rebel: Melville, Dostoevsky, Kafka, Camus.* Chicago: University of Chicago Press, 1970.

Friedrich, Gerhard. *In Pursuit of Moby-Dick: Melville's Image of Man.* Wallingford, PA: Pendle Hill, 1958.

Gaines, Kendra H. "A Consideration of an Additional Source for Melville's *Moby-Dick.*" *Melville Society Extracts* no. 29 (January 1977): 6–12.

Gallagher, Susan VanZanten. "The Prophetic Narrator of *Moby-Dick.*" *Christianity and Literature* 36 (1987): 11–25.

Garrison, Daniel H. "Melville's Doubloon and the Shield of Achilles." *Nineteenth-Century Fiction* 26 (1971): 171–84.

Geist, Stanley. *Herman Melville: The Tragic Vision and the Heroic Ideal.* Cambridge, MA: Harvard University Press, 1939.

Gilmore, Michael T. *The Middle Way: Puritanism and Ideology in American Romantic Fiction.* New Brunswick, NJ: Rutgers University Press, 1977.

Glenn, Barbara. "Melville and the Sublime in *Moby-Dick.*" *American Literature* 48 (1976): 165–82.

Golemba, Henry L. "The Shape of *Moby-Dick.*" *Studies in the Novel* 5 (1973): 197–210.

Gravil, Richard. *Romantic Dialogues: Anglo-American Continuities, 1776–1862.* New York: St. Martin's Press, 2000.

Greenberg, Robert M. *Splintered Worlds: Fragmentation and the Ideal of Diversity in the Work of Emerson, Melville, Whitman, and Dickinson.* Boston: Northeastern University Press, 1993.

Grejda, Edward S. *The Common Continent of Man: Racial Equality in the Writings of Herman Melville.* Port Washington, NY: Kennikat Press, 1974.

Grenberg, Bruce L. *Some Other World to Find: Quest and Negation in the Works of Herman Melville.* Urbana: University of Illinois Press, 1989.

Grey, Robin, ed. *Melville and Milton.* Pittsburgh, PA: Duquesne University Press, 2004.

Grove, James P. "Melville's Vision of Death in *Moby-Dick*: Stepping away from the 'Snug Sofa.'" *New England Quarterly* 52 (1979): 177–96.

Halverson, John. "The Shadow in *Moby-Dick.*" *American Quarterly* 15 (1963): 436–46.

Hartstein, Arnold M. "Myth and History in *Moby-Dick.*" *American Transcendental Quarterly* 57 (July 1985): 31–43.

Hayes, Kevin J. *Melville's Folk Roots.* Kent, OH: Kent State University Press, 1999.

Hayford, Harrison. *Melville's Prisoners.* Evanston, IL: Northwestern University Press, 2003.

Heflin, Wilson. *Herman Melville's Whaling Years.* Edited by Mary K. Bercaw Edwards and Thomas Farel Heffernan. Nashville: Vanderbilt University Press, 2004.

Heidmann, Mark. "The Markings in Herman Melville's Bibles." In *Studies in the American Renaissance, 1990,* edited by Joel Myerson, 341–98. Charlottesville: University Press of Virginia, 1990.

———. "Melville and the Bible: Leading Themes in the Marginalia and the Major Fiction, 1850–1856." PhD dissertation, Yale University, 1979.

Heimert, Alan. "*Moby-Dick* and American Political Symbolism." *American Quarterly* 15 (1963): 498–534.

Herbert, T. Walter, Jr. "Calvinist Earthquake: *Moby-Dick* and Religious Tradition." In Brodhead, *New Essays,* 117–26.

———. "Homosexuality and Spiritual Aspiration in *Moby-Dick.*" *Canadian Review of American Studies* 6 (1975): 50–58.

———. Moby-Dick *and Calvinism: A World Dismantled.* New Brunswick, NJ: Rutgers University Press, 1977.

Higgins, Brian, and Hershel Parker, eds. *Critical Essays on Herman Melville's* Moby-Dick. New York: G. K. Hall, 1992.

———. *Herman Melville: The Contemporary Reviews.* New York: Cambridge University Press, 1995.

Hirsch, David H. "*Hamlet, Moby-Dick,* and Passional Thinking." In *Shakespeare: Aspects of Influence,* edited by G. B. Evans. Cambridge, MA: Harvard University Press, 1976.

———. *Reality and Idea in the Early American Novel.* The Hague: Mouton, 1971.

Hoffman, Daniel E. *Form and Fable in American Fiction.* New York: Oxford University Press, 1961.

Hoffman, Michael J. "The Anti-transcendentalism of *Moby-Dick.*" *Georgia Review* 33 (1969): 3–16.

Holman, C. Hugh. "The Reconciliation of Ishmael: *Moby-Dick* and the Book of Job." *South Atlantic Quarterly* 57 (1958): 477–90.

Horsford, Howard C. "The Design of the Argument in *Moby-Dick.*" *Modern Fiction Studies* 8 (1962): 233–51.

Howard, Leon. "Melville and the American Tragic Hero." In *Four Makers of the American Mind: Emerson, Thoreau, Whitman, and Melville,* edited by Thomas Edward Crawley, 65–82. Durham, NC: Duke University Press, 1976.

Husni, Khalil. "The Whiteness of the Whale: A Survey of Interpretations, 1851–1970." *College Language Association Journal* 20 (1976): 210–21.

Hutchins, Zachary. "*Moby-Dick* as Third Testament: A Novel 'Not Come to Destroy but to Fulfill' the Bible." *Leviathan* 13 (June 2011): 18–37.

Isani, Mukhtar Ali. "The Naming of Fedallah in *Moby-Dick.*" *American Literature* 40 (1968): 380–85.

———. "Zoroastrianism and the Fire Symbolism in *Moby-Dick.*" *American Literature* 44 (1972): 385–97.

Jeske, Jeffrey M. "Macbeth, Ahab, and the Unconscious." *American Transcendental Quarterly* 31 (Summer 1976): 8–12.

Jones, Joseph. "Ahab's 'Blood-Quench': Theater or Metallurgy?" *American Literature* 18 (1946): 35–37.

Joseph, Vasanth. "Some Biblical Nuances in *Moby-Dick.*" *Osmania Journal of English Studies* (India) 8 (1971): 69–77.

Karcher, Carolyn. *Shadow over the Promised Land: Slavery, Race, and Violence in Melville's America.* Baton Rouge: Louisiana State University Press, 1980.

Keller, Catherine. *Face of the Deep: A Theology of Becoming.* New York: Routledge, 2003.

Ketterer, David. "The Time-Break Structure in *Moby-Dick.*" *Canadian Review of American Studies* 19 (1988): 299–323.

Kirkham, E. Bruce. "The Iron Crown of Lombardy." *ESQ* 58 (1970): 127–29.

Kreitzer, L. Joseph. *The Old Testament in Fiction and Film.* Sheffield, England: Sheffield Academic Press, 1994.

Kulkarni, H. B. *Moby-Dick: A Hindu Avatar: A Study of Hindu Myth and Thought in* Moby-Dick. Logan: Utah State University Press, 1970.

Lee, A. Robert. "*Moby-Dick:* The Tale and the Teller." In *New Perspectives on Melville,* edited by Faith Pullin, 86–127. Kent, OH: Kent State University Press, 1978.

———. "*Moby-Dick* as Anatomy." In *Herman Melville: Reassessments,* edited by Robert A. Lee, ch. 4. Totowa, NJ: Barnes and Noble, 1984.

Lee, Maurice S. *Uncertain Chances: Science, Skepticism, and Belief in Nineteenth-*

Century American Literature. New York: Oxford University Press, 2012.

Leiter, Louis. "Queequeg's Coffin." *Nineteenth-Century Fiction* 13 (1958): 249–54.

Leonard, David Charles. "The Cartesian Vortex in *Moby-Dick*." *American Literature* 51 (1979): 105–10.

Leonard, James S. "Melville's Ahab as Marlovian Hero." *American Transcendental Quarterly* 62 (December 1986): 47–58.

Levin, Michael. "Ahab as Socratic Philosopher: The Myth of the Cave Inverted." *American Transcendental Quarterly* 41 (Winter 1979): 61–73.

Lord, George de Forest. *Trials of the Self: Heroic Ordeals in the Epic Tradition.* Hamden, CT: Archon Books, 1983.

Lorentzen, Jamie. *Sober Cannibals, Drunken Christians: Melville, Kierkegaard, and Tragic Optimism in Polarized Worlds.* Macon, GA: Mercer University Press, 2010.

Lukacs, Paul. "The Abandonment of Time and Place: History and Narrative, Metaphysics and Exposition in *Moby-Dick*." *CLIO* 20 (1991): 139–55.

Mancini, Matthew. "Melville's 'Descartian Vortices.'" *ESQ* 36 (1990): 315–27.

Mani, Lakshmi. *The Apocalyptic Vision in Nineteenth-Century American Fiction: A Study of Cooper, Hawthorne, and Melville.* Washington, DC: University Press of America, 1981.

Mariani, Giorgio. "'Chiefly Known by His Rod': The Book of Jonah, Mapple's Sermon, and Scapegoating." In Bryant, Edwards, and Marr, *"Ungraspable Phantom,"* 37–57.

Markels, Julian. *Melville and the Politics of Identity: From* King Lear *to* Moby-Dick. Urbana: University of Illinois Press, 1993.

Marovitz, Sanford E. "Ahab's 'Queenly Personality' and Melville's Art." *Melville Society Extracts* 65 (February 1986): 6–9.

———. "Correspondences: Paranoiac Lexicographers and Melvillean Heroes." In Bryant, Edwards, and Marr, *"Ungraspable Phantom,"* 100–113.

———. "More Chartless Voyaging: Melville and Adler at Sea." In *Studies in the American Renaissance, 1986,* edited by Joel Myerson, 373–84. Charlottesville: University Press of Virginia, 1986.

———. "Old Man Ahab." In *Artful Thunder: Versions of the Romantic Tradition in American Literature in Honor of Howard P. Vincent,* edited by Robert J. DeMott and Sanford E. Marovitz, 138–61. Kent, OH: Kent State University Press, 1975.

Martin, Robert K. *Hero, Captain, Stranger: Male Friendship, Social Critique, and Literary Form in the Sea Novels of Herman Melville.* Chapel Hill: University of North Carolina Press, 1986.

Matteson, John T. "The Little Lower Layer: Anxiety and the Courage to Be in *Moby-Dick*." *Harvard Theological Review* 81 (1988): 97–116.

Matthiessen, F. O. *American Renaissance: Art and Expression in the Age of Emerson and Whitman.* New York: Oxford University Press, 1941.

McCarthy, Paul. *"The Twisted Mind": Madness in Herman Melville's Fiction.* Iowa City: University of Iowa Press, 1990.

McElroy, John Harmon. "The Dating of the Action in *Moby-Dick*." *Papers on Language and Literature* 13 (1977): 420–23.

McIntosh, James. "Melville's Use and Abuse of Goethe: The Weaver Gods in *Faust* and *Moby-Dick*." *Amerikastudien* 25 (1980): 158–73.

McLoughlin, Michael. *Dead Letters to the New World: Melville, Emerson, and American Transcendentalism.* New York: Routledge, 2003.

McMillan, Grant Edgar. "Nature's Dark Side: Herman Melville and the Problem of Evil." PhD dissertation, Syracuse University, 1973.

McSweeney, Kerry. Moby-Dick: *Ishmael's Mighty Book*. Boston: Twayne, 1986.

McWilliams, John P., Jr. *The American Epic: Transforming a Genre, 1770–1860*. New York: Cambridge University Press, 1989.

Meldrum, Barbara. "Structure in *Moby-Dick*: The Whale Killings and Ishmael's Quest." *ESQ* 21 (1975): 162–68.

Melville, Herman. *Correspondence*. Edited by Lynn Horth. Evanston and Chicago: Northwestern University Press and the Newberry Library, 1993.

———. *Moby-Dick; or, The Whale*. Edited by Harrison Hayford, Hershel Parker, and G. Thomas Tanselle. Evanston and Chicago: Northwestern University Press and the Newberry Library, 1988.

———. *Moby-Dick; or, The Whale*. Edited by Luther S. Mansfield and Howard P. Vincent. New York: Hendricks House, 1952.

———. *Moby-Dick; or, The Whale*. Edited by Hershel Parker and Harrison Hayford. 2nd ed. New York: Norton, 2002.

———. The Piazza Tales *and Other Prose Pieces, 1839–1860*. Edited by Harrison Hayford, Alma A. MacDougall, and G. Thomas Tanselle. Evanston and Chicago: Northwestern University Press and the Newberry Library, 1987.

Michael, John. *Identity and the Failure of America: From Thomas Jefferson to the War on Terror*. Minneapolis: University of Minnesota Press, 2008.

Milder, Robert. *Exiled Royalties: Melville and the Life We Imagine*. New York: Oxford University Press, 2006.

Miller, James E., Jr. *Quests Surd and Absurd: Essays in American Literature*. Chicago: University of Chicago Press, 1967.

Miller, Paul W. "Sun and Fire in Melville's *Moby-Dick*." *Nineteenth-Century Fiction* 13 (1958): 139–44.

Moore, Richard S. *That Cunning Alphabet: Melville's Aesthetics of Nature*. Amsterdam: Rodopi, 1982.

Morse, David. *American Romanticism, Vol. 2; From Melville to James*. Houndmills, Basingstoke: Macmillan, 1987.

Moses, Carole. *Melville's Use of Spenser*. New York: Peter Lang, 1989.

Mudgett, Kathryn. "'I Stand Alone upon an Open Sea': Starbuck and the Limits of Positive Law." In Bryant, Edwards, and Marr, *"Ungraspable Phantom,"* 132–44.

Mulqueen, James E. "Ishmael's Voyage: The Cycle of Everyman's Faith." *Arizona Quarterly* 31 (1975): 57–68.

Mushabac, Jane. *Melville's Humor: A Critical Study*. Hamden, CT: Archon Books, 1981.

New, Elisa. "Bible Leaves! Bible Leaves! Hellenism and Hebraism in Melville's *Moby-Dick*." *Poetics Today* 19 (1998): 281–303.

Norsworthy, Scott. "Melville's Notes from Thomas Roscoe's *The German Novelists*." *Leviathan* 10 (October 2008): 7–37.

Olsen-Smith, Steven. "The Hymn in *Moby-Dick*: Melville's Adaptation of 'Psalm 18.'" *Leviathan* 5 (March 2003): 29–47.

———. "Melville's Copy of Thomas Beale's *The Natural History of the Sperm Whale* and the Composition of *Moby-Dick*." *Harvard Library Bulletin* 21 (Fall 2010): 1–77.

Otter, Samuel. *Melville's Anatomies*. Berkeley and Los Angeles: University of California

Press, 1999.

Pardes, Ilana. *Melville's Bibles.* Berkeley and Los Angeles: University of California Press, 2008.

Parker, Hershel. "Damned by Dollars: *Moby-Dick* and the Price of Genius." In *Moby-Dick,* ed. Parker and Hayford, 713–24.

———. *Herman Melville: A Biography.* Vol. 1, *1819–1851.* Baltimore: Johns Hopkins University Press, 1996.

———. *Herman Melville: A Biography.* Vol. 2, *1851–1891.* Baltimore: Johns Hopkins University Press, 2002.

———. "Melville and Domesticity." In *Critical Essays on Herman's Melville's* Moby-Dick, edited by Brian J. Higgins and Hershel Parker, 545–62. New York: G. K. Hall, 1992.

Peach, Linden. *British Influence on the Birth of American Literature.* New York: St. Martin's Press, 1982.

Percival, M.O. *A Reading of* Moby-Dick. Chicago: University of Chicago Press, 1950.

Person, Leland S., Jr. "Melville's Cassock: Putting on Masculinity in *Moby-Dick.*" *ESQ* 40 (1994): 1–26.

Philbrick, Nathaniel. *Why Read Moby-Dick?* New York: Viking, 2011.

Pommer, Henry F. "Herman Melville and the Wake of the *Essex.*" *American Literature* 20 (1948): 290–304.

———. *Milton and Melville.* Pittsburgh: University of Pittsburgh Press, 1950.

Porter, Burton F. *The Head and the Heart: Philosophy in Literature.* Amherst, NY: Humanity Books, 2006.

Porter, Carolyn. "Call Me Ishmael; or, How to Make Double-Talk Speak." In Brodhead, *New Essays,* 73–108.

Post-Lauria, Sheila. *Correspondent Colorings: Melville in the Marketplace.* Amherst: University of Massachusetts Press, 1996.

Powell, Timothy B. *Ruthless Democracy: A Multicultural Interpretation of the American Renaissance.* Princeton, NJ: Princeton University Press, 2000.

Putz, Manfred. "The Narrator as Audience: Ishmael as Reader and Critic in *Moby-Dick.*" *Studies in the Novel* 19 (1987): 160–74.

Radloff, Bernhard. *Will and Representation: The Philosophical Foundations of Melville's Theatrum Mundi.* New York: Peter Lang, 1996.

Railton, Stephen. *Authorship and Audience: Literary Performance in the American Renaissance.* Princeton, NJ: Princeton University Press, 1991.

Reddick, Marcia. "Something, Somehow like Original Sin: Striking the Uneven Balance in 'The Town-Ho's Story' and *Moby-Dick.*" *ATQ 10* n.s. (1996): 181–89.

Rees, John O., Jr. "Spenserian Analogues in *Moby-Dick.*" *ESQ* 18 (1972): 174–78.

Reeves, John D. *Windows on Melville.* Danbury, CT: Rutledge Books, 2001.

Reno, Janet. *Ishmael Alone Survived.* Lewisburg, PA: Bucknell University Press, 1990.

Reynolds, David S. *Beneath the American Renaissance: The Subversive Imagination in the Age of Emerson and Melville.* New York: Knopf, 1988.

Reynolds, Larry J. "Melville's Use of 'Young Goodman Brown.'" *American Transcendental Quarterly* 31 (Summer 1976): 12–14.

Rice, Julian C. "*Moby-Dick* and Shakespearean Tragedy." *Centennial Review* 14 (1970): 444–68.

Richardson, Robert D., Jr. *Myth and Literature in the American Renaissance.*

Bloomington: Indiana University Press, 1978.

Roberts, Terry. "Ishmael as Phallic Narrator." *Studies in American Fiction* 20 (1992): 99–109.

Robertson, Lisa Ann. "'Universal Thump': The Redemptive Epistemology of Touch in *Moby-Dick*." *Leviathan* 12 (June 2010): 5–20.

Robillard, Douglas. *Melville and the Visual Arts: Ionian Form, Venetian Tint*. Kent, OH: Kent State University Press, 1997.

Robinson, Douglas. *American Apocalypses: The Image of the End of the World in American Literature*. Baltimore: Johns Hopkins University Press, 1985.

Rogin, Michael Paul. *Subversive Genealogy: The Politics and Art of Herman Melville*. New York: Knopf, 1983.

Rose, Edward J. "Annihilation and Ambiguity: *Moby-Dick* and 'The Town-Ho's Story.'" *New England Quarterly* 45 (1972): 541–58.

———. "Melville, Emerson, and the Sphinx." *New England Quarterly* 36 (1963): 249–58.

Rosenfeld, William. "Uncertain Faith: Queequeg's Coffin and Melville's Use of the Bible." *Texas Studies in Literature and Language* 7 (1966): 317–27.

Rothschild, Herbert, Jr. "The Language of Mesmerism in 'The Quarter-Deck' Scene in *Moby-Dick*." *English Studies* 53 (1972): 235–38.

Saiki, Ikuno. "'Strike through the Unreasoning Mask': *Moby-Dick* and Japan." In Barnum, Kelley, and Sten, "Whole Oceans Away," ch. 13.

Sanborn, Geoffrey. "The Name of the Devil: Melville's Other 'Extracts' for *Moby-Dick*." *Nineteenth-Century Literature* 47 (1992): 212–35.

———. *The Sign of the Cannibal: Melville and the Making of the Post-colonial Reader*. Durham, NC: Duke University Press, 1998.

———. "Whence Come You, Queequeg?" *American Literature* 77 (2005): 227–57.

———. *Whipscars and Tattoos: The Last of the Mohicans*, Moby-Dick, *and the Maori*. New York: Oxford University Press, 2011.

Sattelmeyer, Robert. "'Shanties of Chapters and Essays': Rewriting *Moby-Dick*." *ESQ* 49 (2003): 213–47.

Schneider, Herbert N., and Homer B. Pettey. "Melville's Ithyphallic God." *Studies in American Fiction* 26 (1998): 193–212.

Schroeder, Fred E. H. "*Enter Ahab, Then All*: Theatrical Elements in Melville's Fiction." *Dalhousie Review* 46 (1966): 223–32.

Schulman, Robert. "The Serious Function of Melville's Phallic Jokes." *American Literature* 33 (1961): 179–94.

Schultz, Elizabeth A. "Melville's Environmental Vision in *Moby-Dick*." *ISLE: Interdisciplinary Studies in Literature and the Environment* 7 (Winter 2000): 97–113.

———. "The Sentimental Subtext of *Moby-Dick*: Melville's Response to the 'World of Woe.'" *ESQ* 42 (1996): 29–49.

———. "'The Subordinate Phantoms': Melville's Conflicted Response to Asia in *Moby-Dick*." In Barnum, Kelley, and Sten, "*Whole Oceans Away*," ch. 14.

———. *Unpainted to the Last:* Moby-Dick *and Twentieth-Century Art*. Lawrence: University of Kansas Press, 1995.

Schwab, Gabriele. *Subjects without Selves: Transitional Texts in Modern Fiction*. Cambridge, MA: Harvard University Press, 1994.

Scott, Sumner W. D. "Some Implications of the Typhoon Scenes in *Moby-Dick*." *American Literature* 12 (1940): 91–98.

Sealts, Merton M., Jr. "Melville and the Shakers." *Studies in Bibliography* 2 (1949–50): 105–14.

———. *Pursuing Melville, 1940–1980.* Madison: University of Wisconsin Press, 1982.

Seelye, John. "The Golden Navel: The Cabalism of Ahab's Doubloon." *Nineteenth-Century Fiction* 14 (1960): 350–55.

———. *Melville: The Ironic Diagram.* Evanston, IL: Northwestern University Press, 1970.

Sewall, Richard B. *The Vision of Tragedy.* 1959. New Haven: Yale University Press, 1980.

Sheldon, Leslie E. "Messianic Power and Satanic Decay: Milton in *Moby-Dick*." In *Melville and Milton,* edited by Robin Grey. Pittsburgh, PA: Duquesne University Press, 2004.

Sherwood, Yvonne. *A Biblical Text and Its Afterlives: The Survival of Jonah in Western Culture.* New York: Cambridge University Press, 2000.

Shillingsberg, Peter. "The Three *Moby-Dicks.*" *American Literary History* 2 (1990): 199–30.

Short, Bryan. *Cast by Means of Figures: Herman Melville's Rhetorical Development.* Amherst: University of Massachusetts Press, 1992.

Shuffelton, Frank. "Going through the Long Vaticans: Melville's 'Extracts' in *Moby-Dick*." *Texas Studies in Literature and Language* 25 (1983): 528–40.

Shurr, William H. *The Mystery of Iniquity: Melville as Poet, 1857–1891.* Lexington: University Press of Kentucky, 1972.

———. *Rappaccini's Children: American Writers in a Calvinist World.* Lexington: University Press of Kentucky, 1981.

Slade, Leonard A., Jr. *Symbolism in Herman Melville's* Moby-Dick*: From the Satanic to the Divine.* Lewiston, NY: Edwin Mellen Press, 1998.

Smith, Gayle L. "The Word and the Thing: *Moby-Dick* and the Limits of Language." *ESQ* 31 (1985): 260–71.

Smith, Henry Nash. *Democracy and the Novel: Popular Resistance to Classic American Writers.* New York: Oxford University Press, 1978.

Smith, Richard Dean. *Melville and Science: "Devilish Tantalization of the Gods!"* New York: Garland, 1993.

Spark, Clare L. *Hunting Captain Ahab: Psychological Warfare and the Melville Revival.* Kent, OH: Kent State University Press, 2001.

Stanonik, Janez. *Moby-Dick: The Myth and the Symbol: A Study in Folklore and Literature.* Ljubljana, Yugoslavia: Ljubljana University Press, 1962.

Sten, Christopher. "Threading the Labyrinth: *Moby-Dick* as Hybrid Epic." In *A Companion to Herman Melville,* edited by Wyn Kelley, 408–22. New York: Wiley-Blackwell, 2006.

———. *The Weaver God, He Weaves: Melville and the Poetics of the Novel.* Kent, OH: Kent State University Press, 1996.

Stone, Edward. "The Function of the Gams in *Moby-Dick*." *College Literature* 2 (1975): 171–81.

———. "Melville's Late Pale Usher." *English Language Notes* 9 (September 1971): 51–53.

Stout, Janis. "Melville's Use of the Book of Job." *Nineteenth-Century Fiction* 25 (1970): 69–83.

Sweeney, Gerard M. *Melville's Use of Classical Mythology*. Amsterdam: Rodopi, 1975.

Taketani, Etsuko. "*Moby-Dick*: Gnostic Re-writing of History." *ATQ* 8 n.s. (1994): 119–35.

Tally, Robert T., Jr. "Whale as Dish: Culinary Rhetoric and the Discourse of Power in *Moby-Dick*." In *Culinary Aesthetics and Practices in Nineteenth-Century American Literature*, edited by Monika Elbert and Marie Drews, ch. 4. New York: Palgrave Macmillan, 2009.

Thompson, Lawrance. *Melville's Quarrel with God*. Princeton, NJ: Princeton University Press, 1952.

Tolchin, Neal. *Mourning, Gender, and Creativity in the Art of Herman Melville*. New Haven: Yale University Press, 1988.

Trimpi, Helen P. "Conventions of Romance in *Moby-Dick*." *Southern Review* 7 (1971): 115–29.

———. "Melville's Use of Demonology and Witchcraft in *Moby-Dick*." *Journal of the History of Ideas* 30 (1969): 543–62.

Ujhazy, Maria. *Herman Melville's World of Whaling*. Budapest: Akadémiai Kiadó, 1982.

Van Cromphout, Gustaaf. "*Moby-Dick*: The Transformation of the Faustian Ethos." *American Literature* 51 (1979): 17–32.

Van Nostrand, A. D. *Everyman His Own Poet: Romantic Gospels in American Literature*. New York: McGraw Hill, 1968.

Vargish, Thomas. "Gnostic Mythos in *Moby-Dick*." *PMLA* 81 (1966): 272–77.

Vincent, Howard P. *The Trying-Out of* Moby-Dick. Boston: Houghton Mifflin, 1949.

Vogel, Dan. "The Dramatic Chapters of *Moby-Dick*." *Nineteenth-Century Fiction* 13 (1958): 239–47.

Walcutt, Charles C. "The Fire Symbolism in *Moby-Dick*." *Modern Language Notes* 59 (1944): 304–10.

Wallace, Robert K. "Bulkington, J. M. W. Turner, and 'The Lee Shore.'" In *Savage Eye: Melville and the Visual Arts*, edited by Christopher Sten. Kent, OH: Kent State University Press, 1991.

———. *Melville and Turner: Spheres of Love and Fright*. Athens: University of Georgia Press, 1992.

Ward, J. A. "The Function of the Cetological Chapters in *Moby-Dick*." *American Literature* 28 (1956): 164–83.

Ward, Joseph Thomas. "Herman Melville: The Forms and Forces of Evil." PhD dissertation, Notre Dame University, 1959.

Watters, R.E. "The Meanings of the White Whale." *University of Toronto Quarterly* 20 (1951): 155–68.

———. "Melville's Metaphysics of Evil." *University of Toronto Quarterly* 9 (1940): 170–82.

Wenke, John. *Melville's Muse: Literary Creation and the Forms of Philosophical Fiction*. Kent, OH: Kent State University Press, 1995.

Werge, Thomas. "*Moby-Dick* and the Calvinist Tradition." *Studies in the Novel* 1 (1969): 484–506.

Wilson, Eric. *Romantic Turbulence: Chaos, Ecology, and American Space*. New York: St. Martin's Press, 2000.

Wilson, James D. *The Romantic Heroic Ideal*. Baton Rouge: Louisiana State University

Press, 1982.

Winnick, R. H. "Melville's 'The Candles' and the Easter Vigil." *Nineteenth-Century Literature* 53 (1998): 171–87.

Wolf, Bryan. "When Is a Painting most like a Whale? Ishmael, *Moby-Dick*, and the Sublime." In Brodhead, *New Essays*, 141–79.

Wright, Nathalia. *Melville's Use of the Bible*. Durham, NC: Duke University Press, 1949.

———. "*Moby-Dick*: Jonah's or Job's Whale?" *American Literature* 37 (1965): 190–95.

Yothers, Brian. "One's Own Faith: Melville's Reading of *The New Testament and Psalms*." *Leviathan* 10 (October 2008): 39–59.

Young, James Dean. "The Nine Gams of the *Pequod*." *American Literature* 25 (1954): 449–63.

Young, William A. "Leviathan in the Book of Job and *Moby-Dick*." *Soundings* 65 (1982): 388–401.

Zoellner, Robert. *The Salt-Sea Mastodon: A Reading of* Moby-Dick. Berkeley and Los Angeles: University of California Press, 1973.

Index